Moving Psychotherapy

Theory and Application of
Pesso System/Psychomotor Therapy

EDITED BY ALBERT PESSO
AND JOHN CRANDELL

BROOKLINE
BOOKS

Library of Congress Cataloging-in-Publication Data

Moving Psychotherapy: theory and applications of the Pesso System/Psychomotor
    Therapy/edited by Albert Pesso and John Crandell.
             p. cm.
     Includes bibliographical references.
     ISBN 0-914797-72-7
     1. Psychotherapy. 2. Substance abuse. 3. Sex abuse. 4. Pastoral counseling.
   5. Feminist psychotherapy. 6. Movement therapy. I. Pesso, Albert. II. Crandell, John S.
     [DNLM: 1. Movement. 2. Psychotherapy — methods. WM 420 M935]
RC489.M66M68 1991
616.89'16 — dc20
DNLM/DLC   91-1623
for Library of Congress   CIP

To my wife, Diane Boyden Pesso,
without whom the process of Pesso System/Psychomotor
and this book would not be possible
A.P.

To Pia,
who has given me place and validation and limits in turn,
and to Alethea and Matthew
who model the expression of developing self with moving vitality
J.C.

Acknowledgements

With great gratitude, Albert and Diane Pesso wish to thank the many people who have helped, in so many different ways, the advancement of PS/P over the last thirty years. In addition they want to express their appreciation to the following people while apologizing in advance to any whose names they may have unwittingly omitted.

G.W. Arendsen Hein, Iman Baardman, Robert Beloof, Nancy Campbell, Carl Clarke, Arthur Cobb, Olga Currier, Marcel Cuvelier, Jacqueline Damgaard, Ed Daniels, Michael DeSisto, Kenneth Druck, Bernt Due-Tonnessen, Joen Fagen, Rhoda Falk, Ruth Fordon, Matthew Fried, William Friedman, Gerald H. Gammell, James Garland, Victor Gelineau, Helen Gilbert, Ira Goldstein, Joyce Goldstein, Samuel Grob, Russell Haber, Grace Hadeed, Helen Hafner, Armen Hanjian, Henry Harsch, Jean Harsch, Jakob Hartman, Ken Holme, Dennis Houff, Verna Houff, Martin Howald, Louisa Howe, Frederic Hudson, David Israel, Erik Jarlnes, Vann Joines, Tjeerd Jongsma, Michael Katz, Gus Kaufman, Bernhard Kempler, Ann Knott, F. Will Larson, Ray Leibl, Naomi Levitan, Daniel Malamud, Scott McNairy, Tilmann Moser, Augustus Napier, Marc Nevejan, Ellsworth Neumann, Carol Parker, Lowijs Perquin, Richard Peterson, Charles Pinderhughes, Lois Reiersol, Niko Roth, Jenner Roth, Peter Runde, Meghan Ruthman, Han Sarolea, Jennifer Savitz, Bruce J. Schell, Paul Scott, Myron Sharaf, Daniel Shaw, Glenn Shean, Irma Lee Shepherd, Judith Small, Eugene Smith, Janet Smith, David Stewart Jr., Jens M. Stranheim, George Taylor, Suzanne Tignor, Marleen V. Asperen Vervenne, Willy Van Haver, Ardry Vermeer, Cor Vreugdenhil, Han Wassenaar, Robert D. Williams, Harold Williams, Wright Williams, Joan Winter, Naomi Young, Wilson Young, Anne M. Zanes, Joan M. Zilbach. They especially give thanks to their daughters, Tana, Tasmin and Tia who have contributed immeasurably with time, energy, thought, patience, and emotional support.

They reserve special thanks for all their colleagues who wrote chapters for this book, and most notably to John Crandell whose indefatigable energies and efforts made the creation and culmination of this project possible.

Table of Contents

Applications of PS/P

Foreword

Nearly ten years ago, when I first saw Al Pesso lead a *structure*, I knew immediately that I was in the presence of an extremely gifted clinician. As he engaged a small circle of *accommodators* in helping a client enact a core problem, I was intrigued by Pesso's insightful reading of the client's dilemma, and his sure, compassionate guidance of this person through a labyrinth of possibilities — into a resolution that seemed safe, just and eminently deserved. So powerful and so moving was this work that I assumed it was essentially unteachable; all I could do was admire.

As I have learned more about Pesso System Psychomotor, from its origins in Diane and Al Pesso's work with their student dancers at Emerson College to its current complex and clearly-defined form, I have become convinced that not only is this exceptional approach teachable, but that it is applicable to a wide variety of emotional dilemmas. For clinicians of every stripe, it offers many possibilities which our usual approaches lack.

The vocabulary of the system reveals its comprehensiveness and its high purpose: There is *shape and countershape*, the *center of truth*, the *possibility sphere*, the *true scene*, *ego-wrapping*. There are *witness figures, resistance figures, fragment figures, ideal figures*. Carefully guided role-players (this approach bears little resemblance to more casual use of role-playing) represent negative and positive aspects of parents, engage in "crossfire," enact dreamed-of, but never before experienced, ideal scenes.

The essence of PS/P is its attempt — through reading the client's body energy; through "staging" internal constructs and dilemmas in an external, visual way; through offering an empathic "witnessing" and labelling of the client's experiences; through providing crucial physical and emotional support — to help the client face the truth about his or her present life. Often this truth is powerfully colored by the traumas and betrayals of the individual's childhood. Working carefully, and with a sharp eye on what seems believable, the PS/P therapist then helps the client, through the use of *ideal figures*, expand what seems possible. Often, these explorations of a wished-for reality recast the old foundations of doubt and uncertainty, and open up new space for more productive living. This exciting work allows clients to experience a world which the limitations in their families of origin have previously denied them; and these symbolic journeys create the beginnings of a new mental architecture, a new internal map.

As a family therapist, I am particularly grateful for the opportunities which this system provides us in working with the family of origin problems which underlie so many current conflicts — without having to reshape the actual historical family. I believe that PS/P supplies a vital "missing link" in family work: We can help our clients discharge primitive feelings about family figures without assaulting them, in the process often uncovering hidden caring. We can also assist in the creation of "ideal" internal images, which interrupt internal negative scripts, and which can initiate the construction of new interpersonal bridges in the present. In these *structures*, a client may unburden himself of long-accumulated anger at parents, discover loving feelings that have also been submerged, and begin seeing positive alternatives which can find their ways into real relationships with partner, parents, and children.

While it is tempting to see this therapeutic system as a collection of techniques, it is far more than that. Pesso System Psychomotor is really a set of working principles (supported by techniques) which are dedicated to promoting a kind of interpersonal justice, and to the liberation of what the Pessos call the *soul*, or all the genetic potential with which the individual enters life. While the family is seldom the ideal environment for the human spirit, the Pessos' *possibility sphere* forms a micro-ecosystem where it may take a firmer, more hopeful hold. In the construction of this alternative reality, this approach can help us begin to reshape the family itself.

Augustus Y. Napier, Ph.D.
Director, The Family Workshop
Atlanta, GA

Introduction

"Another factor...seems to have played a part in bringing about the formation of the ego and its differentiation from the id. A person's own body, and above all its surface, is a place from which both external and internal perceptions may spring...

   The ego is first and foremost a bodily ego; it is not merely a surface entity, but is itself the projection of a surface." (Freud, 1923/1961, pp.25-26)

"Stand up—close your eyes—and relax all parts of your body." These brief instructions to the "species stance" were my introduction to body/psyche in "psychomotor" psychotherapy many years ago. Stand up? And relax? How can this possibly access the unconscious? Freud's famous and oft repeated concept, "The ego is first and foremost a bodily ego" is and was quite reassuring to me, a traditional psychoanalyst, as I participated in and learned about Pesso System/Psychomotor therapy. Shortly thereafter I began to hear terms which were strange and unfamiliar. These included "structures," "accommodation," and many other Pesso System/Psychomotor (PS/P) terms. (Among the more difficult ones was the concept of "ideal parents!") The intricate, complex, and wonderful journey starting from the body and leading to various aspects of the unconscious became evident in the course of my first and many subsequent workshops.

   Freud put the body to rest, prone on a couch, as he ventured into then unknown territory, the deep layers and intricacies of the conscious and unconscious processes of the mind. Freud was first a neurobiological researcher and became a listener, thinker, and first psychotherapist. Al and Diane Pesso were initially dancers and became listeners, thinkers, and psychotherapists. For them the body was from the beginning the primary expressive tool and later a way of understanding and integrating mind and body. The art and science of reading and using body signals became and continues to be a central part of PS/P theory and practice.

   Over many years Al and Diane Pesso have enhanced and enlarged their unique form of psychotherapy. Fortunately their energy, intelligence, and intuition has always been accompanied by and integrated with exquisite sensitivity to the intricate workings of the mind or the "psyche" and as mentioned, fueled from the body — the "motor." Thus the name "psychomotor" recently has been aptly joined with the founders in the term "Pesso System/Psychomotor" therapy, or PS/P, as abbreviated in this volume of readings.

   The language and terminology of PS/P is strange at first. For example, clients/patients participate in *structures*, utilize *accommodators* and create as roles, among other figures, *ideal parents*. These special terms are old friends to readers who already know PS/P. They are indeed useful in creating the particular kind of psychotherapeutic situation which is central to PS/P. Other readers will become familiar with these terms in the course of reading the contents of this volume. (The glossary may be useful to read first as an introduction for the uninitiated reader, and italicized words will be briefly defined in the glossary.) The term "structure" is apt for the individual psychotherapeutic endeavor created by a particular PS/P client. A "structure" includes the therapist, client, and group (usually present) within which a structure is created.

Structure implies a therapeutic form which is inclusive of the varying kinds of verbal and non-verbal interchange of all elements within and surrounding the central therapeutic dyad of client and therapist. A structure is a psychotherapeutic episode created by an individual with the assistance of all of these elements: the therapist, accommodators, and the group as a whole. The richness of PS/P is communicated in the language and special terms which have evolved over the years. As mentioned previously, the glossary is useful as a start, but the richness is conveyed in the many aspects depicted in the broad range of articles included in this volume of readings.

The many threads of PS/P which have been dispersed over the years of their development are gathered together in this reader. During these years PS/P has expanded in theory and practice. This large volume of readings attests to that growth. The contributions range widely over theory and practice. PS/P is linked with contemporary theories, object relations among others. The range of applications represented in this volume is impressive. The opening historical essay amplifies in depth the path of discovery traversed by the founders of PS/P, Al and Diane Pesso. The following comments are not a complete review of all chapters. This would require too extensive an elucidation for an introduction, though each chapter is certainly worthy in and of itself.

Theoretical Issues

The opening chapter in the section on theoretical issues on the "History of Psychomotor" by Louisa Howe, one of the early trainees and continuing central member of the PS/P endeavor, provides a thorough and fascinating history intertwined with clearly elucidated development and exposition of theory underlying psychomotor therapy. Dr. Howe draws upon extensive knowledge of psychoanalytic and sociological sources in her historical account.

The next 3 chapters by Al Pesso amplify PS/P theory with emphasis on his understanding and expansion of the function of ego in PS/P theory and practice. The first of these three basic chapters by Al Pesso, "The Relationship between Pesso System Psychomotor Therapy and a Neurobiological Model" explicates the philosophy, structure and terminology of PS/P. These concepts are connected to an emerging neurobiological structure and system within PS/P. In the second chapter, "Ego Function and PS/P" the clinical example of therapeutic work will be clear to all readers, including those who have not experienced this form of psychotherapy. The therapeutic situation and rationale is expanded in the third of these basic contributions, "Ego Development in the Possibility Sphere."

Though research on PS/P has been scanty, the next contribution, "Childhood Loss and Postural Insecurity" by Gus Kaufman represents such an endeavor. There are references in other chapters to the few other research studies. (See Chapters 1, 9, and 15).

Integrating PS/P with Other Approaches

In the chapter on "PS/P and Object Relations Theory," John Crandell provides a description of therapeutic work in a summary of a structure with an accompanying theoretical description using Object Relations theory to explain the therapeutic work. Overall, he emphasizes the compatability of PS/P with a psychoanalytic orientation.

Tilmann Moser's chapter on "Staging the Unconscious: Impression of Psychomotor as Seen by a Psychoanalyst" may be particularly intriguing to psychoanalytically oriented psychotherapists. His statements about psychoanalysis and PS/P are challenging. They seem to me to be the beginning of a fruitful theoretical and practical collaboration, though they leave many questions unanswered. His discussion of the protection of defenses in PS/P, in contrast to other expressive therapies, is of particular import with regard to the safety of this form of non-verbal/verbal psychotherapy which is so heavily oriented towards and directly utilizes the body in the psychotherapeutic sessions.

Applications

The applications section opens with a strong and in some ways frightening exposition of work on "Abuse" by Al Pesso. The power of the forces released in this work is combined with careful exposition of the safety aspects which must be present and in place in order to accomplish safely the goals of PS/P for clients with abuse as a significant aspect of their history.

The last two application chapters may frighten some readers. They are self reports of PS/P work which include joyous, vicious, sad, happy, rageful, and many more emotions very directly expressed by the authors. The authors in the chapter by Glenn Shean are anonymous. Debra Antari provides a moving self report. The authors are to be congratulated in writing from themselves and giving to us, the readers, their therapeutic journeys. The actual tale of the therapeutic endeavor usually remains behind the privileged client/therapist door. These reports allow us to see with particular clarity PS/P as a therapeutic modality.

Conclusion

Some years ago in Al's seminal publications, *Movement in Psychotherapy* (1969) and *Experience in Action* (1973), he wrote about the basic fundamentals of PS/P theory and practice. These volumes have continued to be a basic foundation of this psychotherapeutic modality. Over subsequent years, PS/P has expanded in theory and practice. This volume of readings attests to that growth. History, theory, and practice all contribute to a rich brew. This introduction has sampled only some of the ingredients.

Many chapters in this volume deserve extensive comment, as I mentioned earlier. However, the primary function of this introduction is to lead the reader into the unexplored territory of these readings. I hope you are intrigued and will make the exciting, at times difficult, and potentially rewarding journey into *Moving Psychotherapy: A Pesso System/Psychomotor Reader.*

Joan J. Zilbach, M.D.
Boston Psychoanalytic Institute
Fielding Institute

References

Freud, S. (1961). The ego and the id. In J. Strachey (Ed. and Trans.), *The standard edition of the complete psychological works of Sigmund Freud* (Vol. 19, pp. 3-66). London: Hogarth Press. (Original work published 1923).

Pesso, A. (1969). *Movement in Psychotherapy.* New York: New York University Press.

Pesso, A. (1973). *Experience in Action.* New York: New York University Press.

Contributors

DEBRA ANTARI, Client, psychotherapist for developmentally disabled, Carmel, NY.

JUDITH BARNITT, Psychologist, Minneapolis, MN.

ROBERT BELOOF, certified PS/P therapist and trainer, Professor of Rhetoric, Emeritus, University of California, Berkeley; Fulbright Professor of American Literature in Naples.

DORIS CHAVES, Assoc. Professor, University of Tennessee, Memphis, College of Nursing.

CARL CLARKE, Executive Director, Telles Institute, Atlanta, GA; certified PS/P therapist.

JOHN CRANDELL, Clinical psychologist, Winchester, VA.

RUTHANN FOX-HINES, Psychologist, University of South Carolina.

GAIL HAGLER, Family Therapist, Atlanta, GA.

ARMEN HANJIAN, Pastor, First United Methodist Church, Montclair, NJ.

VICKY HANJIAN, Assistant Pastor, St. Mark's United Methodist Church, Montclair, NJ.

LOUISA HOWE, certified PS/P therapist; recipient of 1989 Distinguished Career in Sociological Practice Award, American Sociological Association.

GUS KAUFMAN, PS/P trainer, Atlanta, GA; coleader of PS/P certification programs, Atlanta, GA, Basel, Switzerland.

TILMANN MOSER, Psychoanalyst, Freiburg, Germany.

JÖRG MÜLLER, Professor of Law, Berne University; consultant to Swiss government.

LOWIJS PERQUIN, Senior Psychiatrist, Faculty of Medicine, Free University of Amsterdam and Psychiatric Center of Amsterdam; registered PS/P supervisor; chairman of the board, Dutch Association of Pesso System Psychotherapy.

ALBERT PESSO, cofounder of PS/P therapy.

GLENN SHEAN, Professor of Psychology, College of William and Mary, Williamsburg, VA; Professor of Psychiatry and Behavioral Science, Medical College of Hampton Roads.

HAN WASSENAAR, Professor of Neuroscience, University of Groningen.

Theoretical Issues

Chapter 1

Origins and History of Pesso System/ Psychomotor Therapy

by Louisa P. Howe, Ph.D.

Pesso System/Psychomotor (PS/P), or Psychomotor therapy, as it was called during its early years, has fascinated me from the time I first heard about it in late 1961. A friend and neighbor of Diane and Albert Pesso, Ellsworth T. Neumann, M.D., who was Administrator of the Massachusetts General Hospital and a guest lecturer in a community mental health course I taught at the Harvard School of Public Health, told me that Dr. Erich Lindemann had been much impressed by this new method of therapy and said that if the Pessos were doing what he thought they were doing, they should be given a Nobel prize. Not long afterwards there was a write-up in *The Boston Globe* of Diane and Albert Pesso as dance and movement educators who had developed a largely non-verbal method of psychotherapy. I learned also that Dr. Charles Pinderhughes, Chief of Psychiatric Research at the Boston V.A. Hospital, had commented that the Pessos' work was "opening up a whole new world."

Mind and body, and especially emotions and bodily movements, tensions, or sensations, were then and still are a primary focus of PS/P. This focus was not all that initially attracted me, however. Although I am licensed as a psychologist, have taught and supervised psychologists, and have also been trained in psychoanalysis, my academic training has been mainly in sociology and I consider that to be my primary field. What particularly appealed to me in descriptions of this new kind of therapy was its sociological character, its emphasis upon interaction: in PS/P an individual's expression of emotion or of need was responded to by one or more specially designated other person(s) in such a way as to provide satisfaction of the individual's need or a satisfying validation of his or her emotion.

This occurred, furthermore, on a symbolic level, not literally; it involved having the assisting person(s) play roles, and was an example of what George H. Mead, an influential figure in sociology, called symbolic interaction. In the early 1960s psychologists and psychiatrists for the most part gave little attention to interaction (except for transference), and were unacquainted with the sociological concept of role; rather they prided themselves on being concerned only with what was inside the individual human being and on ignoring "the empty spaces between individuals." To learn of an approach to psychotherapy that matched my sociological orientation was quite exciting.

From what I had heard about PS/P as a primarily non-verbal form of psychotherapy, I wondered if it might offer a way to reach troubled people often thought to lack the verbal skills necessary for "talking therapy." While this may well be true, PS/P has become increasingly a verbal as well as non-verbal therapy. This now strikes me as one of its outstanding strengths: information comes in and goes forth through verbal and non-verbal channels. Words convey meanings and bodily sensations or movements convey meanings, of which the person may or may not be conscious.

This chapter traces the major elements and stages in the development of PS/P therapy, drawing on my own experience, certain written materials, and accounts provided by Diane and Albert Pesso during interviews in 1975 and 1989-90.

My Introduction to Pesso System/Psychomotor Therapy

My first contact with PS/P therapy occurred during January, 1962, when — after calling to express my interest — I was invited to join a recently formed group that met weekly in space belonging to the Charles Street Meetinghouse, a Unitarian-Universalist church where the Pessos were members.

The Pessos greeted me and introduced themselves and the group members — eight or nine men and women in their late twenties or early thirties, most of them engaged in academic or professional work.

Al was a broad-shouldered man in his early thirties, strongly built. His brown eyes were alert and glinting, and over his nose a straight vertical furrow bespoke concentration. He was conventionally dressed, his tie slightly loosened at the collar.

Diane was about his height but of a more slender build, with hazel eyes, an attractive face, and with a softly rounded figure. She had a strong, flexible body and moved with grace and spontaneity, finding evident pleasure in her own physical capabilities. In their different ways they conveyed a sense of kindliness and gentleness combined with modesty and eagerness to learn and develop more.

The first exercise was to assume the species stance, or reflex-relaxed stance, as Diane prefers to call it. Everyone in the group was following Al's instructions to stand while being as totally relaxed as one can be without falling over, maintaining the upright stance that is characteristic for the human species. Heads were dropped forward, arms hanging loose, stomachs sagging, bodies occasionally teetering back and forth as the group members let their reflexes keep them upright. Total relaxation when standing is somewhat different from relaxation when lying down; one's standing reflexes have to be allowed to function freely so that one does not fall over. These reflexes are not a matter of conscious effort or voluntary control. "The floor is there and the force of gravity is there," Al explained, "and you can trust them to be there. You can also trust your reflexes to keep you from tipping over, even when all conscious controls are relaxed."

Out of the corner of my eye I watched others in the group being taught other exercises while I continued trying to meet Al's exacting requirements for the species stance. "Your right arm isn't relaxed," he would say, returning to me after coaching some of the others. "Your head isn't relaxed." I stood for long minutes trying to let myself go more and more loose. Finally I achieved what felt like complete relaxation, gently swaying as I stood there droopily. Al returned and scanned me from head to foot. "Your tongue is not relaxed."

Of all things! Startled questions came to my mind. How can he tell? How can he see inside my head? What does it mean if I do feel tension in my tongue? So what if I'm verbal, not physical? What kind of procedure is this, anyhow? I resolved to find out, and have been doing so intermittently, with growing conviction and enthusiasm, ever since.

What is it, and Why Call it "Psychomotor?"

Since its beginnings around 1960, PS/P has developed into a comprehensive, flexible, subtle and finely-tuned instrument for accomplishing therapeutic change or, in Diane's words, "emotional re-education" or "emotional growth." It has become a system of formulations and practices based mainly on many years of empathic observation of people's bodily movements, listening to their reports of physical sensations, discovering what these sensations and movements meant emotionally to people, and experimenting with diverse ways of facilitating and responding to the expression of feelings through bodily actions and wished-for interactions. Such interactions, the active *accommodating* (that is, satisfying) responses of one or more persons playing roles which precisely fit and match one's own emotional interests, actions, and impulses toward action, offer an exceptionally persuasive invitation to the expression of feelings.

Simply expressing feelings is not enough, however. Through *structures*, which are episodes of therapeutic work, usually involving role-played figures, that take place in a carefully controlled setting and on a symbolic, emotionally powerful level, provision is made for resolving an individual's past conflicts, satisfying his or her previously *unmet needs*, healing past emotional injuries, and enabling hitherto unborn parts of the self to emerge and become integrated into the being and functioning of the whole person.

As new issues, puzzlements and challenges have arisen over the years, the Pessos have tried out and thoughtfully assessed various modifications of their ways of working. New techniques and modes of understanding continue to be introduced or elaborated. One element that remains constant is the care taken in PS/P to ensure that each person who engages in this form of therapeutic emotional re-education is treated with thoroughgoing acceptance and respect.

The relationship of the PS/P therapist with the client — the conscious, rational part of the client, the *ego* — is one of collaboration in the task of enabling that client to develop more fully the capacity to find satisfying ways of interacting with the people who constitute his or her world. In Al Pesso's words, the therapist does not "lead" clients in PS/P therapy but "follows the person very closely," giving special attention to bodily cues while making sure the client's ego is aware of and is in charge of whatever happens. Clients are asked to work with the therapist to ensure the structure is completed in a positive and satisfying way.

Diane Pesso (Note 1) sees the PS/P process as assisting a person in doing his or her own emotional improvisation. The therapist makes contact with the rational, aware part of the person and makes sure that other group members provide the needed *accommodation* (emotional interaction) to satisfy symbolically the person's spontaneously expressed needs. She says this feels much like being a coach for the client, a stage manager for the setting, and a director for the accommodators, all at the same time.

The "psycho" part of Psychomotor refers to the psyche (soul or mind; that which is psychological). The "motor" part refers to bodily sensations and movements — motoric actions — including incipient or blocked actions, powered by sources of energy connected with the psyche. The word "emotion" quite literally means the outward expression ("e" from the Latin "ex") of that which "moves" us, whether by way of an external stimulus or an internal need. We respond with motion or with various degrees of bodily preparation for emotional expression; we engage in motor activity, including vocalization. We may, however, try to suppress or hide or detach from emotions, sometimes to the point of rendering them unconscious. Under the latter circumstances emotions can appear in the resultant form of psychosomatic illness or as pain or tension. When the client finds that feelings can be satisfyingly expressed and responded to in the course of a PS/P *structure*, the symptoms' basis for existence is counteracted and symptoms tend to diminish or disappear.

Europeans use the term "psychomotor" to refer generically to a variety of body-oriented methods ranging from massage to martial arts. In Europe people now speak of "Pesso Groups" or "Pesso Therapy" to distinguish it from what the French call "Psychomotricité."

In the United States the Pessos decided to call their method "Pesso System/Psychomotor therapy" (PS/P), retaining the original designation of "Psychomotor," but emphasizing the extent to which it constitutes an articulated system of psychotherapy rather than merely a set of techniques.

Diane and Albert Pesso's Backgrounds: Significant Influences

Diane Boyden (Pesso) and Albert Pesso were both born in 1929, Al in New York City and Diane in Boston, Massachusetts. Although their childhoods seem quite different, both had interests and engaged in activities that contributed to the later development of PS/P.

Al, a youngest son struggling to keep up with his older brothers, grew up in the Bronx and Brooklyn, in a family of Sephardic Jewish descent that had come to the United States from Bitola, Jugoslavia, fifteen years before his birth. At age five he began a disciplined regime of body-building, going daily to a nearby park to work out on ladders and parallel bars. Being able to "do strong things that his brothers couldn't do" (Note 1) became a source of considerable satisfaction to him. As time went on he aspired to fulfil the Greek ideal of a strong mind in a strong body; he excelled academically as well as physically and was sufficiently gifted in science and math to win admission to New York's Stuyvesant High School.

During Al's mid-teen years a weight lifter named Dan Lurie, who had a national reputation as "the most muscular man in America," opened a gym nearby. Al worked with him, and soon found himself running the studio, teaching acrobatics and various methods of body building. Al started a boys' club which he coached in these activities, and also developed a hand balancing team whose members did handstands on each other hands. In all of this, Al has later commented, he was very much aware of the aesthetic aspects of acrobatic and other physical activities. Diane comments that Al's physical sense of line was unusually well developed, as documented by weight-lifting photographs of him at the gym which look like "wonderful Greek sculpture" (Note 1).

Al was seventeen when he was first introduced to the world of dance. Dan Lurie's girl friend gave Al his first exposure to modern dance, which she was then studying with Gertrude Shurr. Much intrigued, Al attended a class taught by Gertrude and her teaching partner, May O'Donnell, who were both disciples of Martha Graham and had been in her early company. They were impressed by Al's physical skills, drew him into their group, and for two years served as his mentors. Within a month of attending his first dance class, Al started teaching dance to youngsters in his neighborhood. One of Al's older brothers undertook to pay for his dance lessons for a brief period; thereafter he was given scholarship assistance and in exchange swept the floors, washed windows, etc. Gertrude Shurr used numerous photographs of Al doing exercises in her book *Modern Dance: Techniques and Teaching* (1949).

With this introduction to the world of art and theater, Al left the family home in Brooklyn and moved to Manhattan. He was excited to be immersed in the avant garde of the time, and read extensively, including works by Freud and other psychoanalytic writers.

Diane grew up as the eldest of three children in a financially strained upper middle class Protestant family. Her mother had trained to be a concert pianist and her father had wanted to be an artist. By age five Diane knew she was going to be a dancer and loved to give spontaneous improvisations for her appreciative grandparents. She entered public school in the second grade, having been taught by her mother at home the first year. During the school years she studied piano, then violin and cello. In dance she studied tap, acrobatic and then ballet. As a young child, she knew her mother was unhappy. Her father was prone to sudden violent outbursts of temper, and she learned early to keep quiet and not disagree with him, although at times she found him playful and fun. In the early years, there were frequent crises and her mother would periodically prepare to leave with Diane and occasionally did leave for short periods.

In her teens, while attending Woodward School for Girls, she studied ballet in Boston with Harriet Hoctor and had occasional classes with Russian ballet stars. To ease the financial pressures she thought were the cause of her parents' conflicts, at age 14 she started the Diane Boyden School of the Dance. By age 16, she had a hundred dance students and occasionally danced at night clubs to earn more money. She still studied the cello (which was very important to her mother) and commuted to Boston for dance classes with José Limon, becoming a member of his Boston dance company, and with Barbara Mettler.

Diane choreographed and designed costumes for several productions, concert pieces for herself, and a show for eighty of her students. During this period she was buoyed by the knowledge that many people expected her to become a notable concert dancer in the tradition of Isadora Duncan.

Diane attended Bennington with scholarship assistance and help from philanthropist Helen Frick. Miss Frick sponsored the concert careers of several young women artists and also sponsored a summer camp for underprivileged girls where Diane served as dance counselor. Diane loved Bennington; she gained from the dance teaching style of Martha Hill, and was strongly influenced by the educational philosophy of the faculty and the college.

Al studied for a year with Martha Graham, on scholarship, with the expectation of becoming a member of her company. At her suggestion and recommendation, he was awarded a full scholarship to Bennington College, where he and Diane met. Although they were not drawn to each other romantically at first, they talked often as friends. They could hardly help recognizing attributes they shared in common. Both had disciplined themselves to perform feats of physical prowess when they were very young. Both had started in their mid-teens to teach others what they had learned. Both felt they had the wherewithal to undertake important innovations; both harbored within themselves a sense of destiny; both wanted to be their unique selves in life and dance. And both felt they had formed their personalities, and were on their way, at an early age.

Although Al feels he gained much inspiration and support from his Bennington experience, he left after one year; he wanted to face more challenge and difficulty. He taught dance for a year at Davis and Elkins College in West Virginia while Diane taught at the Frick summer camp and returned to Bennington. He also opened a dance school, and choreographed the West Virginia State Forest Festival, using, for the first time in that area, a dance group in which black and white dancers performed together.

The bond between them, already formed at Bennington, resulted in marriage, and Diane left Bennington.

They established themselves in New York, dancing professionally, teaching, learning and enjoying the excitement of the New York dance world. Diane took dance courses with Alwin Nikolais and music composition with John Cage at the Henry Street Settlement. Diane's married status resulted in the loss of her Frick sponsorship and they found they could not make a living through concert dance.

For six months they were acting/dancing members of a touring company of "Kiss Me Kate." Al choreographed several off-Broadway productions, taught at settlement houses in New York, and was persuaded to do some musical comedy style dancing with Diane at night clubs. As he says now, at first this felt like sinning because in his view dance represented something so pure (Note 1).

Their first daughter, Tana, was born. As she began to approach school age, her parents realized their lifestyle would have to change as they wanted to have more children. They moved to Quincy, Diane's home town in Massachusetts, and started a dance school.

Their first years in the Boston area were emotionally difficult. Giving up the creative, artistic dance world of New York — and even more, giving up their hopes of becoming great dancers — was devastatingly hard and painful. Al, after two years of struggling with palpitations, a "loss of meaning" and rage that was not clearly felt as rage, sought psychotherapy. He found it helpful, though as he began to understand the process, he felt a sense of dismay about certain aspects of how it was carried out. The Pessos' discussion after each session sometimes evolved into processing the emotions through action and sound. This was an important prelude to the development of PS/P.

While in New York, Al had taught a class in creative dance at a halfway house for former mental hospital patients. In Boston, he volunteered to do the same at the Center Club, a rehabilitation and resocialization center for former mental patients. The Center's executive director and its staff psychologist, Al wrote,

> made strong note of my apprehension of members' states of mind and my ability to relate to this in the class... In retrospect it is probable that their approval of this skill motivated further exploration in the therapeutic milieu (1966, p. 12).

By this time he was also aware of Marion Chace's pioneering work in applying dance-based experience to therapeutic purposes. Others to whom he gives special credit as sources of influence on their development included Merce Cunningham and Barbara Mettler, the writings of Delsarte and Stanislavsky, and Isadora Duncan as a founder of modern dance.

While the aim of the Pessos' approach to dance was, in Al's words, "to give students tools of body and feeling which they could use toward communicating their visions, images, ideas, etc., to an audience," the aim of PS/P was not only to enable people to communicate with others but also to communicate

> with themselves or various parts of themselves; the self of the past with the self of the present; the impulses of the past with the thoughts and feelings of the present; the sensations and needs of the past with the body and thoughts of the present. This communication and interaction of various parts under the aegis of awareness, or the ego, is an important integrating act. No part of the being is left in isolation...(1966, p. 15).

In their first dance school they tried to maintain the high standards of artistry and creativity that meant so much to them. As Al put it,

> What we had in New York we tried to bring to these students, and we had to refine and define the basic ideas behind the way we taught; we had to simplify. We had to rediscover dance and the reasons for it by ourselves. It was like being in the wilderness. Out of these two facts — the breakdown of my meaning and the attempt to reconstruct it through movement — we began to really understand the organization and generation of movement very, very clearly, which was the first step that led to Psychomotor... This happened awfully fast; it seemed like an eternity... It never would have happened if we hadn't had those losses... (Note 2).

Their school, the Wollaston Dance Center, included a concert group, the Pesso Dance Company, directed by Al, in which Diane danced, choreographing her own solos. Over a period of several years their teaching activities kept expanding as they instructed some five hundred students per week. Al recounts that he himself taught as many as forty classes a week. Diane would have preferred to focus on her own concert work but could not find time due to her heavy teaching schedule and her primary responsibility for management of the home and children.

In the late 1950s the parents of some of the students joined a creative movement class led by Diane. This later grew into an experimental group mainly led by Al that included older students. Diane and Al were devising many new exercises involving movement and emotional expression. This was the ongoing "experimental group" I eventually joined.

During the years they lived in Quincy, Diane taught dance at Wheaton College, transferring this to Al when she gave birth to their second child, Tasmin. Then Al accepted a faculty appointment in the Theater Division at Emerson College, later being appointed associate professor. He established a dance major and became head of the dance department. Diane later joined Al in teaching at Emerson. Their third daughter, Tia, was born, and that year they began a gradual transition: their main center of activity shifted to Boston. They moved to Beacon Street and after a year closed the Wollaston Dance Center. They had become active with the Unitarian Church at the Charles Street Meetinghouse. Diane was invited to teach part-time at Sargent College (Boston University). The basis for the new therapy was developing and was beginning to become the main focus of their energy.

Only after the basic system of Psychomotor was established did Al continue his education, taking courses at local universities and, as a non-resident student, obtaining a degree from Goddard College in Vermont. He read widely in the field of psychology: not only psychoanalytic writers but also James, Watson, Skinner, and others. Eastern philosophies also drew his attention. Besides carrying a full teaching schedule, Diane took courses in anatomy, art, literature, and in Hindu and other styles of dance. By devising emotional sound and movement exercises for herself and her students she continued her exploration of the physical aspects and origins of emotional expression.

Modalities
of Movement

What Al and Diane Pesso had concluded through the explorations they undertook in the process of training dancers was that the body utilized three distinguishable *modalities of movement*: *reflex*, *voluntary* and *emotional*. Although this was not wholly original — Delsarte's school had arrived at a similar formulation — they felt they had contributed by developing exercises and practices "which tended to sharpen awareness of motion and expression and the concomitant subjective states experienced during the performance of these exercises" (A. Pesso, 1966, p. 10).

Their formulations of the three movement modalities were first presented in a 61-page essay they distributed privately, entitled "New Perspectives in the Generation of Movement: With Implications Important to Dance Composition, Criticism and Appreciation" (A. Pesso, 1963).

They saw these modalities as constituting three interwoven strands, the first of which is *reflex movement,* epitomized by the reflex-relaxed (species) stance:

> The stance is the first exercise in combining awareness with freedom from inhibition, or restraint. If consciousness were reduced then there would not be the element of communication between one part of the brain and another and integration would not be furthered. Even when the subject is doing extremely primitive movement his awareness is perceiving himself doing that movement and this can be a very educational experience (A. Pesso, 1966, p. 21).

A second strand is controlled, or volitional movement, in which the subject attempts to consciously program an action in advance of performing it, and in carrying it out takes care to turn off feelings and associational imagery, thereby attempting to avoid emotional coloration of the movement. Volitional or *voluntary movement*, "is isolated from the internal environment and exercised for itself. This develops mastery of the body and in a sense mastery of the external environment" (p. 27). Voluntary movement may be considered as a prerequisite for abstract thinking and as a sort of "abstract behaving" that is impaired in brain-damaged persons and in schizophrenics.

The third strand is emotional movement. Whereas voluntary movement is oriented to the external environment, emotional movement relates to that which is felt or sensed about the internal environment, and is need-oriented. "After a subject can achieve the species stance and reflex movement and after he can control his body and move it in an affect free and image free manner, he is given the opportunity to explore and discover the relationship between strong emotional states and subsequent action" (A. Pesso, 1966, p. 29). And further, "It is important to stress that in Psychomotor Therapy all movement modalities are exercised with awareness so that 'acting out' behavior in an unconscious form [is] reduced" (p. 30).

One of the emotional movement exercises starts with the reflex/relaxed (species) stance; subjects are then asked to generate a feeling such as fear and then to allow it spontaneous expression (*direct emotion*). If they cannot generate the feeling or emotion they can be asked to imagine a situation that would arouse the feeling. After this emotion has been expressed people move on to the next, such as anger. After that they are asked to generate a feeling of love in each of two forms: love being given and love being received. The final emotion to be generated and allowed expression is joy.

The Pessos used the exercises for diagnostic purposes and as a starting point for the kind of psychotherapy occurring in *structures*. They considered the exercises a necessary preparation for doing structures — a preparation that clearly carried an important therapeutic impact of its own. *Movement in Psychotherapy* (1969) was written to guide therapists in teaching the exercises and subsequently leading structures but did not include the sort of rationale for the exercises that is presented in the 1966 paper.

The Pessos' interest in disentangling the three strands of movement arose from the needs of dancers and other performers who found that what they intended to convey to an audience could be different from what the audience experienced.

> If conscious intent is not the only source of movement and expression, what are the other sources and how can one isolate and gain control of their expression? There seemed to be three motor systems constantly operating and interweaving with one another which could be explored individually for understanding and control... While attempting to move in and explore one modality and to eliminate behavior arising out of the other two modalities, one could note the appearance or lack of appearance of [actual] or nascent movement in the other two modalities (A. Pesso, 1974).

Through Psychomotor exercises, awareness of such movement could be enhanced and with it control over what might otherwise appear as at least minimal "acting out."

Al Pesso argues, in his 1966 paper, that "an emotional action would be more capable of evoking and unfolding to awareness an unconscious impulse than would a thought or words." He notes that in real life, actions sometimes have a way of getting out of hand. This has led therapists to shy away from action despite the feeling of many that "words by themselves are insufficient in treating mental illness" (p. 35).

The Transition From Dance To Psychotherapy

Various components of PS/P gradually began to emerge as a result of the Pessos' experience in teaching dance and in working with their concert dance company, a group which "received rave reviews for its honesty of expression" (Note 2).

While teaching a highly disciplined class in dance technique, Diane gave her students a brief period of spontaneous emotional improvisation as a way of discharging tensions. This improvisation was *not* dance, but a use of the third modality of movement: direct emotion. She told the students they were not literally to hit or hurt anyone but were free to move and make emotional sounds; it seemed that this rule would allow all emotions to be safely expressed. She noticed, however, that although the expression of most feelings resulted in a sense of satisfaction, students seemed to lose energy after moving in ways that expressed anger. The next day she tried the exercise out with the children in her creative movement class, and then with one of her college classes. In all three groups the students lost energy after expressing anger and many eventually sat on the floor, some slowly rocking back and forth. This seemed to be an undesirable result; she realized that it came from the frustration of expressing anger toward someone who did not respond in a satisfying way.

Recalling children's way of playing "Bang, bang! You're dead!" with the target person pretending to have been shot and tumbling to the ground, Diane told the group doing emotional improvisation that any time angry gestures or sounds were being made toward them by a group member, they should put their own feelings "on hold" and respond by pretending to succumb to the anger. Then they could again go back to the expression of their own feelings. Getting this kind of response made a notable difference; the person expressing anger no longer suffered a loss of energy and the whole experience became quite enjoyable. A corner of the room with a barricade was available as an "off limits" safety zone for anyone who didn't want to play the "game."

This was an early version of what was later to be called *negative accommodation*. Clearly no specific role-playing was involved, and the person who had pretended to be attacked quickly went back to doing his or her own emotional improvisation again. All of this activity, which could appear to be wild mayhem, was within the conscious awareness and control of the students. They would stop immediately when Diane gave the designated signal of raising her arm. Certainly there was no question of any uncontrolled "acting out" on anybody's part. The group or class would then return to whatever they had previously been working on, finding that tensions had been relaxed and that they could now perform their exercises with greater ease and clarity.

Diane, working by herself in the Quincy studio, was doing direct emotion (emotional improvisation in movement and sound). She found herself vividly re-experiencing a long-forgotten, frightening event that had occurred on a Memorial Day many years earlier, following a visit to her grandmother's grave. She realized this was a way of enabling lost memories to be relived and remembered.

Another piece of important learning came when the Pessos asked their students to work with a partner, one pair at a time, doing emotional movement and sound improvisation. A tall young man and a short older woman ended up intently gazing at each other, both with a discontented look. When asked, each reported that the partner had been perceived as a parent figure. This showed them how readily another group member could serve as a stimulus for projection. They further realized that two people who were improvising simultaneously would only rarely happen to act in ways that would provide fully satisfactory experiences for both partners. This was a step toward the decision that only one person at a time should have a turn while others would remain available to provide satisfying responses. Later this was formalized as accommodation.

The creative movement class at the Charles Street Meetinghouse also played a part. Diane's class was attended by the Pinderhughes children. What they had to say about activities there prompted their father (psychiatrist Charles Pinderhughes) to make inquiries about the work the Pessos were doing and to attend some sessions of a class taught by Al.

Some time later another precursor of a structure took place. At a meeting of the experimental group Diane decided to explore her lack of feelings at the funeral of her dearly loved grandfather when she was ten years old. She suspected there were some strong emotions she had never consciously experienced; in her family it had not been acceptable for her to show emotion.

Enlisting the help of the group, she set up the scene to depict the funeral parlor with people attending the service, and someone lying down to represent her grandfather in the coffin. Diane said,

> I felt in my body as if I was my ten-year-old self again. I told that child part of myself that it was OK to go ahead and do "direct emotion." A torrent of emotional movement and sounds came out of me, with enormous feelings of anger, grief, need, and rage switching back and forth. Meanwhile another part of myself was observing — and this was the same type of observing process that Al and I both used when developing a new emotional dance sequence. Now I had access to feelings that were repressed before. I felt free and safe in that room with today-level friends that I knew cared about me and wanted to help. I was also aware that they, including Al, were very puzzled about how to help. Al was reassuring them and telling them just to be there, so I felt I could let my ten-year-old self continue to use my body and learn from the

feelings that came. Later, after I had huddled with my arm around a pole in the middle of the floor and grieved, Al and the group members stayed with me and gently touched me. It was very important (Note 1).

Diane had been trying between sessions with her psychiatrist to recover memories of her childhood. She remembered very little of her life prior to the age of fourteen. She had learned about Freudian ideas first from a friend at Bennington who talked about her psychoanalysis, and then from discussions with Al. It made sense that early events shaped people's later patterns of behavior, and that current problems needed to be traced back to their roots in the past. She also now knew from her experience that through spontaneous emotional expression memories would surface. In her words, "the memories came up as I did the action" (Note 2).

It was during a vacation absence of her psychiatrist that the improvisation having to do with her grandfather's death occurred. The sense of relief afterwards was extraordinary, and she eagerly awaited her psychiatrist's return to tell him of the exciting material she had unearthed, thinking it would help her progress in her work with him.

His response, as Diane remembers, was "You *know* I don't like that type of thing, and if you do that again you can not come back, and you must pay for the next two appointments." She continues, "I felt that the movement exercises Al and I were developing, in conjunction with what I was doing with my psychiatrist, would move me much more rapidly. When forced to make a choice between the two, I felt that what Al and I were doing would take me further" (Note 2).

Al chimes in: "He really put her on the line... That was a *terrible* thing to tell her after she had been in therapy twice a week for two years, because of the transference that had developed... That manipulation was dreadful; it was very hard for her to make that choice and it resulted in a painful loss."

Diane's response to the ultimatum of her psychiatrist about doing "that type of thing:"

> I told him that I wouldn't do any more before I came in for the next appointment. When I next arrived, I said I had chosen the movement work, but that I thought the two together would be best and really wanted to continue working with him. He suggested I wait until I had completed my work with him, and when I told him I had decided not to wait, he told me that I would be back. I never went back. All those needs that got put on him, the effect of the transference... I learned to hate the effects of transference... the less transference there is to the therapist, the safer and better (Note 2).
>
> Subsequently, I have always emphasized getting the transference off the PS/P therapist and onto the role-players as soon as possible. I believe in the power of the caring part of human beings, the therapist and the other clients, but using transference on the therapist as part of the therapy is fraught with danger, provides no opportunity for reality testing and is bad for the therapist who can't behave as his or her imperfect real self (Note 1).

Diane remembers the first Psychomotor *structure*. It occurred one week after the improvisation connected with her grandfather's funeral:

> Al suggested I try doing direct emotional expression from the species stance. I started moving with anger and Al got somebody to stand in to respond as if the anger was effective. As the anger was expressed I realized that it was my father I was angry at, so that person was now standing in for him. When my anger was over I was left with

the still unsatisfied emotional need that had caused the anger, and the wish for my father to behave differently. Al and I were perplexed about what to do about this. We knew it wouldn't make sense to change the behavior of my real father because that wouldn't be true; there was no way of changing his past behavior in the current situation. But the need was very strong and was directed toward that figure. We wanted that need satisfied and we looked for ways to make it happen. I knew that other parents, if I had been their child, could have treated me differently. We came up with the idea of having someone represent a brand new father. Then the problem was for me to get my child self to give up trying to get needs satisfied by my role-played "real" father and to turn my needs toward my new "alternative" father. I did so and it was wonderfully satisfying (Note 1).

The Pessos began to recognize that two kinds of figures were needed: a responsive target for the satisfying expression of anger and a strong, positive figure who could provide an antidote for past hurts, deprivations or losses. This they saw as a bodily as well as a psychological need. Since early negative experiences very often had to do with parents, the polarized figures were likely to be designated respectively as "bad" mother or father and "good" or "wished-for" father or mother. The "good" parents not only counteracted the influence of the "bad" parents but also were a source of acceptance, support, and validation that were especially needed after a "bad" parent or other figure had been symbolically attacked through angry gestures and vocalizations.

Knowing that accommodating responses would occur made it easier to express emotion spontaneously. This expression in turn helped structure *enactors* to summon up recollections of events in childhood which were still charged with their original emotional meaning, even though the events and feelings might have long been absent from conscious memory. These early, remembered events usually set the stage for the structure that would then be enacted. From the development of accommodation to the enactment of structures was a short step; one led almost irresistibly to the next.

Training was necessary for the *negative accommodators* who represented "bad" figures: they were not to retaliate, nor defend themselves, but were to let themselves be defeated, responding to each angry sound, statement or gesture with a body movement and vocalization modulated to match the intensity of the attack against them. Structure enactors were repeatedly reminded of the "four foot rule": the "attacker" was to maintain a distance of at least four feet from the person being "attacked" by hand and arm gestures or by kicks.

Also useful for structures were exercises, originally designed for dancers, that sensitized participants their bodies' reactions to other people's locations — whether nearer or farther away, whether standing higher or sitting lower than one's self, whether located in front, in back, or by one's side — and what the significant feelings were that these positions evoked, to say nothing of how it felt to have an "accommodating" person faithfully follow one's bidding. Thus exercises designated as *controlled approach* and *stimulus figure* were performed, as well as various circle exercises which emphasized the difference between inner and outer, and between acceptance and rejection. (These exercises are described fully in *Movement in Psychotherapy*, 1969).

Positive accommodation in PS/P structures was modeled on the normal, healthy kinds of physical contact that occur between parents and children in the real world. Parents could touch children in caring, non-sexual ways; members of the group could accordingly touch each other in ways that were equally non-sexual when they were enacting structures or serving as accommodators.

Dancers being trained by the Pessos had started to do structures and some had been surprised at the lessening of their tension and anxiety and at the notable changes in their flexibility, strength and performance. Gradually the Pessos began to realize that they had discovered and created together the foundation for a new method of psychotherapy.

First Version: Early to Mid-'60s

At the time of my first contacts, the essential elements already described were well in place, although some things were quite different from what has since evolved. First, PS/P was then considered to be "non-verbal," a designation that in the 1990s would hardly seem apt, even though the underlying emphasis upon spontaneous emotional expression through movement and sounds remains. In 1966 Al wrote, "Psychomotor Therapy, as it is now practiced, proceeds on a primitive non-verbal base, with words used only as expletives by the patients and as instructions by the therapists" (p. 88). And in 1973 a statement concerning the purposes of the Psychomotor Institute described it as "devoted to the development and furtherance of non-verbal techniques in the broad field of human development — psychotherapy, education and the arts."

Second, as the reference to "expletives" suggests, considerably more emphasis was placed on the expression of anger during this early period than was the case later on. During my first experiences with structures, I found it impressive that while enactors gave full vent to their anger, their sense of current reality remained wholly intact. If, for example, the "four foot rule" was accidentally overstepped and a slightly miscalculated "blow" happened to graze an accommodating "bad" figure ever so lightly, the rage would be interrupted by a crestfallen apology: "I'm so sorry!" as the structure enactor stepped back and then, again at a safe distance, resumed the furious symbolic attack as before.

Shortly after I had joined the Meetinghouse group, the Pessos invited me to come to the Wednesday evening "experimental group" that met in their apartment on Beacon Street in Boston. Here now familiar exercises were done and new ones were tried out: one member of the group would be lifted and supported at shoulder height by the others; or one would lie on the floor looking up while the rest of the group stood in rectangle formation looking down at the recumbent one's face. The purpose was to see what feelings, associations, memories, or emotional behavior would be triggered by these exercises.

In this group, the Pessos took turns with the rest of us in doing therapeutic work (structures) for themselves. Often we stayed afterwards, over coffee in the kitchen, trying to understand what seemed to be going on and how it could best be formulated and perhaps improved.

The effects of PS/P on the participants were impressive, but it seemed to me that only the Pessos could lead Psychomotor sessions — especially structures. Only someone trained as a professional dancer would have keen enough awareness of body movements and the ways in which emotions affected the body to be able to lead this sort of therapeutic group.

Psychomotor exercises served powerfully to strengthen group members' trust in one another and in ourselves. We were helped to realize that it was permissible, safe, and rewarding to express positive and negative feelings toward the figures that accommodating members of the group agreed to represent symbolically. And in doing structures, what a satisfaction it was to have a whole array of clearly defined transference figures, rather than just one whose identity seemed to shift so that there was no way of knowing whether one's feelings were toward that "real" person or were products of unwitting transference. Increasingly we could let ourselves get in touch with forgotten or unrecognized feelings by following the leads given by impulses we became aware of in our bodies, and could let these impulses move us into symbolic actions and interactions we would never have anticipated. Doing a structure was always a voyage of discovery. Somehow it tapped another level of consciousness, something like a trance state, or a waking dream. But it simply expressed our own inner, often previously unconscious, feelings — and there was always a positive outcome at the end.

The Pessos' insistence that both the preliminary training exercises and structures should always end positively was one of the things that very much impressed me about their method. In contrast to some other (verbal and nonverbal) group approaches, in PS/P groups no one was allowed to end in a negative situation. If someone was ejected from the group, she or he was always brought back and made welcome again. If a person wanted everyone else to leave the room so that she or he could be alone, that person was persuaded to keep at least one positive accommodator in the room to call on in case of need. If someone wanted to end a structure by "dying," he or she was encouraged to look for an alternative means of expressing what felt like a wish for death. This might be done either by turning self-destructive impulses outward in an attack upon a negative target or by understanding the wish to die as a wish for symbolic rebirth — for reunion with a "good mother" — who could then be accommodatingly supplied.

The positive ending of a structure was due not so much to the therapist's insistence but to reliance on information furnished by the structure enactor's body. Al Pesso has commented, "We've never changed in that belief — that the [pathogenic] experience was in the body and that the *solution* was also in the body, and that when we stayed close to that we always had an outcome. I was *amazed* that we always had a positive outcome, so long as we stayed with the body... Truth was in the body" (Note 2).

Also impressive was PS/P's ingenious multiplication and polarization of transference targets. Ambivalence no longer blocked the expression of feeling because negative and positive emotions had different targets to interact with. One could experience purely negative feelings from — and toward — a "bad" figure and purely positive feelings toward — and from — a "good" figure. They were separate, and neither interfered with the other. Giving vent to negative feelings toward one symbolic person opened the way to expressing and experiencing positive feelings toward — and from — another symbolic person. Getting the wished-for positive response sometimes reactivated negative feelings — "Why couldn't my real mother (or father) have been like this!" — and the enactor of the structure might again make angry gestures toward the "bad" figure, who would revive and accommodate to the renewed symbolic attack. After this the enactor returned with even stronger positive feeling to the "good" mother and/or father, who would respond in ways that seemed suitable. Although either Al or Diane Pesso or the structure enactor suggested responses the "good" accommodators might make, the latter still, at this stage, remained free to respond in a way they thought fitting although any harmful response would be stopped. In deference to the view that this was an essentially non-verbal method, however, words were used sparingly.

A "bad" father could be chosen from among the men in the group; a "good" father could be another male; "bad" and "good" mothers were selected from the women, and "good" and "bad" versions of a brother or sister or other significant figure could be chosen as well. A woman was never asked to accommodate in the role of a male figure, nor a man in a female figure's role. Generational identities were also made clearly explicit. "Good parents" in a structure related to each other in ways that they did not relate to their "child" (the structure enactor), but the "child" could be assured of some day having a contemporary partner of his/her own. Meanwhile the "good" parents provided for the satisfaction of all the *basic needs* of their "child." (How extraordinarily much simpler and easier this was, it seemed to me, than having one lone, ambivalently regarded therapist, with his/her single gender and generational identity, transiently take on and then give up one after another of these manifold transference roles!)

Starting in the autumn of 1964, Al Pesso had been asked to try out Psychomotor techniques with a few patients at McLean Hospital, a psychiatric teaching hospital. He subsequently brought Diane to assist him and later to run independent sessions with patients. The patients chosen for them were usually, predictably, the ones the staff found most difficult to deal with. Working with the Pessos, many of these patients began to make noticeable improvements.

The following year, in the spring of 1966, Jim Garland, then Director of the Activities Department at McLean, invited Al Pesso to conduct a series of ten training sessions for staff members. I was asked to help as an accommodator and to evaluate the sessions' effectiveness. This series marked the beginning of the Pessos' efforts to train other people in the use of PS/P techniques, and we kept careful notes on what was done.

Around this time Al Pesso, sometimes joined by Diane, started giving lectures that included demonstrations of certain PS/P techniques and exercises in psychiatric settings, university psychology departments, and for the American Occupational Therapy Association. As a result of presentations for the Advanced Pastoral Counseling Association, PS/P was prominently mentioned in Clyde Reid's book *Groups Alive — Church Alive* (1969). Other cities in which he gave workshops included New York, Boston, Atlanta, Winston-Salem, Chicago and Philadelphia.

During this mid-sixties period, a few psychiatrists who had referred patients to PS/P groups had found this to be a valuable adjunct to the treatment they were conducting. Patients whose therapy had slowed to a standstill overcame whatever was blocking them and then continued to move ahead very rapidly in their treatment, according to these psychiatrists' reports. PS/P was beginning to be seen as a valid treatment method in its own right and as the treatment of choice for some clients.

Work with psychotic or other seriously impaired patients continued, but it was difficult to treat them in a group because they were not well enough attuned to each other to be able to accommodate adequately. A number of individual sessions generally had to precede the psychotic patient's introduction into a group, and since additional, relatively normal, accommodators had to be brought in, this kind of treatment was likely to be quite costly. Alternatively, a psychotic person might be included in a group of non-psychotic people. I recall Al Pesso once remarked that any group could handle *one* psychotic member. There were Psychomotor techniques available to handle whatever quasi-psychotic states of mind that might occur in group members whose behavior was reasonably normal.

The question of who benefits most from PS/P therapy (or emotional re-education) was often raised by people associated with the Pessos[1]. People with a wide variety of problems and diagnoses have found their way to PS/P, apparently with benefit, and with no indication

---

[1] An intake process has been developed in the Netherlands that is designed to indicate whether or not individuals are ready to undertake the Pesso therapy.

of harm.

During the later 1960s, referrals and self-referrals grew apace. Neither Pesso, however, devoted full time to PS/P. Besides his private practice, Al was a full-time faculty member teaching dance at Emerson College, seeing patients at McLean Hospital, consulting at the Boston V.A. Hospital and pursuing his studies for Goddard College. Diane had her practice at home and at McLean Hospital.

Intermediate Version, 1969-76

After a two year absence, I joined a PS/P group led by Al Pesso and was astounded. No more preliminary exercises! Even no more species stance, unless someone was at a loss about what to do in a structure. Then it could be used to discover unnecessary tensions in the body that could point toward action or toward wished-for accommodation.

There were other changes. Negative accommodation now utilized large foam-filled cushions on which kicks or blows were inflicted while a role-playing *negative parent* or other figure winced and cried out with each impact. It was no longer necessary to worry about accidentally hitting the accommodator; also, hitting a yielding substance gave some people more satisfaction than striking the empty air four feet short of the target.

A further major change had to do with sexuality, which had not been a topic dealt with directly in structures at the earlier stage. Now it was taken for granted that parents and children were likely to have sexual feelings toward each other, and these feelings were given clear symbolic expression in the structures that were carried out. Earlier the issue of sexuality had not come up in structures because the Pessos believed that what might seem sexual was actually a disguised need for *nurturance*, which they regarded as a young child's principal need.

A particular kind of positive accommodation known as *limiting* had been developed. A precursor of limiting had occurred earlier, when accommodators playing *"good" (ideal) parents* (often assisted by others in the group acting as extensions of the parents) lifted up tumbling mats as a barrier so that the anger expression or furious onslaught of their "child" (the structure enactor) could take place safely. During this symbolic attack the "good" parents murmured sounds such as "Um hm" to indicate that they acknowledged the expression of anger by their child and were not letting themselves be harmed by it.

Another early form of limiting occurred in response to a structure enactor's Oedipal strivings. A person might become aware of having had a childhood impulse to push his or her parents apart. The therapist would then instruct the couple accommodating in the roles of "good" parents to hold each other firmly around the middle, asking help from others in the group if their "child" had unusual physical strength. The *enactor* could then try with all his or her might to separate the parents, and would inevitably fail. This experience offered a wholesome corrective to the person's past situation if real parents had not been emotionally close to each other and had all too readily allowed their child to come between them.

The need for limiting is one of several *basic needs* of the growing individual, needs which, before birth, are satisfied by the mother's body, and usually by the mother or by both parents after the baby is born. Besides the original need the Pessos had identified, the need for *nurturance*, they now specified three more: the need for *support*, for *protection*, and for *limits* or containment. Two further needs were subsequently added: the need for a *place* (where one belongs), and the need for *respect*. The identification of these needs resulted from attention to the question of what kinds of response (interaction) would best match or satisfy each emotion that people might experience. As the "good" parental responses of providing support when the child felt insecure, protection when the child was frightened, and nurturance when the child was hungry or in need of comfort were experienced and internalized, the child was enabled increasingly to be self-supporting, self-protecting, and self-nurturing.

Recognition of the human individual's need to be limited, to have what might be called a "holding environment," was a particularly significant development in PS/P. Parents' provision of limits for their child enables the child to internalize the meaning of this particular interaction with the parent(s), so that from this time on the child can impose appropriate limits on his or her own behavior in similar situations. Lacking adequate experience of such limit-imposing interactions, the child is unsure of his or her own boundaries and vulnerable to a sense of *omnipotence* on the one hand and total powerlessness on the other.

During this middle period the enactor of a structure in which limits were to be imposed on the expression of anger was asked to lie on the floor on his or her back. "Good" or positive parents then usually limited the person's arms, assuming positions that allowed them good leverage. "Extensions" of the "good" parents held the person's head and legs. Not until everyone was in place did the struggle begin. When it ended the exhausted enactor realized with surprise and gratification that his or her anger was not, after all, so powerfully dangerous that it could destroy the world; instead, a mere handful of ordinary mortals were able to deal with it calmly and kindly. As a result there was less need to deny anger or hold it back inappropriately and the person felt a new sense of validation and empowerment.

Except for the Oedipal limit structures already described, sexual limit structures came along well after the limit structures for anger had become part of the PS/P repertoire. One sort of sexual limiting took place with the enactor lying on his or her back on the floor. Then, *ideal parents* (as they were beginning to be called) placed their hands over the enactor's hip bones to limit his or her pelvic thrusts toward either the ideal mother or father. Statements made by the ideal parents validated the enactor's sexuality at the same time that their superior strength kept the person's sexual energies appropriately limited, or contained. The meaning of this external, interactive restraint could then be internalized so that the person no longer needed to fear sexuality, hold sexual feelings back, or punish him- or herself for having them.

Another kind of sexual limit structure entailed recognizing and respecting the structure enactor's wish to invite sexual contact with a parent but not permitting this to happen. Originally the response in this situation was to have ideal parents wrap their arms firmly around the enactor's knees, saying that it's all right to want to open up sexually to, say, the ideal father, and it's all right to try to do so with all one's strength, but they won't *let* the enactor literally do that. Ideal parents then add that they have literal sex only with each other, which they very much enjoy, and that neither one of them would ever do anything literally sexual with their child, no matter how appealing the child might be. More recently Al Pesso has shifted to sometimes asking only women to do the restraining of a woman's knees in order to limit her openness.

His second book (Pesso, 1973) referred to what he called a "species ego," describing it "as a system for catching the interactive energies that slip past the ego and would seem to endanger the species... a massive circuit breaker for the emotional system [that] works for the safety and satisfaction of others rather than the safety and satisfaction of the self" (p. 145).

Limit structures are designed to repair gaps or deficiencies in the ego which permit interactive energies to move toward infinity and omnipotence, a movement that the species ego would otherwise counter either by turning off the energy or by deflecting it back toward the self, perhaps giving rise to fantasies or hallucinations.

At a later period limit structures tended to be carried out with the structure enactor remaining in whatever position he or she had assumed, rather than being asked to lie down on the floor and wait for accommodators to assume the positions that made limiting relatively easy. This shift avoids the break in continuity required by the earlier method and works well when there are enough people in the group.

Establishing the Institute

By 1969, there were several people who had been trained to conduct PS/P exercises and structures. The process of teaching, along with presenting lecture-demonstrations, challenged the Pessos to work out increasingly clear concepts and theories concerning PS/P and its effects. The pattern of a formalized two-year training program was beginning to emerge from the informal apprenticeship type of training the earliest students had experienced.

It seemed essential to set up an organization explicitly devoted to Psychomotor teaching, practice, and research. The Psychomotor Institute was established during the summer of 1970 and approved as a nonprofit corporation the following year. In 1971, the Psychomotor Institute bought a handsome former residence — most recently a music school — at 251 Commonwealth Avenue in Boston, a six-story building containing numerous large wood-paneled, virtually soundproof rooms. Here trainees could learn, be supervised, and practice Psychomotor.

In early 1973, I became a member of the Institute's staff charged with filling gaps in the conceptual and theoretical background of some of the newer trainees. Guarding the integrity of PS/P, and establishing a theoretical and research-based foundation seemed the most promising way of attracting well-qualified psychotherapists to seek PS/P training.

A training committee recommended that intensive training in PS/P should be offered only to people already professionally trained in psychotherapy and certification standards were set. Trainees under supervision were expected to lead PS/P workshops and therapy sessions, but were not granted the right to claim they were Psychomotor therapists until they had completed the certification training program.

The Pessos' involvement with trainees and others helped in clarifying, extending, enriching and refining PS/P theory and practice. During the late 1960s, for example, Nat Hollister, a neurologist who had attended PS/P groups in Ohio with his wife, Jane, came to realize that a large number of his patients suffered from emotional rather than neurological problems. They came to Boston so Jane could enroll in the Psychomotor Institute's two year training program and Nat could be trained in psychiatry and attend the first year of PS/P training. He decided to focus on the treatment of chronic atypical pain patients and used PS/P as a major treatment modality. A special unit at the New England Rehabilitation Hospital in Woburn was established, which later moved to Massachusetts Rehabilitation Hospital (now Spaulding Hospital) in Boston. When New England Rehabilitation Hospital appointed a new psychiatrist for the Pain Unit, they recruited one of the Pessos and their trainees to provide the PS/P component.

While Director of Psychomotor Therapy at the Pain Unit, Diane Pesso found that patients' great difficulty with anger expression interfered with the usual structure work.

Needing to find a way for patients to access their emotional needs without triggering the blocking effects of anger, she devised two new exercises, the *ideal parent* and the *self/self - self/other* exercises. These made it possible for patients to go directly to positive structure experiences, while they were still in the process of learning to express their anger.

Jane Hollister, whose orientation was Jungian, recognized that what the Pessos had been calling "good" or "wished-for" parent figures could be considered to be "archetypes"; the concepts of "animus" and "anima" were also useful in illuminating the "phallic" attributes of women and the receptive, nurturing and creative qualities of men.

Jane was one of the early graduates of the training program and a member of its teaching staff. Other early graduates were Arthur Cobb, Ph.D., David Doolittle, M.A., Gail Murray, M.A., Charles Nordby, Ph.D., Rufus Peebles, J.D., and Michael Werle, Ed.D.

Rather than judgmental terms such as "good" and "bad" parent figures, I preferred words like "positive" and "negative" parents. It became clearer that these were *aspects* of real parents which it was useful to polarize (or "split"). In addition, there were the *ideal*, archetypal parent figures who could be constructed to supply precisely what the negative aspects of real parents had failed to provide. Though the reference was at first to archetypes, it seemed simpler to speak of them as "ideal," rather than archetypal, parents.

I continued to be impressed with the close correspondence between PS/P and Freudian theory, especially if the latter were augmented by a sociological emphasis on *interaction* and its internalization — such as has been more recently supplied through the development of object relations, self psychology, and family systems theories. Further extension of psycho-analytic views occurs through PS/P's emphasis on the body and its ways of moving and acting, an emphasis that seems quite compatible with Freud's views even though it was not developed by him beyond his statement that "...the ego is first and foremost a bodily ego."

Although the use of limiting figures to help structure enactors to handle their sexual and aggressive energies seems compatible with Freud's designation of them as "instincts," PS/P's postulation of the child's inherent *basic need* to have such limits imposed is significantly different from Freud's view. Freud saw the child's wish to murder one parent and marry the other as opposed only by the fear of punitive retaliation — castration anxiety — subsequently internalized as a guilt-laden superego. By contrast, it is the Pesso System's more optimistic view that a need to experience opposition to these omnipotent wishes exists innately within the child. There is something within the child, the Pessos believe, that welcomes the firm and kindly parent figures' non-punitive, non-retaliatory, non-judgmental and non-guilt-arousing imposition of limits on his or her wishes.

Freud saw the ego as a "surface entity"; Al Pesso similarly referred to it during this period as "the skin of the self," later using the term *ego-wrapping* to describe how, through the loving, care-giving, and validating responses of parents, ego is wrapped around the individual's *soul* or core self. As for gaining access to unconscious thoughts and feelings, for PS/P it is primarily the body and its sensations and movements, rather than dreams, which represents "the royal road to the unconscious."

Out of a wish to remain hospitable to all possible theoretical views that might be held by potential PS/P trainees or clients, the Pessos deliberately chose not to align themselves with any particular school of psychotherapy. They readily acknowledge that many elements of their approach are also found elsewhere.

PS/P Paradigms

During the course of Gus Kaufman's and my training in the mid 1970s Al Pesso arrived at a new formulation he was eager to share with us: that whatever happens to the human individual from the time of conception somehow leaves a record of that event within the organic-chemical corpus[2] of the individual. Such an event may not be fully, consciously experienced, or felt, by the individual. Even if it is experienced, there may not be an adequate opportunity for the person to express his or her feelings about the event; under these circumstances there is likely to be denial of feelings, or feelings are displaced from their original object to something or somebody else, or they are otherwise defended against. The result is an inaccurate *map* of what the world is like. (Originally Al referred to this as a cognition, later substituting the word "map.") Then, "We no longer see things as they really are, but instead see them in terms of how we were conditioned to see them by our early history... All the events of our childhood are used as map-making elements for how we should behave in the future...as predictors of our future" (Pesso, 1984a, p. 5).

These four steps in the processing of events formed a schema that paralleled the earlier *Cycle of Becoming* paradigm: **Energy—> Action—> Interaction—> Meaning/Internalization**. In this sequence *energy* is seen as equivalent to emotion, which may or may not be consciously felt as emotion.

An implication of the new sequence of steps is that it is not enough to become aware of buried feelings (to experience them), nor is it enough to express them toward an appropriate target; besides both of these it is essential to have a new kind of experience that can counteract or provide an *antidote* to the hurtful experience of the past so that the old *map* can be put aside as a "program" for behavior and a new one created to take its place. It is *ideal figures*, most often *ideal parents*, who provide the interactive experiences on which this alternative map of what the world is like can be constructed.

Al Pesso had worked out a rather complex scheme consisting of magical, counter (or defensive), symbolic, and literal sexual organs. He theorized that, apart from the functional real or literal organ, each psychologically healthy person has internalized *both* a symbolic male and a symbolic female organ. Extrapolating from the first as a thrusting, penetrating organ and the second as open and *receptive*, it was his view that healthy persons of both sexes have the ability to assert themselves appropriately and be aggressive in their own defense, and also, under other circumstances, to be open, sensitive, and able to permit the other a place in their interior life. On another level, whatever bodily parts protrude, whether they belong to a male or a female, can be symbolically phallic; whatever is an opening or an indentation can serve as a symbolic vagina. The eyes are of special significance because they can function both ways: the eyes receive impressions; their gaze also can be penetrating.

When a parent is absent because of death, divorce or separation, military service, illness, workaholism, or other forms of psychological withdrawal, a child is likely to be drawn into the parental role that has been vacated. If a father is the absent parent, the child (whether a boy or a girl) is likely to develop a "magical penis;" if it is the mother who is absent, the child tends to develop a "magical vagina." These magical organs are not present in the consciousness of the boy or girl, but the child's behavior indicates the unconscious presence of the magical organ, which confers an exciting feeling of omnipotence on the one hand and a frightening sense of erotic arousal on the other. The appropriate PS/P response is to have ideal

---

[2] Credit is due Robert Beloof for this phrasing.

figures (and their extensions) limit and contain the energies of the magical organs.

Counter organs serve to defend the child from the impact of a parent who is too much present, who does not respect the child's boundaries, or who is intrusive or invasive. A counter-penis is developed by the boy or girl when the father is the invasive parent, while an invasive mother is warded off by a counter organ resembling hers — a counter-vagina. An ideal father responds to his child's counter-penis by actions and words that signify, "You can keep me out," while an ideal mother responds to her son's or daughter's counter-vagina by making it clear that she will not let herself be swallowed up by the child.

To the best of my knowledge no other theory of psychotherapy has arrived at this formulation, which impresses me as both subtle and profound.

Al Pesso's formulations often go by fours. What he now calls "symbolic operations" he referred to during the '70s as "metaphors" — the ways in which a child acquires and possesses the qualities of another person, typically a parent: by "eating," "merging with," "marrying," or "murdering." There is, however, one trio of concepts: to "predict," "produce," or "recognize." Ideally a structure enactor (or the energies of an enactor) can predict what will yield the satisfaction that is sought; can produce it; or at the very least can recognize the action that will yield satisfaction when it is suggested by the therapist. These concepts presuppose a basic unity of life, that life is an organic process in which the parts are related to the whole as in a hologram, where the smallest part of the organic process has information about all the other parts and about the whole.

Other Mid-70s Developments

Looking back now on my experiences as a trainee, I am impressed both by the extent to which present-day PS/P understanding had already evolved at that time and the degree to which practices during the 1970s differed from what they have subsequently become. Some videotapes from this era are striking in the differences they reveal. In 1979, Al commented on three 1974 videotapes, indicating what he would do differently some five years later. Since the Pessos only rarely played the roles of ideal parents during recent years, it now seems strange to see how often they did so in the past. At that time some accommodators responded to a structure enactor by saying what they thought was needed. This was a criticism Al Pesso now made of his own former behavior: that he would no longer make statements as an accommodator that had not been requested or agreed to in advance by the structure enactor, nor would he heedlessly mix in statements he was making as himself or as a therapist.

One of the 1974 videotapes showed the enactor at the end of his structure being embraced by his ideal parents and then giving a deep sigh of contentment. They stay there a few moments more and then someone says, "Shall we go get something to eat?" Everyone arises and begins to leave the room as the tape ends.

It seemed to me that having accommodators ceremoniously give up their roles and resume their own identities would highlight the important passage between the symbolic reality of the structure (with all its transferences) and the everyday reality of the here-and-now to which the enactor must return. The Pessos agreed that this transition needed to be marked by a ritual divestment of roles that would be faithfully performed at the end of every structure. Negative figures and the cushions representing their extensions were de-roled first, while ideal parents were the last to de-role, doing so in unison so that their "child" would not be left in the company of just one of them.

A new technique also devised in this period consisted of having a *resistance figure* for the structure enactor to push against, when there were indications of a need to push but the target figure was still unclear. The therapist often assumed this role in order to provide a neutral target for the enactor's energies. In the process of pushing, the enactor was likely to recall some figure or event from the past. This would clarify whether the resisting figure was positive or negative and who the figure was, at which point a negative or ideal figure could be substituted for the one initially offering resistance.

Other developments that occurred during these years can be noted. For example, the introduction of the "negative voice," a voice that the structure enactor hears as if it were his or her own inner voice and may only later identify as having had an external origin. Externalizing the negative voice by having it role-played by an accommodator makes it easier for the structure enactor to deal with such a voice.

Giving attention to *self-self/self-other* interaction was another. Often finding out what one part of the body is doing for another part, *self-self*, such as one hand holding the other, or *self-other*, such as grasping the arm of a chair, can link to unmet historical needs which can then be satisfied in a structure with ideal figures.

By the late 1970s PS/P techniques were "cleaner" and more focussed than they had been earlier.

PS/P in the 1980s: Concepts and Techniques

People whose only contacts with PS/P occurred prior to the 1980s would be surprised to return to a session with Al in the mid to late '80s and find him speaking of the *possibility sphere*, the *center of one's truth*, the *true scene*, *shape and countershape*, *ego-wrapping*, the *witness figure*, "containing," *contact*, and "comfort" as well as *resistance figures*, to say nothing of numerous *fragment figures* or *voices*, plus a *pilot*.

Some of these designations derived from Al's efforts to let trainees know more about the thoughts and feelings he experienced — and had trained himself to experience — in the course of working with a structure enactor. The aim was to help trainees become more fully attuned to what was happening in the client's mind and body.

One concept of this sort was that of the *possibility sphere*, which was considered applicable to any sort of psychotherapeutic work and not just to PS/P. The emptiness of the possibility sphere is welcoming; it says, "Here living is possible." The client is surrounded with something potentially fertile; metaphorically the possibility sphere represents a womb which is there to help the individual realize possibilities. It provides an accepting, nourishing, life-supporting arena in which to work, and it is conducive to the birthing of the unborn parts of the self into reality and consciousness. It offers a safe "holding environment" where clients can become aware of how they actually experience their lives in the present moment, can explore painful, submerged parts of their personalities, and can experience the symbolic satisfaction of previously unmet basic needs. Al Pesso's paper on "Ego Development and the Body" (1988), revised for this volume, includes a more extensive discussion of the possibility sphere (see Chapter 4).

The *negative voice* was the forerunner of what in the late 1980s might become one or several voices that were given more specific designations, such as the voice of shame, the voice of family tradition, the voice of caution, the voice of negative prediction, etc. Like the original negative voice, these voices often represent the structure enactor's resistance to the therapeutic process. Having the voices be role-played so that the person hears them from outside rather than just from inside helps significantly in dealing with such resistances. These voices are referred to as those of *fragment figures*.

Their use is in line with a principle derived from work with the behaviorist, Leo Reyna: to proceed in small steps, in small increments. A client may recognize that an inner voice is saying "Don't make a fool of yourself!" but not yet realize that this voice of warning represents an internalized negative aspect of a parent. *Fragment figures* let the sources of early programming about how to conduct one's self in the world be externalized, perhaps becoming part of the *true scene*, well before the client is ready to ask someone to role-play this aspect of a parent.

It is much the same with the *ego-wrapping* figures. To the earlier *resistance figure* there have now been added figures providing comfort, contact and containment. These similarly become available to the client at an early stage of the therapeutic process, often before he or she is ready to accept the emotional reality of a pair of *ideal parents*. The same is true of the *witness figure* whose perception, naming and assessment of the client's emotion gives it external validation. These figures supply other portions of the information needed for constructing the true scene. Creating a witness figure also furthers the Pessos' aim of reducing transference as far as possible: with a group member playing this role there is someone other than the therapist who is available to perform this essential, and basically parental, ego-wrapping function.

Although the phrase *shape* and *countershape* was new in the '80s, the emphasis on shapes was not. Referring again to Leo Reyna, Al remarked that he (Reyna) "was always aware of the shapes of the behaviors and of the shapes of the programs, and I think of a metaphor as a shape" (Note 2).

Another way of working that was new in the early 1980s was sometimes to have positive figures partly restrain a structure enactor when he or she was having difficulty expressing angry feelings toward a negative role-player, with the latter responding as if smitten by the client's words or blows. Previously the client's anger had either been expressed toward ideal parental figures who limited the anger or toward a negative target who accommodated with sound and movement. Now both could happen at once.

The positive voice whose messages supported the structure enactor's best interests can probably be considered a forerunner of another recent development, that of the *pilot*. The pilot exists within the client and can be trusted to steer that person's actions and guide his or her understanding, thoughts and feelings toward a positive outcome. The pilot must, however, have adequate information about early programming, about the old *map* that had been formed. When this information has been made available by constructing the true scene, the pilot can then make decisions that lead to a positive outcome.

Al says of the pilot that he and Diane have always trusted in and helped people to discover that inner wisdom of the body which enables structure enactors to find their way to a positive outcome. As he puts it: "we always had a positive outcome, so long as we stayed with the body... *Truth* was in the body" (Note 2).

Research

In 1964, at the Boston V.A. Hospital, Dr. Charles Pinderhughes, with Leo Reyna and Al Pesso, was funded for a research program designed to explore the use of PS/P exercises and structures with hospitalized psychiatric patients, most of them chronic schizophrenics.

The nature of the research, which had originally been quite broad, was progressively narrowed to one specific goal: studying the species (reflex/relaxed) stance as a diagnostic instrument. A research report was prepared but never published.

Gus Kaufman (1981) completed a dissertation that was both theoretical and experimental: *Body signals of childhood loss: How relational deficits and stress lead to tension and postural insecurity* (see Chapter 5).

Melvin L. Foulds and Patricia Hannigan (1974, 1976) conducted research on students at Bowling Green State University's counseling center. In each study, one group was composed of students randomly assigned to be a waiting list control, while the other group was involved in 32 hours of PS/P exercises and structures as described in *Movement in Psychotherapy* (Pesso, 1969). PS/P participants showed increases in positive perceptions of themselves and others as compared to control subjects; significant results were maintained during retesting 6 months later (1974). Changes were also examined using *Rotter's* Locus of Control and the Marlowe-Crowne Social Desirability scales (1976). PS/P participants became significantly more inner directed, and their increases in sense of personal control of life events remained on 6 month follow-up while the control group was unchanged. PS/P participants showed significant changes on the Marlowe Crown scale toward decreased social desirability ($p=<.01$) which was maintained 6 months later, again with no change having occurred in control group scores. The authors conclude that

> Psychomotor group therapy may be an effective method for facilitating change in the self-descriptions of growth-seeking college students in the directions of increased internality and a decreased tendency to present oneself in a socially favorable (but probably untrue) light (Foulds and Hannigan, 1976, p. 87).

Robert Sokolove's dissertation (1975): *Verbal and motoric styles of therapy: An outcome study* included three therapy groups and a control group: a Psychomotor (verbal and motoric) group, a body movement (motoric only) group, and a verbal therapy group. Thirty-one subjects were randomly assigned to one of the four conditions. Subjects who rated high on the pre-post measure of autonomic arousal did better in Psychomotor therapy than in verbal or body movement groups.

Dissertations and theses on PS/P have been completed by Oelman (1978), Ellingsen-Greenwood (1978), Levenson (1981), Meyer-von Blon (1986), Scott (1987), and psychology students in the Netherlands and Sweden. Dutch Pesso therapists publish *Het Pesso Bulletin*, which contains articles on Pesso therapy.

Glenn Shean has collected descriptions of their experiences written by people who have done PS/P structures (see Chapter 23).

Acceptance of PS/P in Europe

Certain events had laid the groundwork for the Pesso's first European trip in 1973. *Movement in Psychotherapy* (1969) had been published simultaneously by the New York University Press and the University of London Press, which made it available in Europe. (Later it was translated into Dutch). An American psychologist, Jacob Stattman, who had attended a number of PS/P workshops, began to use PS/P exercises and techniques in his own presentations at European growth centers. Along with Al Pesso's book, these presentations aroused a great deal of interest. The Pessos began receiving letters from Amsterdam, London, and Paris asking when they would be able to present their work in person.

The Pessos received a warm welcome when they described and demonstrated Psychomotor therapy. Their presentation for Quaesitor in London was followed by a sympathetic write-up of their work in the English journal *Self and Society*, (Francis, 1973). Through Jacob Stattman, they made contacts at the Tavistock Clinic. They learned that in England twelve therapists had formed a study group that met weekends to learn about Psychomotor. Similar groups were meeting in Paris and Groningen. For several years after their first visit the Pessos returned three times a year to meet with these groups.

Their work won them immediate acceptance from many leading psychiatrists, psychoanalysts, psychologists, and others as important innovators in psychotherapy.

Han Sarolea, a psychologist on the faculty of the University of Groningen, came to the United States for training during 1975, and was later one of the first Dutch therapists to receive certification. She helped organize training programs in the Netherlands, and she and Tjeerd Jongsma provided supervision for certification training groups in the Netherlands, and then in Belgium, Switzerland, and Norway.

Tjeerd Jongsma, a psychiatrist trained in psychoanalysis who headed a therapeutic community for treating drug addicts, was early certified in PS/P. He found the use of Pesso therapy with drug addicts to be promising, commenting that it brought about a marked change of mood toward greater trust. Sarolea and Jongsma helped establish the Vereniging voor Pesso Psychotherapie (Association for Pesso Psychotherapy).

During the late 1970s the Pessos decided to concentrate on developing the training program in the Netherlands, rather than in Paris or London. The opportunities for widespread application of PS/P in the Netherlands, and eventually in Europe, seemed to be much greater.

During the course of the first Dutch training group, and thereafter, the requirements for training, the content and sequencing of training elements became more clearly specified. Certification training groups meet with the Pessos (sometimes just Al) three times a year for three to five days each time. They also meet with each other in so-called intervision (peer supervision) groups, and with supervisors. Candidates for certification are asked to provide a videotape of their work and a transcription in English. These are then evaluated with reference to criteria that the Psychomotor Institute's training committee had worked out. The first certification of Dutch trainees in Pesso therapy occurred in 1981. Several three-year certification training programs have been completed in the Netherlands. Many hospital psychiatry departments, clinics and other mental health treatment programs have at least one trained Pesso therapist on their staff.

From the Netherlands, interest has spread to Belgium, where a training program was set up and coordinated by Willy van Haver. Swiss psychoanalytic supervisor Niko Roth, who had been in the Belgian group, stimulated interest in PS/P among Swiss psychiatrists; this led to the establishment of a training group in Switzerland which was coordinated by psychologist Martin Howald.

In Norway, Jens Stranheim, administrator of a drug and alcohol treatment facility, sponsored several PS/P training workshops which paved the way for a certification training program coordinated by Lois Reiersol. Training workshops are conducted in Israel, though a certification training program has not been established there. In Denmark, BODYnamic Institute is sponsoring a one year program.

West Germany has been a center of strong interest. Arthur Cobb contributed a chapter on Psychomotor to a German book on body therapies (1977). A vivid account of the Pessos' work, written by M. and H. Portele (1978), was published in *Integrative Therapie*. More recently, German interest in Pesso therapy has been greatly stimulated by the publication in 1986 of a translation into German of the majority of Al Pesso's two books combined into one, by Tilmann Moser, a psychiatrist and analyst.

The European training programs attract about 35% psychiatrists and about 40% psychologists, the remainder being social workers, movement therapists, and others.

A recent letter (Note 3) from Dr. Charles Pinderhughes described his visit a few years ago to a back ward of a mental hospital in South Africa, where he had been sent as a member of an American Psychiatric Association committee to investigate mental health care in that country. He was surprised and pleased to encounter a Dutch trained psychotherapist using Psychomotor (PS/P) therapy.

The annual conferences of the International Congress on Psychomotricity invited Al Pesso to address it on three occasions — 1984, 1986, and 1990.

Training in the United States

The Pessos' travels within North America also stimulated greater knowledge and interest in PS/P. They had presented their work within the U.S. before 1973, but after that year went further afield, conducting workshops at the University of Alaska in Anchorage, Houston, St. Louis, Denver, Boulder, Winston-Salem, Columbia, Tampa, Orlando, and Minneapolis. The Pessos led several two-day Institute programs for the American Academy of Psychotherapists and the Association for Humanistic Psychology. In February, 1990, they conducted a two-day Institute for the American Group Psychotherapy Association.

Atlanta has been a major center of interest, starting in 1969 with a workshop at the Adanta Center, where the staff were associated with the clinical psychology doctoral program at Georgia State University. PS/P work then shifted to the Pine River Center, with the workshops being coordinated by George Taylor and then by Jackie Damgaard, who later became certified in PS/P. Currently the coordinator of training programs in Atlanta is Gus Kaufman, Jr. Each January Al gives a one day program for graduate clinical psychology students at Georgia State University. Among the strong supporters is family therapist Gus Napier, whose book, *The Fragile Bond* (1988) contains two engaging and graphic descriptions of PS/P structures. Atlanta is the site of the first "European model" training program to exist in the United States; its first graduates received certification in 1990.

Active centers of interest in PS/P exist in Northern California, where three therapists have been certified (including Robert Beloof), San Diego, Minneapolis, Chicago, Albany, N.Y., South Carolina, North Carolina, Virginia, New Jersey, New York City, and the Boston area.

In the early summer of 1976, the Pessos relocated the PS/P headquarters to Webster Lake in Franklin, New Hampshire, 94 miles north of Boston, and ran their first workshops there in the setting they would later call Strolling Woods.

Training requirements in the U.S. and Europe have been coordinated, using the European model. According to that model, at least three-fifths of the training is to be done by the Pessos and up to two-fifths by other designated trainers, who also provide supervision. The trainees periodically meet as a group for "intervision" (peer supervision) hours. Applicants for certification training need to commit themselves to continue the training for a full three-year period.

There are less intensive levels of commitment to training. *Level One* training, with primary emphasis on the exercises; *Adjunct* level training marks roughly the halfway point on the way to certification. Beyond certification are two additional levels, *supervisor* and *trainer*.

The three-year certification program requires about twenty-six days of training per year: six with Al Pesso during a training week at Strolling Woods; three with Al Pesso locally; six with other PS/P trainers; three with a supervisor; and an average of eight days per year meeting with a local intervision group.

In the first two years of training, emphasis is placed on PS/P sensitization exercises and on PS/P theory, as presented through lectures, readings, and audio/videotapes. Trainees have three trainer-led structures each year, as well as opportunities for short structures led by trainees under the supervision of a trainer. A trainee first leads fellow trainees in structures, then leads or co-leads members of an outside group. Trainees are supervised by peers and trainers, both live and from their videotapes.

At the end of the first and second years, each trainee is individually evaluated. After completing the third year, trainees submit a videotape for review based on a standard structure evaluation check list. Certification follows if the videotaped work is acceptable.

Another model for training was developed during the summer of 1990, when people enrolled in an initial training week decided to meet for a week twice per year for four years with Al at Strolling Woods. They are also making arrangements to meet for intervision and with other supervisors or trainers.

Writings are now becoming available through the PS Press. *PS/P News* is available from Strolling Woods, Franklin, NH to keep interested persons informed of new developments and of scheduled programs for training as well as structure workshops.

Carl Clarke, an Atlanta psychologist and certified PS/P therapist, has been developing audio, video, and written materials through the Telles Institute that he directs.

Therapists who wish to sample PS/P techniques prior to committing to training can attend an experiential structure workshop or a summer training week at Strolling Woods.

As another decade begins, PS/P seems solidly established although still not widely known. About one hundred therapists are currently enrolled in certificate training programs in the Netherlands, Belgium, Switzerland, Norway, and the United States. Numerous other therapists are enthusiastic about the method and use its techniques even though they may not have chosen to complete certification training. Large numbers of former clients, or "explorers," as David Campbell (1989) calls them, also have warmly positive feelings about their experience with PS/P.

For my own part, during the twelve years that followed my first introduction to Pesso System/Psychomotor therapy I believed it was a method of working that I would never be able to master adequately, though I did try bits of it now and then. Repeatedly during those early years I concluded regretfully that I should stay with the kind of verbal psychodynamic therapy that was more familiar to me. Learning to identify and track energies in the body, as the Pessos did with such extraordinary skill, seemed quite impossible for someone as verbal and sedentary as I was. As a result of my training with Al and Diane I think I have managed to learn PS/P pretty well, however, and both my clients and I are glad that I did.

References

Campbell, D. (1989). *Touching dialogue.* New York: In Hand Press.

Cobb, A.L. (1977). Transference and systematic Psychomotor Therapy. Ubertragung und das Pesso-System der Psycho-Motor-Therapie. In H. Petzold (Ed.), *Die neuen Korpertherapien (The New Body Therapies).* Paderborn, West Germany: Junfermann.

Ellingsen-Greenwood, C. (1978). Psychomotor: A psychotherapeutic approach. Unpublished master's thesis, George Williams College.

Foulds, M.L. & Hannigan, P.S. (1974). Effects of Psychomotor group therapy on ratings of self and others. *Psychotherapy: Theory, Research and Practice, 2,* 351-353.

Foulds, M.L. & Hannigan, P.S. (1976). Effects of Psychomotor group psychotherapy on locus of control and social desirability. *Journal of Humanistic Psychology, 16,* 2, 81-88.

Francis, M. (1973). Psychomotor. *Self and Society,* London.

Kaufman, G.B. (1981). *Body signals of childhood loss: How relational deficits and stress lead to tension and postural insecurity.* Unpublished doctoral dissertation, The Fielding Institute.

Levenson, R. (1981). Psychomotor therapy. Unpublished master's thesis, Cambridge College.

Meyer-von Blon, M. (1986). Pesso Psychomotor Therapy: An Apologia. Unpublished master's thesis, St. Mary's College.

Napier, A.Y. (1988). *The fragile bond.* New York: Harper & Row.

Oelman, R. (1978). *Object relations theory and experiential psychotherapy.* Unpublished doctoral dissertation, Union Graduate School.

Pesso, A. (1963). New Perspectives in the Generation of Movement: With Implications Important to Dance Composition, Criticism and Appreciation. (Unpublished).

Pesso, A. (1966). The Development of a Theory of Psychomotor Therapy. Submitted to Goddard College Adult Degree Program. (Unpublished).

Pesso, A. (1969). *Movement in psychotherapy: Psychomotor techniques and training.* New York: New York University Press.

Pesso, A. (1973) *Experience in action: A Psychomotor psychology.* New York: New York University Press.

Pesso, A. (1974). Appendix for Grants and Chapter for Ed Smith Book. (Unpublished).

Pesso, A. (1980). Pesso System Psychomotor Therapy Video Tape Annotations. Transcribed by Robert Beloof.

Pesso, A. (1984a). Introduction to Pesso System/Psychomotor. Transcribed by C. Marchessault. Franklin, NH: PS Press.

Pesso, A. (1984b). Touch and action: The use of the body in psychotherapy. Paper presented at the Fifth World Congress of Psychomotricity, the Hague, the Netherlands.

Pesso, A. (1986). *Image of the Self and the Body.* Paper presented at the Seventh World Congress of Psychomotricity, Nice, France.

Pesso, A. (1986). *Dramaturgie des Unbewussten: Eine Einfuhrung in die psychomotorische Therapie. (Dramaturgy of the Unconscious: An Introduction to Psychomotor Therapy),* T. Moser, (Ed. & Trans.) Stuttgart: Klett-Cotta.

Portele, M., & Portele, H. (1978). Eindrucke und Erfahrungen mit der Psycho-Motor-Therapie von Al und Diane Pesso. (Impressions and Experiences with the Psychomotor Therapy of Al and Diane Pesso), *Integrative Therapie, 5,* 123-129. (English translation by Dorothy Prickett, unpublished).

Psychomotor Institute Newsletter (1973). Vol. 1, No. 1.

Reid, C. (1969). *Groups alive - church alive.* New York: Harper & Row.

Scott, P. (1987). *The Ego in Psychomotor.* Unpublished master's thesis, Lesley College Graduate School.

Shurr, G., & Yocom, R.D. (1949). *Modern dance: techniques and teaching.* New York: A.S. Barnes and Ronald Press.

Sokolove, R. (1975). *Verbal and motoric styles of therapy: An outcome study.* Unpublished doctoral dissertation, Boston University.

NOTES

Note 1. Pesso, A. & Pesso, D. (1989-90). Personal communication.

Note 2. Pesso, D. & Pesso A. (1975). Personal communication.

Note 3. Pinderhughes, C. (1989). Personal communication

Note 4. During the 1980's, Diane Pesso helped her mother to battle against advanced breast and bone cancer. In addition to medical treatment and surgery, her mother moved to Strolling Woods for several months so Diane could work with her, using PS/P structures and exercises to foster changes in emotional programming that she hoped might improve her mother's physiological functioning. Twice a day they did a humorous, emotionally cathartic exercise Diane had devised, using whoever was available to role-play "negative, nasty cancer cells." Her mother then "destroyed" them by means of symbolic hitting, tearing, biting, etc. Daughter Tia videotaped most of the sessions, including her grandmother's participation in several of Diane's weekend groups. Tia was able to witness the resolution of generations of negative mother-daughter issues through the symbolic interactions of ideal mothering and to see the positive impact the work had on her grandmother.

Chapter 2

The Relationship Between PS/P and a Neurobiological Model

by Albert Pesso and Han Wassenaar

In recent years I have become interested in finding ways to describe the processes and metaphors of PS/P in scientific terms so that professionals in other sciences could more readily relate to PS/P theories and techniques from the standpoint of their own disciplines, theories and research. Those disciplines that I hope to reach are neurobiology, computer languages, artificial intelligence, and psychotherapeutic research in general.

In this attempt I hope to achieve even further effect and application of the work, thus adding new elements to the rich pool of knowledge about how human life proceeds.

In 1975 I first met Han Wassenaar in a PS/P group. He was then entirely involved in neurobiological research, especially on the level of synaptic organization, research on psycho-active drugs, and discussions in the field of biological psychiatry. As we grew to know each other better some cross fertilization began to develop. He became interested in what I did, because my work concerns people which are psychosomatic and neurobiological entities. It was natural for me to be interested in what he did for I wanted to know what it was from the viewpoint of neurobiology that might support the psychological processes with which I had become so familiar. This paper presents our ideas together, hopefully in a way that will be illuminating to both neurobiologists and to psychotherapists of all kinds.

Our collaboration culminated in the development of a sensor-psycho-effector model. This model attempts to bridge and connect the two fields of neurobiology and psychotherapy. This model is presented in this paper. The model represents the psychic domain, which is directly and completely connected with the central nervous system. In this psychic domain we postulate two essential terms, filters and gates.

We have defined filters as the derivatives of that neuronal circuitry (most probably cortical with many subcortical connections), which controls the entrance of messages with potential meaning coming from the outside world (environment and body) into that part of the psychic domain where levels of meaning, cognition and attention are added to these messages. There, these messages become images combined with meaning. Filters, in PS/P terms, are connected with the notion of receptivity and experience based on memory.

We have defined gates as the derivatives of that neuronal circuitry (most probably cortical with many subcortical connections), which control and modify the expression of meaningful messages or images. Gates, in PS/P terms, are connected with the notion of expression and self realization.

With these two definitions we can make a connection with the PS/P principle of vulnerability related to the filter functions and with the principle of *power* related to the gate functions.

In PS/P, we use the terms *power* and vulnerability to represent the polarities in the continuum of compelling forces residing at the soul of human beings.

Core is the name given to that particular collection of evolutionary history deposited in an individual by that unique combination of genes inherited from one's parents. It includes those tendencies which incline human beings to take in the world, and those pressures which push it to be born into the world, into reality, into consciousness. Core is another word for all the human potentialities arising from the continuum between power and vulnerability.

In neurobiological terms, vulnerability is expressed by receptivity in open filters. This is an analogue for activated sensors, including their neuronal networks. This sensory input is combined with old information. The combined information leads to new messages which can result in the opening of gates for the expression of power. This is an analogue for output. In other words, the reception of stimuli initiates a process which finally may lead to an expression — output. We conclude with a relatively simple statement: activated filters may lead to activated gates.

In summary, the essential features of the core are reflected in and modified by the filters and the gates. There is ongoing activity between filters, taking in the world, and gates, permitting expression.

In PS/P the term *ego* signifies the conscious, learned self and includes the information about life collected and recorded from individual experience and history that is stored in the memory of a person. We use the term *self* to indicate the combination of the core and ego. The ego is that part of the self that is created by the core's contacts and interactions with the outside world. The ego is that part of the self that is conscious, that exercises control and capacity to moderate the energies of the core that converts reality into meaning and symbols. It is the agency by which we consciously live the core and have the image and identity of ourselves as beings separate from the rest of the world.

Each psychosomatic entity is dependent on two realities, the environmental and the body reality. That is, the sensory information coming into the psychic domain arrives from both the environment and the body. Not either/or, but at the same moment. The representation of this reality in the brain is in terms of first order symbols.

We further note that the information stemming from these two realities is modified by genotypical (core) and phenotypical (ego) filtering. This modifying activity is a result of the well integrated complexity of the neuronal structures and networks in the brain. This complexity induces a new emerging property or a new dimension in the brain which we denote as the above-mentioned psychic domain.

The model reflects basic principles in the organization of pathways in the central nervous system — from the level of sensory input down to the level of effector output. Stimuli from the outside world and from the person's own body induce constructions of images of the outside world and of the body in the brain. Both sets of images stemming from the realities mentioned above exist only, of course, in the brain and in the mind of the individual. In other words, we only know the world from our symbolic construction. We can never know the world "purely as itself" or as pure reality. Also, we can know ourselves with our intentions, needs, and wishes (core) only from the internal formation of self images (ego).

The model, of course, is an abstraction which gives us a way to understand how the here and now, the actual moment of experience, is modified and seen through the lens of history: evolutionary history and personal history. When events are being experienced by an individual and they enter the area of the filtered psychic domain, they immediately awaken those patterns in the memory system that are similar to those new events. The patterns of history are instantly intermingled with the present experience. The *shapes* of the present are matched with the appropriate *countershapes* of the past in the filters thereby allowing these events to enter consciousness and be given names, dimension, and place in conscious existence. The memory systems induce in the actual moment the emotional force and impact of similar past events.

Thus, one can say, in the healthy, "normal" individual the filters and gates function well. And in such an individual there is no tendency either to hold the world out at the impressional sensory level (the filters) or to hold the self in at the expessional effector level (the gates).

With all this in mind, we look at the issue confronting therapists who must treat individuals whose functioning is impaired by their negative history. How are they to help those clients make changes that would allow the input of new experiences and the outgo of new expressions beyond the narrow range of options offered by their relatively closed filters and gates? Or, in simpler language, how are they to help clients feel more connected and open to outer and inner reality and more able to express who they really are in the world.

In considering the filters, we have to ask ourselves what happens to the information that is coming in from the outside world and from the body that may *not* be allowed access to that part of the psychic domain where cognition, memory making, and awareness are available and ready to give the appropriate meaning to that information? This non-included information does not disappear but has already entered that part of the psychic domain where non-emotional (non-affective) memory, and consequently meaning, cannot be added. Then this non-integrated information will show up as inappropriate energy, sensations, behavior or tension in the body. In PS/P we begin the work of therapy by looking for just that kind of information, which we call *energy*. Certain recognizable ranges of body signals, such as medically unexplainable tremors or numbness, and certain recognizable ranges of verbal behavior, such as unexpected shifts in volume or speed in speaking, betray this condition of non-inclusion.

In fact we are talking about the first cause of symptoms showing up in the body. This non-including phenomenon might well be a route or source for the development of neuroses and other psychopathological conditions.

We have to ask ourselves a further question: what happens to the information that has successfully passed through the filters? Of course this information will now be processed, which means that meaning stemming from the memory system is added to that information. This information, however, is sometimes allowed by the gates to express itself and sometimes it is not. Once again, what we know now is that nonexpressible information does not disappear, but that it remains in this part of the psychic domain, which is in between relatively open filters and closed gates.

This information resides there as not consciously expressible and with as yet not fully named and noted meaning. This will be another cause of symptoms and inappropriate sensations in the body. This is the second cause of psychopathology.

In conclusion the body becomes the storehouse and source of information about what has not yet been allowed conscious processing of events (closed filters) and what has not yet been allowed conscious expression of aspects of the self (closed gates). In this conceptualization, the body — through its capacity to feel pain, tension, temperature shifts, etc. — provides access to what is usually called the unconscious.

That stored information in the body is referred to as energy in PS/P. When I speak of looking for energy in PS/P I do not refer to the ordinary background sensations in the well functioning individual during unconflicted moving, breathing, digestion, cardiovascular activity, etc. The sensations I speak of are those related with discomfort — a too rapidly beating heart, labored breathing, pain, tension, heaviness, coldness, unexpected and un-planned movement — unease, having little or nothing to do with ordinary functioning. All sensations beyond normal body functioning signs can be seen as indications of unprocessed perceptions and unexpressed actions and a lot of people have these sensations without attending to them or knowing it.

The underlying assumption in all of this is that there is an ongoing innate pressure and drive for being and becoming originating from our genetic structure which has determined how our brains and bodies are organized and constructed. That pressure is also in the symptom. Thus the basic given of this model is that there is a fundamental evolutionary push toward becoming that is hardly to be denied, and if denied, dearly paid for in terms of diminished functioning, body complaints, and diminished pleasure.

Although the discomfort it gives is an impediment to normal functioning, the symptom in PS/P is also understood to contain valuable life information that could lead to the reduction of its associated discomfort. Not through its removal but through the procedure of allowing its information, experience, and expression to pass through the inhibiting filters and gates with the help of PS/P role figures and techniques.

That leads us to consider what standards are used by the filters and gates for refusing entry and exit. How do the filters and gates become the way they are? What positive purposes do the filters have if one of their functions can result in discomfort and unease?

The answer to the first question is that the standards are created both by genetic structuring and by contact with external events with significant individuals. The genetic information about elements that have shown survival value is kept and passed on through evolutionary processes. That historical information that significant figures in our lives have sanctioned, named, and recognized then become embedded in the filters and gates by virtue of the memory system.

The answer to the second question is that the positive purpose of the filters and gates is to prepare us to live in the world as it has been understood and managed through evolutionary time and further to be understood and managed according to the conditions that have been met in our own particular lifetime.

Let me return now to the words core and ego and demonstrate the relationship between the two via two images and then link those images to the model. One, the image of *shape/countershape* — shape being the core and countershape being the ego. And two, the image of the ego as the skin of the core. In the first image, if the core is metaphorically understood as the shape of the body of an infant as it seeks satisfaction in relationship with figures in the outside world, then those figures can be seen as the countershape that meets and supplies the needs of the infant with what it requires to grow. With such countershaping satisfying interactions, all the surfaces of the child, reaching toward the outside world for realization, are sanctioned. In this metaphor countershaping meets and matches the needs which then gives sanction to the expression and satisfaction of that need. In the best of all possible worlds, the shape of the core should be accurately represented by the countershape of the ego.

In relating this image with the model, we can say that the memory system and its effect on the filters and gates is a record of how the outside world provided or denied appropriate accepting countershapes to the reactivity of the core. These countershapes are internalized in the ego, which resides in the memory system and is present in the filters and gates. A fully countershaped core would be the description of the healthy individual whose filters and gates permit maximum access to what can be experienced and expressed. This condition would arise if all the elements of the core had shown themselves to the parent figures and the parent figures had subsequently accepted all those parts, given names to them, given meaning to them, giving place to them in the world of external reality, thereby giving those parts license to live not only in the world, but in the consciousness of the child. That child's history still lives in the psychic domain and body of the client.

Now let us look at the second image, the ego as the skin of the core. If the core were seen as a single celled organism, then the ego would be the membrane which defines it and separates it from the rest of the world. The ego then, would act as the interface between the core and the world, in touch with and able to modify and communicate with the interior and exterior realities. With ego boundaries the core remains singular, resistant to the possibility of fusing and merging with the rest of the world.

In relating this image with the model we can easily see the filters serving as a kind of boundary around that part of the core represented in the central nervous system. Thus, becoming the internalized skin (with its sensors) of consciousness and choice around the core. There it acts as a modifying membrane at the interface between the internalized world and the outer realities.

Let us return now to the word energy. In relationship to the first image, energy is that part of the core that has not yet been countershaped by the outer world and therefore by the ego. In relationship to the second image, energy is that part of the core that does not yet have an ego skin.

Thus, energy, in this definition, is that alien part of the core having had no satisfying or validating relationship with the outside world, therefore no countershape. Having been given no skin, therefore has no place in the consciousness, energy lives as a symptom in the body, without a name, without a place, without meaning, without memory or history.

Figuratively, parents, and all those who are entrusted with the care of children, are like the God of the Old Testament presiding over the creation of the universe, but who now preside over the creation of the child's psyche. What that old testament God has given names, dimension and function to, and has blessed with the phrase, "And it is good," is allowed to exist in the universe. What the parents of a child have named, given dimension, function, and blessing to is allowed to live in their universe and therefore in the universe of the child's ego. To extend this image further, the ego becomes the god of the psyche, deciding what shall or shall not exist in experience, expression and consciousness. The ego is able to ban parts of the core from conscious existence with the same finality that God would throw sinning Adam and Eve out of the Garden of Eden. Such an ego would throw the unacceptable parts of the core out of the garden of ego.

Another metaphor used in PS/P is called *ego-wrapping*. The wrapping meant here is the wrapping of the core with ego. It is a similar concept as that of having an ego skin, but now refers to a procedure and technique, rather than science. One of the goals of PS/P is to wrap those parts of the core, found through the energy in the body, with meaning, words, consciousness, etc., as one would wrap a naked child in a blanket, or wrap a nearly frozen ship-wrecked sailor in warmth and safety, or wrap a precious gift in protective materials, carefully and with respect.

Now we are in the position to begin the description of the theories, techniques and in the PS/P therapeutic process called a structure and relate them to the model.

A *structure* is a controlled, organized psychotherapeutic/symbolic event that includes the restructuring of past emotional reactions and expressions during significant historical moments which resulted in the creation of important life channelling patterns (filter and gate biases). In a structure, all the unprocessed energy (information) that has been stored in the central nervous system (and therefore in the body) as symptoms are given access to conscious experience and expression, are given names, and allowed to have significance and meaning attached to them. Further, a structure includes the creation of a new symbolic event to provide those kinds of essential, countershaping interactions via the use of role-playing ideal figures who provide antidotal behavior to counteract the toxic behavior of the original negative figures.

The following are PS/P words which represent the sequence that structures follow and also the sequence that actual life follows in laying down memories. The words are Energy-Action-Interaction-and then the last word is a combination word Significance/Internalization.

In our picture of actual life, Energy represents the potentiality of *power* and *vulnerability*. I must include here the element of hope. The energies of the core imply that there could be a future where the satisfaction of those energies can be anticipated and realized. This is not just a fond hope for we know that anticipation is one of the properties of neuronal networks. One might say that the core has some form of information (anticipatory energy) in it about how the outer world should respond to its appearance. Something of this hope shows in the stubbornness of symptoms. Action represents the body behaviors and motor activity supporting experience and expression. Interaction represents the responses of the significant figures in the outside world. Significance represents the ego addition of conscious meaning. And internalization represents the storage of the meaning into the memory system.

Those four steps are fundamentals in raising a child in reality. A child first comes with its core or potential reactivity (energy and action) to its parents or caretakers. The parents respond with words, touch and behavior (interaction), in ways that are accepting or non-accepting of the feelings or behavior of the child. In other words they provide countershapes to the actions of the child that either satisfy and validate those shapes or frustrate or invalidate them. Those interactions are converted into meaning and stored as memory (internalization) which will influence the characteristics of its filters and gates when, in the future, similar figures are present. Those feelings and behaviors that the parents accept with satisfying countershapes are thereby ego-wrapped.

When a client is ready to do a structure they are working on a response to the questions: "What are you feeling in your body? What is in the foreground of your mind?" This is an attempt to seek for the Energy as a way of determining what will be worked on.

The question for the Action step is, "What does that feeling in your body want to do?" Whatever behavior comes out, sadness, fear, anger, love, etc. the next question is asked: "Who do you wish to have respond to this action?" If there is no one brought to mind the therapist can suggest a preliminary accepting figure, called the *witness figure* to be enroled who will respond in a caring, accepting and defining way whatever comes out. This supplies

Interaction. That figure is the first step in ego-wrapping. If the client is sad, the figure can say, "I see how sad you are," thus assuring that the emotion is conscious, named, and given dimension and meaning.

That simple step can lead to expression to some extent, but then memories of suppression may surface which lead the client to have the notion that crying is ridiculous, or some other such negating idea. That leads to the enrolement of figures who simply symbolize those notions and ideas and repeat back those statements. This process makes consciousness visible by having figures represent each facet of consciousness as it arises in relationship to those feelings and energies. Once those figures are externalized the client tends to associate those words and attitudes to historical figures and events of the past where those lessons were learned about how the world reacts to their feelings. This brings in the fourth question, "What does it mean?" The Internalization part is attended to in making a new memory of the synthesized antidote event.

The role-players in a PS/P structure are called *accommodators* and their function is to provide the precise interactions that will satisfy the actions that well up by giving them the countershapes that most perfectly match the shapes coming from them. The setting is always arranged so that positive countershaping and therefore ego-wrapping is constantly provided.

When we find those early reality and emotion defining situations, we encourage the client to follow all the body sensations that arise during them and to follow all the ideas and comments they hear in their minds. The witness figure supports the core feelings or the felt affect and countershapes them, and the other figures present the template and model upon which their images of themselves and the world were formed by those events.

Part of the consciousness of the client returns to the level of the age when those events took place, but another part of the consciousness is observing it from their adult place, with the help of the witness figure who is an ally to their true feelings. With that combination the client can redo those old events to process and express all that might have been suppressed in the original event. In interaction, a symbolic antidote is created in the structure offering the experience of countershaping through ideal figures.

But we do not stop there. We create a symbolic counter event (an antidote event) with ideal satisfying countershaping, caretaking figures and situations involving *ideal mother*, *ideal father*, or whatever relationship that is parallel to the original relationships which stifled or did not stimulate the growth of parts of the self.

All along the way that observing, adult part of the client — in combination with the ideal figures and the consciousness and attention of the therapist — is placing meaning upon all the events: meanings that extend and expand the original ones and via the ideal event, meanings that supplement the original ones. In this way, we are making new symbolic memories to plant beside the original ones. This carries out the step of Significance/ Internalization.

Thus, while the old event is made visible so that unfinished affect and expression can finally take place, a parallel counter event takes place which would allow those developmental needs to be satisfied which might not have been satisfied in the first place.

That step is called *re-mapping*. The old event, having given rise to an image of the world and the self that is negative and life suppressing, is recorded in the memory and affects the functioning of the filters and gates now and in the future. That image is called a *map*, which others may call the memorized Gestalt. The new ideal image creates a new map which is laid down, so to speak, beside the old one. Those events in the present or future that call up the old map for determining how to respond, will also call up the new map which will provide alternative ways of looking at the world and reacting to the world. In other words, the filters and gates will have new information by which to determine how much to allow the information from the world and the self in and the reaction of the self out.

We started this paper with the question: "What is the relationship between PS/P structures and the model?" The combination of support and care offered by the therapist and the group combined with the techniques lend themselves to the creation of a level of consciousness where the memory and affect of past conditioning events can be made alive and visible in the room. It is a kind of symbolic time machine that allows the client to visit the past, live it out fully, and then provide themselves and their memory systems with a synthetic piece of memory. This synthetic memory will be laid down in the psychic domain beside the memory of the original events. This provides the client with an alternative set of "facts" to create new views and attitudes toward the outside world and of the self. Thus when new present events are met which evoke the inhibition causing memories of the past, the new symbolic memories created by the structure will also be evoked, because they have been placed beside the earlier ones and they too will have an effect on the filters and gates performance and selectivity. It is as if their observing ego as an adult is in an alliance with the therapist and the group to provide the child with experience of this new more satisfying, more validating interaction. That makes the experience of the present difficulties appear more manageable. After a structure, the unfinished feelings of the past, the symptoms, have been rescued from their hiding place in the emotions, given a place in consciousness, and are no longer having the effect of static in the system. With the new map, (expanded filters and gates) new experiences become more possible and more parts of the self are expressible. Belief in the future — hope and anticipation — is enhanced.

Chapter 3

Ego Function and Pesso System/ Psychomotor Therapy

by Albert Pesso[1]

PS/P Therapy uses the information in the body as a way of acquiring information about the unconscious. As therapists do this, they stay in contact with the ego processes of the client. In this chapter, we discuss the importance of the balance between body work and ego processes.

To illustrate this, I present an example of a female client, 25 years old, in the 5th year of university study. This was the client's first *structure* in an open workshop group. She described a history of intense, long-lasting headaches and pains in her jaw and chest. The client had undergone an extensive neurological check-up which revealed no medical reason for her complaints. While the client talked in the first part of the structure, I watched her body as she unconsciously showed different variations of intensity connected with what her conscious ego was saying. When I talked to her about what I heard from her story, I talked, so to speak, to her conscious ego. In this case I simply stated that it was possible that her physical complaints were an expression of an unconscious conflict and the consequence of unexpressed emotions.

When she finished telling this preliminary history, I asked her, as an exploratory technical step, to tighten the muscles in her chest and jaw (where the pains were) to see what came out — in terms of emotions, movements, sounds, or associations. She did so and began to cry. I asked her if she knew what she was crying about. She had no idea. This meant that at that moment her emotions came directly to expression without ego participation. Her emotions were living in her, but she didn't know or recognize them as a meaningful part of herself. That is, when the tears came up in her, her ego didn't connect with them. Or, perhaps you could say that the conscious part of herself didn't call that emotional part of herself "I". Without the extra impetus of the instruction to tense those facial and chest muscles, her defense mechanisms and the unconscious restraint of the voluntary muscles in those areas would have kept that particular kind of crying successfully inhibited, not permitting those emotions to be expressed. The symptoms of pain she complained of, I surmised, were the result of the muscles of her jaw and chest (the locus for the expression of crying) being blocked by their

[1] Interviewed by Lowijs Perquin, M.D. Edited by Perquin, Gus Kaufman, Ph. D. and Pesso.

antagonistic muscles, successfully neutralizing the expression of the apparently conflicted impulses.

In trying to determine for myself what the mysterious crying was about, I recollected that at several points during the telling of her story, her gaze had gone upward in that certain manner which I have come to understand as indicative of the client thinking about someone significant who has died. In such a gaze, the eyes lift upward with the whites of the eyes showing prominently on the bottom of the eyeball and not on the top, for the eyeball is rolled up and the pupil is almost covered by the edge of the upper eyelid. It is not as if they are actually seeing something above them with their eyes — ordinarily, when people look up to see a plane or the roof of a tall building, they tip their heads upward and their eyes clearly focus on something. This other kind of look, seen on prayerful figures in religious paintings, gives the appearance of someone far away, in a kind of reverie — as indeed people in that state are.

Of course it is not a cultural or social norm to look upwards in that way when one is preoccupied with the memory of a significant person who has died — it was unconscious body language and she didn't realize this connection.

Her answer to my question about what she felt or associated with her crying however, indicated to me that an "understanding" of the meaning of that gaze existed on an unconscious level. I pointed out to her that I had noticed her consistent manner of looking up, and that in my experience this could mean that she was thinking about a loved one who had passed away. She answered indifferently, "Now that you ask this, my brother died when I was fourteen."

Then she further volunteered information about her family. Her parents hadn't permitted any strong emotional response whatsoever in the family. They never openly acknowledged that her brother was severely handicapped by heart disease. Thus, the children never got the opportunity of experiencing and expressing all their worries about him before he died; and any feeling of jealousy or anger towards him was also impossible after he died. Her parents had flown with her brother from Holland to the United States for him to undergo an operation at a famous heart clinic. He died during the operation. The parents announced his death by telephone from the States. And, so as not to disturb the children's party where the children were playing Monopoly, they tried to tell the story of his death in a casual way in order not to make it "too horrible" for them.

Try to realize the impact of these events in terms of implicit messages to the children: "Strong emotions are not to be expressed." And, "The death of one of our children is not important enough to interrupt a party or grieve about." These would seem to be condensations of the family patterns that existed before the brother died. Her ego accepted the messages of the family: "You cannot have contact with that part of yourself. It's a forbidden part" (the emotions, feelings). Another way of saying this is that parts of the *soul* of this child had to live in a hidden way. She had to be dissociated from the emotions of grief.

After recounting this story, she told us that she could understand the reasons for her parent's action. They both had had very traumatic experiences in a Japanese prison camp, and they didn't want to burden their children with the hard experiences of life. A tragic solution: the parents, with their bad history, intentionally giving their children a "bad history," simply by not allowing them to experience the bad events that happened to them. By "protecting" their young children from the experience of grief, they destroyed the necessary relationship between the children's inner experience and a parent's outer permission to emotionally feel that experience.

With therapy we have to expand the borders that are built up by the conscious ego, supported by such unconsciously internalized "messages," so that the "real self," or the *soul*, is allowed to come out in such a way that it can be recognized by the person as a true part of the *self*. You have to give a client a corrective emotional experience, and new emotional and rational reasons that are strong enough to counter the original messages which have become blueprints or *maps*. At some point this client has to recognize that, in fact, "their system was wrong" and come to discover that she is angry at "that part of my parents which taught me such dissociation."

There was a second critical point further in her structure. She had chosen one of the group members to role play her dead brother. She looked at him and said: "I am totally indifferent. I hardly knew him, I was only fourteen when he died." At that moment as therapist, I had to oppose her rational, reasonable belief system. It was important to remind her that she had lived with him for fourteen years, a long and important period of her life. Seeking bodily confirmation of my assumption, I asked her again how her body felt while she was looking at her dead brother (the accommodator in a role). She reported a pain in her chest again and tension in her face (forehead, eyes, and mouth) which I speculated might be signs of an impulse to cry and a simultaneous struggle against crying. I asked her once again to exaggerate the tension in the affected areas, and unexpectedly, she started to laugh. There were now two possibilities: either the laughter was an expression of primitive victory that it was her brother who was dead and not she, or her ego again wouldn't allow the grieving to take place and instead converted the rhythmic sounds and movements of crying into a contradictory and unexpected laughter. As it turned out the laughter was a precursor of crying. For suddenly, her laughter changed into deep sobbing which she quickly stopped. She somehow managed to turn off the emotional process that she had just begun.

This was the third difficult spot. One possible solution was for the therapist just to ask her to go on and work from the bodily feelings, more or less saying, "trust what comes out of you." The danger in that course would have been that she might experience very strong emotions without the permission and the rational acceptance of her own *ego*. This could result in a situation where even if she did express the underlying feelings, she would not integrate that new experience as her own. The other way would have been to convince her with reasons: to explain why the grief had to come out and why her belief system (that her brother's death was not important enough to grieve about) had to be attacked. This is a point where I had to balance "body work" and "ego work." Arguing too forcefully on a rational level might have strengthened her defenses, helping her keep her beliefs as they were and fixing the symptoms as they were. On the other hand, too much pressure to express on a bodily level could have resulted in an emotional happening, an outburst of unintegrated expression not in accord with her ego and therefore not able to be internalized. That is, if I had helped her just let loose or blast the feelings out, she might then feel about this experience, "I didn't do that, something or someone else organized it, it was not me." Or, following such forced expression, she might later block it out and possibly not even remember that she had ever experienced or expressed it. Or, it could so shatter her to find these alien forces screaming inside of her that she could have felt, and even temporarily become, crazy. None of these outcomes would be useful or desirable.

Let me now describe a general principle — that of bodily *contact* during the experience of strong emotions. This kind of bodily contact is a way of organizing a context in which the emotions can not only be safely expressed physically and emotionally, but the client also feels validated and accepted with those feelings by the appropriately appointed role figures.

Furthermore, bodily contact given by other people in roles provides a temporary replacement or supplement to the ego, which otherwise tries to control, by muscular inhibition, the free motoric expression of the emotions.

This type of bodily contact is what I decided upon for this client at that moment. When she had first started crying, her shoulders shook and heaved forcefully, but she didn't make any sound of crying, pain or grief. To deal with this level of emotional force, I suggested that she choose two people in the group to take positive roles in order to interact with that uncontained action of her shoulders by placing their hands there and applying some pressure. With the external, containing aid of this contact and pressure, she was able to cry and sob with clearly integrated and felt emotion. The counteraction provided by the pressure from outside replaced the effort of her own antagonistic muscles fighting against the movement of the agonistic muscles. The agonistic muscles that could give expression to her emotions were in her case the expiration muscles of her chest and shoulders. The antagonistic muscles create the counter-movement of inspiration. When both sets of muscles are working at the same time the consequence is a neutralization of the impulse, resulting in tension or shaking. By giving resistance from outside to the antagonistic muscles, we stop their effect and as a consequence the agonistic muscles are then free to do their work: expiration, crying, screaming.

These are the technical reasons for the necessity of bodily contact when a client is expressing her emotions: the contraction of the antagonistic muscles has to be stopped in order to give freedom to the muscles which are actually ready to express the sound and movements of the specific emotion.

The second argument for the use of bodily contact is the symbolic meaning of that contact. Let us say that the client chooses a group member in a positive parent role. When this role figure makes such body contact and is closely present while the client expresses his emotions, the client will experience this close contact as a symbolic permission for what she is expressing. This symbolic permission can be integrated as a new alternative for the client. It will help her to accept her feelings and emotions as being legitimate, meaningful, and sensible in her actual life.

The ego is expanded by such experience, getting to know that this positive contact exists and by realizing therefore, that contacting the "hidden self" can be safe. The ego can, so to speak, "grow" through this type of bodily interaction with other human beings. When primitive impulses and emotions are being expressed, bodily contact is necessary to integrate these forces into the ego. We can see this happening in small children who are sad or angry and are held by their parents in an adequate way. The client in a structure is feeling and behaving according to these child needs, while at the same time she is reflecting as an adult on this experience. The adult ego is awake in a structure. There is no decline of consciousness.

We could see a new awareness on the face of this client: part of her looked as if she was in shock (feeling the impact of her long repressed grief), and at the same time she appeared to be outside, hearing herself doing something that existed inside her (which had been an unfelt and unregistered part of her past experience). She was hearing new sounds and assessing whether or not she was going to accept them as a real part of herself. You have to help the client to realize, as she hears the sounds, that it is legitimate to cry in this way, even though she had never heard herself make those sounds before. She is hearing her *true self*, but it is unfamiliar to her existing image of herself. So we have to help to make the client consciously accept that she is expressing her emotions and that it is right to express them: that the death of a family member is a very painful experience and creates a great deal of sadness and anguish. When this woman was crying in anguish over the death of her brother, she was also crying about never having cried. There was also anguish at the stillbirth of that part of her own soul which had not been accepted, not only in the case of the death of her brother, but all through her life. Not until this moment, I think, had she allowed such strong feelings to be expressed.

While working with a client you have to keep attending to the signs of tension and stress, so that you can monitor when all of the expression is finished. Do not end the procedure until all the tension that was registered on the body as visible and reported symptoms is expressed, for otherwise the *new map*, the outline of new possibilities, will include the fact that (even with all this therapeutic help) it was not possible to integrate the old unexpressed experience. Thus, we have to make sure that in the new structure experience the expression is complete and not partial. The client will not construct that new map as a "partial one," but as "the one," and the fact that she could only express herself partially will be encoded in the new map.

Therefore, I kept noting whether there was still a residue of pain and grief showing on her body (by the way she breathed, held herself, and moved) and I encouraged her to keep working with the feelings, tensions, and sensations in her body until all the feeling was expressed. When creating a new map it must be in contrast with the old one. It mustn't include the kind of partial and unfinished expression our old experiences have led us to have. In PS/P we move towards relief and satisfaction, for it is in that moment of relief and satisfaction in a structure that the corrective emotional experience can be paired with changes in cognitive sets and life attitudes. I believe that one consequence of emotional expression completion is that, on a biological level, the endorphins and enkephalins "kick in," providing the chemical background for feelings of pleasure and relief.

All kinds of instinctual or genetic "gestalts" like crying and anger expression have to come to a climactic end. This is where I think Reich made an error because he believed that the only therapeutic climactic end to attend to was literal orgasm. Instead of looking upon the orgasm as perhaps a metaphor for climactic closures in general, he sought to bring his clients to the state where literal and complete orgasm was the outcome, assuming, I suppose, that this orgasmic capacity would then generalize to all other climactic outcomes. But of course we have dozens of climactic closures that are not and should not be looked upon as "pseudo-orgasms". Each has its own rhythm and pattern. The closure of crying in response to loss or pain, with all its tears and upheaval, reaches a peak and then organically dwindles down in its own rhythm. The same is true with laughter which is the climactic response to happiness, pleasure, or joy. And when someone is feeling affection, there is its need for climactic closure, not of orgasm, but of caring contact, caressing, and the vocal and active expression of pleasure.

The need for completion when people feel angry is made visible when the hidden wish to destroy the object (victim) is given permission for overt, albeit symbolic, expression in a structure. The satisfaction that anger expression gives is very clearly seen when clients express it motorically in that safe setting. There, they get the completion requirement of the felt impact of apparent bodily contact when the client punches a cushion while a role-playing negative accommodator acts as if he has been punched and is really hurt.

In this example the completion requires the symbolic death of the negative accommodator. The client's consequent feelings of triumph, relief, and satisfaction lead toward the integration of those aggressive feelings and death wishes. To motorically enact the completion of those aggressive feelings in this type of context is an ego building process.

Carrying out decisions through voluntary motoric action is a basic, early learned ego function. For every motoric action one can schematically outline four steps: the decision, making a program, implementation of the program, and verification that the program was carried out. Finishing the entire sequence results in a feeling of satisfaction, called function pleasure in PS/P, at the completion. This feeling of satisfaction is like that experienced when actions, such as sneezing, swallowing, laughing, etc., are concluded, following the prior experience of itching, thirst, happiness, etc. Something is finished and completed — satisfaction and relief are the result.

A part of psychological growth and feelings of competence and confidence come about when children carry out these ordinary completions in conjunction with their being told (one way or another) by their parents, "That feeling you are having is good, that expression you are making is good...and you are good for being like that." Thus, children grow accustomed to sequences such as this: feel hunger, reach for food, chew; food tastes good, swallow, food felt going down — completion, satisfaction, and pleasure. Later, the food is fully digested, the child feels the mounting pressure in his rectum, the child decides to defecate, the anal sphincters open, feces are pushed out, the sphincters close down again, the pressure in the rectum is relieved — completion, satisfaction, and pleasure. Through these kinds of acts the ego is consistently developed as all these completion processes are experienced by the child, in participation with his conscious and volitional choices. Most importantly, he is validated by his parents as all this goes on. The parents, as representatives of the environment, must welcome the child's learning of these sequences: eating, defecating, sneezing, swallowing, crying, laughing, getting angry, etc.

In the process of learning these simple actions there is always conscious ego involvement; the actions don't just instinctively "happen." The parents and other care-givers help by permitting these impulses and actions to arise by saying "yes" to the child as she feels them, but also by teaching the child to modify those actions, so she will be able to tolerate postponements and to control emotions. For instance, when the child is angry it can learn that it can scream or punch in the air but not smash its brother in the face. The child can carry out the behaviors of anger but with enough ego control to create safe distances from the object. Children can learn to shift from strictly literal action to an equally satisfying symbolic motoric level of expression.

To continue the story of the structure of my client as an example: she finally emitted a very loud and long-lasting scream, finally able to surrender to her grief. The scream sounded as if torn from her, perhaps because her emotions had so much pressure, or perhaps from having been buried for so long.

It was important that she make the connection (via her adult conscious ego) with her memory of herself having the impulse to scream in anguish at the age of fourteen when she had first felt the grief, but hadn't been able to cry or doing any mourning whatsoever. It was important that she not place her grieving in the context of herself now — the 25 year old woman she is — but in the context of the memory of herself as that 14 year old girl. Her conscious ego, overseeing the structure, had to place the experience of grieving going on at that moment in her adult body, at the right psychological age level when it should have first come out, had it been permissible to do so.

If the affect is not consciously connected to that 14 year old context and age level, she may not fully register that she is in a structure, recalling an old event and feeling at that age level once again. Instead she may feel like a fool "making all that noise about something that happened so long ago." To avoid this unnecessary confusion and self-ridicule, her ego has to provide her with the clear distinction between her memory of herself and her repressed feelings at that time, and her experience of herself in the present. That conscious ego choice helps her know that now, in the structure, she is being given the opportunity of feeling the physical sensations of that repression, and this time allowing the full expression of grief. By that expression and its consequent relief of symptoms she comes to know that it was the previous non-expression of grief that created those physical sensations.

The therapist has to assist the client in the creation of a clear time frame for the experience of the feelings in a structure. If not, the experience might induce a regression and the client might think she is 14, rather than knowing that she is remembering and consciously feeling back and experiencing as that child of 14. Then the client's ego can frame the experience in its proper perspective and the client can come to know that what is happening now in the structure would have been a legitimate experience for back then.

For the client to believe it is useful to experience all those painful feelings, several things must happen. First, I as the therapist must ally with both the primitive forces and the ego. When the client feels the upwelling and pressure of the emotions I tell her that this pressure is good. When she can express her emotions in a clear context, i.e. in a safe symbolic environment with appropriate role figures offering the right *accommodation* for that expression, then she will feel better. This helps make it possible for her to accept that it is she, the adult, who is feeling and experiencing.

When training new clients in Psychomotor Therapy, it is important to let them know that their body experience is a legitimate part of them. When you give reasons on a cognitive level why this is so you become the ally of the ego. As a PS/P therapist you have to switch between the two positions, helping weave the unconscious emotion and body level with the ego level. This process helps people in PS/P groups develop the understanding and experience that powerful impulses — sadness, fear, anger, joy, and pleasure — can and should be trusted.

The relief the client felt at the end of her structure (also the disappearance of the physical pains that she had for months) had much to do with the expression of grief, but it also came as a consequence of her letting herself, further in the structure, express the loving feelings she had bodily felt but never expressed towards her real parents (also present via role-players). By the family rule of repressing strong emotions, she had not only held back her grief, but also much of the love she felt towards her real parents. Thus, she couldn't psychologically grow away from, or leave, them. She was still bound to them by the force of the unexpressed feelings toward them. The unfinished expression of love for them was an unfinished gestalt which would not let her fully leave. Those unconscious feelings were still looking for closure. The uncompleted expression still caused her to "hang around in my parent's house," although she didn't know why. Perhaps the only way one can really say "goodbye" is to first say, "I love you," and maybe also, "I hate you." The amalgam of unexpressed feelings and unfulfilled needs makes a very tight, though unpleasant, bond with persons associated with those feelings and needs.

I am near the end of this discussion, but I don't yet feel the closure, although I don't know precisely what I am missing. This is the same way it feels near the end of a structure. The therapist knows that the end of the structure is imminent, but something yet has to be done to complete the closure which will bring the satisfaction that arrives at the end. When you don't feel that quality of impending closure and satisfaction near the expected ending, it's important to see that as an indication that something is lacking and be willing to wait and to trust your own inner processes. We PS/P therapists also need to attend to and trust the organismic sequences we have genetically encoded in our own bodies. This attention helps us not only as therapists but also to continue being who we really are.

Look at a healthy child: when it is sad it cries and seeks comfort in bodily contact with its parents. When we learn more about all these and other organismic patterns we will be able to raise our children without so much frustration and harm, without philosophies hostile to our current organismic functioning.

When I look at my own process of growth and maturation, it is easy to now see that what I once labelled as Al Pesso was too limited. Further, I hadn't then realized that we are all carrying thunder and lightning inside our souls — my conscious ego awareness about what was inside was so narrow. The more I am able to let my own conscious ego sufficiently trust the creative source of my interior, the more I can open that barred door and get into contact with the reservoir of unconscious information. In such a way, my ego can begin to trust and use this source of knowledge, enabling me to expand my possibilities for solving actual life problems, bringing me greater happiness.

Yet, I suppose there will always remain in every person a part of the self that will never be known and which will never get enough ego around it. None of us will ever be finished or complete. However, it will always be an adventure to work in a structure, finding the courage to dare to trust unconscious parts of myself and — with the help of a supporting and safe environment consisting of the group and therapist — to be able to call a new, no longer hidden, part of myself, "me."

To review, I want to again emphasize the necessity of bodily contact and muscular effort in developing the capacity of the ego to contact the unconscious material and learn from its knowledge. Mechanisms of defense like denial, reaction formation, repression, are not simply organized in "the mind." They are developed, as all ego-functions are, in and by the movements of the body in reaction to the inner impulses and the demands of the outer environment the child finds itself in. The child learns and grows up in verbal and sensory-motoric interaction with the parents. The psyche of the small child is not organized by the body movements coming from his own self alone. He needs the support and protection of the body movements coming from the outside, from his loving parents, who act on behalf of, and then become, extensions of the child's ego. As this benign interaction happens, the child's ego develops and becomes strong enough to permit the full experience and expression of its own powerful feelings and impulses.

A child who has been abandoned by his parents early or for long important periods of his life; and who has never had the possibility of expressing the feelings of grief about that period of time, cannot really be helped sufficiently by verbal psychotherapy alone. Such clients need caring and powerful physical contact as they experience and express what they have missed. I cannot imagine that the intensity of crying and anger expression we see during structures can be safely and satisfyingly expressed in a purely verbal setting — one that doesn't include any body contact or externally applied pressure. Without some literal holding, clients coming into visceral contact with what they really feel would likely go into panic.

I am inclined to believe that in verbal psychotherapy clients dare not fully get in touch with their really strong destructive impulses. Only with the aid of loving, benign *limits* can those feelings safely be contacted. Hovering around those vaguely felt but not physically expressed destructive impulses in traditional, purely verbal therapy would lead clients to the unconscious conclusion that neither they nor the therapist is able to handle them. Those feelings then remain an unintegrated "dangerous power." Such a person can be in verbal psychotherapy for extended periods without daring or being able to contact that part of his or her real self. For without the technique of limits, the client and the therapist find out quickly that it is simply too dangerous to release, motorically, that part of the hidden self.

Without the inclusion of some body techniques, the client in traditional therapy might experience incredible amounts of pain and frustration, important parts of psychotherapy experience to be sure, but not necessarily followed with any promise of relief or satisfaction. Such clients might accept that painful condition as a basic requirement for their therapeutic growth, never suspecting that they have not been given sufficient possibilities for alternative solutions to their painful condition. When the traditional, verbal psychotherapist disallows physical contact and yet seeks as a goal the strengthening of the ego of the client, he seems to simply have forgotten that the client's ego was originally built in the physical interaction with the first objects, his parents. In PS/P we have the combination of emotional working through of the old conflict, the cathartic expression, and the "ego repair" experience. The ego repair is directly related to the inclusion of the body in this therapy.

Simply being ready to touch and to move with clients is not sufficient. There is a technology involved. It is very important that group members playing roles do not touch the client with the wrong pressure or in the wrong place, as such touch can become an imposition and, with inept use of body contact, messages can be communicated to the client that are totally different from what is either needed by the client or intended by the therapist. That is why PS/P therapists have to be extensively trained in awareness of bodily signs and signals. With such training and awareness, catharsis and ego repair in the context of bodily contact are interwoven.

Chapter 4

Ego Development in the Possibility Sphere[1]

by Albert Pesso

Since the time a client spends in psychotherapy is so short compared to the time they spend on the rest of the activities in their lives, something must happen in psychotherapy that is heightened, special, and intensely to the point. But at the same time it must not be hurried. A special arena must be created where this is possible. In fact, the name I have given that arena is the *possibility sphere*.

The possibility sphere is not a fantasy world ride although I can imagine such a thing in a fantasy world. You walk into this great big globe which is glowing with a lovely light. There is freshness in the air; there is a promise of pleasure, satisfaction, and the expectation that something wonderful will happen: excitement, maybe even a bit of dread, because we all know that fantasy world rides are sometimes scary. Tourists in the fantasy world know they are in a special place and their senses are heightened and they are aware of everything around them.

You don't have to be a fantasy ride inventor to create the possibility sphere; you can develop that atmosphere where the client, not a tourist, feels that something important can happen. What the therapeutic possibility sphere does is that it offers the client the possibility that there they can really be themselves. That's what begins to make it special. The possibility sphere invites out the parts of the client that are in trouble — that are hurting, that are tense and aching for resolution — and parts that are not yet found, like power. It offers it first by its emptiness, and then by its unspoken and implicit promise of awareness and reactivity.

In a way, a person with emotional difficulties is like a person in a tight fitting suit. Think of their bodies as their *true self*. Their bodies are being pinched by the too tight suit. The suit is their ego, and it really doesn't match the body underneath it as a good suit should. Or they may have an even more dreadful ego which is a prison to their true nature. Or worse, their ego may have been constructed by such cruel interactions with their parents or parent substitutes that it constantly punishes and wounds the person so they are in never-ending pain.

When such a client steps into the *possibility sphere*, they should feel something like this, "This person must be able to see how bad my suit fits." Or, "This person must see how much

[1] This article was adapted from a lecture given for the Studiedag (Study Day) on "Body Aspects of Psychotherapy" held at the Vrije Universiteit in Amsterdam, May 30, 1988. Copyright Albert Pesso, 1988.

like a criminal I feel and how imprisoned I am." Or, "This person must see how much pain I am living with." Maybe they don't put those things directly into words but I am sure they have a wordless hope that perhaps here they can get out of the discomfort they are in. Certainly their eyes and their body posture and their gestures speak for them.

One of the messages given by the possibility sphere is that here the person can be as they really are, and that not only will they be seen, but they will be able find a suit here that really fits. That is, they will be responded to as they really are and therefore they will be able to find an *ego* that truly represents their *soul*.

When someone is being as they truly are, we call that being in the *center of their truth*. That means they are in touch with what they really feel, in PS/P terms that means in touch with the feelings and emotions in their bodies. But not only that, it also means that they are in touch with what they find themselves thinking about how things actually are in reality. By that I mean in touch with the messages that have been laid down in their egos by important life events — events that have told them what their value is, what they are like. Their identity has been mirrored back to them by their parents and caretakers. Those life events also tell them what the world is like, based on their experiences with how those parents behaved and acted in real life.

You, the therapist, at the other end of the possibility sphere, may be able to sense all of this, just because you see and feel that person in front of you. It is incredible how much information we get about a person just from being in their presence. It is your heightened awareness and consciousness that is your most important tool at this time, for it will tell you so much about the client from how your possibility sphere vibrates in reaction to the information pouring into it from the client.

In this way you can think of the possibility sphere as a heightened field of awareness filled with the energy of your consciousness, intelligence, sensitivity and reactivity, but empty of your troubles, your needs, and your expectations.

We encourage the client to be in the *center of their truth*. In the therapy we encourage contacting their center by asking them to report what is in the foreground in the feelings in their body and what is in the foreground in their thoughts, memories, and associations.

Once the client is in the center of their truth, the next step is the creation of the *true scene*. The *true scene* is the beginning of building a situation that will result in producing change. The true scene makes the center of truth visible, illustrated and illuminated by role-playing group members who play the parts in the interactions that highlight exactly the state of the client at that moment.

We do that with the help of role-playing figures. The role players are called *accommodators*. The word accommodator implies that the role player will not improvise, but specifically adapt their behavior according to the needs and wishes of the person whose structure it is. In this situation the accommodation means that the role-played responses, in action and in words, will exactly match — that is, accommodate — the actions and words, feelings and truths of the client. This matching idea is captured in the notion of *shape/countershape*. If the client's actions and words are the shape, then the accommodator's perfectly tailored counter-actions and words are the countershape.

Let me give you an example of *accommodation*. Let's say the client feels sad and frightened. Can you see the shape of the client crying, huddled in fear, saying, "I'm terrified and don't know where to go?" What do you think the wished for countershape to that shape would be? The one that most accurately fits that shape in my mind would be an accommodating figure or figures who would embrace and encircle the huddled, fearful person, their arms creating a haven into which the frightened person could snuggle. The implicit comforting, protective, accepting behavior would be accompanied by words. This makes the message of acceptance and care explicit and therefore more likely to be remembered consciously later. The typical words that are used at those moments are, "We care about you and can handle how frightened you are. We can protect you. It is okay to cry and come to us." Of course it is the client who is the one who finally determines what the wished for countershape will be, for the client is always in control of the accommodation and the *structure*.

What would inappropriate countershaping of parents look like? That's easy, just remember some of the situations your clients tell you about when they were children. Or think of a real child huddled in fear and crying. Brutal parents may beat such children for making too much noise. So instead of their bodies, their shapes, being respected and outlined by caring arms and hands, that is, carefully countershaped, those children may instead experience their bodies being attacked, their shapes not validated but punished and injured for being the way they are. Their tears not soothed but hated and ridiculed. Their feelings not accepted and treated gently, but ignored and asked to go away.

Before going on to describing the true scene, I want to carry the shape/countershape metaphor a step further. If we think of the soul as the shape, then the well fitting ego would be its proper countershape. Remember that the ego is constructed by the relationship, verbal and non-verbal, between a child and its parents. If that is how egos are constructed, and if well fitting or healthy egos are the appropriate countershapes of the soul, then we can see that poor egos or ill fitting egos are formed in relationship with those negative kinds of parents who provide inappropriate, self denying countershapes.

So talking about countershaping is another way of talking about constructing egos. If there is poor countershaping, there will certainly be poor egos. Or to combine this image with earlier metaphors, if parents provide poor countershaping to their children's truth there will be tight fitting suits — or prisons for the soul.

Now let us apply this shape/countershape metaphor to the concept of the possibility sphere. Remember the possibility sphere has an emptiness that is filled only with awareness and consciousness. Emptiness means it has no shapes in it, only the possibility of shapes. Having the possibility of shapes means that it can represent the basic stuff or the universal template from which all countershapes can be formed. The emptiness of the possibility sphere carries the promise that all necessary countershapes needed to make a good fitting ego suit can somehow be constructed. This is another way of saying that the possibility sphere, the fundamental unspoken relationship between you, the therapist, and the client, is the foundation of hope and belief upon which all the future interactions with accommodating role-players will be built.

Now for the *true scene*. First let me say what the *true scene* is not. It is not a primal scene, it is not a traumatic scene. It is not even a scene of something that has happened in the past. It is a scene that illustrates the truth of the client at the very moment they are in now: now, in the therapy, in the session. Sometimes people come into a session knowing exactly what they want to work on. Everything is prepared and worked out in their minds. They know what they want to feel, what they want to do and how they want people to react. If we followed this plan the structure or therapy work would be a kind of self manipulation process. They would put themselves through this and this situation in order to have a predetermined outcome. That is all very fine, but it has nothing to do with the truth of the moment. That kind of pre-planned self programming may lead to little therapeutic outcome.

For the true scene, the therapist asks, "What are you feeling now, in your body, what is in the foreground in your mind?" We assume that this particular *now* will contain all the learned meanings of past situations, both good and bad; also, all the hopes and longings of those parts of the soul that have never been met and properly countershaped.

There is an innate push from the soul toward realization — the soul would become real and not merely potential. We become real in response to the soul's genetic pressure towards action directed to the outside world — creating relationships. We are pressed from our core to seek contacts with people which result in the creation of satisfaction and meaning: thus ego is fashioned. With ego, soul energies are accepted into reality and consciousness.

The client may say, "I am feeling kind of uneasy and tense in my stomach. There is pressure on my chest and my throat feels closed." Your possibility sphere surrounding the client is receiving messages telling you how they feel. And through your possibility sphere you are in touch with how you feel about him. With this information you can consider the client's symptoms and combine that knowledge with how he looks and sounds to you on the emotional level. I'll tell you what happens to me when I hear those kinds of messages from that position. I think of feelings in the stomach as coming from unspecific emotions, the combination of feelings in the chest and throat indicate that the potential action might be something that includes the breath and therefore some sounds might be coming out of the throat. That could be forceful talking, crying, shouting, or singing. But the closed throat indicates that there may be ambivalence, or at least inhibition about letting the feeling, emotion, or energy come out of the throat. The pressure may come from the feelings in the stomach, be mobilized in the chest for the forceful expression of air and sound, but stifled and choked off in the throat.

And as I look at him, his posture, the look of expectation, hope or dread, I consider: what emotion might come out of such a body? How does my body feel when I see a person in such a state in front of me? Do I feel like I would be afraid of such a person, or do I feel I would want to protect such a person? My body reactions and conscious speculations prepare me for what might actually come out at those times and gives me a range of possible interventions to suggest and offer the client.

But I might only say, "What do you think your body wants to do?" They might say, "I don't know, but my breathing feels kind of shaky." That would lead me to say, "Tighten or exaggerate the feelings in your chest and see what happens." This is a basic intervention which amplifies the tension temporarily and tends to push the potential expression to the threshold of action. If the intervention works, the emotional action, and the sound that accompanies it may come out.

I won't go through all the steps that such a procedure might require, but let us say that it results in the client making sounds and beginning to feel an emotion about which they had ambivalence, but which nonetheless was pressing for expression in the body. When there is inhibition, it could be because when such an emotion had surfaced sometime earlier in their lives, it had not been acceptable, or it had been ignored or they had been punished for having it. In other words, it may never have been properly countershaped. Let me bring in another term that has a similar connotation to countershaping — that is the term, *ego-wrapping*. Ego-wrapping means to wrap the soul with ego. Do you know what I mean by wrapping? Wrapping is what you do when you put beautiful paper around a gift. Or what you do when you put a blanket around a baby. You wrap the baby in a blanket. So ego-wrapping means you wrap the shapes of the soul in those well fitting countershapes which lead to a well fitting, healthy ego.

There are steps that must be followed in having the soul fully ego-wrapped. One step is to give it a place. The soul must have the feeling that it is accepted *inside* something. If it is inside something then it has a place in that something. Just as a foetus inside the uterus is given the feeling that it has a place inside the uterus.

The second step is to give it a name, just as a child is given a name when it comes into the world. The name of the new part of the soul coming out might be the name of an emotion, or an action, or it might be the name of a body part. What's the implication in giving names? Everything that has a name has a right to exist in consciousness. If it doesn't have a name it cannot live in consciousness.

The third step is to define its dimension, giving it boundaries. When children are taught about their body parts, they must be told what those parts do, what their function and limits are. Otherwise, the parts may appear endless, doing unknown and unexplainable things.

The fourth step is to give a license. This gives it the right to exist. That is given by such words as, "It's alright to be angry. You have the right to be angry."

The fifth step is to give a blessing. Blessing comes from words that say, "It's good what you do."

All those things together add up to ego-wrapping.

So here we are in the therapeutic session, and we therapists are inviting the client to come out with a new part of themselves, or an old part of themselves that has been in hiding in their body as symptoms. Who is there to welcome those parts into the world? Who will do the ego-wrapping? The therapist? His or her presence does give the client the courage to begin in the first place. What would happen if it was only the therapist who provided all the ego-wrapping? It might make the therapist too important and all powerful for the client. He or she would become so personally necessary for their future development.

We solve this through the use of symbolic figures role-played by group members. When the feelings are first showing up in the body, the client can ask for someone to role-play someone called the *witness figure* to be the verbal ego-wrapping, welcoming figure. That figure witnesses the truth of what is in the body, it is an ally of what is true for the person. What they witness is the emotional truth and they begin the process of ego-wrapping it.

If the client begins to feel tears, the witness figure can say something like, "I see how sad you are." This names the emotion and also gives a dimension to it by noting the amount of sadness in the word *how*.

The witness figure is only the first part of the ego-wrapping process, other figures might come in which are called containing figures, or contact figures, comfort figures, or *resistance figures*. Those figures are used to make actual physical contact with the client, literally countershaping them with their bodies and movement as all those names imply. Further in the process they may evolve into full fledged *ideal figures* who are used to counteract the original negative figures of the past.

All well and good, we have these figures ready to receive and accept all that is coming out of the client, but the client and the client's history isn't that ready to have that happen. Remember the client was inhibited and ambivalent about the expression that was about to come out, and for good reason. There was a lot of pain involved in learning how not to let those feelings out. How is that part of the truth of the client made visible if this is supposed to be a true scene?

Here we bring in what we call *fragment figures*. We call them that because they are only fragments of attitudes and values, not actually people yet.

Let's say the client is now in the midst of feeling that forbidden emotion, let's say it was fear and vulnerability. The witness figure has noted it and the client has felt seen and accepted for a moment about having that feeling. Then the client has the words going through their mind, "This is ridiculous, you are an adult, what are you doing crying in the middle of the floor?" Those then become the lines for the fragment figure which will be named according to its function. The function of this particular figure is to ridicule the client, so it may be called the ridiculing figure. After such a figure is enroled, it says back exactly the words in the client's mind, "This is ridiculous, you are an adult, what are you doing crying in the middle of the floor?"

Or there might be a guilt giving figure, if the emotion was anger at one's parents, that figure might say, following the thought coming up in the client's mind, "You are bad, you should be guilty for having such a feeling about your mother."

Do you see the psychological function of such figures? They represent the conscious negative record of events having to do with those feelings now rising in the body in that moment in the session. So here we have the witness figure and all the other allies and champions of the soul — the potential positive countershaping figures — and on the other side, we have the fragment figures who represent the negative countershaping attitudes of the past that were relevant to those emotions and feelings. Now we are in the true scene. We have made visible, illustrated, and illuminated the true state of the client right now. We have externalized the internal drama, illustrating the conflict between the unwrapped soul parts and the old ego. The witness figure is the ally of the unrecognized soul parts. The ridiculing and guilt giving figures represent the internalization of the negative messages. The emotional process and thoughts going on inside the client are now perfectly represented in the room. This is the true scene.

The client is in the center of the tension of the truth of their soul and the historical truth of their negative ego. But this time there are allies on their side: the therapist with the possibility sphere, the witness figure and the potential ideal figures are there too.

Now the client is in the emotional and psychological state which will generate vivid memories of those past events that are the roots of the present conflict between their emotions and attitudes.

As they talk about those events of the past, an interesting thing begins to happen. They start to feel some of the same emotions that they felt then and also their bodies begin to have some of the same reactions and feelings that they had then, especially if the memories were when they were beaten and abused or when they were longing for the satisfaction of their *basic needs* and those needs were denied and frustrated.

We began with the center of truth, and the true scene which illustrates it, and we suddenly arrive at an intense historical moment that is associated with it. We are in two intense moments, powerfully linked. The client is in their present consciousness, and because the true scene has been so vividly illustrated and illuminated, it induces them to remember themselves in those earlier, similar life conditioning moments of the past. It is as if the true scene was an unexpected doorway into history. Being in both those places at the same time, the client can do some important work with the help of the therapist and the accommodators.

The original event is now the past but its lessons have become embedded in the client in a way that it affects his present and future. A *structure* presents a "time machine" opportunity.

The client can symbolically and emotionally go back in time and be in that state of consciousness where he remembers and feels his past state of being while still in touch with his present consciousness and reality. He can, step by step, with the help of the therapist and the group, review and process the feelings left in his body at that earlier age. He can also reprocess the attitudes in his mind produced by those events, thus changing the ego lessons.

There is a present true scene and now a parallel historical scene can develop. Group members are asked to enrole as aspects of those people in the past who damaged them or denied their needs. The ridiculing and guilt giving figures can be expanded to the negative aspects of the parents in the historical scene — which we call the old map.

Once again the guide to the development of this structure is the feelings in the body and thoughts in the mind of the client. So when the clients report what they are feeling right now, it is the combination of the *now* of the present with the *then* of how they felt in their bodies as a child, because some of the same feelings are in their bodies at the present moment in the structure. If they report trembling in their arms or shoulders and the therapist asks them to amplify the trembling, the therapist may come to realize that they wish to attack their parents for having beaten them. When the client swings an arm at the negative parents, the accommodators react as if the blow landed on them, making the sound as if they had really been hit.

Further ego-wrapping is done by the witness figures who note how angry they are. The contact figures limit the blow, by holding the client's arms, defining the extent of the rage, saying "We can help you handle how angry you are. We will not let you literally kill them." That is the message they give by literally holding him back at that moment, at the same time giving room for the emotional expression.

As the structure goes on, the client gets very aware of how bad things were and how much they missed having the kind of childhood that they saw other kids having, or read about in stories, or saw in the movies: parents who would have been kind to them, treated them with respect, who would not abuse them, who would satisfy their basic needs.

When the client is in contact with that needy state, the therapist can ask, "Would you like to choose group members to role-play parents who would have treated you the way you needed?" The client can now experience and interact with those giving parents in their child consciousness. Much of the structure now deals with getting all those needs met in this symbolic setting. These *ideal parents* are the symbolic fulfillment of the promise offered by the possibility sphere. The therapist neither role plays or attempts to literally become the *ideal parent*, but the character and personality of the therapist, in combination with the caring of the group, supports the belief in the possibility of the principle of *ideal parents*. This human principle of caring and nurturing is very real and is directed in the structure to the child part of the client still living in the body and mind of the adult.

By providing the new input to the client while he is in the context of the old event which denied those needs and feelings, we will be affecting future present moments. Because as you remember, the present moment is dependent on old events. While the old map of the past is made visible and available for study and evaluation, we are in the position of helping the client create a new symbolic history and therefore have a new *map* intimately associated with the old one. More important for the client than the thought of a new map is the experience that the frightened child in him has been sheltered, that the abused child could scream with pain in caring arms, which gave dimension to his agony. That he found relief in loving faces and loving touch, which he soaked up through his skin, nerves, and muscles.

The structure is over, the role-players de-role. The clients return to the present, figuratively climbing out of the time machine. They leave the place of heightened special intensity where there is the possibility to do and feel the things that may deeply affect their lives.

But they are not the same. They speak of seeing the room differently, they are aware of more light and color in the room that they feel lighter in their bodies. Indeed their faces may have more color in them — which fact group members often comment on following a deeply satisfying structure. Contact with, and expression of, the newly born parts of the soul often brings a feeling of deep contentment and centeredness that is reflected in both the perception and appearance of the client.

Later, after the session, when the clients are in the real world, they will experience new events that will partially arouse the old negative reactions and lessons. However, they now have this new symbolic memory, reinforced with deep bodily sensations and satisfactions, which is clearly linked to the old one. With this they have more hope, and expectation that they will be treated well. They have more positive self images and anticipations about the world and people which give them a broader range of alternative behavior. Their bodies feel different, their souls have better fitting egos and they feel more ready to meet what life has to offer.

Chapter 5

Childhood Loss and Postural Insecurity:

A Theoretical and Empirical Validation of Pesso System/Psychomotor

by Gus B. Kaufman, Jr., Ph.D.

The primary goals of this research were to 1) demonstrate scientifically (via an experiment with a control group and statistical analysis of results) that the Pessos' observations and hypotheses of the relationships between events in a person's life and body signals *are* accurate and 2) trace and enrich the connections between the Pessos' work and other research on life history, psyche and soma. This research project was reported in detail in *Body Signals of Childhood Loss: How Relational Deficits and Stress Lead to Tension and Postural Insecurity* (1981).

Usually, knowledge that leads to therapeutic technique comes from clinical observation — a clinician sees a number of people with symptom *x* and history *y*, and says, "Ah! *Y* must cause *x*!" (especially if the clinician can hypothesize a likely method of causation). In this research I use a more sophisticated method to validate hunches arrived at in this way by the Pessos. I first review a wide and disparate range of studies to help me more accurately state and qualify those clinical hypotheses. I then gather one hundred persons' reports of their symptoms (body experiences) and histories and analyze these statistically to determine which historical and current factors reliably go with which body signals. Synthesizing these ideas and observations and clinically testing them extends and enriches Pesso System/ Psychomotor therapy (PS/P), and increases our knowledge of its validity.

To accomplish these purposes I study responses to the species/reflex relaxed stance, a PS/P exercise (Pesso, 1969). In this diagnostic exercise the Pessos correlate individuals' reports of sensations experienced in a relaxed standing position with salient emotional issues and typical historical antecedents. One set of sensations I group and label "postural insecurity." This includes 1) reports of shaky feelings in the knees and legs, dizziness and a tendency to collapse; 2) rigidity and tension in the legs, knees and back (torso); and 3) pain in these areas.

Building on the Pessos' work (1973), I hypothesize that this syndrome indicates needs for emotional support and often protection, derived originally from not having enough parental support and protection. Symptom one above is a direct expression of these feelings; two and three are at the same time expressions of and defenses against overwhelming feelings and unacceptable actions. They indicate even more severe neglect or abuse.

In seeking to develop and corroborate these hypotheses, I looked first to folk wisdom, for example, the Mother Goose melody "Rock-a-bye Baby" (1765) which in its words and use by parents connects falling anxiety and parental support. The first scientific report of these phenomena was Darwin's *The Expression of Emotions in Man and Animals* (1872). He points to fear as the most likely source of trembling and concludes that movements of expression in the face and body "serve as the first means of communication between the mother and the infant..." (p.364).

More intensive study of these phenomena began in the 1880's and '90's with Breuer and Freud's "On the Psychical Mechanism of Hysterical Phenomena: Preliminary Communication" (1893/1966) and *Studies in Hysteria* (1895/1966). In the first of these they coin the term "...conversion to signify the transformation of psychical energy into chronic somatic symptoms" (p.86). They base this on Darwin's principle that the overflow of excitation leads to the physical expression of the emotions. In these two works Freud and Breuer, neurologists, are keen observers of bodily experience who have also learned to listen to life stories.

They gradually realize that motor symptoms "...have an original or long-standing connection with traumas, and stand as symbols from them in the activities of memory" (p.95). As an example, they talk of Lucy R. whose "painful legs began to 'join in the conversation' during our analyses" (p.148). One of her symptoms was astasia-abasia defined as "combined incoordination on standing or walking, or a mental conflict making it difficult to stand or walk without swerving or swaying" (*Taber's Medical Dictionary*). Reading case reports by Freud carefully, we can see that he clearly connects somatic symptoms with meaningful trauma in earlier life about which the symptom "speaks."

Felix Deutsch (1959) began to extend Freud's theory of conversion in the 1920's. It was his belief that conversion is a defense against the experience of loss, and that "if no surrogate object is available, conversion symptoms are formed..." (p.77). Deutsch came to believe that conversion is a normal and continuously operating defense.

The psychoanalytic community, as had Freud by about 1900, largely rejected any touching between therapist and patient. Wilhelm Reich did not accept this stricture, and maintained a lively interest in bodily experience at a time when cognitive ego psychology was on the rise. He was driven from the fold, and interest in bodily phenomena in the analytic community was confined to the practice of psychosomatic medicine, which incorporated medical, physiological, and psychological research findings largely within a pathology-based model.

From this school Dunbar (1954) stated that "changes in muscle tone are the most frequent mechanisms of psychic expression..." (p.217). Jacobsen (1967), a physiological researcher, studied action potentials of muscles as early as 1927; he found that persons characterized as "tense" and "anxious" have "excessive muscular contraction" (p.67). Two later physiological researchers using biofeedback discuss "bracing efforts...by which we hold the body, or part of the body, rigid or 'on guard' ...representing efforts...by which we bring forth within ourselves, in substitute form, objects or events or phenomena that are not at the moment impinging on our sense organs" (Whatmore and Kohli, p.38).

It was Reich (1942), though, who discovered the fundamental identity between chronic muscular tensions and emotional blocks. He found that in certain threatening situations a child inhibits motoric and emotional expression. If this becomes chronic it may be called characterological defense or "armor." Alexander Lowen, Reich's student, gives a concrete example of this in *The Language of the Body* (originally *The Physical Dynamics of Character Structure*, 1958):

> The child who learns to walk at a time when the muscles are not strong enough or coordinated enough develops severe tensions in the quadriceps femoris and tensor fascia lata muscles to give it support. This will happen if an infant is left alone for it will make some move to get up and go toward its mother. The tension of these muscle groups will give the leg the rigidity needed for support but at the expense of natural balance and grace. When one attempts to induce relaxation of these muscles one meets with a resistance proportional to the falling anxiety present (p.27).

In *Bioenergetics* (1975) Lowen adds to this scenario:

> The early deprivation may be due to the actual loss of a warm and supporting mother figure by death or illness or her absence caused by the need for work. A mother who herself suffers from depression is not available to a child (p.158).

Psychologically, we defend against falling anxiety with denial and counterdependency. The physical defenses — stiffening the legs and locking the knees — cause a loss of flexibility and increased stress, increasing the danger of physical damage. A person letting go of locked knees may feel shaky and fear falling, yet actually be more secure than one who is unable to let go and has become deadened to chronic tensions of the back, legs and knees.

Since absence of *support* was hypothesized to be the major antecedent of postural insecurity, I reviewed studies of "object" loss and maternal deprivation. These studies seldom concerned themselves with physical, nonverbal behavioral outcomes. However, Kestenberg and Buelte (1977) elaborated on Winnicott in asserting that the 'holding environment' in infancy is "the mainstay of future holding-oneself-up and feeling self-reliant" (p.352). Early failures in mutual holding (the parent supporting the child, the child holding onto the parent), they suggest, lead to adults whose "body attitudes reveal their attempts to hold themselves up by putting strain on their neck, back or shoulders" (p.369).

Two mediating factors, I believe, are likely to affect this relationship between childhood object loss and postural insecurity in the reflex relaxed stance. Recent life stress should lead to greater postural insecurity, while strong social support should prevent or minimize it. Many studies establish the deleterious physical and emotional effects of stress. Other studies reveal the buffering or protective effects of even one significant relationship for human beings and other animals.

As summarized above, I was able to find many works that tended to validate and in some cases extend the Pessos' observations and hypotheses. Yet overall I found none matched their movement-based observations of the parent-child relationship and its sequelae (outcomes) in all their physical, psychological, sculptural, choreographic, sensate, and physiological dimensions.

Working from these sources, I created a new set of hypotheses (simplified here):

1. Childhood relational deficits are likely to result in postural insecurity, defined roughly as a tendency to collapse or to brace against collapsing.

2. This relationship will be more in evidence when there is strong current/recent stress and less evident when strong supportive relationships are present.

3. Childhood relational deficits are likely to lead to psychological insecurity, which should

be correlated with postural insecurity, but these relationships are likely to be more tenuous and complex. (This reflects my belief that psychological tendencies, as measured by verbal self-reports, are modified primarily by verbal inputs, while sensorimotor-postural functioning is modified primarily by tactile-symbolic interactions. Since our culture tends to limit communication between adults to verbal interaction, psychological self-reports are more likely to be modified in adulthood than is sensorimotor-postural functioning.)

To test these hypotheses I conducted an experiment in which two PS/P therapists, Louisa Howe and I, each led adults in academic classes in the reflex relaxed stance. Dr. Howe was not told the hypotheses being tested. She led two classes and I three, comprising in all one hundred subjects. Fifty of the subjects completed a battery of test instruments before experiencing the stance, fifty after. All completed open-ended questionnaires and checklists about their experiences in the species stance. They also completed the *Adjective Check List* (1965) (a psychological trait index), the *Holmes and Rahe Schedule of Recent Experiences* (1976) (a measure of recent life stress), and an inventory of current social support and childhood object loss.

Results

A remarkable finding was that species stance responses labelled postural insecurity, when subjected to factor analysis (a statistical technique) clumped in the three categories predicted. Collapse responses, including dizziness and falling feelings, were the most prevalent. Another factor was injury and pain, and a third substantially separate factor was tension and rigidity. It tended not to be present if the "dizzy-fall" factor was. This finding makes sense in light of the theory that tension is a defense against the collapse tendency; the defense (rigidifying) and the experience defended against (falling anxiety) are not likely to be reported simultaneously.

All of the object loss indicators except neglect were found in simple analysis of variance (another statistical technique) to be significantly related to tension. Neglect was significantly related to general postural insecurity. These results confirm that a variety of childhood relational disturbances (experienced neglect, parental death or divorce, frequent punishment) predispose one to postural insecurity reactions as an adult.

As for the buffer factors, the presence of a satisfactory primary relationship proved to be a major buffer against postural insecurity. I conducted multivariate analyses, using the multiple regression statistical technique. Here object loss alone was again likely to be associated with tension. Significantly, the individual most likely to be severely symptomatic (injury-pain responses) was one who had object losses in childhood, a high level of recent stress, and was relatively without social support.

Most of the *Adjective Check List* scales were not significantly related to either object loss or postural insecurity factors. A number of explanations are possible. As mentioned above, it may be that most people have been able to modify their beliefs about themselves since childhood. Further, psychological self-attributions may include a significant element of denial, especially perhaps for those with greater childhood trauma. In support of this theory were the significant correlations between high scores on the "Autonomy" and "Self-Confidence" scales and the injury-pain factor. My experience in working with chronic pain and injury-prone patients (see Chapter 15) was that they tended to deny any need for others' support.

Conclusions

This study provides research evidence for an articulated set of relationships between life experiences and body experience. The existence of normative conversion processes is strongly supported by the results; their workings are documented so that we can follow events through the life cycle as they express themselves in our somatic experience. The results show that the species stance is a valuable diagnostic tool for these relationships. Critical life issues, both historical and current, are revealed in their effects through this simple, brief, non-threatening exercise. It provides client and therapist a precise readout of an individual's current adaptive level and specific vulnerabilities, often prior to the onset of more serious symptoms. The Pesso System of Psychomotor Therapy gives the client (assisted by the therapist and other group members) excellent tools for healing the damages we have found.

Appendix

The Use of the *Species Stance* (Reflex Relaxed Stance) in Clinical Practice

I have written the following directions for the species stance with the assistance of Diane Boyden Pesso. Before beginning, we suggest you give the group a bathroom break so there are no physiological distractions irrelevant to the exercise.

Directions for the *Species Stance* (Reflex Relaxed Stance): A Script

In this exercise we will try to relax our musculature as much as we can while in a standing position. Basically, there are two parts to it. One is that I'll talk you through a head-to-toe relaxation; then the second is, I'll ask you to tune in on what part or parts of your body didn't relax — any place you notice any sensations that stand out against the general background of relaxation. This might be a pain, or tension, or tightness, or shakiness in a part of your body; it might be a hot or a cold feeling, or a heavy or light feeling, sweatiness — any kind of thing that stands out, just note it.

O.K., stand comfortably with your feet six to nine inches apart. If any of your clothing is constricting, for example your belt, loosen it. If you have high heels on, take them off, as they tend to throw you forward. And begin to let yourself just relax in place; let your head and neck relax and your head will tilt forward towards your chest. Let your eyes close, if you want to...let your forehead relax and your cheeks...and your mouth and jaw and tongue...and just relax every part of you. Relax your shoulders, upper arms, lower arms, hands, fingers. Relax as much of your musculature as you can while still remaining standing.

And let your upper back relax, the middle of your back and your lower back. Let your rib cage and your chest relax. Let your gut relax, don't worry about appearances. Relax your abdomen. Relax your hips, your buttocks and your sphincters.

Let your thighs relax; let your legs remain straight but relaxed. Your knee muscles should be relaxed, but not locked, so that your legs remain straight. Let your calves relax and let your weight remain centered between the balls of your feet and your heels. Let yourself be as relaxed as you can possibly be and still remain upright.

You may notice that in this position, you tend to sway. If you start to tilt off-balance backwards or forwards you've got reflexes that will send you back into balance.

And in this rather relaxed position, begin to take a tour of your body and notice what parts of you *aren't* relaxed: where you feel tightness, hot or cold, heavy or light, moisture, pain, movement or a tendency to movement, any sign by which a part of your body calls attention to itself. Just make a note to yourself of that and later we can use this information towards considering what action and interaction is implied in it. Now I'll stop talking and give you time to experience and monitor your body. When you've explored as much as you want, just sit down quietly so as not to disturb others' concentration.

If you are using this exercise with clients, you may choose to vary the script a little. In doing so, take care to maintain two essentials. First is to say, "to allow" or "let all body parts relax," rather than "putting yourself" in a particular body placement. The second key distinguishes this exercise from relaxation techniques, for we focus awareness on that which will not relax. The suggestion to experience the sensations and tension as energy which can lead to action and interaction is the genius at the root of Psychomotor. The job of the leader is to enable the client to understand the possibility of allowing this energy to go as it will, toward whom it will, in future symbolic work. To develop this ability, it is useful as a second version of this exercise to practice the species stance with the additional instruction to actually allow the tension to move one into action. As a third stage you can encourage the participant to imagine what would be a satisfying interaction. Still later, one might start a full structure from this exercise, using accommodators to provide the wished-for interaction.

As PS/P has grown more complex and finely articulated, the danger may have increased that therapists using it without the deep emotional movement awareness of the Pessos will follow cognitive false trails. Practicing the species stance yourself and with others will keep you in touch with the embodied physical roots — the basic *Energy-Action-Interaction* sequence — upon which a true PS/P structure is built and monitored. Using the species stance as a lead into structures, one is far less likely to create "as if" structures based on the therapist's or the client's distortions.

Careful study of the Pessos' writings on body signals and their potential meanings and on the uses of the species stance is a necessary adjunct, but not a replacement for actual practice with this exercise. The Pessos' insights arose from direct experience. These experiences were not at first in the complex milieu of therapy, but came through their long experience performing and teaching in the field of emotional movement and dance. This was followed by years of use of this exercise and other motor and spatial sensitization exercises with hundreds of people in a therapy setting. These exercises, as every PS/P trainee learns, help one isolate emotional sources of movement, their effects on one's bodily state and how these show up in the social arena.

If we wish to have the knowledge and skill of a Pesso, we need similar experiences. The species stance is the first door to and the foundation of such experience.

References

Darwin, C. (1965). *The Expression of the emotions in man and animals.* Chicago: University of Chicago Press. (Originally published, 1872).

Deutsch, F. (Ed.), (1959). *On the mysterious leap from the mind to the body.* New York: International Universities Press.

Dunbar, F. (1954). *Emotions and bodily changes.* New York, Columbia University Press.

Freud, S. (1966). Freud's selections in Breuer and Freud's *Studies on Hysteria.* In J. Strachey (Ed. and Trans.), *Standard edition of the complete psychological works of Sigmund Freud* (Vol. 2). London: Hogarth Press. (Original work published 1895.)

Freud, S. (1966) On the psychical mechanism of hysterical disorder: Preliminary communication. *Standard edition of the complete psychological works of Sigmund Freud* (Vol. 2). London: Hogarth Press. (Original work published 1893.)

Gough, H.G., & Heilbrun, A.B., (1965). *The Adjective Check List manual.* Palo Alto: Consulting Psychologists Press.

Holmes, T.H. & Rahe, R.H. (1976). The Social Readjustment Rating Scale, *Journal of Psychosomatic Research, 11,* 212-218.

Jacobsen, E. (1967). *Biology of emotions.* Springfield, IL: Charles C. Thomas.

Kaufman, G.B. (1981). *Body signals of childhood loss: How relational deficits and stress lead to tension and postural insecurity.* Ann Arbor: University Microfilms International.

Kaufman, G.B. & Aronoff, G.M. (1983). The use of psychomotor therapy in the treatment of chronic pain. *Psychotherapy: Theory, Research and Practice, 20,* 449-456.

Kestenberg, J.S. & Buelte, A. (1977). Prevention, infant therapy and the treatment of adults. *International Journal of Psychoanalytic Psychotherapy, 6,* 339-396.

Lowen, A. (1958). *The language of the body.* Originally published as *The physical dynamics of character structure.* New York: Collier.

Lowen, A. (1975). *Bioenergetics.* New York: Penguin.

Pesso, A. (1969). *Movement in psychotherapy.* New York: New York University Press.

Pesso, A. (1973). *Experience in action: A psychomotor psychology.* New York: New York University Press.

Reich, W. (1942). *The function of the orgasm.* New York: Farrar, Straus, Cudahy. (Earliest edition, 1927).

Whatmore, G.B. & Kohli, D.R. (1979). Dysponesis: A neurological factor in functional disorders. In E. Peper, S. Ancoli, & M. Quinn (Eds.), *Mind/body integration.* New York: Plenum Press.

Chapter 6

PS/P — Its Impact on Law and Society

by Jörg Müller[1]

As a politically active lawyer and professor, I would like to point out some of the practical and theoretical implications of PS/P in regard to law and society. I believe the Pessos' method contains undreamed of possibilities for improving our understanding and for rational change in our everyday practice of law, our social reality, and our understanding of what it means to be a democratic legal community. I am not here interested in an exposition or discussion of PS/P as a school of thought; instead I want to outline the pragmatic perspectives in the Pessos' approach to man which may be usefully applied to justice, politics, and government — areas where I, myself, am active.

Using a *Structure* to Point Out Conflicts of Power

Psychomotor can be fruitfully applied to overcome political conflicts, and the accompanying personal issues. At the end of one of our workshops, I expressed fear at the thought of having to return to my job because, in recent weeks, one of my faculty colleagues had attacked me in an unusually severe and public manner. At the same time a campaign had been launched against me and the commission I presided over by a broad segment of the Swiss public, especially from within the press. I felt victimized by my colleague, whose actions seemed so inexplicably aggressive toward me, and by the other politicians who attacked me. Al Pesso invited me to explore my problem in a mini-structure. I enroled my colleague and behind him, looming tall, were the social powers which — in my imagination and in reality, to some degree — backed him: powerful banks, mighty trade associations, and the whole of traditional jurisprudence. It seemed that my cause was lost against such overwhelming odds. Yet Al insisted that we explore how it was that these powers reacted to me as a source of fear. What was it to which my opponents reacted? Further analysis brought out that backing me were a couple of thousand radio and television journalists, for whom I had recently taken a stand in a scientific and political discussion concerning the control of the media. With this perspective, the reactions of my opponents became quite understandable. I had learned that I was by no means a lonely, idealistic fighter who had been unjustly turned into a sacrificial lamb. Instead, I was the spokesman for enormous social powers to which the other side

---

[1] Translated by Eva Christianson. Edited by John Crandell.

reacted with a wide array of weaponry. By recognizing and accepting the true power that I represented, I was able to take steps toward a realistic solution to the problem that troubled me. In exchange for my gains in facing reality I had to give up my role as victim, and I had to recognize and accept my own potential for aggression. My opponent became more human in that he became more visible and his anxieties could be reviewed in the structure.

Law — Alienation or Self-Determination: The Rule in Life History and Political Reality

Those who are familiar with Psychomotor know about "the rule" — the old *map*, or the law — which dictates a certain behavior or world view. An example would be the woman hearing the command: "Do not become like your mother!" Such a law can be externalized in a structure by localizing it in an enroled object or person. The law is based on historical experience activated, perhaps unconsciously, in the present moment. From time to time the law is reinforced in the real world by recognizable cultural forces. (As an example, one could take the taboo against a woman showing sexual desire or pleasure.) Or a man finds himself adhering to a rule from his mother, who had suffered from the uninhibited aggression of her husband and who, consequently, had instructed the child: "Never become like your father!"

In the structure, such profoundly intense laws can be traced back to their roots in life history and to interaction with the very earliest human contacts. The rule can be represented in human form, opening up a chance for change. Al Pesso time and again contrasts "the old map and the new map, the old rule and the new rule, the old construction and the new construction." In the structure, the roles of *ideal parents* or other ideal personalities are appointed as instant partners for catalyzing change.

In analogy to life history analysis, social laws can be understood as an accretion of historical experiences. This could be discussed using various examples of constitutional law, civil liberties, or the constitutional principle of the division of powers. We know that laws can be understood either as God-given, unalterable, metaphysically founded rules or as the result of secular communication among real people. Depending on the specific understanding, the rules either seem changeable by means of democratic processes or they appear petrified and remote from the politically active person. This analogy applies to whole political systems. People cannot topple an authority instituted by the grace of God. Only the understanding of a political order as a fabric shaped and formed and legitimized by people will lend itself to questioning and change in the law by people.

Only after an institution, a complex of rules (for example, today's relics of a patriarchal order), has been experienced as being unsatisfactory and alien to life does the possibility of change present itself to political or personal life. However, pressure through suffering will not, in itself, lead to change in either the social or personal domain. A prerequisite for the possibility of change is that I, in my imagination, no longer cling to the existing personal or legal systems as alienated and inaccessible in their magnitude. As long as I am fixed in the viewpoint of a child, to whom the parents seemed indeed overly powerful and absolutely unavoidable, the prospect of change remains totally remote. On the other hand, as I learn to look at the historical conditions under which a rule became valid and upon which the law was founded, and when I consequently question the actuality of the existing requirements as a mature person, the horizons of possibility for change will expand.

Immediately this leads to fear, just like any other prospect of freedom. In the structure, the first steps into this new freedom are explored by means of the role of the *ideal parents*. It is fundamental to PS/P that these ideal persons are not going to act out the ideas of the therapists about how they would like to see their clients act and the system of rules to which their clients subject themselves. Instead, the ideal parents — in their gestures and positions, their words, in the inclination of their voices, etc. — faithfully respond to what the working client experiences in the structure as the life-history deficit.

The ideal persons in a synthetic parent-child relationship open up the chance for true communication and interaction to take place, and this provides an alternative to the scenario formerly enforced by the restrictive law. By representing in the structures the clients' life histories of experienced subjugation as well as their still alive — however buried — autonomy, the ideal persons are indeed a turntable for possible change. They are pointing out the present dissatisfaction at the roots. At the same time they show it to be a system of rules fashioned by humans and formed by interaction. The premise: **that which was created by interaction can only be altered by means of new interactions**. The clients in effective structures have no doubt whatsoever about what the healing interactions would be like and they feed on that.

It is most decisive for the clients who, following their newly discovered needs, are working to construct the ideal parents who introduce the corrective elements. With this help they can assume responsibility for their future life. Now their processes are no longer the blind executions of plans introduced by historical parents. What happens then?

I am only too well aware of a general opposition to work with the ideal figures. Nevertheless, personal experience shows that the formulation within the structure of all I once needed from real people, the lack of which resulted in a traumatizing deficit which determined my actions, can subsequently change my perceptions in daily life. I am beginning to notice women who are different than my historical mother. I am hearing words spoken by men that differ from those spoken by my father. My usual interpretations of the environment are changing. I am discovering new aspects of real people and new people in my world which up until recently did not fit into my "picture."

At first success comes only in small pieces: to come to know anew, to learn from real interactions that which had been missing for having lived so long under the old rule: "you must not be aggressive — or you will not be loved." In this way, the structure has an effect on everyday life: there, the ideal parents do not exist; however, by means of discovering my most basic needs and the construction of their gratifications, chances are opened for the detection of real possibilities of interactions of a new kind in everyday life — which prove to be more satisfying than all that which was possible under the old law.

Democracy is based on the theory that people have the right to free themselves from the alienated and inhuman forces which are a feature of feudal, tyrannical, and ideological systems. People have the right to arrange the order of their community based on an understanding of their own needs as articulated in free discussion. In the political area, as in the personal, the same parameters apply: discovery of private needs, dissolving alienation, and realization of self-government in the social sphere by way of interactions which permit people to uncover and assert the validity of their individual needs, and to strive for optimal satisfaction by voting on the presented interests.

In view of the politico-social relevance of psychotherapeutic work, my preference is for work done in groups as opposed to work done individually. I suspect better results from the former method. A democratic political community draws its sustenance from individuals who dare to step forward and express their needs and fears, who take heart and express their demands or requests (which are usually common to all) in the precarious area of political discourse. The therapy or training group offers the ideal transition from the more isolated client-therapist relationship into the open arena of political discussions. The group as a place of sheltered social communication is well-suited for broaching ideas which are still unfinished and vulnerable in a social sphere to experience the reaction of our fellows — their solidarity and occasionally their rejection. This opportunity is offered in the shelter of a stable group which has developed intimacy, is united in common purpose. Self disclosure can be helped along if the need arises by the correcting hand of the therapist. Mature personalities will be able to incorporate this "shelter" within themselves as they move on to the harshness of social and political discussions. They can rejoin the nurturing, supporting, and secure environment of the group where solidarity with their concerns may be expected. One further point deserves attention: politics seldom involves dispute between single individuals with their own specific needs and interests; rather, it takes place in a contest between alliances of groups (political parties, factions, special interests, churches, etc.) which carry into the political dispute their mutual interests. Work within the group offers training for the work of politics.

Summary Thoughts

1) In the non-judgmental attitude of the therapist toward the human experience laid out in the structure lies the prospect of gaining access to human reality, including the hidden and buried needs of man. To make these experiences visible is a prerequisite to bring about changes in the personal and social spheres. The same holds true in therapy and in politics: movement toward a more humane and satisfying order, indicated by greater freedom on the inside and tolerance toward the outside, can take its course only from what is already there — the crooked and secret, but also the living and that which strives for a new gestalt. The reactionary remains rooted in a reality which has become history within its ossified legalities. The idealist is thinking in the context of ideal conditions which are not "grounded" and rooted in the soil of reality, and by doing so evades change as well. Real change evolves from the inner and outer reality found, e.g., in a structure. In this environment, the roots of personal and social growth can be uncovered. The atmosphere within the group, as well as the *possibility sphere* created by the therapist, opens up the potential for real growth.

Inner restraints that we occasionally suffer personally and social rules, including rules of law, are more closely related from a psychological point of view than is generally assumed. Introjects that we experience as inwardly oppressive quite often correlate to cultural precepts and regulations on the outside. The explicit or implicit commandments to which children have to submit themselves are by no means capricious whims or neurotic constraints imposed on them. Instead they represent cultural legitimacy in the same manner that legal procedure is marked by it. Without this kind of imperative, a culture of justice and law would probably not be viable. In other words: every order of law and justice depends on childhood training and internalization of its basic tenets as a set of basic rules, values, ideals, or taboos. However, a rule can become overly oppressive on the inside as well as on the outside; this, then, will lead to much unnecessary suffering, individually or collectively.

2) Ossified rules or norms will hinder individual and collective processes of development. It is a human characteristic that we are able to discern the difference between an existing

condition and one that "should" be. We can find a way to accomplish this in therapeutic work, for example, where, with the help of ideal parents in the structure, the innermost deficits and needs can be experienced and resolved. The ideal parents become catalysts in the process of dissolving ossified life history rules, while at the same time they assist in the formulation — born out of the client's own competence — of the client's basic, private, and up until now buried needs. Ideal parents can point up real possibilities for satisfaction of repressed needs. The neurotic defenses of the individual as well as the social system lose their dominance and space is created for a free social order, which is based on the competence and communication of inwardly satisfied people. In the same manner in which a structure set up to foster human development cannot start out with the ideal parents — but instead must find a way to display the energies, inhibitions, rules, anxieties, and desires that are really present — likewise political change can not arise from a system of rules of any ideologic, religious, or political party nature, but instead must start with a profound comprehension of human reality. Possibilities become apparent in individuals who are aware of their identity, social ties, and real dependencies.

In this sense, all the judges, legal scholars, politicians, and legislators who work at shaping our legal order should first of all strive to attain the non-judgmental and unprejudiced attitude of the therapist — and then get some practice in it — before attempting to work the instruments of legal and social design, and before starting to pile burdens or hand out privileges to their fellow men. Only the law which seks out its beginnings time and again in the forever evolving and newly emergent basics of human nature is a democratic law. This would be a law which does not reproduce fossilized interests and ideologies, but instead would be open to the basic needs of a law-abiding people. Furthermore, democratic politics — just like therapeutic work — must start from the premise that in a secular society no one knows authoritatively that which is good for the development of their fellow man, that which is their nature and very being. Therefore it follows that where rules are to be established — as in legislatures and executive branches — which will affect everyone, all must competently express their needs, desires, difficulties, anxieties, and hopes and bring them into the democratic discourse. Democracy as a community of mature people will not tolerate a condition of guardianship — the big brother mentality. There is no other way to go in a democratic society than the protracted, wearisome, tedious, and troubled road of dialogue. This is not to say that work on the political order could be reduced to psychotherapy. Rather the appreciation of basic needs becomes the necessary prerogative of a real democratic order of mature people.

I do not mean to say that we can get along in politics without long term projects, nor without visions or utopias. Our democratic constitutions are themselves visionary projects of the human community promising to acknowledge liberty, equality, and dignity for all people. The human ability to differentiate between what actually exists and what could be influences our actions. However, for a political utopia to become decisive, actively realistic, and productive of social change, it must be formulated by means of communication and interaction among men who are sure of themselves, who know their *center*, who know from personal experience the ever-present task of dismantling alienation and ossification, who are attentive to inner movements and energies, and who are at the same time aware of the dangers of rationalization as a defense mechanism.

3) Al Pesso's recent therapeutic work has emphasized the democratic element by working with the client's *pilot*. This comes from the conviction that the patients alone know

what to relate to in the structure, how to demonstrate the life-threatening or life-impeding problems, where they can attend to surfacing energies, and how to relate that which they need to draw from their social environment (via the ideal persons) for greater fulfillment in life. The competence of the therapists stands even further behind the competence of the clients. Acceptance of such competence in each partner — be they client, colleague, or simply another creature endowed with a human face — forbids that one decide for another, simply because only the individuals can fathom the course and meaning of their life or know the direction of their needed development. In this particular point, the therapeutic principle meets the inalienable premise of a democratic community where neither the all-knowing priest, the monarch marked by birth, the ideologically legitimated central office of the party, nor the arbitrarily constituted majority of the people has automatic validity or respect. Direction comes from the consensus achieved in human assembly by means of the difficult discourse between mature people. Even the social order established through such free communication must be constantly kept open lest the capacity for new learning be diminished or lost through ossification. Karl Deutsch, the great political thinker, wrote: "Power has he who can afford not having to learn" (1963, p.111). The humanist goal aimed at in psychotherapy is the constantly renewed achievement of freedom, in the sense of an absence of power. The foremost task of democratic politics is to constantly point out concentrations of power, in the sense discussed above, to denounce them and dismantle them so to give the communicative flow of mature people the chance to evolve a more human order: that is to say, one that remains forever mobile rather than rigid, one that does not claim to be absolute in the area of families, communities, governments, or world order.

Fascism lives on the elemental energies of people — energies such as the need to belong, for love, for meaning, for togetherness. Such feelings have never been *ego-wrapped* and so remain inaccessible to control by reason within the individual, and yet are susceptible to uncontrolled projection onto the all-promising leader or onto "the enemy." The historical reworking of such feelings in a structure will alleviate the defensive displacement — at least for a time. It will take away the unconscious and dangerous (especially in politics) projection onto a leader, a caesar, a people's tribune, or onto the collective of a party or a fundamentalist religious group.

References

Deutsch, K. (1963). *Nerves of government: Models of political communication and control.* New York: Free Press.

Chapter 7

PS/P as a Model for Pastoral Care:

A Feminist Perspective

by Vicky Hanjian

In this chapter the benefits of PS/P from a feminist, Christian, pastoral perspective are discussed. I will first consider the theme of patriarchy with which feminist theological thought is deeply engaged. I will then describe the usefulness of PS/P as a therapeutic modality for healing which is compatible with the feminist orientation toward the liberation of human consciousness from the patriarchal effects of orthodox Christian religious tradition. Finally I will make some assessment of PS/P as a paradigm for effective pastoral care.

Christian tradition as most widely understood and practiced is characterized in feminist thought as a "patriarchal" tradition. Shaped by the Hebrew and Christian scriptures which were transmitted in patriarchal social structures, the tradition celebrates its foundations in a male deity revealed in human form and substance which, historically, is also male. Patriarchy is a form of societal organization in which what is male is normative, honored, respected and valued. What is female is negated, trivialized, subjugated and feared. Patriarchal structures find their ultimate justification in a male deity.

The nature of the effect of patriarchal structures of thought is illustrated in the following text from the book of Judges (11:29-40):

> Then the spirit of the Lord came upon Jephthah, and he passed through Gilead and Manasseh, and passed on to Mizpah of Gilead, and from Mizpah he passed on to the Ammonites. And Jephthah made a vow to the Lord, and said, "If thou wilt give the Ammonites into my hand, then whoever comes forth from the doors of my house to meet me when I return victorious from the Ammonites, shall be the Lord's, and I will offer him up for a burnt offering."
>
> So Jephthah crossed over to the Ammonites to fight against them; and the Lord gave them into his hand. And he smote them from Aroer to the neighborhood of Minnith, twenty cities, and as far as Abel-keramim, with a very great slaughter. So the Ammonites were subdued before the people of Israel.
>
> Then Jephthah came to his home at Mizpah; and behold, his daughter came out to meet him with timbrels and with dances; she was his only child; beside her he had neither son nor daughter. And when he saw her he rent his clothes, and said, "Alas, my daughter! you have brought me very low, you have become a great trouble to me; for I have opened my mouth to the Lord, and I cannot take back my vow." And she said to him, "My father, if you have opened your mouth to the Lord, do to me

according to what has gone forth from your mouth, now that the Lord has avenged you on your enemies, the Ammonites." And she said to her father, "Let this thing be done for me; let me alone two months, that I may go and wander on the mountains, and bewail my virginity, I and my companions." And he said "Go." And he sent her away for two months and she departed, she and her companions, and bewailed her virginity upon the mountains. And at the end of two months, she returned to her father, who did with her according to the vow which he had made. She had never known a man. And it became a custom in Israel that the daughters of Israel went year by year to lament the daughter of Jephthah the Gileadite four days in the year.

A cursory examination of this text from a feminist perspective raises several dynamics inherent in the patriarchal religious and social mindset. The god whom Jephthah acknowledges is masculine and militaristic and is perceived as one who can be manipulated by vows and promises. It is interesting to note that although Jephthah makes a vow to his god to be fulfilled in exchange for a military victory, this god neither requires, nor acknowledges, nor responds to Jephthah's vow.

However, Jephthah attributes his victory to the effectiveness of his vow. What happens next becomes a point of focus for understanding the nature of the effect of patriarchy for women and for men as well.

The first "whatever" to greet Jephthah in celebration of his victorious homecoming is his first born and only daughter. She greets her father with joy and he blames her for his devastating predicament. He must keep his vow and she will have to be sacrificed and burned. Without any greater consciousness of herself than that which the prevailing culture has fostered and reinforced, Jephthah's daughter submits to her father's authority requesting only that she be permitted some time to mourn with her female friends that she will never fulfill that for which she was born — to marry and give birth to sons, to become someone's wife and someone's mother.

The characteristics of patriarchal culture are visible in the story of Jephthah's daughter. She is property. Her life is subject to her father's wisdom (or lack of it) and to his control. He has the power to make life and death decisions about her. The culture supports his authority in a religious system which understands god as all-powerful, all-knowing, and male. This same culture also understands that if god is male and carries these attributes, then males must be like god. While this becomes very apparent in the story, the more subtle effect of the patriarchal system is visible in the dynamics of the daughter's response. There is nothing to indicate that she has any consciousness which would lead her to considering another option. She does not point out the absurdity of her father's vow. She does not respond with resistance to his blaming her for being the first one to greet him on his victory. She does not use the two months which she is granted to save herself in any way, but rather to mourn with her friends that she will not ever fulfill what the culture expects of her. Except for her young friends, who are as powerless as she is, she has no female support. Indeed, if a mother were present, she too would have accepted the tragedy as part of the meaning of being female and would have counseled obedience to Jephthah. So, Jephthah's daughter dies a virgin, and she is never given an identity beyond that of being Jephthah's daughter.

The story exemplifies the negation, disrespect, and devaluing of the female in the patriarchal system. However, we must acknowledge that Jephthah is equally oppressed by the cultural structure which negates the feminine. At some level this father will always mourn the loss of his daughter's dancing and joy and laughter because he had to sacrifice her to the religious and cultural expectations of the patriarchal system in which he lived.

It is known by feminist thought that patriarchy is alive and well and continues to exert its effect on the lives of women and men. Indeed, a central task for feminist theological reflection is to bring focused attention to bear on the present patriarchal structures which continue to oppress both sexes, but predominantly females. Feminist thought works to either dismantle, or to reconstruct existing patterns of theological thought to reflect a more sane, balanced and wholistic theological perspective which will permit healing of the human spirit and move humanity toward wholeness.

To make the connection between the efficacy of PS/P as a therapeutic modality which is both compatible with and enhancing of the feminist perspective, I use the story of Jephthah's daughter as a reference point.

The feminist perspective in Christian theology seeks equality and mutuality in human relationships. This quite naturally implies the dismantling of hierarchical structures which require that there be a "top" and a "bottom" in the structures of human relationships. The hierarchical nature of human relationships in the patriarchal system is illustrated in the story of Jephthah's daughter. The all-powerful god is in the most superior position, exercising influence over the life and death of his creatures. Next in superiority is Jephthah, who communicates with this god and derives power from him to exercise decisions over life and death regarding his family members. In the ancient tribal customs, this influence would extend over the patriarch's entire household which might have consisted of many wives, sons, daughters, slaves, livestock and so on.

If feminist influence were brought to bear in this story, the scenario would be significantly different. Jephthah, in his conversations with his god would seek not the destruction of his enemies, but perhaps ways in which to live together to their mutual benefit. If the story unfolded to the point of his realizing the foolishness of his vow, he and his daughter might have sat down and looked at the problem together and come to a more humane and mutually life enhancing solution. A feminist influence would construct an ameliorating and balancing female presence which is lacking, perhaps as a wisdom figure or a strong mother.

PS/P and the Patriarchal Mindset

The PS/P perspective challenges every assumption of the hierarchical, patriarchal mindset exemplified in the story. This is one point at which its compatibility with feminist theological reflection becomes apparent. The dynamics of the guide-client relationship provide one antidote to the patriarchal assumptions inherent in hierarchical relationships. Basic to the effectiveness of the work done in a PS/P structure is the willingness of the guide to honor and respect the client's inner capability for choice making at every step of the way during the work done in the structure. In effect, the guide works in a realm of cooperation between her own skills and intuitive knowledge and the client's own internal wisdom. The therapeutic work done in this dynamic exhibits a mutuality of concern and effort in which neither party exhibits a dominant role with the other being subject to the power of an external, superior authority.

In addition to mutuality and cooperation in relationships, feminist theological thought seeks a dynamic which Nelle Morton has aptly described as "hearing one another into speech"(1985, p.202). The assumption underlying this dynamic is that each human being is a story waiting to be heard. When that story is effectively heard, healing of the deep wounding of the soul is effected. In the patriarchal construct exemplified in the biblical story of

Jephthah's daughter, the daughter's story is never sought. Beyond her request for time to mourn her impending loss, her voice is not heard. She is not permitted to give voice to her story and thus the possibility of a different alternative is eliminated.

The PS/P methodology of identifying the *true scene* of the client's state of consciousness honors the story and "hears" it into speech with presence and compassion and without judgment. Each nuance is witnessed and responded to in some way which validates its reality for the client. Employing the *witness* and *fragment figures* permits a precise articulation of the inner scene of consciousness. The client's affect is seen, her internal voices of injunction or control or warning are externalized in the symbolic figures.

For women particularly, this special "hearing" enables the naming of the various and multitudinous strictures placed on the energies of the soul in a patriarchal culture. As the *structure* progresses, a new reality more suited to the present life of the client emerges and more energy becomes available for possible alternatives. The feminist principle of "hearing one another to speech" finds apt expression in the PS/P process.

Feminist thought is also concerned with relationality. It acknowledges that human beings affect one another and that this affecting can be both positive and negative. Human beings function in relationships which either enhance and validate or negate and destroy. The energy in interaction flows both ways and requires some cooperation, whether creative or destructive, on the part of each participant in the relationship. Each participant then is subject to change relative to how she engages in a particular relationship. In the dynamics of hierarchical relationships, the balance is heavily tipped in the direction of the inferior member of a relationship adapting in deference to the superior member. Jephthah's daughter fully adapted to the demands of her father.

The dynamic of the relationality sought by feminist theology is demonstrated again in the guide-client relationship in PS/P structure where, in the activation of the *possibility sphere*, the guide consciously permits herself to be affected by the client, to allow her own energy system to be impacted by the client's energy. In this process, a creativity is generated which permits both the client and the guide to emerge from the work changed, affected in some mutually enhancing way as a result of having been related during the process of the structure. The point is, the client is not the only one who benefits from the guide. The process is mutually beneficial.

Feminist theological reflection has many expressions and emphases, far more than can be addressed within the scope of this essay. It is as varied as the personalities, histories, and understandings of the women who address themselves to women's issues. I cannot begin to do justice to the full range of feminist thought here, but would be remiss if I did not acknowledge that fundamental to every strain of feminist thought is the movement toward justice for all of humankind. And fundamental to this movement is the honor and respect, the support and encouragement of the surfacing of the rage which females have repressed, perhaps from the beginning of time.

Orthodox Christian thought traditionally has honored the body/mind split to which it fell heir in its close relationship with Greek and Gnostic influences early in its evolution. Inherent in this split is the denigration of the body in deference to the superior nature of the mind. It follows fairly congruently, that the subjugating of the body involves the subjugating of the emotions, especially the "negative" ones of grief, sadness, fear, indignation, anger, and rage.

Feminist thought seeks to restore body/mind unity and to honor the "negative" emotions as a route to a higher degree of morality in human life together. The recognition of feminine rage is increasingly understood as the first step toward the empowerment of females toward creative action in behalf of economic and political justice, not only for women, but for all people who continue to struggle for fullness of life under the oppressive limits of patriarchal social structures.

Perhaps in PS/P's honor, validation, and support of the raising to consciousness of the powerful energy of rage within the safe boundaries of structure work, PS/P comes closest to being the therapeutic model of choice for feminist theological reflection. It has the potential for empowering women's and men's response to the patriarchal structures which continue to have their devastating effect on life on this planet.

Feminist Christian ethicist, Beverly Wildung Harrison writes: "We must never lose touch with the fact that all serious human moral activity, especially action for social change, takes its bearing from the rising power of human anger. Such anger is a signal that change is called for, that transformation in relation is required" (1985, p.14).

Perhaps at no time in history has the mobilization of creative rage been so desperately needed as it is now when the fate of the planet is so severely compromised.

PS/P and the Pastoral Relationship

Given the above discussion, PS/P becomes a viable and desirable paradigm for feminist pastoral care. It provides a model for pastoral relationships which replaces the orthodox, hierarchical model. Under the influence of feminist theology, the nature of pastoral care necessarily comes under close scrutiny. The patriarchal, hierarchical model still prevails. It thoroughly colors the distorted understanding of the meaning of "pastoral authority" enabling pastors and persons entrusted to their care to cooperate in ineffective relationships which perpetuate a denial of the fullest realization of the human soul.

As a more effective model for pastoral care, PS/P demonstrates the possibility of equality and mutuality between pastor and people, where neither has power over the other and where each is informed and enhanced by the other. Whether in the counseling setting or in a board meeting, the model of the *possibility sphere* opens up the range of interactions to creativity rather than conflict. It permits a quality of mutual respect which is absent in the more hierarchical models of pastoral leadership.

With PS/P as an operative model for pastoral counseling, the pastor is no longer the one with all the answers. There is an acknowledged respect for the parishioner's ability to discern for herself, with the support, guidance, and attentive listening of the pastor, the direction in which her life must go. The strength of the PS/P model in this regard supports the feminist goal of empowerment of the individual.

Perhaps one of the most significant areas of pastoral intervention is around the issue of forgiveness. This is a particularly sensitive area for feminist theology. Christian orthodox theology, still the primary foundation for pastoral counselling, permits the spiritualization of wounds to the soul. It assigns the healing of inner pain to the realm of spiritual suffering, self-sacrifice, and prayer. As such, orthodoxy continues to function out of a body/mind split which perpetuates partial healing and often reinforces ineffective and destructive patterns, particularly where women's issues are concerned. The inadequacy of this traditional pattern becomes acutely evident when an abused woman is counseled to pray for patience and to forgive the abusing spouse.

Feminist theology insists on the integrity of the body/mind relationship as a basis for healing both the individual and society. PS/P uniquely facilitates this process through the attention to and respect for body energy, for the symbolic process which accompanies it, and for the individual who embodies the entire process. As a pastor with concerns for and commitment to the agenda of feminist theology, I appreciate the integrity of PS/P which allows for the experience of the soul's wounds to be raised to consciousness in the environment of the Psychomotor *structure*. Healing can be set in motion which does not require the negation or the trivialization of the original trauma. Forgiveness in the traditional understanding of orthodox Christianity circumvents this healing which feminist thought recognizes as critical for the transformation of persons and of society.

PS/P permits the naming and the owning of pain. It permits the accessing to consciousness of the existential rage which accompanies the denigration of the soul and thereby allows the creative energy which accompanies the utilization of such rage to become available for the transformation of human life, both individual and societal. As such, it is a powerful modality for feminist pastoral care in the light of the feminist theological agenda.

References

Harrison, B.W. (1985). "The power of anger in the work of love." In C. Robb (Ed.), *Making the corrections*. Boston: Beacon Press.

Morton, N. (1985). *The journey is home*. Boston: Beacon Press.

New Oxford annotated bible with the apocrypha, revised standard version. (1977). New York: Oxford University Press.

Chapter 8

A Study in Symbolic Action:
A Predecessor for Pesso System/Psychomotor

by Robert Beloof

Hope deferred maketh the heart sick;
But when the desire cometh, it is a tree of life.
      Proverbs 13:12

I

One way to appreciate the completeness and significance of Pesso System therapy is by an examination of the largely forgotten work of two women in their struggle against the forces of mental disintegration. Out of their experience they came to a real if primitive comprehension of how the symbolic, expressing itself through the body, can create movement toward health. And both their achievements and their failures serve to highlight the major advances in the system of therapy developed by Albert and Diane Pesso.

Two books appeared in English in 1951 which recounted the work done by a Swiss psychoanalytically oriented therapist, Margeurite Sechehaye (1951) and her client, known only as "Renee" (*Autobiography of a Schizophrenic Girl*, 1951/1970). Ms. Sechehaye reappears in this second book, taking roughly the last third of it with an analytic interpretation. The struggle of these two people to comprehend the function of symbols and the centrality of the body in the symbolic matrix offers both an invaluable validation of the Pesso system and, by contrast, an appreciation of its present level of professional power and sophistication. And Renee's autobiography offers a brilliant view of the way, in the symbolic world, that a self-destructive present reality can be reversed as, played out in the body, symbolism becomes curative.

II

The nature of the symbolic level of the psyche is much misunderstood. The position is often taken, consciously or unconsciously, that the saner a person gets the less of a symbolic level there is. This error arises from two occurrences. First, as a person becomes adequate to the world around him or her, that person's symbolic language more and more coincides with "plain language" or is adequately served by figures of speech. And symbols as seen in bodily gesture become so culturally acceptable and expected that they no longer excite notice. Second, the symbolic layer becomes so functional, so (if one may use the term) accurate, as to virtually disappear from sight. One might almost take it as analogous to the traffic light that escapes conscious notice till it malfunctions; but that is not quite accurate. For the traffic light is more like a well functioning ego. The symbolic level is the level where the decision was made that the world is a world where traffic lights are needed. Such a decision is so right in so many ways that one fails to see that a symbolic decision was made.

Thus a symbolic decision is a meta message. It directs the course, energy, and target of other messages. It becomes almost like the ROM memory in a computer. Almost, because it can be altered, though with great difficulty. For example, a client, after work with a persistent dream, recalled being taken to a hospital at age two years to have her tonsils removed. She recalls that, left alone in the dark, she came to the conclusion that she was supposed to die. To put it more precisely, she believed that if she were to be an obedient daughter, a good girl, she would do what her parents wished her to do, namely, to die. Though her parents certainly did not wish her to die, hers was not an altogether irrational conclusion. A highly active, volatile child with a persistently inquiring mind, she was really too much for her placid mother whose mind seldom missed an opportunity for a conventional word or deed. The child drove her to distraction, and though she undoubtedly loved the child, she probably didn't much like her. The father was a cold, controlled alcoholic. Thus it was not so unreasonable for a two year old with such a pair of parents to assume, since they had removed her to this dark, lonely, hostile place, that they had left her to die. But that conclusion was not a symbolic decision. That was simply an operational adding up of data, however mistaken, with an operational conclusion, a conclusion that required a response. She wrestled with the question whether to live or not live all the night, till finally as dawn touched the window she decided to defy her parents and live, and that was the symbolic decision, as the result of which she had lived her life up to the time she entered therapy in alternate modes of defiance. Once a symbolic decision of this sort is made, incoming data will be distorted to confirm it, and, of course, it will create behavior that will cause the world around literally to act in a confirmatory way. Further, and most important, the body will adopt the posture, pulse, chemistry, suitable to a life lived on the basis of that decision. The symbolising level of the human psyche is, then, the level of meta decision, where rules for action that support self-identity and survival are embedded. And at this level what seems sensible may look very different from accepted sense.

Ms. S. found in Renee a client who taught the therapist how to do symbol-body therapy, as Freud was taught the "talking cure" by the lady who told him to shut up and listen. Unfortunately (though fortunately for us) Renee was by her demons denied the use of direct words (p. 75), and so the learning was long, perilous, with several nearly irrecoverable setbacks.

Renee explains very clearly why analysis would never have achieved any results with her, and in doing so she opens a window to the motor symbolic level as it processes "sense" and "reality":

> "I was glad that Mama changed her method at the end of the first year of analysis. In the beginning, she analyzed everything I said, my fear, my guilt. These investigations seemed to me like a bill of complaints, quite as though in looking for the cause of feelings, they became more at fault and more real. As if to say, 'Find out in what instances you are guilty, and why.' This for me was proof that the guilt existed, that the System was really there since one could find the reason for its actions. From these sessions I went home more unhappy, more blameworthy, more isolated than ever, without any contact, alone in my own unreal world" (p. 39).

What could have been liberating for another, i.e., "discovering causes," was for her counter productive because such "causes" reified the feelings of fear and guilt. To put it figuratively, digging in the ground to examine the nature of the worms simply confirmed and emphasized that the worms were really there, that they were her fault, that she was evil and must be punished. But how else, if not by the conventional route of "discovering causes" can so profound a guilt and shame be alleviated and such an overpowering omnipotence (disguised as total vulnerability) be limited? Before proceeding to such issues I shall outline briefly the "causes" that were there to be found.

III

A Summary of Renee's History

This history omits the various symptoms manifested by the child through the early years.

1. Parents upper middle class, mother Swiss of aristocratic South-of-France ancestry. Father a Swedish industrialist who, in addition to his business, studied Russian, Chinese, and the violin for recreation. Both lived in a "dream world" (Sechehaye, p. 21) and were unused to difficulties of any kind. The wife became pregnant almost at once.

2. Only the mother found the baby ugly. Fed her with a bottle. Unconsciously watered the milk so much the baby, starving, came to hate the bottle. A doctor, diagnosing a stomach disorder, recommended further dilution of milk.

3. A grandmother arrived, recognized that the child was starving, and since the child hated the bottle, she fed her from a bowl, having to use two spoons "so that there was no interval between swallows, otherwise the baby howled with anxiety" (p. 22).

4. This grandmother left suddenly at baby's age eleven months.

5. The child, hitting her head and looking everywhere for grandmother, is placed in the parents' bedroom where the parents not only laugh at her hunger, but father threatens to take mother away because she belongs to him, pretending to bite the mother hungrily. She interprets the primal scene as "the father enters into the mother with a 'spoon to eat her'" (p. 87).

6. At fourteen months received as a playmate a pet white rabbit. The father killed the rabbit in front of the child. She developed a fever with delirium, believed to be meningitis.

7. At eighteen months a second baby was born, absorbing mother's attention.

8. Father, to amuse himself, would lift up the child's clothing and tease her about her nakedness. She was told by a servant girl, "Someone must have cut something off you!" (p. 23).

9. Two more children were born (sons) and the father began to frequent another woman, which led to arguments in front of Renee. When mother would threaten to leave, father would comfort Renee by telling her the mother would be replaced by a negress with big teeth, who would bite her, or, alternatively, Renee would be placed on a farm where cows would eat her.

10. When depressed, father would propose mutual suicide to the child. Father eventually left home.

11. At nine years, mother informs Renee that she was an unwanted child, and that mother had considered her to be a hideous baby. Frequently and insistently mother reproaches Renee for not loving her enough, and accuses her of "tendencies toward inversions" (p. 27). She frequently threatens that after she dies she will return and "pull her by the feet for having loved someone other than her mother" (p. 27).

IV

With such a severely negative environment, pathology was evident from the beginning. However, it is not part of my purpose to trace, with Renee, her descent over the years into the isolation of madness. It is my purpose, rather, to trace from the beginning Renee's discovery of how to use symbolism, how to discover its meaning and its curative powers if used through the body in interaction with symbolic objects. Using both Renee's recollection and Ms. S's professional self-examination, I will concurrently follow Ms. S's gradual comprehension, through many errors, of some of the principles of that therapy.

In Renee's history there are many early evidences of symbolic projection. An example would be the appearance of her perception of her shadow as another self, a doppelganger which "might be filled with evil intentions for her" (Sechehaye, p. 24). But the arrival of Riquette was, according to Renee's account, the first prefiguring of what Ms. S. later called the symbolic method. Diagnosed as having tuberculosis, Renee was in a sanitorium where "by mistake" (*Autobiography*, p. 30) she was sent a large and beautiful doll, which she called Riquette. After leaving the sanitorium she began to be concerned with the doll, spending a good deal of time caring for her — but surprisingly in only one dimension. "But this was because my love for Riquette was very one-sided, and was concerned only with temperature. To every other consideration of appearance, of cleanliness, of feeding, I was completely indifferent" (p. 3l). One can speculate that the more profound issues of *nurturing*, *validation* and *support* were too forbidden, too loaded, and were condensed into the safer issue of warmth, a condensation which would account for the intensity of the energy within this narrow range. In any case, we see that without doubt Riquette was an outer object which, projectively, Renee was trying to use in order to work out symbolically some new decision about the world — to find a way to satisfy needs which she had decided, on the meta message symbolic level, that she was unworthy to have fulfilled.

Subsequent to this period she entered analysis with Ms. S:

> It was in the course of the first year of analysis that I realized the danger I was in. For me, madness was definitely not a condition of illness; I did not believe that I was ill. It was rather a country, opposed to Reality, where reigned an implacable light, blinding, leaving no place for shadow; an immense space without boundary, limitless, flat; a mineral, lunar country, cold as the wastes of the North Pole. In this stretching emptiness, all is unchangeable, immobile, congealed, crystallized. Objects are stage trappings, placed here and there, geometric cubes without meaning (*Autobiography*, p. 33).

So it is that analysis is capable of sharpening her sense of what is true for her, and in so doing confirms her culpability. She tells Ms. S., "In fact, you will take away all the badness and then there will be nothing left in me, because there is nothing good in me" (Sechehaye, p. 34). It is indicative of the general professional resistance to the idea that salvation is to be found (in the clinical setting) in anything but mental activity, that when after three weeks, and with the client growing more and more removed, "I [Ms. S.] consult the psychiatrist who considers the case very serious, and sees his diagnosis of schizophrenic disintegration confirmed. However, since the young girl wants to come for the treatment, he feels that it is necessary to continue to ease her mind" (p. 37).

It is very difficult to sort out the precise road toward the critical moment when both Ms. S. and Renee see fit not only to allow Renee to call her "Mama," but for Ms. S. to name herself as such in relation to Renee. Apparently Renee makes the transference when, after three and one-half months, she begins to make a series of symbolic drawings (included as an appendix in *Symbolic Realizations* and of great clinical interest). Ms. S. encourages this non-verbal activity, with the result that "she came very regularly and had difficulty in leaving" (p. 38). But Renee tells her later that "after leaving the session she would jump up and down in the street shouting: 'I have a mother! I have a mother!'" (p. 38).

Over a half-year later Ms. S. decided to modify treatment a little. "The position of the analyst in back of the patient has left Renee with a feeling of complete abandonment; when she did not see me, she thought I was not there. I therefore have her sit next to me on the couch; she then observes that she is listened to and that she has a partner. She feels less lonely and more protected against fear" (p. 42). Renee summarizes this entire sequence as follows:

> Against this enlightenment I waged a battle with the help of the analyst who later became my 'Mama.' Only near her I felt secure, especially from the time when she began to sit next to me on the couch and put her arms around my shoulders. Oh, what joy, what relief to feel the life, the warmth, the reality! From the moment I left her at the end of the session, I began to count the hours and the minutes: only twenty-four hours, only twenty-three and a half hours, only eighteen hours (*Autobiography*, p. 34).

But this momentary island against the world of brilliant emptiness was insufficient and Renee's condition deteriorated for two years into institutionalized madness.

At this point several items need to be noted concerning the touching and holding in the therapy sessions, and of Renee's calling Ms. S. "Mama" and of Ms. S. so referring to herself, items which the Pesso System therapist will be able to put in perspective. First of all the use of herself directly as "mother" is an error, however necessary an error at the time. Many later developments with Renee make that point clear. As a therapeutic maneuver it is a triumphant step over the nothingness of the usual physically unresponsive transference/countertransference. Here is a paradox, yet it is a paradox beautifully resolved by Albert and Diane Pesso's key discovery of the clinical use of real persons enroling as *ideal mother*, *ideal father*, or other *ideal figures*. It is a resolution which allows for the physical contact, and it is that which conveys the messages of *support*, *nurturing*, *protection*, *limits* as well as a sense of personal *place*, *respect* and *validation* to the deep symbolic level, where symbolic decisions may be restructured. At the same time it allows the client a deepening comprehension of the difference between reality and those aspects of her symbolic decisions which are non-functional. Such experiences, with real people enroled to receive the transference, can be provided in a therapeutic group. They can also be approximated using PS/P in individual psychotherapy (see Chapter 18).

Two years of deterioration in Renee's condition are perhaps to some extent attributable to the failure of Ms. S. to make the above distinctions, though nothing should take from her our praise for the courage to move in directions which must have been quite antithetical to her training.

V

For a deeper key to Renee's continued downward spiral we must look at two profound double binds to which she is subjected. In response to orders from "the System" (her system of paranoic self-persecution) to burn her hand, she finds herself caught thusly:

> An indescribable anguish squeezed my heart, an anguish no resolve could allay. If I refused to obey, I felt guilty and cowardly for not daring, and the anguish mounted. Then the order became more insistent. If, finally to obey, I went to the fire and stretched out my hand, an intense feeling of guilt overcame me as though I were doing something wicked, and the anxiety waxed in proportion (*Autobiography*, p. 41).

While that double bind caught her in inescapable guilt, the second double bind, also linked to the "System" and its orders, attacks the integrity of her personality:

> I had too the conviction that my behavior was deceitful. In reality, it wasn't anything of the kind. I was deeply sincere. But if I disobeyed the System to maintain the integrity of my personality, I was deceitful since I acted as though I had no considera-tion for the order. If I obeyed it, I was equally deceitful, since I did not agree to burn myself. I suffered horribly from the orders and from the feeling of treachery so contrary to my character (p. 42).

The powers of the rational mind in these circumstances are finally turned on the more powerful of her worlds, the symbolic world of punishment and nothingness, with unfortunate results:

> In the system a formidable interdependence existed. Without knowing it, I had ordered that people be punished, and in my turn, I was to be punished. Those who had received punishment from me had the right to punish, but for each punishment they meted out, one was incurred. When I understood the mechanism of the System of Punishments which engulfed me, I fought less and less against the orders (p. 43).

Pesso therapists will recognize all too well the dilemma of a client caught in the hopeless need to self-limit an omnipotent guilt without a physical system within which to construct an adequate response.

During the period of institutionalization following an attempt to burn her hand Renee relates that one nurse, aware of her drive to burn herself, would follow and stop her when she left the lounge or her own room. "How relieved I was when I realized how altogether impossible it was to carry out the orders! — When, then, the nurse placed an obstacle in the way I no longer had to struggle against them" (p. 46). Contrarywise, the director of the hospital, intellectually interested (as Renee put it) in such psychological abnormalities, would allow Renee to "reach my objective and only interfered at the last moment when I reached toward the flame or match box. Sometimes I sensed her behind me and hated her for letting me struggle alone against the impulse to carry out the order, a struggle moreover in which I was always vanquished" (p. 47). These occurrences give evidence of the necessity for and comfort of *limits*, though there is, as usual, at this point in Renee's awareness, no comprehension that such limit-giving might reach beyond mere temporary relief if applied, as in Pesso work, in safe physical restraining by *ideal figures*.

None of the above, necessarily so selective, gives any concept of the complexity or dynamic movement of Renee's pathology. In the midst of Renee's agony Ms. S. makes a direct intervention by taking Renee with her to the seashore for a holiday, and this episode gives another opportunity to look at the problems that arise from Ms. S., in her person, being "Mama" and not role-playing a symbolic ideal mother:

> But I was amazed to discover that the longed-for constant nearness to Mama did not bring the happiness I had anticipated. Quite the contrary; I was disappointed. Before, during our sessions together, Mama had been just 'Mama'; now on the trip and at the hotel she became 'Mrs. Sechehaye,' so that in spite of my wanting it, and her kindness and affection, I had no contact with her. She was disguised as a 'lady' and in vain I looked for 'Mama'. Fortunately we had a treatment session every day and I was able to regain the relation, but apart from the sessions she was a stranger. And all my attempts to alter this painful situation were fruitless (pp. 59-60).

Pesso therapists will readily understand why Renee was able to maintain the "Mama" relationship in the therapy hour, at which time she could unconsciously regard the relationship symbolically, and why she could not retain the "Mama" in her "real time" with Ms. S.

Ms. S. eventually was able to place Renee in the home of a nurse, at which time her condition was fundamentally catatonic in its outer appearance. At this point three years had passed, and Ms. S. had finally grasped the meaning of a significant part of Renee's symbology. She attempted to explain rationally the meaning of the symbols to Renee. "But we reached only an intellectual and fleeting comprehension and often I was met with nonreceptiveness..." (Sechehaye, p. 48). It was at this time that the first active therapist-client interactions on the symbolic level took place, but each tells a somewhat different tale. I will follow Renee's account of these events first:

> ["Mama" gives Renee a] little plush monkey of which I was at once afraid. When he had his arms up, I was anxious lest he hurt me; and then, he had a most shockingly unhappy expression. Oddly, at that very moment, I felt the impulse to strike myself. I realized full well that my own arms were delivering the blows, still I was sure the monkey was attacking me. Nonetheless I did not know that he was a symbol of myself, nor in any case that I should have known what he meant.
>
> I said to myself 'I am I and he is he and there is no relationship between us'; however the confusion as to who was who was complete. He had the same troubles as I and moreover he wanted to hurt me, to destroy me, and I dreaded him without holding it against him for I realized it was not his fault.
>
> When I related my fears to Mama, she did something extraordinary. She took the monkey's two arms, lowered them around his little knees and said, 'Mama's little monkey, Mama asks you always to keep your arms down to comfort Renee. Then Renee will not be afraid of you, do you see?' The little monkey agreed; I could see it in his eyes. It is hard to express how relieved I was that Mama made him take this position. At any rate, from that moment, the impulse to self harm left me abruptly.
>
> I was very careful to see that the monkey kept his arms down. Were they perchance up I was forced to strike myself since the monkey wished it. Then I would

run to him and lower his arms. And everything was well again (*Autobiography*, pp. 65-66).

The projection and identification are obvious to all. What is perhaps clearer to a Pesso therapist than to most others is the manner in which the symbols work with the "Mama" to resolve pathology. When "Mama" lowers the monkey's arms and lectures it on keeping its arms down "to comfort Renee" she makes an observable, experienceable alliance with that part of Renee which does not wish to damage herself, and limits the threatening gesture of that part of Renee which has perforce accepted alliance with external historic destructive forces. Destructive and divisive forces from persons and events had, through the instruments of powerful double binds, forced upon a part of Renee a denial of self, so that the only hope of survival, of beingness, was to ally a part of herself with those evil forces. "Mama" demonstrates that there is a force now in the picture which can perceive the split and move decisively to protect that part of the self still struggling for self-validation. And that is why "the little monkey agreed; I could see it in his eyes."

I say that this new force, the "Mama," could protect the divided self. She could not yet serve to provide Renee with the experiences needed for her to unify herself. We shall later see why this is so and what wrong and nearly disastrous turnings were taken before the method that led out of the labyrinth could adequately be learned.

The monkey was preparatory to the first major breakthrough both for Renee's ability to communicate her need adequately through a symbol, and for Ms. S. to comprehend how the body and present reality were to be used symbolically for healing purposes.

VI

In the chapter called "The Miracle of the Apples" Renee herself points out how the preliminary figure of the monkey played the major role in creating the symbolic framework within which the primary and most deeply poisoned developmental stage could at last be approached and dealt with, and she could begin to take, on her own initiative, unworthy food (unripe apples plucked from a tree) from a neutral mother (the earth):

> The monkey was unhappy because he had nothing to eat; everything was forbidden him except apples and spinach. So I went to the orchard to gather an apple or two from the tree; these I ate voraciously. In taking these apples, I had no sense of guilt for the tree was part of my country, the land of Tibet I called it, of which I was queen. Indeed, I had the clear impression of living in a desert country, desolate, rocky, unreal, where I had one right - to eat the apples of my tree. Nevertheless, despite the tree, I was abandoned, miserable, left only the right to eat the apples; everything else was denied me (p. 66).

It is interesting to note that Ms. S. misses entirely the vital preparatory role of the monkey. The eating of the apples appears suddenly, in her account, as it were out of the blue:

> For three years now I have been doing my best to save Renee. The wall of guilt which I have come up against is still there. The main difficulty of the moment is getting her to eat. She is now in this boarding house in the country (next to a farm), where she is able to accept green vegetables; not being nourishing, they do not cause feelings of guilt. She is also able to eat them because they are products of the earth (mother).

Renee can also eat apples, provided that they are green, that is to say, not ripe. (Green apples hold to the tree, i.e. to the mother. It is the milk from the mother's breast. But ripe apples are detached from the tree, have fallen to the ground; they represent boiled milk, cow milk. Green apples also represent a symbolic food, the food of autism which is permissible, because being autistic is being in the mother's body.) (Sechehaye, pp. 49-50)

Pesso therapists are constantly made aware by the body energies which their clients exhibit of the prime importance of the oral stage. In Erik Erikson's (1950) developmental schema, this is the age when trust is established. And the trust that must be established is, in all its complications and implications, a trust in the rightness of the self (beyond mere survival-feeding needs), its rightness in being where it is when it is on this earth. So it is not simply a question of adequate nurturing. *Reactive Attachment Disorder* is a diagnostic label that has only recently appeared in the literature. What it so minimalistically implies is that the child has been neglected or abandoned or by circumstance cut off from a consistently caring parent. But the sense of trust is disrupted not simply on the feeding level nor on the macro level of abandonment. The infant must have validated its power, in D.W. Winnicott's (1965, 1975) formulation, to both create and obliterate the giver of loving support (it must be securely and lovingly held, supported in proper relationship to the breast, without subtle or unsubtle nervousness or rejection on the mother's part). When the infant looks at its mother's eyes it needs to see the mother gazing at it with a calm and validating love. It needs to experience these things with a certainty that the mother and father are capable of protecting it from distracting as well as outright hostile forces. In short, it is not merely gross neglect or abandonment which can create critical flaws in the foundation of the psyche. *Nurturing*, *support*, *protection*, and, a little later, adequate *limits*, are all vital elements the baby begins to integrate on the symbolic level during this foundation period for all later development. And all come through body-information, not reason-information.

As we have seen, Renee's oral stage was a disaster, with a mother who looked at her with dislike if not hatred, who unconsciously starved her, who allowed the sadistic father to psychologically torture her. So Renee felt profoundly unworthy. Her needs, which apppeared as demands rather than as rights, create unmanageable guilt and shame. So she has incorporated on the symbolic level the double bind "how can I eat and not eat?" or "how can I make not-eating an eating?" But there is yet a prior double bind on an even deeper layer of the symbolic level, and that is, "since my being is bad yet I am here and must be, how can I make non-being a being?" or, more critically, how can I make non-being a being, so that I may exist enough to make non-eating an eating?"

It is in resolving the primary paradox or double bind that the monkey as symbol becomes critical. It provides a way to be and not-be. It is the monkey who is unhappy because it cannot eat. Renee, then, is free to resolve this problem for the monkey, but only within a certain narrow range created by a symbolism of the earth as an indifferent non-human mother. But this symbolism must be even more narrowly conceived. Non-human as the earth-mother is, even it cannot conceivably *give* the good milk to the monkey. No, Renee must seize the not-so-good milk, unripe, and paradoxically both willingly and unwillingly, from the safely indifferent mother. It is impossible to take ripe apples because that would imply that the mother was giving them to the monkey, and that would set up unbearable guilt.

At one point a serious setback occurs. The tree from which Renee has been taking the green apples is on an adjacent farm, and one day the farmer's wife comes and berates Renee for taking apples that do not belong to her. (Once again we see the problems arising from a confusion of the real with the symbolic.) Ms. S. believes that this is the first crisis in the affair of the apples — but such is not the case. Renee relates how Ms. S. failed at first to see the apples, and the whole manner of getting them and eating them, as symbolic. Like a sensible person she:

> brought me pounds of magnificent apples. But I could not touch them, for I was allowed to eat only my own apples still attached to the Mama-tree. I should have liked so much to have Mama give me apples, real apples I called them. But, alas, Mama did not understand. Amazed, she cried, "But aren't all these apples that I bring you real? Why don't you eat them?" Her words irritated me and I removed myself more and more from Mama. I had no more contact with her except when she took the little monkey in her arms and talked to him, a thing she did too rarely to suit me. I was extremely unhappy. I felt myself getting younger; the System wanted to reduce me to nothing. Even as I diminished in body and in age, I discovered that I was nine centuries old. For to be nine centuries old actually meant being not yet born. That is why the nine centuries did not make me feel at all old; quite the contrary... More and more I lost contact with Mama and it often happened that I avoided her and even forgot the visit, something practically unheard of for me. For Mama remained the sole being to whom I still clung in despair (*Autobiography*, pp. 66-67).

First, Ms. S., stuck in the confused role of real-symbolic Mama and failing to distinguish between her therapeutic role of ideal mother, Renee's transference Mama, and her own countertransference Mama, thinks, as one does in the "real" world, "if green apples are acceptable, then beautiful, nourishing, ripe apples must be more acceptable." Such obtuse insistence drove Renee further and further in upon her unreal world of guilt, for the matter went beyond Mama not understanding; Mama became a danger, thrusting forward dangerous food that threatened the solution of how to be and not-be so that one could eat and not-eat.

It was at this point that the negative intervention of the farmer's wife took place:

> The horror that gripped me on hearing these [the farmer's wife's] words is impossible to describe. Shame, rage, the deceit, and above all an intolerable burden of blame struggled in my heart — The one favor, my only remaining sanction, had just been brutally wrenched away and my awful guilt put in its place. But she had done it, had robbed me; she must then be right and I wrong to want the apples... The more I wanted them, the more I demanded 'my apples' back again, the heavier lay the load of guilt (p. 68).

After several reactive crises, she runs, under pressure of her need for her apples, to Ms. S's house. And it is at this point that Ms. S. finally moved to the symbolic level, whether or not she understood what she was doing or why she was doing it. Here is Ms. S's account of that moment:

> Renee runs away and arrives at my house all alone, at nine in the evening, in terrible agony. I persist in trying to understand the symbolism of the apples. To the remark that I gave her as many apples as she wanted, Renee cries: 'Yes, but those are store apples, apples for big people, but I want apples from Mummy, like that,' pointing to my breasts. 'Those apples there, Mummy gives them only when one is hungry.' I

understand at last what must be done! Since the apples represent maternal milk, I must give them to her like a mother feeding her baby: I must give her the symbol myself, directly and without intermediary - and at a fixed hour. To verify my hypothesis I carry it out at once. Taking an apple, and cutting it in two, I offer Renee a piece, saying, 'It is time to drink the good milk from Mummy's apples, Mummy is going to give it to you.' Renee then leans up against my shoulder, presses the apple upon my breast, and very solemnly, with intense happiness, eats it (Sechehaye, pp 50-51).

I am going to emphasize this moment by giving Renee's account of the same event. I do so because her words describe so eloquently the sort of occurrence which Pesso therapists see not infrequently, if less dramatically. I use this re-telling also to emphasize that, while in the world of symbols it is possible for anything to represent anything, in the world of Pesso therapy we know that the healing will not work till the pieces of the client's symbolic world are so emergent to the consciousness of the client that they may be assembled in proper patterning — the word, the body, the mind. That pattern of word, body, mind then functions to present to the client, not an abstract idea, but a physical action in symbolic reality. That action-in-reality, because wholly constructed from the client's experiential historic needs, symbolically fulfills with great accuracy a developmental need in the client's own system-world. As a result, that action-in-reality penetrates in most persuasive terms to the deep symbolic decision-making level of the psyche-soma:

> Mama tried affectionately to calm me, but without success. 'Why,' she said, 'don't you take the apples I bring you?' 'I can't do that, Mama,' I answered. And while in my heart I was outraged that Mama too wanted to force me to eat, my eyes fell to her bosom, and when she insisted, 'But why don't you want the apples I buy you?' I knew what I was yearning for so desperately and I was able to bring out, 'Because the apples you buy are for grown-ups and I want real apples, Mama's apples, like those,' and I pointed to Mama's breasts. She got up at once, went to get a magnificent apple, cut a piece and gave it to me, saying, 'Now, Mama is going to feed her little Renee. It is time to drink the good milk from Mama's apples.' She put the piece in my mouth, and with my eyes closed, my head against her breast, I ate, or rather drank, my milk. A nameless felicity flowed into my heart. It was as though, suddenly, by magic, all my agony, the tempest which has shaken me a moment ago, had given place to a blissful calm; I thought of nothing, I discerned nothing, I reveled in my joy. I was fully content, with a passive contentment, the contentment of a tiny baby, quite unconscious, for I did not even know what caused it... I left with the nurse who had come to fetch me, and when we were outside I realized that my perception of things had completely changed. Instead of infinite space, unreal, where everything was cut off, naked and isolated, I saw Reality, marvelous Reality, for the first time (*Autobiography*, pp. 70-71).

VII

But Ms. S. had understood the moment without fully understanding the principle of healing through bodily action in symbolic reality, an understanding which is both at the heart of Pesso therapy and is also at the heart of why it takes years of training to become a competent facilitator-therapist in this powerful method for change. As Renee, through symbolic association with the apples (representing the mother's breast), was able slowly to expand her range of food and eating environment, a new direction for healing arose. It took the natural developmental path of cleansing her body as a rite of self-love and self-acceptance. "Some time later, my interest in maternal nourishment waned and I focused instead on my body" (p. 73).

Renee felt so little justification or right to exist that use of the personal pronouns "I" or "you" always caused an increase in pathological symptoms. By extension any suggestion that the body had enjoyments was, paradoxically, what Pesso therapists call a *negative reconstruction*, which is, simply, allowing the client to act out symbolically the historic neurotic pattern without a new and positive outcome. To understand how this can be so we must return to the basic double-bind: "I am forbidden to be, but I am," or, to put it actively, the problem is "how to not-be while being." To experience pleasure is, *ipso facto*, a simple, straightforward assertion of being. Such assertion is impossible for Renee to obey because it raises the intolerable guilt and shame of beingness. If the ideal mother insists that the client satisfy the need for pleasure, then the client is relieved of moral responsibility, and a way is opened out of the double binding maze. A good example of a similar double bind which Pesso therapists encounter frequently is the inability of a client to beat a pillow (symbolically representing a negative aspect of a parent), while finding it acceptable that an ideal parent can administer the punishment — an answer to the client's double bind "how to punish the unpunishable."

So it is that when Ms. S. insists that Renee bathe, Renee is free to enjoy this self-affirming enhancement of the body. "She now had the right to live, it was necessary to acquire the right to enjoy living" (Sechehaye, p. 57):

> Mama was present at one or two baths; she said 'Mama wants Renee to be clean and neat, Mama wants Renee to take a bath so she will be.' What a satisfaction to lie in the lovely, warm, fragrant water, as though I lay in Mama's arms. Just the same, the privilege of washing with this soap, of washing at all, was not for me. But I could accept the nurse's washing me because under these conditions I was not responsible for the pleasure I experienced in being clean (*Autobiography*, p. 73).

Unfortunately, Ms. S., as I have said before, had not grasped the basic principle:

> Catastrophe! I had just repeated the mistake made in connection with the apples ('give her as many as she wants'). I had made Renee responsible for bathing; that is to say, I had loaded her again with feelings of guilt. The 'attention of the voices' was attracted and suddenly the improvement was stopped short (Sechehaye, p. 57).

How does Renee respond to this error?

> Unhappily, Mama did not comprehend the intense culpability ready to sweep over me the moment I took the initiative in creating the pleasure myself. She said something dreadful: 'Bathe Renee only when she wants to; she loves it don't you Renee?' A tearing rage against Mama rose up in me. How could she do anything like that to me, anything so shameful! To declare openly that it was I, Renee, who wanted the pleasure of a bath! The blame attached to this was immediately reawakened and I vehemently refused to bathe. At once contact between Mama and me was disrupted; abruptly wonderful reality disappeared, to be replaced by the old cinematographic scene. I was crushed by the responsibility she had laid on me and deeply wounded that she had said aloud in front of the nurse that I enjoyed the bath and wanted it.

However, by refusing to bathe and remaining quite passive while the nurse washed me, I managed to temper a little my unbearable guilt. As a consequence of this break of contact, I turned more toward the nurse who took care of me and whom I liked very much. In spite of this, hostile impulses against her would surge up suddenly for no apparent reason (*Autobiography*, p. 74).

As Ms. S. says, "Because of my clumsiness, the matter of the bath, which seemed so promising, became a failure. Renee dropped this symbol, so to speak, to take it up again later with gymnastics and massage" (Sechehaye, p. 58).

VIII

Ms. S's failure to take her cues from Renee, voicing instead her own real-world wishes, had brought a promising development to failure. And that failure presents a window on what was, from a PS/P perspective, the great flaw at the center of Ms. S's treatment, a flaw which remained despite the profound courage and honesty which led her to ultimate success. I refer here to the actual use of herself in the transference counter-transference as Mama. This fundamental confusion of the therapist with the parent caused great and continual difficulty. We have earlier spoken of how it confused Renee. In the failure of the "bath" symbolic usage we see an example of how such a confusion makes it difficult for the therapist to keep focused on the line of symbolic thought-action arising from the client.

Ms. S. says:

> I thought that the improvement was going to continue of itself and that I would merely have to use a treatment of re-education. — But I was off the mark! — And, like the preceding ones, they [other conflicts] demanded to be settled in the same symbolic manner, so that Renee could progress by stages as she should have been allowed to in her life. I did not understand it at the time, unfortunately, and for lack of adequate care I let our patient slip back into a more serious state than before. I thought that it would be easier to do some re-education if Renee stayed with me. Therefore I invited her to spend a few weeks at our home with us (p. 60).

No more convincing evidence of the continued confusion of Ms. S. concerning the real and the symbolic could be given than this invitation to Renee to live in her home. It is an intervention which will have, as we shall see, dire consequences.

Placing this account next to Renee's we see some significant differences. First of all, Renee is very clear, as Ms. S. was not at the time, that the episode of the botched bathing symbol led to a good deal more than simply the end of the bath as a useful developmental tool. It meant a significant degree of withdrawal of cathexis from "Mama," with a concurrent increase in closeness to the nurse (acting in what Pesso therapists would in some sense see as an extension of the *ideal mother*). Renee says,

> Months passed; then one day my nurse failed to appear as usual. She had gone on vacation, causing me a horrible shock. All night long I sobbed in anger and grief; my whole world had fallen to pieces. Her absence was simply unbearable and my suffering was cruel. Then, too, I was vexed with Mama for allowing her to leave. Though at that time I went to spend several weeks at Mama's home, I felt a pervasive sense of abandonment, for it had been the nurse who had fed me, dressed me and made me work (*Autobiography*, p. 74).

It is important at this point to pause and recall the earlier time, when going to the seashore with Mama forced Renee to distance her, except in their therapy hour. But that was before the Mama changed from being at best a Mama merely of comforting words. Now she had been transformed into the breast-giving, life-giving Mama, and a Mama who at this point had made a major error in the handling of the "bathing" symbolic action. It is at this crucial time, with the symbolic extension of Mama (the Nurse) suddenly gone, that Renee is brought into the real house of the real Mama and is forced to discover that this Mama has other "children" (i.e., patients) — sibling rivals who have their inexorable time with Mama, and that she also has a husband whom Renee calls "the Great Personage" (p. 74):

> Mama I recognized less and less; in her place I perceived the Queen, the Goddess, source of life and joy, yet withal a source of deprivation as well... With each indict- ment I believed the Queen would understand and bestow the precious milk. But, alas, she did not comprehend my language... But the Mama of the apples did not under- stand; the Queen, formidable and terrible, had completely supplanted her (p. 75).

It is most important to understand what a profound effect this confusion of the real and the symbolic had on Renee. Her drift into unreality was hastened by several maladroit occasions with Mama. Particularly disastrous was one episode which illustrates the centrality of the concept of limits in Pesso therapy, and which is also an excellent example (or would be, if the episode were in a Pesso *structure*) of a *negative reconstruction*:

> Finally, one day at dinner, more unhappy and upset about the patients than ordinarily, I refused to eat. Mama, instead of insisting, instead of announcing that she, Mama, gave me the right to eat, exclaimed, 'You may leave it, if you don't want it,' meaning, to me, 'I don't want you to eat!' I rose and ran to my room, weeping and wailing in fathomless despair (p. 76).

Ms. S. as the real woman sitting at the real table and exasperated with this jealous, acting-out child, had said what Renee's symbolic world could only take as a destruction of the way out of the maze, the double bind, "how do I eat and not-eat?"

During this period Renee was twice admitted to a psychiatric institution, returning to Mama "even more rigid, more silent and particularly more inimical and guilty" (p. 76). This profound withdrawal continued for nearly a year. There is not room here to recount the symbolic errors during this time that arose from a continued confusion of the real with the symbolic on the part of the therapist. Particularly vivid was one time when Ms. S., in an obvious effort to recapture the healing of the Apples (oral) symbolic period, offered Renee some cream, which Renee called "snow" and which represented purity. Renee, out of her deep conviction of unworthiness, refused. Mama does not insist, does not actually place the cream in her mouth, and Renee is left in a tumult of self-hatred. "Only one thing absorbed me, to annihilate, to assassinate this ignoble being, this hideous, infamous creature, myself, hated to the point of death" (p. 78).

During this period Ms. S. had a serious physical illness which exacerbated Renee's sense of guilt and of being abandoned. Finally, "Three months later, it occured to me to give Renee a new double of herself. It was again a baby, but this time made entirely of porcelain" (Sechehaye, p. 68). This doll, which Renee named, for symbolic reasons, Ezekiel, presented again a way out of the double bind "how to be and not-be," for if it is too guilt-producing for

Renee to be held by the Mama, and to be tended by her, it is acceptable that a self not-self should receive these life affirming gestures from the symbolic Mama. And as Mama tended and cared for Ezekiel, Renee's symptoms were to some degree allayed.

At this critical moment Renee was visited by a life-threatening illness, which seemed to her another overwhelming proof of her unworthiness. Slowly the medical doctor brought her back from the edge of death; Ms. S. resumed the symbolic treatment with Ezekiel. The straps which were restraining Renee's self-destructive gestures were removed six months after the re-introduction of the symbolic treatment. But the major return to progress lay in a more profound symbolic regression.

IX

One day, when Renee was suffering terribly from her voices I said to her: 'Mummy is going to put a stop to these wicked voices which punish Renee, and Renee will sleep as Ezekiel and Moses [another doll] do in the warmth of their cradle. Mummy is going to put Renee in her cradle.' (I then gave her the sedative prescribed by the doctor. The sedative symbolized the atmosphere of well-being in the cradle.) Her agitation calmed down immediately and Renee repeated with relief: 'It is all green, all green...' She was speaking of the color of the room, which was green because of the green pulled-down shades. I told her that it was mother who had made the room green (in pulling down the shades), so that she could sleep peacefully in her cradle and so that the voices would go away. Green was for Renee (as she explained to me later) the color of the bottom of the ocean and marshland, and 'to be in the green' meant 'to be in the mother's body,' the wished-for paradise. Whenever the voices came back, Renee complained: 'It isn't green anymore! They take away all the color.' And when I put on a compress to relieve her, she said: 'You're making green" (Sechehaye, pp. 72-73).

Renee reports this episode as follows:

One day when Mama was well and I was tortured by their [the voices] persecution, she came to me and announced her intention of banishing the voices, thereby enabling me to sleep like Ezekiel and Moses. After a sedative hypodermic injection, I shortly felt myself slipping into a wonderful realm of peace. Everything in the room was green, green as the sea, quite like being in Mama's body. My pain assuaged in a state of perfect passivity, without want of any kind; Mama had procured this bliss for me. Hence, I thought, she is willing to take me into her body. An immense relief flowed over me; I was in Paradise, in the maternal bosom. From that moment I had unshakable confidence in Mama and I loved her as never before. That she had received me into herself, that she had acceded to my fondest wish filled me with happiness and proved without a doubt that she loved me, that I was loved (*Autobiograpy*, pp. 82-83).

Either through some verbal relationship (the green sea, the amniotic fluid) or some actual primitive remembrance of the light filtering through the mother's skin into the womb, the green room is taken profoundly as a symbol of acceptance into the *ideal mother*'s body. Mama has made the ultimate gesture in the face of the double bind, "Renee is, because in me she cannot not-be."

Ms. S. explained this event by calling it a permission to a return to "autism" (Sechehaye, pp. 73-74). I believe her explanation was flawed, though her symbolic solution was accurate.

A Pesso therapist would interpret this symbolic action not as a "retreat into autism," but as a symbolic re-birth in human physical union with an ideal mother whose loving presence creates the healing double bind "You are because the two of us are together in joyous union." Ms. S. says that, "By the sedatives which I could give her, I showed her my willingness to have her enter the maternal bosom. The tie was strengthened each time I relieved her" (p. 74). Again I believe this explanation demonstrates that she had succeeded, but had not yet learned the primary lesson concerning limits and negative reconstructions. The ideal mother would not be willing, but would rather insist on the child's well-being, will not take "no," will not be put off by the guilt of the child, by its need to placate demonic forces with its own self-destruction. It is interesting to note that the injections have been given before by Ms. S., with no evidence of any symbolic import. It is only when they are given in that matrix or environment of the words from the ideal mother which insist on the child's well-being that the entire gestalt — the words, the ideal mother's physical presence and actions, their precise coincidence with the need of Renee to have the responsibility of dealing with the voices taken from her hands — only then does a "structure" appear: a complete physical-symbolic event which meets with exactness a historic need. Only then can the injection, as part of that whole, have power for change. The ideal mother leaves Renee with no choice but to give up her pain. And by that absolute insistence by the ideal mother that Renee has not merely a right, but a *place* of well-being, she opens the way for the total acceptance of and entrance into the mother's womb. The mother will have it no other way. "Whenever after this the suffering bore me down and the voices afflicted me, by the simple expedient of a sedative hypodermic and arranging the green twilight in my room, Mama placed me in the 'green sea' in felicity, safe from every vicissitude" (*Autobiography*, p. 83). Pesso System therapy is a completely drug free process and I am not suggesting here that it was the drug that made the difference. What made the difference was the language and the symbolic intent of the ideal mother coinciding with the symbolic need of the client. That there is a natural though symbolic developmental process here, and not a case of drugging, is evidenced by the natural moving on of Renee in her physical-symbolic re-creation. "And more and more, I preferred to be *near* her, rather than *within* her... Later Mama gave me a letter in which was noted in detail what food I was to eat, food she herself had prepared, so that even in her absence she was near me" (p. 83). And so we see a clear example of Renee's symbolic integration of the mother which leads to that progressive independence of which Winnicott first spoke so eloquently.

Renee's progression in her symbolic actions from the womb, to being near ideal mama, to being fed by ideal mama, to feeding herself with only the abstract words of Mama present, is an example of the kind of developmental symbolic re-decisioning which is at the heart of clients' work in their *structures* in Psychomotor therapy. Again, the developmental progress in terms of object relations is expressed quite succinctly by Renee:

> At first I could maintain contact with Mama only if she met me on the level at which I was. Any other kind of conversation or social attitude on her part removed me from reality and I could accept her only as part of the outside world. Then by degrees I became independent of her, first through feeding, then through cleanliness and personal care. At length I could think differently from her without endangering clear reality perception (p. 85).

Renee at the point of the womb experience was twenty-three and three-quarters years old, and had begun therapy with Ms. S. just prior to her eighteenth birthday.

Not the least interesting fact of this case is that in a letter to Ms. S., written from a nursing home when she was twenty years old, Renee already knew what her body wanted to experience, what turn her therapy might best take at that time:

> My dear Mummy, I am trying very hard, and it is for you. I want so very much to go into your body. I hate this life. Take me. I rejoice in returning to your body. I shall no longer hear anybody crying. Mummy, I try hard to eat and dress myself, but it is so hard. If I succeed, you will be so happy and we shall work together for the enlightened [mentally ill] people. Naturally even for those enlightened by perversion, but mostly for those having great grief (p. 47).

There were other important symbolic developments as Renee achieved, with occasional setbacks, her sanity. But I leave each person to explore those valuable details. Looking back to the profound truth concerning her needs as expressed in Renee's letter, it is a fascinating if useless speculation to wonder if a Pesso System therapist, so used to validating and knowing how to act upon such symbolic wishes, could have foreshortened significantly the time of the treatment. But there can be no happier conclusion for us than to affirm to that courageous, truthful young woman's spirit, and that of her courageous, caring therapist, that their mutual work is indeed still working "together for the enlightened people — for those having great grief."

References

Autobiography of a schizophrenic girl, (1951/1970). New York: Signet.

Erikson, E. (1950). *Childhood and society*. New York: W.W. Norton.

Sechehaye, M.A. (1951). *Symbolic realizations*. New York: International Universities Press.

Winnicott, D.W. (1965). *The maturational processes and the facilitating environment*. New York: International Universities Press.

Winnicott, D.W. (1975). *Through paediatrics to psycho-analysis*. New York: Basic Books.

Chapter 9

Developments in Psychomotor

An Interview with Al Pesso[1]

by Al Pesso and John Crandell

Prestructural Issues

Using the Crossfire to Frame the Structure Work

John: What we are doing is talking about future directions of Psychomotor, going over some thoughts about where it has been, and where it is going in the future. Why don't we start by talking about some of the developments in the last few years: the *pilot* and *fragment figures*. Maybe you can describe how this is different from what Psychomotor used to be, what it reflects as a change.

Al: The more I do it the more it seems connected to everything I did before. So often I would apologize. In the recent past with groups, I would say how different things are and then people would say that it isn't all that different. So I think that everything that is coming out now was telegraphed by the past. I think I've found better ways of doing things I have always been concerned about. I always was concerned about ego processes and the pre-structural work. I was always concerned about framing, and it seems that now with this *pilot* work and getting to the *center of truth* and setting up the true scene, I'm taking care of all that pre-structural stuff and making sure that someone is really ready and seeing where they are going to work. It's become systematized.

John: And seems much more conscious, planned, and thought through now.

Al: Yes. Again, I didn't know that I was implementing old wishes. When I first did it it seemed like a radical departure. I thought, "My God, I'm leaving the motoric, I'm simply trying to link back to the traditional population of psychotherapists." But, I wasn't moving away. I don't know why I tormented myself thinking that I was. Today, it got perfectly clear to me

---

[1] Edited for publication from an interview done in Montclair, New Jersey on October 14, 1989. A videotape is available through the Telles Institute, 3304 Mathieson Drive NE, Atlanta, Georgia 30305-9996.

that what I called the crossfire is having the emotional status of where the person was clearly felt by the person; clearly seen by the *witness*; and then the witness elaborating through the help of me, the therapist, on the affective qualities — not merely on what the person says they're feeling, but with acute attention paid to the total body posture, the expression on the face, the amount of energy in the whole system, so the witness then is enriching the pilot's inner awareness of where they are. That's one side of the crossfire, and is opposed by what the person is saying that goes counter to the expression of this awareness — which would be the injunctions that say "don't feel like that, you're ridiculous to feel like that." For instance, today, someone was feeling a certain pain at not being as strong as they like, and they were crying with the pain of the injury that they felt, all the while hearing the inner admonishment: "Girls should be as strong as boys," etc., etc. That's the crossfire: where they are feeling exactly what they feel, and it goes counter to what some of their internalized values are. That begins to be the frame for the work itself. I found it so hard to teach trainees how to frame — like what should the *structure* be about, and doing this process of witnessing and having other figures represent the other values just locks that condition in.

John: So as I understand it, the frame has always been a concept of what is the essential issue, the central dynamic a person is working with, where they are plugging into the *old map*.

Al: I didn't even think of the old map. Years ago, I thought, where does the work want to go, and I used to phrase it as "what is this person telling me in their body and in their words about what the work is about," and I would listen, and in a sense I would categorize it. Without defining it I would have kind of unnamed categories about the feeling and the affect of the motoric and listen to what I call "their story." And I did that all internally and never shared it with the client. Then I would look and listen for where I saw the highest energy. After it framed, then I would say, "That's the general theme. Now I see that." I would say "choose this figure because it looks like you're mostly concerned with such and such" and "choose this figure because this figure may be anti it" or whatever, and with amazement people would wonder how we got directly to what they're dealing with. They didn't see the steps.

John: Now you're making the crossfire overt and visible to the person (**Al**: Instantly.) in the scene rather than doing it in your head and presenting them with a conclusion from that.

Al: That's right. In a way I gave away the magic to the client, and now I'm giving it away to the therapist, because the therapist would say, "I don't know how the hell you did what you did." It looked like I was doing all kinds of magical stunts, and now it's so clear to follow.

The Pilot

John: I find the crossfire a beautiful analogy because very literally you can see the person bombarded from two, sometimes four, different directions with contradictory messages. It creates a geometrical frame.

Al: The other geometry I'm thinking of making a diagram for is to show how the setup is enriching the pilot. Again, the *pilot* is that part of the person that is listening to all the different constituencies inside and making assessments and decisions about which way to go. And the pilot is not only listening but also feeling. For me to diagram this, it would be inside the head of the pilot, the central agency, and it's connected to the affective stuff, and it's connected to the injunctions and the values, etc., etc., and the resistances, and that's all inside the person. Although the pilot is receptive to new information and new ways of being, it can only choose out of the information available to it. As it only has information about the *soul* that has been affirmed by past external validators, it may be limited by its interior perspective. It lacks the external validating view of the body that could represent whatever is still unconscious. Now, by having the witness outside, we enrich the pilot's awareness of their affective state. Now there may be feelings running through their body which they are unaware of, but the body may be showing all kinds of things that were never licensed or named or been made at all aware of. So we are now loading the deck with the witness having the acuity of vision and understanding of the therapist. And then, of course, the witness is the template for the construction of the pilot.

By putting outside the person all these injunctions and values, the pilot is hearing that information inside as their own thoughts and then hearing it outside as commands. When it's inside as their own thoughts they attribute it to their values; they don't tend to fight against it. But when it's commands from the outside you can watch on their face how they feel when they are being told these distinctive, nasty things. Their spirit revolts against that.

John: And the witness then feeds back that revolt so they can recognize it.

Al: And then also feel that it is credible. It gives credence to it and somehow a place to it. That's the framing now. It's done right there. What I had concern about in the first flush of the excitement of knowing I could teach this and the excitement of seeing what happens when people are witnessed, I didn't include the motoric all that much and I felt like I was abandoning it and I missed all the gut satisfaction.

Fragment Figures and the Motoric

John: As you were training us in doing this we were deliberately, for a while, de-emphasizing the interactional (with the historical figures at least) as we were working on trying to set the true scene. That was an artifact of a training technique.

Al: An artifact of my getting a handle on teaching all this stuff. I did bring in the allies to the witnessing which are the containing figures, the *resistance figures*, the contact figures we use. So whatever was felt, if it was too charged, we would embrace it with physical touch that would say, in effect, "I can help you handle this," especially if the person was in great distress. Now when people are feeling stuff and they don't know what it is and they contract their muscles I immediately put a resistance figure there, and then that gets back to *shape/ countershape* and *action/interaction* which leads into the structure.

Fragment figures are steps that help people be in the center of their truth. They highlight the old map, giving clear and external dimension to all the old beliefs and commands (as exemplified by the *voice of your truth*). Their externalization encourages the soul to move — to reject or rebel against anti-libidinal messages — and aid in *ego-wrapping* by naming and affirming what emerges into awareness.

In earlier versions of Psychomotor, the *ideal parents* did the ego-wrapping and delivered the *antidote* messages. There are potential difficulties with exclusive reliance on the ideal parents. First, they may not be necessary for a discrete bit of ego-wrapping: why use the whole ideal mother when all that is needed is her fingernail, so to speak. Second, the strong associations and reactions to the ideal parents may distract from ego-wrapping. If they are introduced too soon, they may not be believable. Even if accepted, they might be too bulky, have too many dimensions. So what we did, in a sense, was we tore them into many little pieces. We took all the minute qualities of the ideal parents so that we could be more precise with all the folds of the soul. Third, ideal parents function in history. When people are in the crossfire, when new aspects of their soul are being witnessed and coming to awareness, they need ego-wrapping in the present. Fragment figures provide this in the present. When the shift is made to the historical scene, they may expand to become full-fledged ideal parents — giving human and not magical definition to the source of the antidote. But as long as the action is in the present, the fragment figures flesh out the *true scene*, allowing the soul to move and the pilot to observe it.

But the goal of all this preliminary stuff is to help the client get such a vivid experience and taste of that state of the immediate **now** that all the associations of history related to this — old threads — will go back to the original history that would create this. Then, of course, we would work this out in the traditional way.

John: The true scene becomes then an invitation to dive into a historical scene — setting up history out of current experience.

Al: And then the person is in complete ownership of this status. They're totally conscious so when they plunge into history they don't do it as a regression or as a dive into some condition that has no relevance to the immediate present. They can see the root to that history and the relevance of the structure in the immediate present because the lines are so clear.

John: Come back to the word "ownership," because in my perspective it seems to run through an awful lot of what we are seeing in Psychomotor now. I think that with the pilot, enriched by the witness, there's certainly an attempt to help them own their experience more fully. I also see in the work of talking with the client's pilot about the transferential elements, the energy directed into the transference or the re-creation of history through the transference now is brought back to the attention of the pilot. So it seems to me that the witness takes care of a lot of the emotional. The dialogue with the pilot handles the transferential aspects. So there's a very conscious focus on giving ownership to the pilot of all the information that is available here.

Al: It's the ownership of the power, and I was very vehement — and I don't feel quite so vehement now because I'm past it — when I shifted to not doing "dramatic, exciting structures." Because I felt when I did that kind of structure — I *knew*, since I'd been tracking the body so clearly — I knew where all the power was and I didn't tell them and I didn't help them own their power all the way, and when it busted loose they saw it somehow as in my possession. And — I exaggerate here — in a way I stole their divinity and their power or took a certain ownership of it.

John: In my experience, it's accepting an invitation that came out of their experience of never claiming their power.

Al: I must say it was exciting to know I could do that, and one part of me wanted to get some kind of credit for that, and now I'm appalled at any thought that they wouldn't know that was their power. The true scene is set for the pilot to make an informed choice. I work to cultivate an audience of one: the pilot. Instead of bypassing the defenses, I try to illuminate them so that the pilot can see the energy and choose the direction of the work. Respect its control rather than coopting it. I don't want to rob them of all that because all the energy of the soul is coming out of the body. What we call the divine could be all the genetics stuff that they should know is theirs, and never attribute to the therapist or anybody who is a facilitator in the process. And by doing the work this way, it is less likely that it's attributed to me or to the therapist. The ownership of power is never taken from their hearts. Even though quite often they are waiting. Some clients have been so passive, they are assuming the way they are going to be healed is simply to follow your orders. And if you set yourself in a position of knowing the truth and telling them, the next thing they do is sabotage everything you tell them.

I don't know why this is coming up, but I was asked to do a TV show recently and they interviewed me over the phone and did a little role-play of how I would act with a call on the telephone, after you do the talk. Then they said "Well no, that won't quite work out."

And I'll tell you why. When they usually get these calls, the therapist who answers says "Here's what you ought to do: go tell your husband such and such, and your brother-in-law to do such and such, and you stand up and do such and such, and everything's okay." He takes total ownership. He knows their lives in three seconds; and now that is anathema to me. But so much of the public thinks that is what the expert help is all about: that you submit to this higher authority and just simply follow orders. And it's also in the culture. So here I am, we're offering something with this ownership that is not necessarily wanted. I'm wondering how much of the public really does want to own their power, and take their own authority, and live with that.

John: I'm excited about this idea. People often have had so little experience with ownership, so little experience with ego-wrapping, it's a question of whose control or what control they accept in exchange for their own in giving up their pilot.

Al: So much of what we call education, so much of what we call religion is submission of your pilot to do some other work. So it's a little bit controversial — radical I think. Any real spirituality talks this way.

Ego Construction

John: I'm wondering if you want to say anything about ego-wrapping.

Al: When I talk about *ego-wrapping* I find myself wondering "how do I differentiate what I call a pilot from typical, general ego processes?" It seems that the pilot is some higher level. I think I always did a certain amount of ego-wrapping, and I even did it before I had the notion of the pilot. The pilot is like the ultimate choice and the ego-wrapping has to do, I think, with providing a countershape; ego-wrapping has a lot to do with satisfying the action, and by satisfying it's giving its countershape, its validation, its place, its name, its blessing. You point out that it looks like I do more of the verbal therapy, but I think that ego-wrapping has to be all of that.

Another thing about ego creation. I first started thinking about ego creation as a consequence of satisfying *basic needs*. When we first began this work I never thought about ego. I just thought that therapy had to do with all unmet needs, and when needs are met symbolically the person is healed. I didn't know it had an ego consequence.

Psychomotor has shifted in emphasis. Where initially the focus was primarily on meeting unmet needs, now there is a clearer emphasis on helping the *true self* emerge. This means that the ego must give contour to all the surfaces of the soul. We don't live our soul directly, we live it consciously through our ego. So the ego is the agent that allows us to come in contact with the soul. The myth in Genesis of the creation of the world is really a nice metaphor for the creation of reality: it's got witnessing, it's got validation, it's got naming in it. In Genesis you have God up there saying, "I shall call you day and I shall call you night, and you are good." Wow! Into reality come day and night. All the different qualities of the universe get brought into existence and that's exactly what the ego does. A piece of the soul comes out and the ego says, "I shall call you sadness, and you have a right to be sad." Yeaa! So, when we are constructing the ego, we are constructing a benign God who gives us a right to exist inside of it — in the Garden of Ego.

Psychomotor, Culture, and Metapsychology

And once on that, I want to talk — this may not be within the purview you wanted — about education and what's happening with educational standards in the US. Ego is constructed out of parenting — in having *support*, and *protection*, and *limits* — which then results in having the capacity of thinking abstractly and thinking symbolically. The greatly reduced numbers of intact families in the US — the numbers I saw on TV are in the 40% range, down to 27% of all households, only, are intact families — I think that runs parallel with our educational level. I think that the less ego-wrapping of intact families creating the capacity to think, the more we are going to get a reduction of educational standards. When people talk about how are we going to change that, I don't think educational policy is going to do that worth a damn. I think we have got to do something with our family structure.

John: That's a good link to something I wanted to ask. I'm a psychotherapist, many of the people you work with in your training groups are psychotherapists, and we tend — to use an analogy — to catch people downstream after they fall in the water or half-drown, when they are certainly damaged by their experience. I think there's always been a desire to move upstream and help people before they get in the water, to teach them how to swim, or to do something before a disaster has happened. Maybe the family is the answer. I would like to ask you about your sense of the applications of Psychomotor in a wellness model, in a model of either preventing, or of enriching family life, religious life, educational life.

Al: What first comes to my mind is a heart's desire of Diane, which is to have Psychomotor available in the public school system, particularly in the high school, so that high school students would have the benefits of doing structures so they get their *basic needs* met, if they haven't been met in their own upbringing; and then have them know enough about having *ideal mother* and *father* images internalized so that when they go shopping around for a partner they won't be looking for that in a partner, they'll be getting more of a peer. And then, having had their own basic needs met on a symbolic level, they will have some idea what it is to be a parent and be able to parent better, having been through the experience of structures of parenting. And that should make a change. That would be a wellness model: not something you do to solve their problems, but do it to solve, prevent, the problems of the next generation.

John: Do you have any sense of places where it is being applied or where there is an openness to moving in that direction?

Al: The only place I know where it is applied right now in that age group is in the DeSisto Schools with a particular group of kids who had emotional problems, drug problems, problems with the law. I'm sure they are making better choices as a consequence. It isn't directly being applied in any school setting.

John: The only approximation I'm aware of would be in family therapy sessions where this kind of therapy with the parent is witnessed by adolescent children.

Al: I'm hoping that as Psychomotor is expanding into the family therapy realm it might have that effect.
    You mentioned religion. I'm in a funny religious place right now, where I almost feel blasphemous, I'm just so angry at organized religion for how it robs people. I was raised in an orthodox family, and there is much I have to be thankful for that. But it just imprisons the mind and it channels it so narrowly when you think of the ultimate truths about the whole notion of God and the notion of power. It took me half a century to get some beginning clarity on myself as a member of the human race, and not just a member of a certain religious sect. A loss of universality happens — of them and us — in the religion. And all religions seem to have such an investment in absolutes, in having the absolute truth. It seems to me that things in reality are so evolving, that the notion of a fixed absolute beforehand and afterhand is counter to the reality of endless change. So religion fosters adherence to a fixed image of God that they are the absolute owners of, and you can't tamper with it unless you're in the priest class.

John: We've got a bureaucracy of God as well.

Al: I find that horrifying. The guilt that is instilled in me and in others: if you deviate from that, they just grab you so early, they've got you with creation, life, death, creation of your birth, the creation of love and death, they've got the absolute handle on it. So they grab the highest powers in your self, and it takes forever to get your pilot back.

John: You are not only scrapping with injunctions that are built in by the religion, but you are in some cases dealing with the lack of ownership of the pilot.

Al: That's right. And also the control they have on ultimate reality, because they name God as really It and capture the capital G of Godness, if you deviate from that you are either a Pagan or Heretic. Those are two words which mean that you don't belong and you are outside the pale.

John: Sounds like you've stepped into those words and maybe tried them on, uncomfortable as they are. I think I hear you saying perhaps: give you a little more room to find your own God.

Al: I would think a religion that did that... not to move away from morality — I could hear them fight about good and evil and all that — but I'm hurting from having that religion be forced on me. And the blinders... how long it takes to get loose of those blinders, to see the more fluid world as it is, and then to really dare to own some of your own power — not in a way to say there is no force greater than yourself, but to own that God-force within yourself that you share with all other humans.

John: When you started talking about orthodoxy I was hearing a few other ideas I want to check out with you. It seems to me that as you move away from absolutes you talk a lot more about the present moment as being the act of creation: flux and change as being the creation.

Al: I believe that if there is such a being as God, I don't believe that God is finished. Because life isn't finished, life is an endless evolution of the unexpected due to the incredible juxtaposition of forces which are absolutely not to be predicted beforehand and afterwards about which way they are going to go. I'm reading a little bit about that in this book on chaos (Gleick, 1987); the beauty and wonder and unexpectedness that comes out of the interplay of forces on the real level is absolutely unpredictable. And it seems to me that, the excitement of that, if there was a God, I think that God might be part of that creation and not be a fixed static thing at the end of a line. The old way is a primitive hope in some absolute fixed condition which is so counter to reality.

John: And to the experience in Psychomotor. So I'm hearing a God that's present in the flux of the moment, and that's becoming in the moment, and I think I'm hearing about a God that is very much within us.

Al: And we're part of it, what we're talking about God becoming. We're the engine of the becoming or the tools or the parts of the becoming. The whole universe is in this becoming process and each piece counts. In the true nature of things, everything affects the total web. So the total web is alive, and that might be God. The total is everything that is, and we are a part of that. So everything we do counts.

John: I want to pull you back to a very practical level. It's clear that Psychomotor has things to say in terms of applications in religion situations. Not only in terms of a metapsychology and a kind of belief system, but also in terms of how religion could be structured, or how Psychomotor would become a part of religious experience. Any thoughts there?

Al: It's a little spooky. I get scared when you talk about Psychomotor becoming part of a religious experience.

John: I hear you don't want it to become any orthodoxy, clearly.

Al: No, I would be willing for the thing to just endlessly grow. But I don't think that people who do Psychomotor are any less religious. I think they are far more, because it awakens such a love of humanity, such a caring. When you see the work that goes on, it awakens such tenderness, compassion, and love for the budding of the self. I can't imagine people doing Psychomotor getting less religious on that profound level of loving life and wanting to do things that will enhance life and release the life of others, and cherish the life in themselves and the life in others. I think it creates more social beings, more loving beings. I think that happens. People talk about the safety — I love seeing that. In diverse groups, everywhere I go, there is always a sense of safety and warmth and acceptance and connectedness and belongingness that is an emanation or byproduct of the group.

The Hierarchy of Responsibilities in Psychomotor

John: Is it perhaps worth sharing at this point that hierarchy you put together today at Armen's invitation? I thought that was an interesting comment. It was framed in terms of a hierarchy of a therapist's responsibilities to the client.

Al: I hadn't thought that through, but when he pressed the point I guess the first thing — the emotional responses are the gauge I used to check the truth — is that everyone should have a *place*, so that there's the notion of existence and nobody is outside the circle of existence. That comes back to the pilot, which says "I own all of my self." I think that people who cut off and say "good/bad, good people/bad people," are those who are denying their own badness, and then won't allow anyone else back into the house unless they are "good." That's that universal notion that we are all part, everything is part, of a family of existence and that nobody should sacrifice their self as an avenue or ticket to belonging. It is an embracing of diversity and range of the human spirit. And it leaves room for redemption. Nobody gets locked out. There's no final definition of what is human so that there's no such thing as somebody saying "I'm born outside your definition, therefore I don't fit." A lot of people feel that, because they don't fit with somebody else's definition in the family or the religion.

John: Or they feel that about some aspect of themselves.

Al: Yes. So I think that's the priority one. And then autonomy, or the right for self direction. That would be the pilot — the right to the ownership of your choice and responsibility for yourself.

John: In a very practical way that was illustrated in a discussion of whether a person has a right to say either "I don't want to do structure work now" or "I want to leave."

Al: The right to leave without being thrown out of the family, that they may choose not to be there and that's still acceptable.

John: And the freedom that gives them to choose to stay on their own terms, rather than on your terms as the therapist.

Al: And then, as soon as I think of that — since we're so much saying yes to life — then I think about assisting people in finding the energies that would help them to live. Sometimes people want so badly to die and, rather than say "I can see the best move you can make is to kill yourself because your life is horrible," find ways to use that energy to keep them alive. If there's that much passion toward death, the passion itself must have force and vitality to help people to live, even though they are feeling depressed and wanting to escape and end it all. So we are on the side of hope and the side of continuation of life.

John: It makes me want to pop back to dealing with the suicidal. Are you superseding the article you wrote in '85 on that?

Al: Not at all. I still think that the way we follow that is a symbolic death, because we know that following the passion there will be an answer, at least on the symbolic level. So let them go to what they consider death, because only there have they projected an expectation of release of pain, and people don't get relief of pain except where they think it will be found. So let them follow their impulse, but not so that they are rehearsing for death or literally moving toward death, but let them experience this symbolic death.

The Spokesman for the Genes

John: It seems to me what you did in that article (Chapter 16) — which was using death as a vehicle towards reunion with an image of God — was you went past that even to being reborn in a better, more accepting place — which becomes an elegant way of introducing ideal parenthood.

Al: God, there, is doing what I said the Psychomotor group does with people: nobody gets left out. God leaves nobody out; like death, everybody has a home there. The place of last resort is God and death. How to capture that in the service of life? As I talk now I realize how much I can attach what I'm talking to as being a spokesman for the genes. The genes are, if you want to think of anything as pro life; that stuff is bubbling away and pushing its wants; it's practiced for a couple of billion years on how to keep life going. I feel more and more as I embrace my genes and say that I'm an outgrowth of that, I feel like a conscious spokesman for it. And I will take the power of that thing. My God, look at the power of that! We've all inherited that; we're on the newest, most recent wave of existence and we really ought to know how much we've owned.

John: Interesting, I hear the pessimism about family structure but I hear the vibrancy and exhilaration and the exuberance.

Al: The germ plasm is there, but I think this culture shits! I think that we're rotting. I hate to say that, but I think of Carter's "Malaise Speech." Remember that speech where everyone went "Boo! Wimp! Wimpo!" He was pointing the finger at a real sickness in our culture, and it's there. We are watching it, looking at that educational stuff go down. We won't wake up. We are beginning to wake up when the bottom line of the dollar starts going down and education translates into a reduced industry, etc., etc. in competition with Japan.

John: Again I want to ask, is there another level rather than individual training level at which Psychomotor can speak to these issues? I see people coming to Psychomotor as part of that search for new ways of being that are more vital, that are more alive. But they come in and use it more often as individuals than as groups.

Al: Well, now I get to my pessimism. As we talk about this, I get grandiose. But then in reality I see how few people this is affecting and how grandiose my earlier notions were that some day this would be part of information available to the world at large. I've kind of given up on that. This sort of touches some of that old narcissistic ache, about it being important in the world. So I don't feel like even wanting to think about selling it. In this book on chaos this guy did an experiment on weather. He put in a computer all the 12 weather conditions and certain patterns of ever changing weather came up. Then he wanted to start again and he put in the numbers again. But he left out three digits in the thousandths, thinking that it won't make much difference. And even with that tiny little bit of shift of input the weather patterns were totally different. Even at one-thousandth of a number. That led him to the notion that every variable has an impact, a totally unexpected impact. Even the butterfly wings somewhere in Australia beating one way or another would effect the weather at some point in New York or somewhere else. So what I'm thinking is, rather than saying that I'm going to affect the world, I'll just be doing my little butterfly wings in my local place and no longer trying to...

John: But with the confidence that it is going to have its rippling effect...

Al: It might very well — but it's been such a relief to give up grandiosity and narcissism that I don't want to waken it again and think that I might, indeed, some way or fashion...

John: Sounds like that struggle to find a balance between narcissism and, without becoming pessimistic, correcting what perhaps is part of this rich notion of ownership of the pilot.

Al: I'm coming back down to my own personal issues because when you don't have sufficient ownership of your pilot you might end up with grandiose dreams as compensation. But if you get your own pilot, it's enough.

John: Just parenthetically, this seems to be very close to the stuff you were dealing with in the *Experience in Action* book, the universality versus individuality theme. It's a different language but it's the same issues.

Al: I think I'm pretty consistent, because as I look back in thinking that I've just come across these notions I read the earlier stuff that implied them.

Training

John: We talked about change, and I want to talk about some of the changes in Psychomotor. It certainly is going to continue to evolve and I'd like to get some of your thoughts on where you expect it to evolve in terms of application, in terms of training.

Al: It's so unpredictable, and everything I thought would happen didn't happen. One of the most interesting changes that came about was so unexpected and unpredicted. So I doubt whether I could really predict it. I think it will get clearer, richer, and I think if I still stay active in it, some of it will come out of me. I'm sure it will come out of other people. At this point I have no idea who that will be and who will be the pilot of the Psychomotor process. Right now, I guess that's Diane and me, mostly. It kind of saddens me to think that I won't be, but I know perfectly well, that now that I'm sixty, I will be in the process of preparing for my demise and my decline and actively trying to cultivate strong people, knowledgeable people; I'll just have to trust what happens there, and build it that way. I don't know where it will go, I hope it will be in good hands.

John: I hear the question mark and I think that certain regrets are, obviously,... will hold onto the reins.

Al: Yeah, but I've got to prepare.

John: In some sense that emphasizes training as being the role. I hear you saying that you want to have strong people and try to contribute to that.

Al: Training is where all of my time goes. I hardly do any experiential work. I mostly figure on training. If I could just stop, part of me wants to retire and do nothing because I'm tired, but another part of me thinks that what I'd like to do is get the materials as organized as possible so that it's clearly understood. And I guess having video tapes like this, that Carl Clarke has collected, so that part of the training is seeing how it was done, how I did it, or the spirit with which I did it, maybe that would be a way to keep some of those elements alive.

John: Clearly you are saying there's an awful lot, that training is an apprenticeship, training is watching and watching and watching.

Al: I believe that it is, maybe it's because I was a dancer. I do think that there should be a curriculum and there should be training capsules, and I think more television in pointing out this, this, and this. And the clearer they are the better. But I really do think most serious training is hands on training with small numbers of people.

John: You've really kept emphasizing for me, again and again, the need to read the body and read it with much more refined sensibilities than I brought to the beginning of training. Do you have some sense of the continuing role of dance in Psychomotor training?

Al: I don't know how we can say continuing role, because it has none except with Diane and myself, and that's indirect. Psychomotor is not in dance; but I sure as heck saw and see the need for real body understanding, because it's through the witness seeing the body, and it's through the therapist giving the witness stuff to see, and the therapist knowing enough about how to talk on the action level, that all the juice of this work comes from.

John: I think many of the people who come to these workshops have an interest in the body or have some background in expressive therapies, yet I don't think very many people have that kind of formalized training.

Al: I don't know how to put that in. Maybe because I've been wanting to make it so clear that this is not a dance therapy, I stayed away from out-and-out *giving them dance*. I suppose if I was a psychiatrist I could embrace dance as part of my expansiveness towards the arts, but I'm saying (to dance) "stay back there" because if you're an artist you are not considered much of a professional.

John: I understand that dilemma, but on the other hand I experienced your power yesterday as you were moving me around, as we were wrestling, and that's a very real skill that you bring...

Al: Well, because of that, because of you, and because of what happened, and because I'm getting more and more certain of my worth and not afraid of being diminished by all the professional people, I might reintroduce some of that. I don't know how to bring the full richness of what I know on the motoric level to students.

John: I just wonder about that process and movement in that direction, because I see Diane coming back and doing workshops again after a period where that wasn't something she was doing regularly. I hear more of this, if not in the exercises, at least some of the wisdom that comes from watching the body in those earlier exercises.

Al: She would make some caustic remarks to me about "You know these people you're training, they don't know enough about the body, they are busy with doing your fancy structures and they imitate you with all these mythic characters..." There is some truth in that because when I did those fancy structures, people didn't know how I got it, they would do kind of an imitation of it and she would see it as off-base. I'm getting simpler now. Even though this pilot stuff is in labels and names I'm putting there, she was always for more control in the hands of the client. She hated the idea of calling herself a therapist. She hated the whole idea of the power and the transference because of the injury she got in the psychiatric therapy with transference. It was badly abused by this therapist. So this new stuff should nowhere be construed as a deviation from what our roots were, but more as a clear expression of what was at the heart of Psychomotor.

John: So in some sense it's changing in emphasis but in another sense it's coming back to roots. I always see things as cycles. There's certainly returning and using elements again.

Al: And having the element come at the next cycle, this cycle at a more elaborated, more differentiated level.

John: Maybe this is the time to ask you — in your experience of watching the soul birthing in the structures or in the process of supervising the training, what are the things you find most exciting, where you are in the last weeks or months. I guess I'm trying to project in terms of what's going to be developing in the future.

Al: I think I became a better teacher and a better supervisor the moment I started thinking of extending the *possibility sphere* to the trainee. I used to extend the possibility sphere to the client and had a nurturing, caring thing for them to grow and be themselves. And then when

I'd watch a trainee with a client on videotape I'd be so busy with the possibility sphere of a client that if a trainee made a mistake I'd say "You fool, how could you do that to them" and they'd be blown away. Now I'm thinking "how do I help them to nurture their strengths," which is a whole other way of working. So I see the trainee as my client. The training has shifted and I'm much more caring. I'm watching it have effect. Before I'd want them to be Olympic types. I told them that, and it drove them crazy. They'd say "We're never going to be Olympic therapists. Now stop it. We don't have to have that kind of standard." I'd say "Well, don't you want to be the best?" That's kind of nuts. Now I shift and I help them to be the best *them*. So they're coming out in all different varieties. Rather than making them know what I want them to know, or helping them to know what I think they ought to know, I'm now cultivating what they know and finding out where their learning process is and trying to implement that. That is very varied. I guess that's the most interesting thing, the variation of their learning and how people are just different in how they go about their learning process.

John: I've really felt that difference and really appreciated what I considered the pretty tough lessons done caringly and lovingly in the last months for me. I feel that honoring of, that permission to *be*, not where I'm *supposed* to be. That's a lovely place to be.

Al: I hadn't offered that before to the trainee because I was so busy wanting, if there was going to be a Psychomotor organization I wanted the best... and I think having that attitude had negative results.

John: It reminds me of an analogy to what you talked about today in terms of the structure: the less you expect of a client in a structure, the more freedom there is in the structure to go where it needs to go.

Al: And then the possibilities and the unexpected bounces that come around, which then give me license to go with my unexpected bounces instead of getting angry at myself for being such a labile, volatile, emotional nut.

John: So chaos becomes...

Al: Chaos then shows the order. One of the things they showed is that when they track the motion of what seems like completely random dots and the things that go here, here, and here; then as the dots coalesce, they get these incredible shapes, these incredible leaf-like shapes. Each individual dot was random, but when all the dots accumulated... So I'm giving up linear thinking in a way. The people go in a very odd route.

John: Kind of a fractal geometry of the soul.

Al: It's there. I'm trusting that what I thought before might have been error and mistake and chaos is the only way to get that level of creativity.

John: Which is a delightful answer to the question of "where do you think Psychomotor is going to go in the coming years," because you've just told me, it's a nonsensical question.

Al: That's right. There's no way to know that. It might be predicted later. You might look later and say "of course," because it was predicted in the momentum of the thing, but in this spot it seems to just keep taking its own way.

My interest is in learning more... If I could stop and do nothing I would study quantum mechanics, relativity, and this chaos stuff and tie it together with this neurobiology business. I think I'm getting some idea of basic shapes of the psyche as being like the fractal basic shapes that are built and built and built. There's a part of me that's sniffing around that, to get to a science of what we're doing. But the science of chaos is much more nonlinear than the science of predictability. That's fun for me.

John: What's been fun for me with this process you've been living and expressing in the work this weekend has been that I like synthesizing different theories or different approaches to personality change, and I've seen you do some sublime psychoanalysis and I've seen what I would call Neurolinguistic Programming, and your comment was, "No, no we're not doing this or the other, we're working with the basic constituents of the self. It's going to have commonalities with other approaches." In that sense, in this book, where we're having that section on comparisons, we may be just scratching at some of the areas that get expressed in commonalities.

Al: I think that we were all scratching the same elephant, in different ways.

John: We have gone different places. I'm not sure if we've gone where we expected to or not. I feel a need to wrap it up and give you room to say if there's something we left out that you want to cover, and at the same time hesitating, because I've enjoyed the trip.

Al: What pops into my mind is in my own personal shifts. A couple of weeks ago I was in the midst of despair and anxiety and suffering, and if I were to make a prediction from there it would look like mostly I was going to slow down and things were going to decline in an entropic diminishment. Then I found myself, a couple of week later, swinging with excitement about my impact on a group of people where I can be utterly myself and not have to crank myself up to perform. Not to be frozen — to live in the moment, but not to be frozen in the moment — as if the moment is a prediction of all that's going to come. And to know that each moment, the unexpected and the unpredictable could follow and there's some hope in that.

John: Not a lot of security in the immediate sense.

Al (laughing): Security! What's security! I guess if you grab for security, you're grabbing linearity and predictability, and then there's death. That's the death of possibility.

John: There is the counterword — possibility.

Al: Because only with possibility is there the vividness and fun of life, but there is the insecurity. People have got to live; it's a trade off.

John: That excites me, let me jump in with something. It seems to me you're saying the tool for training people to live with insecurity is to have the fundamental securities that go with internal *ideal parents*.

Al: That's true. Then you've got the portable *place*. You've lived in an externalized space that others have given you, you've lived inside somebody, and then you internalize that sense of place. It's inside of you now so you don't need an external place, because everywhere you go is home. It's a portable place, and that comes through getting all the *basic needs* met. People really have to go through, I suppose, the *nurture, protection, support, limits, place, respect*. That gives the possibility of moving away from home, so to speak. There's that sadness. If you give people a firm enough base, they are going to move away from home. They are going to go to the next possibility, the next unpredicted thing. But if they haven't had it I think they are going to stay holding on to security, and the orthodoxy. You kill your present life, so I guess you have to have dreams of other lives that are going to be fun.

John: There's a richness in the possibilities here. You talk about that portable place. What you're talking about is an aspect of the self, the internalized ideal parents, and I think it also includes almost the sense that the pilot may be an aspect of the self that can be separated from the rest of the self even though in some sense it encompasses...

Al: Run that by again, "separated from the rest of the self?"

John: I find it internally useful to say, "what is my pilot saying about this now," and I almost sense myself stepping back...

Al: I don't quite do it that way. It's "what do I feel when I put myself in the pilot position." I don't think "what is my pilot saying?" Then it's not me, it's talking to me. I don't personally do it that way. I think of myself, my emotional, internal condition when I'm in that pilot place. When I'm in that pilot place, I can feel many things that are going on in me, including some regressive things, but I have a perspective that I am not only in that regressive place, I know there are alternatives.

John: You answered my question about the difference between the pilot and the observing ego.

Al: When I hear all those other injunctions and negative predictions, I don't feel enslaved by it. But my pilot hears and takes note as well: "here come the crazy radicals from the far right of my personality," just reporting in. But I don't have to let them get the levers of power. They may hurt and make me feel awful. I guess I'm treating it like the kind of governmental metaphor when in elections, it's all the different constituencies. They vote, and the crazies come in and the repressive things on the other end come in, and you can know it and feel it and give it room. You're in a nation, but it isn't running the show. Although sometimes when you're in that regressed place you start living just that regressive place, you just don't know there's anything else.

John: It seems to me you're saying in a political analogy, that the pluralism is so necessary. Now in a psychological economy, a psychological analogy, there's something important about talking about the integrity of wholeness of yourself, rather than letting it fragment into different parts.

Al: All these parts have to be ego bound. That's why you do the ego-wrapping. Then the pilot is relating to them, not as demons, but as ego bound aspects of the self that are recognizable, that have a voice, but don't become anarchic and take over the seat of power. But the pilot too is aware, or I am aware when I'm in the pilot position, that I'm in a position of stewardship. So I don't any longer think I have the ownership of life, or even of my life. I'm a steward to what I've inherited. So there's a kind of responsibility to your own life. You can hold a heck of a lot of power that way and not get that sense of grandiosity that you did it. All that stuff you've inherited. You've cultivated and taken ownership and learned how to control it. But you didn't do it; it's just so much beyond you. When I step into a pilot position, I'm also stepping in that which knows life best — which is again the genetic information and the divine parts.

John: I hear that very clearly, that it goes beyond you and your current understanding.

Al: Then I could become a spokesman. Part of me can speak for that. I don't have to just remain my historical self which was told to be one kind of person, in one kind of culture, in one kind of nation.

John: I think it's a lovely analogy for self, which is real and into itself but not an end in itself.

Al: It is part of a huge commonality.

References

Gleick, J. (1987). *Chaos: Making a new science.* New York: Penguin.

Pesso, A. (1973). *Experience in action.* New York: New York University Press.

Integrating Psychomotor
and Other Approaches

Chapter 10

Pesso System/ Psychomotor and Object Relations Theory

by John S. Crandell

Pesso System/Psychomotor (PS/P) has always been attractive to clinicians who identify with psychoanalytic theories. Object Relations (OR) theory and Psychomotor are especially compatible. There is fundamental agreement about the importance of relationships to personality structuring, about the psychopathological consequences of early developmental failures, and about the therapeutic goals of enhanced ego structuring through internalizing new and more satisfying expectations in relating to significant others. Yet the conduct of therapy is very different in these two traditions. Psychomotor offers powerful techniques to handle transference, to directly reconstruct preverbal experience, and to provide through accommodation the symbolic satisfaction of *basic needs* occurring at various stages of development. These contributions resolve concerns raised by OR practitioners and permit more efficient depth psychotherapy. PS/P will be useful to psychodynamically oriented clinicians who are willing to actively manage transference and to apply OR theory with a range of patients, in addition to the most dysfunctional.

Object Relations Theory as an Interactional Psychology

OR theory emphasizes that the relationships experienced within the preoedipal family are the crucial determinants of personality structure. The dyadic interaction with the mothering person, in particular, is pivotal in the process of providing the child with experiences of relatedness which are internalized as lasting expectations of how the self interacts with the other (the object). Such expectations (based on mental representations of relationships) affect not only the quality of the interpersonal life, but also the individual's identity, emotional tone, and degree of psychological health.

Object Relations theory revises psychoanalytic thought in a way that makes it more compatible with PS/P. First, the role of instincts is deemphasized. Freud was a dualist who described the struggle to reconcile opposing libidinal and aggressive (life and death) forces within the unconscious. Conflict, and its control by the managerial and defending ego, are the legacy. This contrasts with the metapsychology of theorists such as Pesso who see a single life force powering development and who believe that the deepest self can be expressed in a relatively direct and prosocial manner. Many OR theorists concur with Pesso, tracing the degree of internal conflict not to the vicissitudes of the instincts but to the satisfactions and frustrations experienced in early relationships (Greenburg & Mitchell, 1983). Instincts become less central. In Fairbairn's words, "Libido is not pleasure-seeking but object-seeking" (1946/1952, p. 137). The psychology of impulse is replaced with one of goal. Second, actual interpersonal relationships take center stage as the role of instinctual patterning of the personality is deemphasized. This is most evident in the infant's complete dependence on the provider. In Winnicott's terms, "If you set out to describe a baby, you will find you are describing a baby and someone. A baby cannot exist alone, but is essentially part of a relationship" (Davis & Wallbridge, 1981, p. 34). The foundations of the self are the mental representations of the satisfactions and dissatisfactions occurring in the child's contact with the parents. Actual experience is introjected, dictating the internal structure of the personality. In this way OR theory becomes a bridge, linking intrapsychic approaches with those based on interaction (Framo, 1982; Meissner, 1978; Slipp, 1984).

Psychoanalytic thought has always acknowledged the importance of relationships with significant others, as evident in the idea of cure through transference. Object Relations theory makes the model more explicit: the "therapeutic matrix" is based on the "maternal matrix." As Horner describes it:

> When it has been determined that there has been a failure or deficit in the organization of the self, we can view the major function of the therapist as parallel to that of the primary mothering person or persons of infancy — that is, as the mediator of organization within the therapeutic matrix (1979, p. 306).

The therapist's role differs from that defined for traditional psychoanalysis. Transference is used to promote integration, and not as a guide to unresolved oedipal issues to be clarified through interpretation. Transference is managed actively: the therapist moves away from analytic neutrality and acts in such a manner as to be a good object for internalization. This revision in psychoanalytic practice by OR theory makes it more compatible with Pesso System/Psychomotor.

The Compatibility of Object Relations Theory and Psychomotor

OR and PS/P share a fundamentally similar view of development, of the requisite parental skills for effective childrearing, and of the psychopathological consequences of failures in integrating a cohesive self in the context of positive relational experiences.

Since the therapeutic matrix correctively reenacts the optimal maternal relationship, OR theorists are close observers of the ideal manner in which to parent the preoedipal child. Caretakers function as auxiliary egos, compensating for unlearned skills while encouraging their mastery. Parenting requirements change in tandem with the child's development. During the symbiotic phase, while the child is only nascently aware of the otherness of the need-satisfying provider, the optimum is "normal maternal preoccupation":

> It starts with, and is a continuation of, "the physiological provision that characterizes the prenatal state." The function of holding in psychological terms is to provide ego-support, in particular at the stage of absolute dependence before integration of the ego has been established. The establishment of integration and the development of ego-

relatedness both rely upon good enough holding (Davis & Wallbridge, 1981, pp. 99-100).

These ideas, here from Winnicott, convey the fundamental importance of nurturance and support, conveyed through physical touch and symbolized by holding. This reliable contact contributes to "hallucinatory or delusional somatopsychic fusion with the representation of the mother" (Mahler, Pine, & Bergman, 1975, p. 45). As the child acquires the mobility to explore and the rudiments of the ability to tolerate frustration, the provider should show "gradual de-adaptation." Winnicott describes this "good enough mothering" as the willingness to allow freedom and self determination within the confines of protective limits. The parent, like the therapist, provides a secure base in dependence and encourages phase-specific manifestations of independence.

Psychomotor also models therapeutic interaction on a similarly defined vision of the parental role. Therapy is based on a reworking of the parent-child relationship during the earliest years. Pesso stresses, "in psychomotor training,... all roads lead to a return to the basic relationship between the child and his mother or mother surrogate." If the therapy is progressing optimally, "Psychomotor training offers an arena where one can finally return to the infancy stage and receive as a child receives, with a sense of endlessness, eternity, and total satisfaction" (1969, p. 100).

In the corrective therapeutic contact, as ideally in the earliest real relationships, the parents operate as auxiliary egos in fulfilling four crucial functions: *support*, *protection*, *nurturance,* and *limit-setting*. Support is analogous to Winnicott's idea of holding, while protection entails averting any overwhelming external stimuli. Miller (1981) and Kohut (1971, 1977) are dynamic writers who are explicit about the need for the mirroring relationship in which each aspect of the developing self is — in PS/P terms — *witnessed*. Nurturance encompasses mirroring as well as feeding, providing the sense of being cherished. The parents encourage autonomy within the range of the child's competence, setting limits to protect against the experience of excessive frustration or omnipotence. Limits channel the child's energy so that it can be productively object-related.

The view of developmental needs is not identical. Psychoanalytic tradition emphasizes the importance of mothering. PS/P uses mothering imagery, especially in regards to support (e.g., the womb as the prototypical model) and nurturance. But PS/P is more explicit about the importance of effective fathering. Protection and limits are traditionally presented using male imagery. The child's sexual identity formation, and the balancing of vulnerability and *power* in the forming personality, require the parenting of two adults of opposite sexes who maintain a primary affectional/sexual link with one another even as they minister to the child's needs.

OR theory traces the growth of the self to mental representations of interaction. The terminology differs from PS/P, but similar issues are highlighted. Fairbairn presents development as proceeding from primary identification with an undifferentiated object, through splitting[1] the object into good and bad aspects (to segregate satisfying and frustrating expe-

---

1 Splitting is important as a normal but primitive defense which must be superseded by more mature ways of handling inner representations if healthy self-esteem and relations are to be realized. Splitting operates by segregating the experiences of love and hate for an object. One of the feelings is dissociated. This reduces emotional confusion but guarantees strong mood swings when the exiled

riences), to mature dependence on ambivalently experienced but unified objects. Corresponding to these stages are personality characteristics respectively labeled schizoid (with an underlying fear of loss of self), depressive (with an underlying fear that the object may be destroyed by hate or consumed and lost), and normal functioning. Paranoid, obsessional, hysterical, and phobic behavior are used as defenses against the underlying depressive or schizoid state.

Most other theorists accept the similar developmental schema of Margaret Mahler and her associates (Mahler et al., 1975). Her account of the separation-individuation process includes the stages of symbiosis, hatching, practicing, rapprochement, and consolidation of individuality.

The essential task of the separation-individuation process is to internalize a unified and predominantly positive view of the self and objects so that relationships can be pursued without risking loss of identity. When successfully completed, first, the child will recognize the separateness of self and others. Failure would be evident in psychosis (e.g., paranoid ideas of control) or in emotional fusion with others (as when the affective tone contaminates the entire relational world). Second, the basis of realistic self-worth is laid down through experiencing the extent and limits of personal power. Lacking this, there are the opposing risks of grandiosity versus a sense of futility with excessive dependence. Third, successful completion of the separation-individuation process also entails integrating the representations of frustrating and satisfying interactions into psychic relationships between a whole self and whole objects. Again, this is predicated on an adequate relationship with the parents: "The establishment of affective (emotional) object constancy depends on the gradual internalization of a constant, positively cathected, inner image of the mother" (Mahler et al., 1975, p. 109). Once internalized, positive internal objects are available to help the child handle frustration and loss without damage to self-esteem or recourse to defensive splitting. Failure would be evident later in narcissistic rages, acute separation anxiety, or schizoid detachment. If the mother is erratic and unreliable, "thinking becomes a substitute for maternal care and adaptation. The baby 'mothers' himself" (Davis & Wallbridge, 1981, p. 54), and the capacity for object-relatedness diminishes except through a "false self." The child is then doubly trapped, turning to an inner world populated by unstable and punitive part-objects out of fear of unsatisfying contact with significant others.

Horner (1979) systematically relates major psychopathology to arrest or regression to different points in the separation-individuation process. After Winnicott and Mahler, she relates autism and symbiotic psychoses to failures previous to and during the stage of normal symbiosis. Schizoid and sociopathic personalities are seen as resulting from varying degrees of rejection of symbiosis evidenced in premature hatching. Character disorders reflect failure during the stage of separation-individuation. The grandiose self is based on pathology in the practicing subphase resulting in the self-object representation being "differentiated in a distorted manner, with the power of the object 'adhering' to the self" (p. 103). Narcissistic and borderline structures show varying degrees of regression from developmental difficulties associated with the rapprochement crisis. While this review is vastly oversimplified, it does

---

affect returns. Splitting destroys the cohesiveness of the representations of self and other (i.e., the hating self and the hated object are dissociated along with the feeling of hatred). So there will remain an instability in mood and identity which will undermine psychological health.

convey the consensus that defects in object relations result in predictably severe psychopathology.

PS/P lacks a detailed diagnostic system, but it strikingly resembles OR theory in its view of the psychopathological results of developmental defects. There is concern about split off aspects of the self, about autistically relating to symbols, and about unrealistic self-esteem in the absence of appropriate early interaction. Deficits in structure (because of ego breaks or lack of *ego-wrapping*) lead to a defense against becoming object-related because of fears of engulfment or grandiose destructive fantasies. Correspondingly, the focus shifts away from seeking gratification to attempts to avert identity-threatening energy overflow. Pesso names the "species ego" those superego precursors which function as a psychic circuit breaker. Although the terminology is somewhat different, the area of concern is strikingly similar to that discussed by OR theorists:

> Whenever the species ego has swung strongly into action, one can assume that there has been an ego break, that there will be symbolic rather than direct expression of powerful feelings, and that the individual will identify more with the universal than the individual (that is, he will develop feelings of omnipotence and personal grandeur). This person will tend to withdraw from interactions with other people and will prefer to interact with his inner self; he will lose a sense of competent identity with other individuals as there will be no external figures powerful and stable enough to orient from, and he will therefore orient from his own omnipotence but without external, concrete confirmation of his power (Pesso, 1973, p. 154).

The similarity of observations in the absence of common theory tends to validate the reality of the underlying phenomenon addressed by both the PS/P and OR theory. There is clear concurrence that developmental defects may compromise attainment of a cohesive and object-related self.

Psychomotor shares the recognition that therapy requires corrective interpersonal contact:

> All behavior is interpersonal. If there is a blocking of intrapsychic energy, there may be body armoring in the individual which shows the location of the block, but that block was created in an interpersonal constellation and it will never do to manipulate away the block without dealing with the interpersonal element (Pesso, 1969, p. 95).

This requires therapeutic reengagement of the positive figures and internalization of enacted parental functions:

> All unexpressed and untested strong reactions are contained interiorly as a way of inflating one's fantasy sense of power. All unexpressed emotions seem to amplify the longer they remain unexpressed. These emotions need the testing of reality, and the limit-setting of the good parents to place them in their proper perspective (Pesso, 1973, pp. 71-72).

Pesso would agree with Horner that the "therapeutic matrix" is modeled on the "maternal matrix," or at least the parental matrix.

Failure to Apply OR Theory to Less Primitive States

Despite similar views of development, OR theorists tend to be more pessimistic about the psychopathological consequences of failures in early relationships. The recognition that some major defects in object relations are evident in apparently successful people does not alter this pessimistic assessment. Horner contends, for example, that fixation or regression to the hatching subphase will activate three ego states: the good self-object, the bad self-object, and the self-without-object consolidated around the autonomous functions. Such individuals may function adequately as long as significant relationships do not impinge on their organizing overinvolvement with their thoughts and projects. Their superficial adaptation and success only disguises the fundamental faults in psychological structure attributable to early difficulties in object relations.

The link between OR theory and severe pathology is a historical artifact that has outlived its usefulness. OR theory is the only applicable psychoanalytic theory for much of the preoedipal period (Gedo & Goldberg, 1973). It has led to the fruitful extension of analytic psychotherapy to a broader class of severely disturbed patients (Giovacchini, 1979; Horner, 1979; Kernberg, 1975, 1976; Kohut, 1971, 1977; Masterson, 1976). But the excitement generated by these efforts has fixed the application of OR theory in an unnecessary way to the treatment of character disorders. Both psychoanalytic writers (Kernberg, 1987; Rangell, 1985) and psychodynamically influenced family therapists (Framo, 1982) have recognized that object relations theory is applicable with less disturbed clients.

The artificial limitation of the theory can be attributed to four features. First, there has been a much too polar distinction between good and bad parenting, with a correspondingly exaggerated schism in self-representations. While it is certainly true that gross failures in maternal function do occur, and regularly result in severe pathology, it should be recognized that less severe parental faults and greater than normal developmental stresses can interfere with the attainment of object constancy. In this connection Mahler et al. (1975) note that the rapprochement crisis is complicated by the child's heightened fear of object loss based on awareness of the conditional nature of much of the parents' love and attention, the struggles around toilet training, and the fantasies associated with awareness of anatomical sex differences. These stresses can propel the child into the oedipal conflict with heightened ambivalence. Similarly, inconsistent parenting, or failure within a circumscribed area can compromise the developing personality without causing a total lack of integration. A more finegrained analysis may show a person to be vulnerable to one type of rejection while relatively unfazed by another. Second, OR theory has sacrificed accuracy for clarity in its exclusive focus on the parents as the source of introjects. There are multiple real objects in a child's life. Pathogenic influences can be substantially counteracted by other and later friends and relatives, as evidenced in the study of children of divorce (Wallerstein & Kelly, 1980) or offspring of alcoholic parents (Werner & Smith, 1982; West & Prinz, 1987). Third, compensatory strategies within the family relationship can be partially successful at healing faults. Mahler and associates (1975) acknowledge the child's ability to extract needed emotional gratification in the face of less than optimal parenting by prolonging the subphase or modifying the subsequent subphase activities to consolidate previous growth. While it may be assumed that there are remaining vulnerabilities, these need not compromise adjustment so long as the adult can contain them within intimate relationships. This is the basis of the observation by family therapists of the complementarity in needs expressed by partners in intimate relationships (Dicks, 1967; Framo, 1982; Meissner, 1978). Acknowledgement of any of these processes would result in the recognition that essentially neurotic levels of adjustment can be achieved in the face of difficulties with object relations.

A clinical vignette may clarify these points. Object relations theory is, in one of its aspects, an explanation of the individual's response to frustration and loss. As such, it influences the grief process throughout the course of life. The inevitable rejections and disappointments of living may be experienced by those with unstable or unintegrated internal objects as persecutory attempts or as life-threatening assaults on the integrity of the self. With greater maturity, similar frustrations activate self-soothing introjects which enable the individual to maintain self-esteem. There are options — choices among introjects — influenced by the accrued experience of a lifetime. Except for the most severely limited, there will be a range of internal objects that can be mobilized. So a young woman, depressed at the ending of a relationship, feels the pull of the self-destructive messages activated by images of her abusive father as experienced at three years of age. The persecutory object coheres with her own sense of being unworthy. Yet she is simultaneously conscious of her core solidity and competence in managing the crisis without resorting to abusive drinking. She is able to accept and feel deserving of the support of a motherly friend who helps tide her through the crisis. There are multiple introjects, and the most primitive are not always activated, nor are they inevitably the most important for understanding the personality.

Conversely, even a relatively integrated personality may regress to marked splitting if the current context matches a vulnerability from early childhood. Gedo and Goldberg recognize this when they comment that, "Functions typical for more archaic phases persist as potential even after the achievement of this more mature position as the 'typical one'" (1973, p. 175). Because regression remains a possibility, even relatively intact individuals may show the evidence of faults in their internal object world. Fairbairn is the consummate detective for such clues. The part-object mode of relating is evident in states of unusual detachment, in dreams, in déja vu, and in any situation in which internal contents are overvalued at the expense of external relationships (Fairbairn, 1941/1952). If primitive object relationships are so readily re-engaged in each of us, then the therapy of those who have progressed beyond a preoedipal character structure will be advanced by attention to reworking damaged internal representations. Recognition that OR theory can be applied with less disturbed patients makes its cross-fertilization with Psychomotor more important.

Technical Contributions of PS/P to OR Therapy

Pesso System/Psychomotor resolves major technical problems in psychoanalysis that have limited the therapeutic utilization of Object Relations theory. First, PS/P provides a means of reconstructing preverbal experience. Analytically influenced approaches rely on the talking cure even while acknowledging that the crucial developmental issues covered by OR theory have not been adequately symbolized in words. Psychomotor not only provides techniques to access such experiences, it helps to link bodily and interpersonal energy to verbal symbols so that a more complete representation of early experience results. Second, alternative means of handling transference are offered in PS/P. Psychoanalysis has relied on the development and interpretation of the patient's transference to the therapist as a way to resurrect and resolve object relations. Because archaic representations are fragmented, unstable, and emotionally charged, it is demanding work for the analyst to foster the desired insight and integration on the part of the patient. By distributing the part-object representations among group members, PS/P allows the therapist to remain a more unentangled ally of the *pilot* (observing ego). Third, PS/P uses the role-players to provide appropriate gratification. By accommodating early needs, and by assuring safety and satisfaction, regression to preoedipal levels can be accomplished without loss of observing ego. Through Psychomotor, early experience can be addressed directly and therapeutically.

The Reconstruction of Preverbal Experience

It is a challenging task to reconstruct early experience so that it can be consciously owned and understood by the patient. Some contend it cannot be done (Brenner, 1971). Blanck and Blanck discuss the technical difficulties in applying psychoanalytic psychotherapy, which is so fundamentally dependent on words, to preoedipal material which is intrinsically nonverbal:

> The early years of life are spent in a special kind of silence... Even after speech is acquired it takes at least seven years for the child to become capable of abstract thought and to be able to communicate it. For the psychotherapist who is to treat an adult patient years later, it is useful to know that, as an infant and a young child, his patient lived in a state in which emotion and complex thought were not cathected to language (1974, p. 205).

Verbal techniques and interpretations will be of limited use in penetrating to experience that is of vital consequence for mental representations. Preverbal phenomena can be hypothesized from the nature of the object relations mobilized in the transference and by the nonverbal behavior of the client in therapy (Anthi, 1983; Blum, 1980). This information can be used diagnostically. But interpretations based on it are unlikely to be accepted or integrated (Basch, 1985; Ornstein & Ornstein, 1985). Reconstruction relies heavily on teaching about preverbal experience or demonstrating its expression in the transference. Because these techniques are indirect, they lack persuasive power. Furthermore, verbal interpretation is unlikely to touch issues encoded through somaticization or preverbal acting out (Gaddini, 1986). Consequently, "successful reconstruction of preverbal experience is yet rare" (Blanck & Blanck, 1974, p. 214). A major impediment in the application of Object Relations theory is the lack of techniques for directly accessing preverbal experience.

Yet psychoanalytically-oriented therapists respond suspiciously to the "body therapies" that do access nonverbal materials:

> From the ego psychological point of view, to be able to communicate and to understand the communications of others in the primary process is questionable therapy except for psychotics, because it would make inroads upon identity, autonomy, and would impair many ego functions... — including ability to distinguish inside from outside — and the defensive function. To put it another way, the ego would be relatively inoperative and structuralization would suffer (Blanck & Blanck, 1974, p. 216).

Some degree of observing ego is necessary if the experience is to be meaningful — that is, to move beyond catharsis to effect internalization.

Psychomotor provides access to preverbal experience without bypassing the ego. Nonverbal techniques are used to elicit strong emotional reactions. But the therapy is directed verbally by both patient and therapist so that the observing ego is maintained. The adult capacity for self-observation is utilized reconstructively:

> The aim of a Psychomotor structure is to release the capacity of the human to recall, not only verbally, but, more importantly, in motor terms, all those events and interactions which have not resulted in satisfaction or pleasure or maturation, experiencing and 'playing them out' again. This time the conscious, rational minds of the client and therapist are available to glean new learnings, attitudes, conditionings, and modelings from the replaying, while permitting in a safe therapeutic environment the expression of energies and behaviors that had not been expressed in the original event, and adding to this memory positive relationships and experiences that had not been available in the original event (Pesso, 1973, pp. 28-29).

The explicit goal of therapeutic interaction is the internalization of more optimal relationships and expectations. What is unique is the reliance on motoric expression: "insight seems to follow action, rather than action following insight" (1969, p. 208).

The metapsychology of Psychomotor assumes that there are five phylogenetically based energy systems in humans. In addition to those shared with other animals — the reflexive/body righting, metabolic/vegetative, and material/impersonal — there are the critical interpersonal/interactive and verbal/symbolic. Because of the absolute dependence of the neonate and the social nature of living, most psychologically significant energy requires interaction with significant others. This is the interpersonal/interactive sphere. The verbal/symbolic system becomes progressively more important throughout life with the shift to representational and abstract thought which lends itself to conscious recall. The implication is that much of the interpersonal energy — especially those crucial patterns arising during the preverbal period covered by object relations theory — is unconscious, not because it is repressed, but because it has never been translated into verbal/symbolic terms. The unconscious can be made conscious if it can be fully accessed through nonverbal techniques, if it can be named (as by the *witness figure*), and if the experience is *ego-wrapped* (See Chapter 4).

Psychomotor theory postulates that there are four steps to complete experience, and these are collectively called the *Cycle of Becoming*:

1) *Energy* (experienced as tension, emotion, or impulse to action) intrinsically seeks expression in

2) *Action* (motorically mediated), which leads to

3) *Interaction* (impact on others, drawing a response which, optimally, is calibrated in intensity and direction so as to satisfy the original tension), which gives rise to

4) *Meaning* (or Significance/Internalization), the symbolic representation of the process, which is internalized and may become consciously available.

With the last step, the nonverbal experience is accessible in an updated context.

Therapeutic effort is directed at correcting distortions which prevent the appropriate unfolding of the cycle of becoming. This includes confusion about the energy (e.g., the person who denies nurturant needs because of their massive frustration), the appropriate organ to channel the energy (e.g., nurturance received through sounds to the ear rather than food taken in orally), the appropriate interactive system (e.g., metabolic shunting of interpersonal energies, as in the gastrointestinal distress attendant on trying to "swallow" and digest anger), and the appropriate expectations for a response (e.g., "eating shit" in the absence of sufficient experience with appropriate nurturant supplies). Lastly, there are distortions of meaning, usually resulting from frustration of object-directed energies (as in the omnipotent fantasies when there has been inadequate experience with testing emotional expression). More globally, PS/P fosters structuring by attending to ego-wrapping so that any emerging energy is named, accepted, and valued for its potential contribution to the client's being. When *basic needs* are met through the completion of the cycle of becoming, previously unconscious aspects of the personality can be consciously owned by the ego.

Therapy which relies on words alone will be less powerful than reconstruction also using nonverbal techniques to access the different energy systems. First, the verbal/symbolic system is regarded as secondary to the interpersonal/interactive system. This is in part a reality based on development: there has been a great deal of interpersonal experience before the verbal/symbolic capacity develops. This is the point developed by the Blancks. Experiences that are processed in sensorimotor terms may simply not be available via verbal symbols. Potentially significant representations are processed somatically, especially if interpersonal energies which have never been ego-wrapped have been shunted into the vegetative/metabolic system. Second, Psychomotor offers a number of hypotheses about the likely meaning of various bodily sensations and postures. Curling of the toes often indicates nursing schemata, eye pain is associated with mischanneled anger ("if looks could kill..."), etc. These potentially rich sources of hypotheses can be explored in trial enactments. Third, nonverbal techniques extend the range of available options for therapeutic work. The client can free associate using body movements, awaiting the surfacing of tension or emotion. Energy can be heightened enough to be clarified, as in requesting that a gesture be repeated or exaggerated. Counterpressure (for example, the therapist's hand pushing against the back of the neck where muscle tension is experienced) may surface an impulse to act. The therapist joins the client in "energy-seeking" (Pesso, 1980), watching for heightened tension accompanying verbalizations. All of these techniques can begin work that could not be initiated verbally.

Fourth, when the verbal/symbolic system is relied on to represent interpersonal/interactive energies, there is a high risk of distortion:

> In Psychomotor, it is not sufficient merely to speak of the emotion that one is repressing. It is felt that since the emotion is considered to be an impulse to behave in certain ways that the behavior itself is the clearest form the impulse can take. Translation of impulses into words can cause semantic confusion, ambiguity, transformation of meaning, sometimes resulting in the camouflage of the original intent... (Pesso, 1969, p. 78).

Energies, means of expression, targets, and desired responses can all have been inaccurately or incompletely encoded during the development of the verbal/symbolic capacity. Clarification requires reenacting the tension-action-interaction sequence, with meaning as the last, dependent step.

Fifth, enactment is more powerful than verbal reporting even when there has been accurate symbolization. Nonverbal behavior is powerful. By experiencing with "all channels" there will be a much more complete investment in that experience. Sixth, nonverbal enactment, precisely because it involves the full participation of the client's body, makes it less likely that the experience will be defensively disavowed. Even the most primitive drives must be owned when they are reenacted:

> Most people, when finally energized and mobilized and interacting in an emotional, interpersonal fashion, will accept that the feeling and behaviors are their own. They may be puzzled by them and bewildered by them but they almost always accept them as their own. So it could be said that a structure is a way of bringing to the surface, to the doorstep of the conscious ego, the interactive energy of the unconscious ego as only the actions and feelings of the body can do (Pesso, 1973, p. 201).

It is clearly preferable for clients to achieve their own awareness through guided action than to attempt to forge links with even the best-timed genetic interpretation. Especially because so much of the psychological material of importance to the object relations theorist is remote from and even repugnant to the adult perspective, techniques that enable the client to own the experience are powerful.

Alternatives to Reliance on Transference to the Therapist

Psychoanalysis, which has provided the basic therapeutic orientation for OR theorists, relies on the interpretation of the transference neurosis to achieve lasting therapeutic change. The transference is the remobilization of significant object relationships, with the therapist as the observant recipient of the projective mechanisms. Therapeutic progress is slow and uncertain because analysis demands high levels of intelligence and verbal skills, the cultivation of an observing ego, tolerance for frustration created by analytic abstinence, and the challenges and delays inherent in developing and coming to accept interpretation. There has been criticism from both analytically-oriented and nonpsychoanalytic theorists of the idea that interpretation of transference to the therapist is the appropriate manner to rework mental representations. What is less often recognized, is that Object Relations theory need not require adherence to even a modified psychoanalytic approach.

The adequacy of traditional psychoanalytic techniques has been generally criticized by OR theorists, at least as they pertain to the more severely disturbed patient:

> Successful therapeutic intervention in patients with relatively archaic organization of the psyche is indeed possible. We have emphasized that success in such efforts depends primarily on the use of technical modalities of treatment different from that of psychoanalysis proper, that is, on interventions other than interpretation (Gedo & Goldberg, 1973, p. 167).

Where analysis works to bypass the ego defenses in surfacing unconscious material, OR therapy more often entails ego building. In their work with preoedipal issues, analysts are "hampered by a constricting technique which was designed for the psychoanalysis of neurosis and cannot be usefully stretched, modified, or expanded" (Blanck & Blanck, 1974, p. 143). Specifically, the analyst needs to be active in "sharpening the differentiation between self and object representations, aiding neutralization, building object relations, furthering the defensive capacity" (p. 123), and otherwise strengthening the ego. The specific sphere of effort is determined by the degree and nature of the defect: pacification for the most primitive psychotic core, being a reliable object to the initially differentiating self, accepting the idealizing transference of the grandiose self, and then optimally disillusioning the patient ready to internalize functions (Gedo & Goldberg, 1973). The therapist's overarching goal is to be a good object who fosters the development of coherent self and object representations. Again, there is a contrast with and a criticism of analytic neutrality: "When the self-effacing attitude of the analyst is combined with a mode of interpretation based upon a psychology of impulse, a considerable strain is imposed upon the patient's capacity for establishing satisfactory object relationships" (Fairbairn, 1944/1952, p. 87).

The thrust of these comments is that the OR oriented therapist manages the transference actively, in accord with the diagnostic assessment of the patient's developmental needs. Other core aspects of the analytic treatment tradition remain unchanged. Therapy remains a dyadic interchange, using the talking cure. It remains lengthy and intellectually demanding.

A more profound re-evaluation of the role of transference is found in the writing of psychoanalytically sophisticated theorists who adopt a family systems approach. Framo questions whether important self and other representations will ever be expressed in the transference:

> ...certain important behaviors and attitudes come into existence only in the actual physical presence of a close other. Many of these attitudes and behaviors of a patient, moreover, are lived through and acted out in relationships and transactions with family members, and therefore are not reproduced in the transference relationship with the analyst (1970/1982, p. 20).

Object relations not expressed can not be resolved in the one to one therapeutic relationship relying on interpretation. Having significant others or their surrogates present enables the therapist to address a fuller range of object representations. Additionally, the emotional fusing that accompanies the transference to the therapist interferes with the patient's capacity to differentiate, and taxes the therapist's ability to maintain objectivity (Bowen, 1978).

A potential solution to these problems is to have the important object relations enacted within the therapy without being focused on the therapist. Such an approach, while a major departure from the analytic tradition, is entirely consistent with OR theory. It would be more flexible (by engaging a fuller range of object relations) and less likely to result in counter-transference mistakes (since the therapist is not the focus of the relationship). To be effective, such therapy would have to engage the patient, both in terms of emotional re-experience and in terms of an observing ego, to foster the ego structuring basic to OR therapy.

PS/P meets these criteria. Transference manifestations are typically handled within the context of a group, with members alternately doing *structures* and *accommodating* in the structures of others. Psychomotor actually is individual depth therapy with accommodators available to provide a range of transference objects.

There are advantages to having the transference directed at the group. First, the mannerisms and appearance of different group members mobilize a range of object representations. Transference can be generated quickly. Second, multiple introjects can be worked on at once. Having several different individuals as recipients of projection makes it easier to separate and clarify the transference manifestations without the contamination encountered in individual therapy, where one therapist must sequentially represent several objects. Third, simultaneously having several transference aspects (especially when they include the loved and negative features of the same person) honors the phenomenological reality of patients for whom splitting is a prominent characteristic. This is the point made by Krystal (1977) in noting the advantage of a clinic setting for the initial treatment of drug dependent or psychosomatic patients: different staff members are likely to mobilize different elements of the polarized intrapsychic world. The same arrangement is effective in more integrated personalities when it is desirable to promote therapeutic regression so that incompletely resolved splitting can be addressed. Fourth, having accommodators act as recipients of the projection process simplifies the role of the therapist, who can be more consistently the assistant of the client's pilot. The working alliance is less likely to be threatened by projection onto the therapist of competing representations from the client's inner world. Conversely, the therapist is less likely to be caught up in countertransference manifestations and so is more likely to be a reliable partner in the therapeutic effort.

Transference remains in PS/P. The positive transference to the therapist undergirds and supports all the other relationships that develop in the structure and in the group. This is the "lively relationship" (Sarolea, 1986) which gives so much of the possibility to the *possibility sphere* (see Chapter 4). Because others are enroled to accept the transference elements, the therapist is less distracted from being midwife to the birth of aspects of the self which were not previously ego-wrapped.

Therapeutic Regression in Psychomotor

PS/P is quintessentially applied object relations in part because it seeks to reenact the experience of the preoedipal child. Significant others are typically divided so that separate accommodators represent the loved aspect and the negative aspect of the target figure. Interacting with one part-object at a time circumvents paralyzing ambivalence and draws out the primal emotions that obtain before object constancy is achieved. The gestures and verbalizations of the negative parent, for instance, are scripted to mobilize old rage. The resulting attack may entail symbolic murder, with the target figure accommodating by writhing or groaning until the primitive impulse is satisfied. But this dramatic action does not leave the client abandoned, because there is always the ideal parent who can perfectly fulfill the needs of the client (Pesso, 1980). Here again the role — in this case by honoring the magical thinking of the earliest stages of development — mobilizes primitive issues so that the basic steps of identity formation can be addressed. Polarization leads to the re-experience of splitting. It calls forth the full range of emotions and bodily tensions that develop in significant early relationships.

Accommodation assures that there is a suitable response to each action impulse. First, by continuing the cycle of becoming, new learning continues. Second, "accommodation enhances the experience of function pleasure" (Pesso, 1969, p. 164). Action that is completed, that generates the desired reaction, carries with it emotional satisfaction. This sets a tone of security. Third, trust that emotional needs will be honored makes it possible to access previously unavailable impulses:

> It is understood in Psychomotor theory that many emotions are not experienced or actions expressed by people because the family setting or circumstances they were raised in did not provide satisfactory accommodation or "matching" responses to their feelings or behaviors. By offering accommodation to as yet unexpressed emotions and behaviors, the Psychomotor process taps the reservoir of repressed, inhibited, and unconscious feelings and permits those aspects of one's being that have yet to be discovered, to be expressed and hopefully, to be integrated into one's life (Pesso, 1973, p. 8).

Psychomotor is able to penetrate successively deeper into the person's emotional and physical tension:

> One of the aims of psychomotor training is to reduce the amount of unnecessary or damaging modification and to reroute pathological modifications and restraints by first finding them in tension and then giving vent to their primary and primitive emotional expression, much as the young infant and child move in primary emotional and reflexive manners previous to the process of acculturation (1969, pp. 76-77).

Because accommodation assures symbolic satisfaction of basic needs, archaic material surfaces — including the splitting typical of the object relations phase. Again, this is not license for acting out or for overwhelming the ego with id derivatives. Behavioral controls are maintained by the therapist through the containing figures or *ideal parents*. But the emotional impulse is responded to. There is catharsis.

Beyond that, accommodation is *validation*. The messages delivered and the respectful manner with which the witness, the permission-giving figure, or the ideal parents respond to the client offer new relationship models for internalization. What is given is empathic mirroring (Kohut, 1971, 1977) in the sensorimotor channels that are most compelling for archaic experiences (Bacal, 1985; Basch, 1985).

Accommodation offers the opportunity to experience the satisfaction of previously unmet basic needs. Where psychoanalysis can help identify old injuries, mourn the losses, and experience a partial and indirect resolution in the corrective transference, PS/P can offer the accommodation that permits the experience of satisfaction. So accommodation simultaneously encourages regression and promotes structuralization. Pesso notes this:

> The positive accommodator must play two distinct roles: one, as the individual who supplies the internal needs as long as they are desired or needed; and two, as the one who supplies the support and belief in an individual's ability to gain his own ends (1969, pp. 191-192).

In this sense the ideal figure assumes the role of Winnicott's "good enough mother," who adjusts her ministrations to the growing capacity of the child for self-care. With this emphasis on preverbal experience and encouragement of splitting, the experience of the preoedipal child is routinely available in PS/P.

Lastly, the security offered by accommodation permits regression without loss of the observing ego. Structure work accesses the unconscious in the service of the client's *pilot*. This conscious, choiceful return to early modes of experiencing contrasts with true regression. PS/P is therapeutic because the archaic needs are understood and satisfied, not just re-experienced. To summarize:

> It is felt that it is not sufficient to merely recapitulate in thought and word the feeling of our infancy and childhood, but to once again experience the powerful forces of the impulses in the most direct and uninhibited fashion, touching once again the raw forces of our being and learning once again with an adult's mind to control and channel these impulses and energies in more suitable and satisfying ways (pp. 106-107).

The corrective re-experience of preoedipal stages is effective because PS/P recapitulates the optimal developmental process. Typically, rage (directed toward accommodators representing the negative aspects of the parents) is experienced and expressed, then given limits (by the ideal parents) so as not to be destructive in fact. This usually mobilizes the depressive position (Fairbairn, 1952), generating fear of abandonment and a desire for nurturance. The ideal parents accommodate these concerns, offering acceptance and reassurance. It is this experience that is then internalized. Psychomotor replicates the ideal developmental resolution, allowing both poles of emotion to be mobilized, but with the assurance that the good object relationship predominates (Jacobson, 1964). This outcome, which includes the redirection of previously shunted interactive energies which are now brought into object relatedness, permits more complete whole-self to whole-object relationships.

Presentation of a *structure* will highlight these features.

Clinical Example of PS/P

This example presents the second of four structures completed by a 26-year-old graduate student. He had initially sought therapy with his wife because of depression and marital conflict. Six months prior to initiating treatment he had returned to school. He had poured himself into his class work, making it clear that his wife was to seek emotional support elsewhere. She sought therapy. There was no history of previous psychological disturbance or prior treatment. In fact both continued to function well in work and social relationships.

In three months of marital therapy they had accessed feelings, clarified communication, and developed a trusting paternal transference to the therapist. While the conflict had subsided, there was still little sense of closeness in the marriage. He found this acceptable, stating he had chosen to marry her, despite her somewhat constricted expression of affection, because he wanted a strong woman who would not become overly dependent on him. There appeared to be projective processes at work, for he clearly was defending against his own dependency: he continued to express anger in situations when hurt or seeking nurturance would have been appropriate, and he would give to her in ways and at times when he wanted to receive. But his habitual style was to restrict emotional contact through intellectualizing or withdrawal. When he described his own mother as emotionally inconsistent and unavailable, the therapist decided that work on relationships with the family of origin was indicated to clarify the sources of the transference to the wife. The client accepted the recommendation of concurrent involvement in a Psychomotor group.

He began his structure by recounting a fragment of a dream about a yellow bird he had the previous night. There were no spontaneous associations to the image, so he was urged to enact the fragment. A small man from the group assumed the role of the little bird and was coached by the client to do a squatting hop into a position immediately in front of the client, who then hugged the little bird and broke into deep sobs. The bird represented his childhood freedom. He spoke of feeling empty, of the oppressiveness of his responsibilities, and his regret at losing the playfulness of his youth. When he said he wanted to run and wrestle, he was encouraged to pick someone to represent a childhood peer. The therapist was surprised when the client selected an obese woman, but accepted the choice without commenting on the apparent intrusion of a maternal object. There was some tentative contact, but then he expressed the desire to wriggle away from the "playmate." He proceeded to crawl on, over, and under a pile of pillows. The therapist was unclear whether this displacement was a defense against oedipal or preoedipal strivings, but it was clear the client was shunting interpersonal energy into the impersonal/material arena. To clarify the target and the nature of the energy involved, the therapist explained to the client that his movements seemed ideally suited to contacting his fleshy playmate. The client did burrow under the side of the reclining accommodator, in a manner perhaps indicative of nursing, and then became fearful and claustrophobic, expressing concern that he might suffocate. It was clear that the client was relating to a negative maternal object. Instead of the freedom and playfulness expected, the enactment portrayed the avoidance of the engulfing mother of rapprochement or the premature hatching subsequent to failed symbiosis.

Several alternative ways to develop the structure suggest themselves. A positive maternal figure who would not be smothering could be enroled to polarize the elements of the object. An accommodator could enact the constriction that goes with suffocation, tightly encircling the client's chest. The resulting breathing could be sounded, in all likelihood resulting in the bellows of surfacing rage which could then be targeted at the playmate (re-enroled as the negative mother). But before these alternatives were suggested the client pulled away from the accommodator and lay prone on the floor, with his head in a small square of light where the afternoon sun streamed through a window. When queried by the therapist, the client recalled an early memory of watching the sunlit patterns around drawn curtains as seen from his crib. He felt a sense of security. The sunlight was "magical" and "soothing." The memory dated back to when he was two and one-half years of age, and staying with his grandparents during his mother's confinement following the birth of his younger sibling.

The memory clarifies the developmental defect and the direction of the structure. The magic sun is symbolic nurturing, replacing the mother lost at rapprochment. Rather than rage at the loss or mourn it, the client had shunted affectional needs into precocious verbal/symbolic development. His academic career continues his preference to relate to symbols rather than people. His withdrawal and renunciation of dependency in the face of marital conflict replicates his childhood decision to opt for premature independence rather than experience the depression of needing the unavailable mother. The reconstruction required is to again experience the possibility of human nurturance. After the therapist explained the sun's symbolic role, the client enroled an ideal mother and father. They merged with the sun, cradling his head in their hands, leaning over him so that they and the sun shared his field of vision — "beaming" at him. They accommodated his requests for reassurance as to their permanence, love, and continuing support. He responded nonverbally with relaxation and smiles. Verbally, he expressed contentment and satisfaction. After five minutes of internalizing the image of the ideal parents, the structure ended.

There was no effort in this structure to enact the rejection of the negative mother. The focus had to be on restoring the nurturant tie. Subsequent work returned to the nursing experience. Only after that relationship was experienced as trustworthy was the client able to deal with negative feelings, projected first onto the sibling and then with the negative mother. The impact on the marital relationship was salutary. The client became more directly receptive and dependent. The internalization of the nurturant image also made him less fearful of rejection and more capable of handling conflict without withdrawal. So there was increased flexibility regarding closeness in the marriage.

This case illustrates several of the important points of this paper. Object relations ideas were applied in the treatment of a client operating at a neurotic level of adjustment. Although somewhat obsessive and rigid, he was clearly reality-related, productive, and capable of intimacy. But there was a fault evident in his counterdependent withdrawal during marital conflict. The nonverbal techniques of PS/P permitted the efficient recovery of archaic material and the reworking of the negative introject of the mother, freeing the client to experience dependence positively and to relate to his wife with less distortion due to maternal transference. Ambivalence about intimacy can be tolerated, even in the face of conflict, when there are internalized ideal parents who confirm the client's worth.

Conclusion

This paper has sought to demonstrate how Pesso System/Psychomotor can be useful to adherents of Object Relations theory. Drawing on the similar view that family interaction leads to internalized self- and other- representations, with attention to similar psychopathological manifestations, with similar emphasis on the importance of preverbal experience, both Psychomotor and OR theory seek to accomplish restructuring of the internal object world through corrective interpersonal experience. Yet they take strikingly different approaches to the conduct of therapy. There are enormous possibilities for cross-fertilization.

Object Relations theory does not require adherence to techniques derived from psychoanalysis. This paper has highlighted three ways in which the theory can be more effectively applied by borrowing the perspective and techniques developed in PS/P. First, OR theory can be more generally applicable than it has been; it need not be limited to the treatment of character disorders. Second, transference to the therapist is not the only — and probably not the most desirable — way to encourage reworking of internal representations. Psychomotor directs transference manifestations away from the therapist, using the group to evoke and enact early object representations. Third, most therapy based on OR theory continues to rely on predominantly verbal therapy when the crucial phenomena are not verbally cathected. Object Relations theory requires a set of techniques that access preverbal experience in such a way that the observing ego can use it reconstructively. The controlled regression and nonverbal awareness generated by Pesso System/Psychomotor make it perhaps the purest existing technique for the clinical application of Object Relations theory.

References

Anthi, P. (1983). Reconstruction of preverbal experiences. *Journal of the American Psychoanalytic Association, 31,* 33-58.

Bacal, H.A. (1985). Optimal responsiveness and the therapeutic process. In A. Goldberg (Ed.), *Progress in Self Psychology: Vol. 1* (pp. 202-227). New York: Guilford Press.

Basch, M.F. (1985). Interpretation: Toward a developmental model. In A. Goldberg (Ed.), *Progress in Self Psychology: Vol. 1* (pp. 33-42). New York: Guilford Press.

Blanck, G., & Blanck, R. (1974). *Ego Psychology.* New York: Columbia University Press.

Blum, H.P. (1980). The value of reconstruction in adult analysis. *International Journal of Psychoanalysis, 61,* 39-52.

Bowen, M. (1978). *Family therapy in clinical practice.* New York: Aronson.

Brenner, C. (1971). The Psychoanalytic concept of aggression. *International Journal of Psychoanalysis, 52,* 137-144.

Davis, M., & Wallbridge, D. (1981). *Boundary and space.* New York: Brunner/Mazel.

Dicks, H. (1967). *Marital tensions.* New York: Basic Books.

Fairbairn, W.R.D. (1952). *Psychoanalytic studies of the personality.* Boston: Routledge and Kegan Paul.

Framo, J.L. (1982). *Explorations in marital and family therapy.* New York: Springer.

Gaddini, R. (1986). Early determinants of self and object constancy. In R. F. Lax, S. Bach, & J. A. Burland (Eds.), *Self and Object Constancy: Clinical and theoretical perspectives* (pp. 177-189). New York: Guilford.

Gedo, J.E., & Goldberg, A. (1973). *Models of the mind.* Chicago: University of Chicago Press.

Giovacchini, P. (1979). *Treatment of primitive mental states.* New York: Aronson.

Greenburg, J.R., & Mitchell, S.A. (1983). *Object Relations in Psychoanalytic theory.* Cambridge, MA: Harvard University Press.

Horner, A.J. (1979). *Object Relations and the developing ego in therapy.* New York: Aronson.

Howe, L. *Psychomotor/Pesso System Psychotherapy.* (Available from Psychomotor Institute, 60 Western Avenue, Cambridge, MA 02139).

Jacobson, E. (1964). *Self and the object world.* New York: International Universities Press.

Kernberg, O.F. (1975). *Borderline conditions and pathological narcissism.* New York: Aronson.

Kernberg, O.F. (1976). *Object Relations theory and clinical Psychoanalysis.* New York: Aronson.

Kernberg, O. F. (1987). An ego psychology - Object Relations theory approach to transference. *Psychoanalytic Quarterly, 56,* 197-221.

Kohut, H. (1971). *Analysis of the self.* New York: International Universities Press.

Kohut, H. (1977). *Restoration of the self.* New York: International Universities Press.

Krystal, H. (1977). Self representation and the capacity for self care. *Annual of Psychoanalysis, 6,* 209-246.

Mahler, M.S., Pine, F., & Bergman, A. (1975). *Psychological birth of the human infant.* New York: Basic Books.

Masterson, J. (1976). *Psychotherapy of the borderline adult.* New York: Brunner/Mazel.

Meissner, W.W. (1978). Conceptualization of marriage and family therapy from a psychoanalytic perspective. In T. Paolino & B. McCrady (Eds.), *Marriage and marital therapy* (pp. 25-88). New York: Brunner/Mazel.

Miller, A. (1981). *The drama of the gifted child: The search for the true self.* R. Ward (Trans.). New York: Basic Books.

Ornstein, P.H., & Ornstein, A. (1985). Clinical understanding and explaining: The empathic vantage point. In A. Goldberg (Ed.), *Progress in Self Psychology, Vol. I* (pp. 43-61). New York: Guilford.

Pesso, A. (1969). *Movement in psychotherapy.* New York: New York University Press.

Pesso, A. (1973). *Experience in action.* New York: New York University Press.

Pesso, A. (1980, September). *Psychomotor/Pesso System Psychotherapy.* Paper presented at the Fifth World Conference of Therapeutic Communities, Hague, the Netherlands. (Available from Psychomotor Institute, 60 Western Avenue, Cambridge, MA 02139).

Rangell, L. (1985). The object in Psychoanalytic theory. *Journal of the American Psychoanalytic Association, 33,* 301-334.

Sarolea, H. (1986). Ideal parents. *Pesso Bulletin, 2,* 1-9.

Slipp, S. (1984). *Object Relations: A dynamic bridge between individual and family treatment.* New York: Jason Aronson.

Wallerstein, J., & Kelly, J. (1980). *Surviving the breakup.* New York: Basic Books.

Werner, E.E., & Smith, R.S. (1982). *Vulnerable but invincible: A study of resilient children.* New York: McGraw-Hill.

West, M.O., & Prinz, R.J. (1987). Parental alcoholism and child psychopathology. *Psychological Bulletin, 102,* 204-218.

Chapter 11

Staging the Unconscious

Impressions of Psychomotor as Seen by a Psychoanalyst

by Tilmann Moser

In the more than fifteen years that I have been active as a psychoanalyst, I have felt a certain deficiency due to the limits of a primarily verbal form of therapy — a form which, at the same time, runs the risk of becoming an exclusive ideal in itself. This feeling has led me to search for experiences with other more dramatizing forms of therapy: Gestalt therapy, psychodrama, primal therapy, bioenergetics, integrative body therapy, and family therapy. I didn't want to renounce the theoretical richness of psychoanalysis with its differentiating exploration into a person's structural depths, formed as they are by his life's history, but I did want to make use of the abundant experience which has been gained in other forms of therapy which include the body and body language.

New understandings in the field of human science arise not only from contemplation, but also by integrating new experiences. I can now say that, having adopted the Pessos' insights into my own theoretical and clinical perspective, my work with patients has changed: taking on a more positive, more creative, and more life-encouraging form. Among the advantages offered by PS/P is the vividness of experience when the unconscious is enacted rather than described or felt in the transference relationship; the ability to find meaning in nonverbal behavior; the speed with which lost aspects of the self can be discovered and integrated; and the sensitivity with which defenses are respected even as awareness is broadened. Perhaps most of all, PS/P contributes by giving access to the body. I am no longer afraid of the patients' bodies, nor of using my own body in therapy. In this context, the great problem of "abstinence" must be rethought. Certainly there is a need for more precise guidance than occurs in psychoanalysis where, fearfully and with a nearly total lack of experience, the problem is solved by the negation of the real body.

Accommodation and the "New Beginning"

Key to Psychomotor is the splitting of early inner and outer objects into ideal and negative aspects, with psychological growth encouraged under the auspices of the *ideal parents*. There is a definite similarity to Balint's "new beginning."

Accommodation permits reworking the early experience of the client. If a protagonist in a *structure* is searching for his negative feelings from either conscious or long-repressed hurts, then it is extraordinarily helpful if another participant, taking the negative role, can react with pain in word and gesture to criticism, anger, hate, or contempt. This then encourages the protagonist to accept and to explore feelings which often have never been verbalized or were even unknown to him. The client has an unconscious picture of the reaction he hopes to attain through his negative affects. His face clears remarkably when, after a period of seeking and trying to find expression for his emotions, he achieves an appropriate response from the accommodator. Importantly, negative emotions are explicitly directed not toward the real parents, but rather toward their isolated threatening aspects.

Ideal parents represent the possibility of archetypically ideal relationships and not simply the idealized aspects of historical parents. These ideal parents are prepared to meet repressed primary needs in order to achieve the first tracings in a *new map* of positive development. As opposed to psychodrama, all participants in the PS/P group completely serve the needs of the protagonists, who may correct and rearrange them as long as necessary (with the help of the empathic therapist) until, out of the fog of the unconscious, there arises a clear picture of an ideal — perhaps a never dreamed of — reaction. By using a range of accommodators, a highly differentiated unconscious scene can be enacted in a short time.

The structure may begin with the protagonist's actual feelings or, quite often, may come from unconscious body language signals. The therapist then may seek clarification through careful exploratory questioning or through the offer of accommodation in search of the yet unknown background scene. For example, on one hand the client may avoid eye contact because he unconsciously believes that his glance is murderous enough to kill. On the other hand it is possible that he has an ominous feeling about his overwhelming desire for instantaneous merging, looking away so as not to lose contour or not to lose the "object" on account of his greed. Accommodation permits a transformation into an expressive area, and does so much more quickly than in individual analysis because it takes much longer for the patient to experience with one person (the analyst) that the analyst can learn to understand the patient's anxieties and is able to survive his attacks.

The client with lowered eyes may also unconsciously fear that the therapist (or, in the past, the parents) through eye contact may see through him immediately, seeing his sexual or anal fantasies, and may punish him; or that his delusions of grandiosity may be read from his eyes, leading to retaliation; or on a more psychotic level, that through eye contact fleeting and uncontrollable parts of the self are rapidly exchanged, or that the client might not be able to defend himself against a magic inundation from the therapist in the form of "bewitchery," attack, poisoning, or dissolution. All these possibilities could be further enumerated, but the point will have become clear: with the help of accommodators, a differentiated unconscious scene is worked out. Negative affects are explored and expressed. A minimal new beginning will be hinted at through the use of ideal figures. To some extent the new beginning may even be "lived out," revealing itself as a shy flaring up of happiness, sometimes in boundless joy, followed often by a deep mourning about long lost potential. Because the patient often cannot bear these affects alone, he is offered support, if he wants it, either of psychological or of a purely physical nature. One or more participants may build what Bion termed "the container" or what Winnicott called the "holding function."

When the protagonist has played through his negative fantasies of killing, his fear of dissolution, his feeling of being seen through and punished (with the accompanying anger), his pain, and his contempt, then he is able to experience with the ideal parents that his anger will not destroy them; that his greed doesn't cause them undue anxiety; that those fantasies which he considers insane or perverse can be coped with and understood. The ideal parents behave toward each other and toward the "child" in such a way that the deforming alternatives — the symptoms, the character contortions — become potentially unnecessary. The whole group can be caught up in the happiness, relaxation, or laughter when the protagonist, after possibly a life without looking, immerses himself in an astonishing, stable, and (to him) seemingly endless gazing at an object that neither punishes him nor overwhelms him, neither takes possession of him nor bewitches him, doesn't mistreat him, but just looks. At this point there might be a few minutes of silent "being," as Winnicott terms it, as well as moments of transition from the sustaining "being" to the inevitably waiting conflicts.

PS/P Demonstrates the Psychoanalytic Unconscious

My encounter with Psychomotor has enriched and changed my own working style. In no way has it undermined my psychoanalytic identity, because the Pessos have tested their technique for too long, working in an American hospital with analytically-oriented colleagues. Quite the opposite is true. My impression is that a great many unconscious constellations and conflicts may be revealed in the group scenes. This search for the traumatic constellations that influence the unconscious is the joint enterprise of the group.

And what is so new about all this? If only viewed superficially, then not very much. What becomes visible in PS/P groups recalls fragments of psychodrama, Gestalt therapy, the various primal scream techniques, bioenergetics, and still other therapy forms. Yet it seems to me that the fruitful combination of these different techniques leads to something new, as shown in the often deeply moving clarity of the unconscious scenes and the refinement of psychosomatic perception. It frees the analyst of those dizzying feelings of flying blind which so often occur in other therapy forms. I have occasionally seen non-analysts with almost acrobatic genius rummaging through the unconscious, their competence limited to one level of the conflict and being quite helpless on other levels. They have neither the support of a well-founded theory nor of the setting which can offer support when orientation is temporarily lost. PS/P offers both the setting and organizing theory.

It wouldn't be inaccurate to call PS/P a radicalized psychodrama. What might cause an analyst to be positively euphoric about the Pessos' work is that the main discoveries of the more recent psychoanalytic theoreticians (Mahler, Kohut, Winnicott, Kernberg, Bion, and even Melanie Klein) can, in fact, be experienced, understood, and clarified within the interaction itself. Constructions appear, taking the form of three-dimensional human pictures: The lost self might, for example, be represented by a tiny voice in the midst of the roaring identifications with the overwhelming aspects of the early parental figures. This shrill concert of false aspects of the self can be made audible. The remaining aspects of the self receive one or more auxiliary egos in helping him defend and assert himself against the encroachment and inundation of the early threatening parental images.

The unconscious delusions of grandiosity in the narcissistic or the depressive patient are allowed to be shown and meet with a boundary that brings him back to earth. The evil introjects are given voices, are localized and examined. PS/P permits reenacting the archaic phases of early childhood where the mother (or substitute figure) is not perceived as a separate entity, but as a partial object, especially in the split form as the idealized good and the bad images. The patient can once again split the inner images into those ghosts and giants, in just the same way as the child experiences the adult world.

PS/P creates, in the animism of the child and his magical thinking, a field on which to experiment freely, because voices, character traits, atmospheric qualities and religious themes can be put into an outer "physical body." All forces and motives that can in any way move the soul get a chance of becoming visual reality. The Pessos, much to their advantage, have worked with psychotic patients for years and are familiar with fragmentation, splitting, the forces in the disintegration of the psyche, as well as with the deep yearnings and attempts toward new integration. Their technique enacts this primal human drama.

I am intrigued by the potential integration of psychoanalytic theory, in its vast complexity, with the sheer representational force with which Psychomotor expresses the early interpersonal conflicts which have resulted in body tension and other abnormalities. Each phase of psychosexual development has its own world of pictures, needs, and dangers. Patients with conflicts on the oedipal level may often be overwhelmed by the desire to see their parents just once being tender to one another, self-confident and unified, but still open to and accepting the child, not using the child too much for their own needs. On the other hand, the patient, taking advantage of his own neurotic wishes and his compensatory life skills, may re-enact in full force his need to deepen the split between the parents. Behind this bitter triumph, deep sadness or perhaps fierce anger can be felt at the unstable family system which had never allowed a childhood within protective boundaries. These feelings can be named, and the yearnings honored through the provision of the needed limits: With the ideal parents, the client can experience the security of being cherished by parents who could not be divided.

One of the most impressive scenes, seen again and again, is that in which the participant is reacting like the child with uncontrollable rage who is held by strong loving arms, held by the whole group while he plunges into archaic anger. At this moment he accomplishes the expression of destructiveness which he has always feared and repressed with incredible energy, only to find his destructive energy in supportive and limiting hands. Six or eight participants, representing extensions of the ideal parents, are sometimes needed to hold the raging protagonist. The ideal parents acknowledge his rage and admit that he must have been deeply hurt. In this way the hurt may be allowed to become conscious. The injury itself has often been long repressed, because the latent rage was considered terrible enough. Very often the image of the hurt can appear only when the situation which caused the split-off rage in the first place can be relived in an non-traumatizing "holding" setting.

I have seen variations of images of God take shape which, in analysis, are seldom brought into the transference. In one person there may be several images of God and these may be at war with one another. I have never seen it so clearly demonstrated as here that the devil is, for children who have been exposed to religious instruction, at least temporarily, a very real person. Some sessions take the form of an exorcism when deeply buried identifications with the devil or with an attribute of God come to light and it becomes clear that half of one's life has been spent running away from God's all-seeing eye.

The superego can be housing a whole zoological garden of ghosts. The earlier the disturbance has occurred, the less the superego content resembles Freud's classic picture of fatherly dictates. The main concept is to make the unconscious content as three-dimensional and as clearly visible as possible, both verbally and through body language, just as it seemed to the child at the time. In disturbances of a more paranoid nature, but long before manifest delusion, it takes a long time for the different voices, played by the participants, to be identified, localized, and connected with persons from the past or connected with split-off introjects.

Because even the classically-oriented analyst behind the couch tends to think and feel with images when working with oedipal conflicts, I would like to consider, in the following examples, constellations that may be experienced less visually in the analytic setting. In analysis, conflicts are dealt with one after the other, the various contents, voices, object representations, and ego representations are handled in chronological order. Important to the staging of unconscious constellations, as opposed to analysis, is that conflict material is brought out simultaneously, presenting a collage of conflicts. Instead of wandering through continually flowing time, the staging is set in space, using a series of images. Although the time factor remains perceptible, the richness of the time sequence is exchanged for the wealth to be found in the simultaneous view of the action.

It is, for example, possible that the patient needs the feeling of being cradled in the uterus, the first really undisturbed place in life, in order to begin facing the trauma of birth or of an unwelcome arrival, or to even imagine alternatives. The group can cradle him. He may have the wish to prepare for his arrival in a discussion with the ideal parents. He may want to articulate the rage which the unloved fetus feels in an anticipatory dialogue with accommodating "bad" aspects of the real parents.

In another case the patient may want to experience again moments or phases of his birth, whereby the group forms the birth canal with their arms or bodies. Re-living one's birth has become a central process in other therapy forms. But only PS/P seems to focus on the availability of an alternative experience.

Another patient may need a time of undisturbed symbiosis to achieve even the first feelings of possible security near a motherly object. It is, for example, impressive to see, in a later stage of symbiotic closeness, the moment in which the patient for the first time dares to make whispering contact with the ideal mother, experiencing an intimacy which had never before been known. There are just as many situations in the separation-individuation phase that can be staged, whereby it can be a relief for the patient if, for example, an auxiliary ego (the therapist, the *witness*, or a support figure) formulates the content of the as yet unspoken "no" or the silent stubborn refusal. In PS/P, images are structured from any of Margaret Mahler's phases, in addition to the oedipal scenes. Patient searching is required to make the scene precise and, of course, to root it in the working through process.

My choice of an example, greatly simplified, is the *structure* of a borderline patient. The patient cannot, at first, make visual contact with others. The therapist suggests that he try to find out what consequences he fears from looking and what impact he secretly hopes to achieve. An accommodator assumes the role of the grandmother who lived in the protagonist's family and asserted herself in a strict and controlling way. She portrays her horror of and being shocked by the protagonist's "evil eye," when he wants to reverse the trauma of being unrelentingly looked at. The problem here is the identification with the aggressor. It is equally possible that other causes might be responsible for the anxiety provoking split-off rage which led to visual blocking. While the accommodator is suffering the effects of the "evil eye" upon her, the protagonist's reaction increases to the point of pure rage or the point of getting ready to take hate-filled action. The protagonist may feel the urge to kill the evil person with the sheer power of his "eye" which he, in magical thinking, experiences to be a death ray.

This is a triumphant moment; the protagonist feeling, for the first time, that he has located and understood powerful and anxiety-provoking inner forces. Directly following this, a sort of stupor may set in, a state of confusion, increased anxiety, or sadness. The stupor shields the protagonist like a wall from the strong feelings of abandonment that occur in connection with the mother who, during the war years, was unreliable, unempathic or unpredictable due to depression, panic, or sickness. Another possibility is that the emotional rigidity cannot be cracked open because it has become a habitual part of his protective shell against those emotions, stemming from the early traumatic phase of the relationship. Still another possibility is that the mother, as an object, has disappeared entirely, her presence revealed only in the basic atmosphere, vaguely remembered from the air-raid shelter: closeness, panic, bodily contact, too little fresh air, and a primitive but frozen feeling of security. Another accommodator may then take this part, giving voice to this close, thick atmosphere. From the child's point of view the mother has literally gotten lost, herself overwhelmed by the situation. In tiny steps the message in the "atmosphere mood" is explored — this atmosphere which is repeatedly sought out as a neurotic, regressive shelter. Hidden behind this feeling of loss there might be a split-off feeling of concern for the mother or even immense contempt for her that has not been allowed to become conscious. Depending on the point of focus, the objects, defense mechanisms, or fragmentary parts may be enacted. In a favorable case, the protagonist is now prepared to accept the symbolic experience of ideal parents and to ask for a simple, primitive form of protection from the overwhelming emotions felt temporarily when giving up symptoms of rigidity, depersonalization, and fragmentation. It is also possible that the protagonist may only want the ideal mother to see him just as he is, which the real mother had not been able to do at the time, because she was in panic herself. To some severely disturbed patients, the concept of ideal parents is an absolute impossibility. As a first step, these patients need an ideal "atmosphere," built by a wall of people to stem the oncoming terror.

When the ideal parents can be accepted, such desires follow as: "Please don't fight with each other; don't feel contempt for one another; I want to hear that you love each other, that you really wanted to have me, that you will stay together always, that you feel that I belong to you." It is often deeply moving to see how children from such split families, where the thematic content has been disloyalty, betrayal, contempt, sadistic tendencies, or power plays, break down tearfully at the sight of ideal parents who are tenderly holding hands with each other. It is not uncommon for them to want to view, for minutes at a time, ideal parents who are looking at each other lovingly, until the wish to be included in the tender scene becomes clear. Occasionally, there are bedtime scenes where the protagonist, perhaps for the first time in his life, can symbolically experience both parents sitting by his bed in complete harmony and, when he opens his eyes a few minutes later, find them still lovingly there. These very intense symbolic experiences can provoke sadness, hate, and doubt, but these are the scenes of the symbolic new beginning.

To return to the borderline structure: if the protagonist can view the enactment of a part of his fragmented ego and can, at least to some extent, connect particular scenes with objects, then he needs the ideal parents in the slow process required for integration. For example, he needs the assurance that they recognize his fragmented state of mind and are strong enough to bear it with him without having to "excommunicate" any emotion. Additionally, it is important that they accept the fact that he may go through crazy phases, that the intensity of his emotions won't frighten them, that, if necessary, they are prepared to physically hold him together (with the help of the whole group, which acts as an extension of the ideal parents). Even though the containing function of the group allows and encourages the expression of extremely strong emotions, it is, however, not meant to be merely a cathartic procedure or a mechanism for letting off steam. Emotions must take their way back into lively interaction, into a significant and meaningful relationship between human subjects.

Transference and Resistance

Should the thesis prove correct that PS/P is a radical group psychodrama equivalent to the analytic technique, then, equally, the basic tenets of psychoanalysis, transference and resistance, must also be present in this work. Spontaneous transference to the therapist, crystallizing at the beginning of a structure, is clearly made use of. At first the therapist is an escort on what may be a hellish trip, later he is available in the search for the first signs of reorientation. He remains an auxiliary ego. Spontaneous and very often intense transference phenomena, as soon as they become clearly felt, are separated from his person and brought into the group scene. The therapist maintains a neutral position to help the client track energy and choose direction for work. Transference is directed toward the original object or partial object, the inner object to which the invested energy is bound. When this energy is brought into the open, and directed toward the object, it functions similarly to what occurs during the structuring of transference with the analyst, but with more emotional power. To express myself more dramatically, Psychomotor supports the return to the blast furnace temperatures of the original scenes, whereas the analyst wants to melt the hardened material in a much more gradual warming up process.

The length of time for the working-through process is most likely nearly the same, because the participant in a group has the opportunity to enact a structure only once every couple of weeks. He must also act as an accommodator for other participants. He gets a more intensive dose of "experience," but in wider intervals.

The true scene (see Chapter 4) dramatizes various types of resistance. There is, in all forms of therapy that utilize role-playing, the so-called "play resistance," a more or less anxious hesitation about becoming involved at all in a scene and taking over a role. Resistance is readily felt before each new step is taken. It may be surmounted, however, not through patient interpretation, but rather through actively encouraging the next gesture, the next point of contact, by encouraging the next words to be placed in the mouth of an accommodator. Important sources of encouragement are, for example, the group itself, the force behind the developing scene, and the following questions: "What do you need now?" or "What do you want to do or to say now?" Also of importance is urging the protagonist to intensify gestures or poses which are not as yet understood until their unknown scenic meaning has been further developed. The therapist, in his role of director and auxiliary ego, displays increasing authority in the form of active encouragement, always bearing in mind the question of whether the next step may be risked. In more prolonged work the patient himself gets a better feeling about which scenes he wants to do. The resistance is given a voice by *fragment figures* (the voice of hesitation, of dissociation, etc.). In the true scene the protagonist can interact with, and often choose to defy, the enacted resistance. And as a final boost, there is always the ever present psychic pain in the background which, in itself, is a tremendous incentive in overcoming resistance. Of additional help is the patient's progressively surer feeling that each structure carries within it the potential moment of a new beginning, that each structure leads to a step forward in development. The ideal figures confirm newly found vitality, hope, initiative, and autonomy. Perhaps this is the clue to the suctional pull that is felt in a structure. Each time fear has been overcome, there beckons a new view, hope and encouragement to the unlived life.

Acceptance of PS/P by psychoanalysis will meet with some difficulty because, although Al Pesso's approach is theoretically not too distant from psychoanalysis, he has, like so many pioneers before him, created his own terminology. The result is that his two books, *Movement in Psychotherapy* (1969) and *Experience in Action* (1973) are, in part, difficult reading. The analyst must first transpose the text into analytic categories until he has become familiar with the conceptual system. Then the feeling of strangeness disappears, leaving only a hint of regret that double work has been done and that not all the well-researched territory that psychoanalysis has covered is included in Pesso's conceptual system.

Respect for Defenses in PS/P

Psychomotor is a gift to psychoanalysis from the world of theatre and dance. It shares its dramatic intensity with other expressive therapies which came into being as a result of anger at and disappointment over the insufficiencies of the couch setting and the restrictions placed on a therapy which limits itself only to verbal exchange — the "talking cure." Many of these therapies are dangerous, especially to the degree to which patient and competent working through of conflicts dissolves into cathartic discharge and emotional trampling. PS/P avoids this risk because defenses are respected.

The new dramatizing therapies focus on the complete expression of negative affects towards the early traumatizing objects, lacking an understanding of the dimensions of the unconscious loyalty bonds. In these approaches it is often as though one were dealing with a separate subject, seen solely by itself, who turns his rage, disappointment, contempt, and suspicion against his parents: screaming back at them, or fighting with them symbolically in murderous emotional and physical attacks (usually directed against plastic foam substitutes). If the deep ties of loyalty are not taken into consideration (in psychoanalysis they turn up quite naturally in the transference, bound on the person of the analyst), then negative affects are directed against the internalized part of the object, too. What follows are guilt feelings, psychosomatic reactions, feelings of emptiness, depersonalization, fear of annihilation, and paranoid reactions. Interacting with split aspects of early objects clarifies where a negative affect serves the purpose of individuation and the restoration of self-esteem and where it futilely and destructively rages against self objects which, in the emotional environments, are not yet outlined as independent objects, even if they have been alleged to be so by the protagonist in the scene. There are two major hazards in the dramatized therapy forms: The patient fears in his rage that he will destroy, through magic, the motherly or fatherly total object, if he does not split it off before the attack; and he is afraid also of damaging self objects on which he is still very dependent and are a part of his inner reality. Group dynamic processes of delegation, however, often result in encouraging or even provoking the protagonist to attack inner objects to which he is still deeply tied and which he still needs. He then fights a war for the co-patients who vicariously watch, regressing at this moment to the consumer level of spectators watching a gladiator in the arena. Latent in every patient is the magic fantasy that it is only necessary to break the Gordian knot towards early objects and then the difficult road to individuation is opened.

I would like to compare the typically negative image of the fighting gladiator, which is acted out time and again in many of the "wrenching out" therapies, with the differentiated structure of a PS/P setting. Here the therapist does not presume to offer the whole parental objects to attack. He respects their intensive unknown qualities of richness, and selects instead single negative aspects which he senses have threatened and hurt the patient. In this way the therapist indicates that individuation does not lead to the expected catastrophe, but that individuation is the slow road of differentiation, of selective identification, of the selective "no." Only in this way can a murderous rage be utilized, instead of leaving a devastated forest in its path or forcing the remaining bonds into the swamp of psychosomatic symptoms. When the inner objects are so massively and unfairly attacked, they regress on their own, so to speak, and cling to the attacker in a much more archaic way.

This is probably the one important explanation for the destructive course taken in some undifferentiated forms of primal therapy in which the unconscious, simply said, is the attic store room to be cleaned out with the use of force. Among the archetypical motherly and fatherly household effects are both the valuable and the dangerous, side by side. Cleaning out with a cathartic garbage removal service often leaves only an empty attic and a psychic hangover. PS/P, in contrast, is careful to work with split objects. It is always emphasized that the confrontation applies only to the negative aspects of the early figures. Therefore, the aggression doesn't threaten the patient with guilt feelings which can occur in the cathartic mother and father-killing orgies occasionally seen in other therapy forms. The patient is spared the partial self-destruction that results from prolonged fusion and identification with the destroyed objects.

Ideal figures are offered in exchange for the negative objects. With their assistance the patient can try to recognize what he would have needed at the time the trauma occurred in order to achieve active, healthy development. He is not offered magical figures to either humor him or to make reparation. On the contrary, it is extremely impressive to see just how difficult is the process of trying to rediscover long lost wishes, or of realizing those wishes that have never been experienced on a conscious level. Only by decoding the body's messages is it possible to arrive at gestures and words which allow the needs to be verbalized. Some patients become literally paralyzed in the face of potentially ideal parents. Being allowed to state a need may cause panic, disbelief, or raise primal distrust. At this point the patient's only desire may be to be left in peace. If this wish is granted, then the seed is sown for the next tiny wish. In other therapies the defense mechanisms might be bulldozed to death, leaving more than a few patients with helplessly exposed insides as they rush from the scene of the action. One of the basic rules of Psychomotor is that the participant himself designates repeatedly during a session just how far he wants to go. The therapeutic contract is being constantly renewed and re-discussed with the adult part of the patient — the *pilot*. Should a profound regression come to happen, then the therapist and the whole group are prepared to offer help to the protagonist. This applies, of course, to many therapy forms, but is particularly emphasized in Psychomotor. In the beginning, some structures serve the sole purpose of trying to use the true scene to identify anxiety and resistance, looking for potential lines of development toward achieving improvement.

Because the Pessos gained their experience in long years of work in a psychiatric institution, they are particularly sensitive to patients who are defenseless against external influences, unless they resort to the total protection of psychotic withdrawal. Once a patient has grasped the idea behind this therapy and has internalized the fact that he may really sit in the stage director's chair or may co-direct until he has found an unknown part of himself in the mirror of accommodation, then he can begin to develop personal solicitude towards his needs for integrity and individuality. A significant number of patients develop guilt feelings at first, when they make use of one or more role-players for the purpose of "only" searching for lost feelings or part of the self. Many want to give up too soon, because they fear the role-players' patience is running out or that it is really wrong or almost immoral to want to clarify their own feelings. Every analyst is familiar with similar situations that occur on the couch. In the intensity of the group scene, they are much more evident.

In the beginning it is difficult for some members of the group as protagonists to patiently wait until the fitting gesture, the right tone, the precise word, or proper pose is actually found. Once it has been found, the protagonist usually displays reactions of relief and gratitude. This is a well-known phenomenon to the therapist, who senses that he is on the right track with his interpretation. The interpretation becomes fully acceptable to the patient only after he has re-peatedly re-phrased it, either expanded or reduced it, and made it more exact. I never thought it possible that such precision work could be accomplished through the staging of previously experienced, feared, or hoped for reactions. Most protagonists are ready to give up or are satisfied with vague approximations, because they have never had the experience of being empathically asked about their exact unknown feelings and wishes. It is, therefore, a tremendous relief for all participants when the tension is broken, after the exact form of the solution has been found and the long search is rewarded. The reaction is similar to that in children, who have lost their way and have been found again after a long search. Of course, the reaction to being perceived exactly as one is and finding the precise solution to a long unanswered question is very similar to a state of shock. It is enough to take one's breath away in amazement and joy, but also in fear that the forthcoming emotions cannot be brought under control. Should it become obvious that anxiety to being "found" is present, then the therapist may reduce the pace or discuss again with the protagonist just how far he wants to go.

In sum, PS/P avoids the risks of some expressive therapies in that individuation is treated as a gradual process, with the important contribution of defenses respected. Selected negative aspects are addressed without jeopardizing needed self objects. Primal energy is contained and channelled back into relationships. The whole object is never destroyed; the ideal parents remain as a secure base for individuation. Lastly, even in regressive work, the pilot of the protagonist remains active in determining the pace and depth of the work.

Advantages of PS/P and Psychoanalysis

Psychoanalytic research is studying ever more complicated disturbances in the protected setting of the dyadic relationship; the sensitivity to transference and counter-transference problems has been refined even in areas that long seemed unattainable within the setting. Concurrently, the more dramatic techniques are developing with the possibility of very rapidly approaching the main conflict through intensive focusing. Each setting has its merits and dangers. In the extreme, an analysis may bring to light increasingly subtle insights without bringing about change. Or, possibly, the therapeutic contract might degenerate to a long lasting folie-a-deux. PS/P offers the element of intensity and drama that leads to quick movement. An important conviction, won in my work with Psychomotor, is that it is considerably easier to find the correct level of the conflict with accommodation than in analysis, due to the integration of body phenomena and the mutual efforts of therapist, patient, and the group as a whole in the progressive work on the structure. In analysis it is only too easy to choose the wrong level of interpretation with a patient with a weakened ego. In accommodation there are so many more criteria in determining the correctness. A patient who has, in analysis, gone through phases of interpretive work which were on the wrong level, experiencing quiet despair, unnecessary rebellion, confusion, or a loss of the self, will certainly appreciate this. The same is, of course, true for the therapist who, in his work with patients, has experienced the drudgery of a dialogue on the wrong plane. A structure could give stagnating analyses new clarity.

Nevertheless, in many cases the analytic couch cure will probably remain the only way to work through deep-seated psychological disturbances. I have not been able to set a precise indication, although my intuitive choice would be analysis in those cases in which extended periods of safe regression and sufficient strengthening of the ego are necessary. It may be similar in cases of deeply rooted character deviation, which require extensive time in reaching a solution. In all probability, analysis is the therapy of choice when an abandonment syndrome requires the slow and steady process of becoming "reattached" to the object. Still, I am convinced that PS/P work encourages most effectively the patient's own self-healing qualities. It seems much easier to break through the shell of ego syntonic neurotic behavior in the group. The structure enables a swift portrayal of the self, exposing the character deformity in one or a series of scenes.

It has not been my intention here to evaluate, compare, or consider these therapy forms as rivals. PS/P and psychoanalysis make use of similarly perceived and diagnosed material, which is then implemented technically in very different ways.

The Pessos' method can be employed for long-term treatment as well as for a brief focusing on difficult conflict situations. The main emphasis in the training seminars lies on the use of the group to achieve emotionally strong and diagnostically valid evidence. PS/P especially emphasizes the useful possibilities of internalization, an implanting of the new experience, so that it may function similarly to time-release pills, having a guiding effect on further development. The experienced conflict, like the new beginning, is directed toward both the emotional and eidetic memory. The emotional evidence remains sheltered in the visual experience of the unconscious.

It is not contradictory to be either in therapy or analysis and, at the same time, a participant in the structure group — quite the contrary. This raises the possibility of combining therapeutic methods, resulting in an enrichment in the therapeutic work.

The attempt to lead the patient in separate scenes toward the ideal object from which he can learn what he would have needed in those moments or phases of despair when he was a child, encourages the growth of lost empathy for himself. This model can be found in role-playing as well as in individual analysis on the couch. The standard question amenable to many variations is: "What, in your opinion, would you have needed then?" This leads to the fantasy of alternatives, to an image of the self as a child who at least belatedly is allowed to feel what was missing then. Once this has been made sufficiently clear, then the question on the actual transference level may be: "What do you now need from me, when you are re-experiencing all of this once more?" The patient can give the analyst important information about what sort of inner position he should take. He might also say: "I cannot even feel, much less describe, what I need." And the therapist may, thereby, draw the conclusion: "The patient is timid, so far from his real needs, so far away from the ability to wish, because he could only survive by giving up his wishing and empathic fantasizing and because he has forgotten about what is good for himself." At the center of the lost ability to wish may be clearly seen the common search for the lost self or for important parts of it. It requires some fantasy on the part of the therapist to imagine the inner life of the patient (particularly if the disturbance is an early one) as a stage on which a chaotic troupe of actors, unearthly shapes, and archaic monsters stagger on unsteady ground; and the patient is standing frightened in the corner, or makes a pact with a monster, or feels himself being shoved back and forth between shapes and figures which he must learn to direct. It is not always advisable for the analyst to wait until all threatening and enticing figures take shape in the transference, because often he, as a companion, has been lost in some frightened way by that time.

Conclusion

I have felt a growth in identity, due to the alleviation of tension between the two poles in me: classical analysis and the dramatic new forms of therapy. My psychoanalytic identity has deepened and my delight in enacting the unconscious, with the additional inclusion of the body in the work, has found its analytical basis and legitimation. PS/P has built the long sought for bridge between the wild richness of the newer forms of therapy and the mainstream of psychoanalytic research. I can remain an analyst and need not close my mind to the new.

References

Pesso, A. (1969). *Movement in psychotherapy*. New York: New York University Press.

Pesso, A. (1973). *Experience in action*. New York: New York University Press.

Chapter 12

PS/P and Bioenergetic Analysis

Judith E. Barnitt

One of the most beautiful sights to behold is the human body when it is lively and vibrant, moves with grace, and expresses a full range of movement and emotion. Two therapies which promote such beauty are PS/P and Bioenergetic Analysis. While these two therapies were created from different thought systems, there are some links that make them cousins in significant ways.

The focus on the body is the main link between the two psychotherapeutic modalities. Much of traditional psychotherapy focuses on the thought processes of clients and ignores the body as a way into the deepest unconscious. Fritjof Capra, in his book *The Turning Point* (1982), focuses attention on how Cartesian thought has influenced treatment. He discusses Descartes' notions that call for the separation of the mind from the body. In doing this, Descartes set the stage for modern Western thought which sets a higher value on mental rather than physical work and recognizes no relationship between the illnesses of the body and the owner's mental/emotional state.

Bioenergetic Analysis and Psychomotor focus on restoring the aliveness of the organism — the movement from the fear of life to the enjoyment of it. Each system teaches that the body and the human mental processes deeply affect one another. Indeed, they are intimately joined. One cannot just free-up the body and its energy and then expect to have a joyful life. Both aspects must be considered in successful treatment. So it is that, hopefully, the body map and the cognitive map become one in the processes of both Bioenergetic Analysis and PS/P. Such unification is the soul of the work.

Overview of Bioenergetics — History and Theory

History: The roots of Bioenergetic Analysis lie deep in the work of Sigmund Freud, with a branching from that body of knowledge, through the work of Wilhelm Reich.

Reich, a graduate of the University of Vienna in 1922 with an MD degree, was an Austrian by birth (1897). When Freud's Psychoanalytic Clinic began its work in Vienna in 1922, Reich became a clinical assistant. He continued this until 1928. During that time he conducted seminars, lecturing on clinical subjects and biopsychiatric theory. He contributed to the literature of psychotherapeutic work by publishing articles and books on the subject. His main interests began developing in the areas of sexology as it relates to neuropsychology and in the notions of characterology.

He developed a system of understanding body armoring and the relationship of that armoring to neurotic functioning. It is out of this study that much of the work of Bioenergetic Analysis proceeds.

> Reich was the first psychoanalyst to formulate a coherent theory of character. He showed that the different character traits were dependent one upon the other, and that taken together they formed a unitary defense against all emotions that were felt to be dangerous in one way or the other. This defense Reich called the character armor. Reich was able to show that this armor had its origin in situations in childhood where the child had been denied satisfaction of some instinctual drive, and that the energy of such a drive had been split up in a way that made one part of it hold the other part in suppression. (Raknes, 1970, p. 21)

He further developed his ideas to include direct work — body manipulation — to loosen the chronically held muscle tensions. As these systems were loosened, memories and emotions were brought to the consciousness of the patient and thus events and emotional scars that were totally repressed were available both to the client and therapist for the process of working through. As these chronic tensions were released, Reich discovered that there were feelings of streamings (a flow of energy in contrast to a feeling of tension) that could be felt as either pleasurable or more anxiety-producing.

> ....when a patient had become conscious of an attitude or manner of behavior, he would often change it, sometimes momentarily, and present a new facade, as it were. When he was made aware of this new attitude, he would change it again for another, or sometimes revert to his former attitude. It was as if the character consisted of inter-changeable layers, or as if it were a fortress with several lines of defense, one behind the other working directly on the tensions would eventually liberate the repressed emotional energies, which also manifested themselves in the "vegetative streamings" (Raknes, pp. 24-25).

As he continued in the pursuit of character analytic body work, Reich also formulated another hypothesis which was a driving force in his material:

> a healthy sex life depends on a complete, convulsive discharge of sexual energy in the embrace of a beloved partner of the opposite sex, with momentary loss of consciousness. The capacity for such an experience Reich termed orgastic potency, which thus became a criterion of mental health (Raknes, p. 27).

Reich, a penultimately curious and inventive being, continued his work and explorations. He wrote, taught, lectured, and continually explored the connection between the physical and the psychological. His work was not always well accepted and he was often persecuted for his beliefs. He died in a federal prison in Pennsylvania in 1957.

One of the people who was deeply affected by Reich was Alexander Lowen. Lowen studied with him from 1940 until 1953. From 1942 to 1945, Reich was Lowen's analyst. It was out of this close association, and his own interest in influencing mental attitudes by working with the body, that Lowen developed the material that is now known as Bioenergetics. Two others worked with Lowen to create the Bioenergetic Institute in New York: Alice Ladas and John Pierrakos.

Lowen is a prolific writer and to this day continues to add to the literature on Bioenergetic Analysis with books and articles. He, and the others who formed the Institute, spoke in public meetings and created a clinical seminar where the work was performed on willing participants for the purpose of teaching and discussing the various techniques and understandings of the psychology of the body. Over time, a faculty was formed and training programs were begun around the country and in Europe. Also over time, there have been differences of opinion in the New York Institute, and other branches of the work have formed with different philosophies which also address the body as the central theme in psychotherapy.

Lowen, in his very pragmatic way of thinking, moved the clients from the couch, in prone positions, to standing on their feet. His thought was that the clients must be able to leave the therapeutic session and stand on their own two feet out in the world. He developed the concept of grounding — the reality concept — so that the clients could immediately begin to deal with the world in a new and more profound way. This movement of the client from a prone position to an upright position of personal command signals a change of philosophy from the dependency of the client on an authoritarian figure to a position of power and self-regulation.

With Lowen as its continuing leader, the Bioenergetic movement, in all of its multiplicity of presentation, continues to grow and flourish as a dynamic form of psychotherapy.

Theoretical Considerations: Bioenergetics places the focus of therapy on the body as an externalization of an internal map. Historical events and the person's response to those events have caused the body to form in certain ways. The person lives his body in these response patterns. There is not only a physical formation in response to external events, but there is also a belief system and a behavioral pattern that become a fixed part of the expression of that life. As psychoanalytic theory and Reichian theory developed, Character Analysis was created to help the therapist understand the problem of the client.

The underlying belief system that is basic to understanding the theory of Bioenergetics is easily stated: The personality is understood in terms of the body and its energetic processes. The processes that are addressed are respiration, which fuels metabolism to produce energy for the life journey, and movement, which expresses the responses one has to the environment.

Bioenergetic Therapy is, therefore, a process of working with both the mind and the body to help people resolve their emotional problems. The hoped for outcome of such work is to be able to live fully and pleasurably in the world, responding in a present-time modality to events in the environment, and resolution of past history that might bind a person in old patterns. The body work that constitutes Bioenergetic Analysis consists of certain kinds of exercises that help the body give up its tensions and chronic holding patterns (Lowen & Lowen, 1977). The therapist also employs some techniques of touching that help muscles soften and give way to ease of movement. Increasing respiration is a key element which allows certain holding patterns to change.

In order to help the reader understand a bit about the structure of thought and theory in Bioenergetics, the following sections are offered with the understanding that these are only brief delineations of character and represent only a very small portion of material that is available. If you are interested in further information, please read *Bioenergetics* by Alexander Lowen, M.D. (1975).

Schizoid Structure

Schizoid individuals tend to deal with the world by withdrawing into themselves. There is a breaking of contact with the environment and those in it. Contact with the body is weak, almost anesthetized. The essential aliveness of these individuals is frozen at the core of being.

The external map presented by a schizoid person is one that looks fragmented. The parts don't seem to fit together. There will be a rigidity on the outside that functions to hold the person together. The face of the individual may seem mask-like with no energy in the eyes.

The etiology of the problem is very early. There may have been some sort of disruption in care-taking, a rejection by the primary caretaker, or external social events (eg., war) that have made survival doubtful. It is also possible that some life threatening events occurred prior to and during the birth process. A history of the person will reveal a lack of strong positive feelings of security or joy. Night terrors would be a common complaint.

The behavior that is noticeable with this kind of problem is that of withdrawal: little social contact, inability to make and maintain intimate relationships, and a penchant for living out of the individual's head or wits, rather than as an embodied being.

The belief that is usually strongest is that if a need for closeness is expressed or sought, existence will be threatened.

Oral Character Structure

The pattern of orality is understood as a problem with its focus during the developmental period known as infancy. Those personalities that have this issue as central will find that being in the world is particularly trying. They will find themselves being unable to be alone, in need of a lot of support from the environment, and have difficulty in standing on their own two feet. Independence is an issue since the core belief is that if one exhibits independence, then needed warmth and support will be forfeited.

Early deprivation is the force that has formed the body and the personality of an orally focused person. Perhaps the primary care-giver was not able to supply the infant with enough food, attention, or body contact. Perhaps the environment was one of poverty of stimulation. The result of such deprivation is often a deep sadness, sometimes depression, and unexpressed grief.

Energetically, the bodily expression will be one of underdevelopment. The musculature will seem young and child like, and the whole system will be undercharged. Breathing will be shallow and the chest will be collapsed. The legs and feet will look weak and not able to support or move the person out into the world in a forthright and aggressive manner.

Psychologically, oral people are rather passive and wait for the world to supply what they need — but with little hope that that will happen. The ability to reach out and supply their own needs has not been developed. Friendships are formed so that other people can take care of them in the hope that all needs will be met without effort. There is a pervading sense of inner emptiness which masks the intense longing that underlies all areas of life. Mood swings are a hallmark of this problem. The answer to all issues is "out there."

The key to understanding this character structure is the conflict of need versus independence: "I can express my neediness so long as I am not independent."

Psychopathic Structure

This character strategy is one that is developed between the ages of two and four. It is during this time that the normal pattern of development confronts issues of autonomy. To successfully negotiate this developmental stage, children need to be allowed to experiment with becoming their own people. They need support of parenting figures to do this, both in modeling of behavior and in the provision of a safe environment for such experimentation. What these children learn during this period is that mother cannot allow differentiation nor can she set aside her own needs to provide safety for them. Father is absent or not emotionally available to the children. Out of this, they learn to manipulate and deceive in order to get what is needed. They learn to deny their own feelings and to conceal any signs of weakness or vulnerability. They learn that in order to survive in this family an acceptable image must be presented. These children learn to become powerful, but in a way that is without feeling.

With all of the maneuvering children must achieve in this stage, the head area of the body becomes overcharged and sometimes will be larger than the body shape and size would indicate. The two halves of the body are disproportionate in development. The upper half is more fully developed and energetically charged, while the lower half is less well developed and undercharged. The eyes are particularly telling, as they are distrustful and ever watchful.

Psychologically, psychopaths must control: others and their environment. This is done without feeling and without any understanding of the feelings of others or the implications to others of their actions. They are masters of the power play. They maneuver others so that they will need them and then their own needs will not have to be expressed. The expression of need would feel devastatingly vulnerable. Rather than allow that, psychopaths out-power or subtly seduce those in their environment into subservience.

The core belief here is: "I can be close to you if I can control you."

Masochistic Character Structure

This character structure is also formed during the time when children are learning to develop independence and autonomy. The moves that they make toward assertion are squashed by the adults in parenting roles. The family configuration that is present here is one of loving, affectionate closeness, with everything the children need being supplied — sometimes, too well supplied. There is an over-protective quality to their care, here.

The damaging process is one of loving too well. The children learn that in order to survive they must please the parenting figures and live up to their expectations. Every area of the childrens' life and development is under close surveillance by surrounding adults. Privacy is non-existent for these children and their experience is one of control by guilt and "sweet" coercion. The only acceptable way of being in the family is to comply with expectations and not express any negative feelings. Expression of anger is not allowed. There is no way that they can take charge of their own lives. Resistance becomes the primary strategy of life. When an opportunity to move out and become autonomous beings presents itself, there is tremendous internal resistance. This character development, then, is one of being stuck.

The energetic presentation of these psychological components is one of closely held energy. There is no lack of energy in the masochist. There is an inability to act and express the energy. The bodily expression, therefore, is heavily muscular and dense. The deep muscles are in a tense state; movement is solid and heavy.

On the psychological level, masochists are compliant, non-assertive, and often passive aggressive. There is a sense of held in anger and profound defeat. Whining and complaining are the forte of this character, as well as spite and joylessness. Life is lived in a morass with little spontaneity and expressed excitement.

The core belief here is: "if I am close to you, I cannot be free."

Rigid Chatacter Structure

The rigid structure is developed around the problem of the Oedipal resolution. Having negotiated the vicissitudes of childhood development, children arrive at the time when they fall in love with, and have erotic feelings for, the parents of the opposite sex. How this love is received and returned helps to develop the rigid structure. The natural proclivity is to reach out to those around them, to give and receive love and affection. When these loving impulses are met with an openness and freedom, the children develop a sense of self and are secure in their sexuality. However, if the parents of the opposite sex do not receive this reaching appropriately and the parents of the same sex do not provide approval, appropriate modeling, and protection during this very vulnerable period, the children do not trust the sexual impulses. They experience a broken heart and rigidify the body in order to deal with the feelings.

While this period has as its focus the Oedipal stage, the creation of the rigid structure spans many years. During this period of time, children seek answers to questions about how to be in the world. The parenting figures and other significant adults teach them by example how to be achievers and be accepted. Maleness and femaleness is learned in more than just the sexual arena. If the children reach out and find that such vulnerability gets the response that injures, then there will be a holding back of such impulses and the body will create itself around such holding.

The body of the rigid structure is well formed, energetic, with a certain grace of movement. There is a freedom to move in the world that the other structures do not have. There is an air of success — of stressed success; there is an air of *having* to achieve instead of achieving because it is pleasurable. Competition is a way of being in the world with very little time to enjoy "smelling the roses."

The core belief that functions here has to do with being free, if the head rules the heart and the children do not surrender to loving feelings.

A skilled Bioenergetic Analyst can read the body by seeing the areas of holding as well as interpret the movement of the body while it is in motion. The amount of information the analyst can obtain through this procedure is quite phenomenal. The first time one experiences such a reading by an accomplished professional, it seems like magic. However, with a thorough understanding of character issues and a keen eye and ear, the analyst puts many clues together that are accurate readings of the map.

It must also be noted that very few people are "pure" character structures. This material provides a way of thinking about and understanding the relationship of the formation of the bodily presence and the psychological and spiritual development of the human being.

Bioenergetics and PS/P

To compare Bioenergetic Analysis and PS/P is like comparing apples and oranges. They are both fruit, but with different textures and flavors. Both are body-oriented psychotherapies, but are quite different in approach and philosophy.

The formula for therapy that is the key to successful PS/P work is known as the *cycle of becoming* : *Energy->Action->Interaction->Significance/Internalization*. This concise formula, used in the context of a participative group where roles are played to enhance the experience, is quite different than the one-to-one way of doing therapy that is the usual pattern for Bioenergetics.

In PS/P, a new *map* is created for the client with the role playing figures, giving the client a way of restructuring history and reforming the psyche around old wounds. The support of the group in that process of restructuring is quite different from the support received by the Bioenergetic client in a one-on-one session. The support comes from the earth, from the interaction with the therapist, and from the new feeling of aliveness in the client's own body.

Pesso has also developed some excellent material around the issue of abuse that adds to the understanding of the process of what happens to the body and what needs to be attended to in the healing of the wound. (Please see Chapter 14 for more information.) This is an area that is still being developed in Bioenergetic Analysis.

Psychomotor pays a great deal of attention to the physical movements that the clients make during the structure time and the significance of each movement is noted and included in the work. For instance, any movement to stroke themselves is replaced with a figure to do the stroking for them and give them the satisfaction that is wanted. In Bioenergetics, attention is directed also to movement, or lack of it, in the clients' bodies, as well as to their posture, holding patterns, tones of voice, and breathing patterns. The therapists help the clients to experience these patterns in a conscious way and then provide options that release those deeply held contractions through physical movement, massage, deepened respiration, vocal sounding, and body manipulation.

Satisfaction is a key word in both therapies. Although the techniques for achieving this state are quite different, the theoretical base is much the same. Both therapies seek to discover and restructure areas in the deep psyche that are unfulfilled. Satisfying these primal needs changes the clients' experiences of every day life and produces happier, healthier individuals. Both Bioenergetics and PS/P address these needs in a physical as well a psychological way.

The basic tools of PS/P therapists are the group energy and the touching, holding, and interaction provided by the group setting. Bioenergetic Therapists use their own energy and body, as well as other physical tools. A couch or bed is used for hitting and kicking as well as for certain kinds of breathing exercises. The Bioenergetic stool, invented by Alexander Lowen, is used to open breathing by extending the body over it. The tennis racquet, or other tools, are employed for the expression of anger and assertiveness. A mirror is sometimes utilized to see the response to emotion in the face or body. A large dowel is used for stretching and to use on the bottoms of the feet to help with grounding. A towel is a handy substitute for a hated person and can be used for biting and twisting.

One of the dangers in doing direct body work in Bioenergetic Analysis is that of transference and counter transference issues between clients and therapists. Touching a client magnifies the transference issues ten-fold. We still don't understand all of the ramifications of touch. It is exceedingly powerful. One psychological study shows that when people are physically touched, they are much more likely to carry out a request than when not touched. So, in therapy where touching is part of the work, clients can give away their power much more easily to the therapist than in therapy where a physical distance is maintained. The PS/P work also has the dangers of transference. However, since the therapists do not touch directly, the issues are somewhat less charged.

Further, the possibility of countertransference is handled in PS/P by the period at the end of the structure when there is a time for sharing of feelings and process by both group participants and therapist. This does not mean that there is no transference or counter-transference in PS/P, it means that there is less opportunity for such to develop.

There is an advantage in the therapist being trained in both Psychomotor and Bioenergetic Analysis. Bioenergetic Analysts can read the body and have a great deal of information about the clients' world view and how they interact with it. When working in the PS/P modality, Bioenergetic Analysts are able to catch on to the clients' situations quickly and, with additional information about character structures, can provide a more direct approach to the problem. With the knowledge of the kind of release that Bioenergetic Analysis provides, along with the techniques of PS/P, clients are well served in moving through issues as quickly as their psyches and structures will allow. PS/P attends to the re-parenting process in a very unique and powerful way. This could be adapted into Bioenergetic Analysis to enhance integration of material revealed in body work and provide a new cognitive map.

Cases

It is difficult to compare these two psychotherapies adequately and, rather than just talk about theory, I'd like to present two cases that are similar in content, but one in which I used Bioenergetics alone as the primary mode and one in which I used both Psychomotor and Bioenergetics.

Conrad, a young man of thirty-two when he presented himself for therapy, arrived in my office because of a depression which seemed to have been an ongoing part of his life. From earliest time, he remembers having to struggle to have enough energy to do the things that he wanted to do. He could not remember a time when he did not have a sleep problem, and he had always felt that there was a dark cloud hanging about his head. There was never enough of anything. and in his life, he was always feeling abandoned.

He looked in some ways like an infant. His musculature was under-developed and slight, his legs looked weak and his feet were long and narrow. In fact, his body had a long, narrow look, with slumping shoulders and a rather lost look on his face. His chest was collapsed and his breathing shallow.

His history was classic, in terms of the diagnosis of oral character structure. His mother became ill about two months after he was born, and family life was a struggle. His father tried to provide the food and nurturing that were necessary, but was over-burdened with a hospitalized wife, a young infant, and a job. He had people take care of young Conrad, but the care was certainly not of the caliber of that which had been provided by his wife. The child entered a time of malaise and had feeding problems. When his mother did return home, she did not have the energy she needed to cope with a growing child. He received enough food, but his parents were not able to give him the emotional closeness and caring that he needed to thrive. Another child was conceived and delivered when Conrad was four, and he had to share the meager parenting that was available with another child.

During therapy, we worked with the inner emptiness that characterized his life. Our first line of attack was to increase the depth and quality of his ability to breathe. Work was slow, but after a while, Conrad reported that he could feel more fullness in his life and more ability to take in that which was offered to him. We also worked with his grounding, using Bioenergetic exercises and encouraging him to develop an exercise regime that included plenty of walking and contact with the earth. Reaching with hands, eyes, and lips helped him to develop a sense of power in being able to get that which he wanted.

During this time, Conrad developed a support system outside of the therapeutic hour. At first he had problems with being too dependent, both on his therapist and others around him. Gradually, with grounding work and breathing work, he developed a sense of independence.

His physical body also changed. He became more developed in terms of musculature and lost the look of neediness that had characterized him. He developed a significant relationship that was sexually and emotionally satisfying. He found work that supported him both financially and creatively.

After three years of therapy, he took time off to integrate what he had accomplished and enjoy the new-found energy that had allowed him to move ahead in his life in fulfilling and joyful ways.

The second case is similar in nature. Karen was a forty-two-year-old married woman when she arrived in my office for therapy. She was in the middle of a life crisis which centered on problems in her marriage. She was a traditional housewife, raising two teen-aged sons with a husband who was beginning to look elsewhere for female companionship. She had always had a problem with lack of energy and had felt depressed most of her life. Her whining voice characterized her communication. She was bordering on being obese and food was used to fill her up so that she did not have to feel her emotional deprivation. Her feet and legs were spindly and did not look as though they could carry the weight of her body. Her overall appearance was that of a lost child.

She came from a very large rural family: the youngest of eight children. Her mother and father were overburdened with trying to provide for this family on a farm that was of poor quality. Her father was an alcoholic and had a ferocious temper. He often physically abused the children and Karen was no exception to the rule. Her mother was typically codependent and tried her best to keep the family together, but was not able to do so.

We began to treat Karen with Bioenergetic body work. She developed her grounding and increased her breathing capacity. During this, her considerable rage at her father and mother began to surface in desires to bite and tear with her teeth. During this stage of her therapy, she had the opportunity of attending a group that was engaged in Psychomotor. The first work that she did was to develop *ideal parents* who could give her the time and love that she needed without competition from the other children in the family or the prodigious work load that characterized her family of origin. This development of ideal parents had a profound effect on Karen. Her self-esteem improved and she began to care about her appearance. She lost some of the needy look.

Other group sessions focused on her rage at God for having placed her in such a family. She was able to develop a new God figure that was one of love and compassion. She lost her biting sarcasm and need to chew on food or other people. During this time, she also developed a sense of her own ground by seeing how she depended, first on her father, then on her husband, currently on her two sons, for her grounding. They were there, in her belief system, to take care of her. As her ideal parenting continued, she gained the confidence that she needed to ground herself and take care of her own needs. Out of this work, she went back to school and developed a career of her own.

The family dynamics changed dramatically during this work. Her husband decided to do some therapy for himself and made some necessary changes that brought their marriage into a much more stable place. As Karen became more independent, he was able to see her in a different way, and was more able to support her growth and development.

In my opinion, Psychomotor work (6 sessions), in conjunction with the Bioenergetic work, provided a support system for growth and moved Karen along more swiftly. She left therapy with no depression evident, with a new lease on life, and a marriage that was thriving. The time frame for this therapy was two years.

Conclusion

Since my main modality of work is Bioenergetics, I am most impressed with the way in which PS/P and Bioenergetics complement one another. PS/P seems to provide a nurturing framework for the direct body work that is dynamic and powerful. Each has strengths and weaknesses, but the combination of work moves people through their issues rapidly and deeply.

References

Capra, F. (1982). *The turning point*. New York: Simon & Schuster.

Lowen, A. (1975). *Bioenergetics*. New York: Coward, McCann & Geoghegan, Inc.

Lowen, A., & Lowen, L. (1977). *The way to vibrant health*. New York: Harper & Row.

Raknes, O. (1970). *Wilhelm Reich and orgonomy*. Baltimore: Pelican Books.

Chapter 13

Hypnotic Process and PS/P:

Similarities and Differences

by Glenn Shean

PS/P attempts to provide an interpersonal context in which participants can release emotions long suppressed and symbolically experience meeting needs that often date back to early childhood. This is accomplished through the collaborative creation of *structures* organized to provide a symbolic interpersonal context conducive to healing/transforming experiences. In this sense PS/P is in the tradition of interpersonal/dynamic therapy rather than more directive approaches usually associated with the use of hypnosis. PS/P does not rely on trance induction or indirect suggestion to bring about change, although participants often do experience aspects of their structure work in a special state of consciousness.

There are several differences between the process of PS/P and directive hypnotic approaches such as Ericksonian Hypnotherapy; these differences, however, are matters of degree rather than kind. One important difference is that there is no intent on the part of the PS/P therapist to induce trance, or to present indirect suggestions for change or paradox. Participants in Psychomotor initiate and select the content of their structures with the assistance of interpretations from the leader, and are ultimately responsible for the process and content of their structures. During structure work bodily sensations, when allowed expression, often result in the recollection of feelings and images that arise out of each person's history. The PS/P therapist acts as a guide and choreographer, within the guidelines of a well defined theoretical structure, for the expression of these emotions/actions and the provision of symbolic healing experiences in an interactive context.

The leader facilitates and helps to choreograph — but does not select — each person's experience of symbolically real settings in order to bring about future change and growth. Participants create their own symbolic drama, with assistance from the therapist, down to the precise placement of *accommodators* in the room as well as their exact words and responses in each situation. The nature and sequence of recollections, as well as the content of the transforming experiences, are the responsibility of the participants; the therapist helps to interpret and guide rather than actively direct the process.

Psychomotor is not a set of strategies designed to directly or indirectly remove symptoms, although this often occurs. Nor is it primarily a form of dyadic therapeutic communication (Gindhart, 1985). There are, however, parallels between the goals of PS/P and Ericksonian Hypnotherapy, as apparent in C. Lankton's description of Ericksonian hypnosis as favoring, "a retrieval and association of experience to help the person continue moving within the developmental continuum, with an understanding that the symptom will fade when more appropriate adjustment is made" (1985, p. 164). This paper discusses some parallels and differences which exist between the two approaches.

The public tends to equate hypnosis with somnambulism, sleep, or trance. Definitions of hypnosis provided by professionals, however, provide substantially broader understandings of this process. Hilgard (1977), for example, regards hypnosis as an altered state of consciousness in which people evidence enhanced capacity for "suggestibility" or "acceptivity". Brown and Fromm describe hypnosis as "a special state of consciousness in which certain normal human capabilities are heightened while others fade into the background" (1986, p. 3). Others, in the Ericksonian tradition, tend to dispense with the notion that hypnosis necessarily requires any altered state of consciousness, and accept Haley's view that hypnotic interaction is simply "an example of the powerful influence one person may have upon another if both cooperate fully" (1976, p.10). Erickson's own description of hypnosis was simply: "hypnosis is the evocation and utilization of unconscious learnings" (Rosen, 1982, p. 28). His view of therapy was, " First you model the patient's world, and then you role-model the patient's world" (Rosen, 1982, p. 35).

These statements suggest an important difference between the two approaches in that PS/P relies more heavily on multiple symbolic interactions in a group context, both cathartic and healing, with a focus on past experiences and their influences on present interactions. The hypnotic process does, however, include elements that are similar to experiences of participants in PS/P structures. Kohn (1984) described hypnosis as involving: 1. a narrowing of attention whereby the person pays less attention to the surroundings or possible distractions and more attention to the events or attitudes under consideration, as though a mental search-light were directed from place to place as needed; 2. the person is more relaxed; 3. there is a temporary relinquishing of some critical attitudes; 4. there is enhanced ability to control many involuntary physiological responses; and 5. there is enhanced ability to express repressed or dissociated material as well as to retrieve memories. Brown and Fromm (1986) have also observed that: 1. hypnotic subjects are less attentive to their surroundings and are instead absorbed in their own imagery and content given in suggestions; 2. information is processed in ways different from those in the waking state so that it is processed more slowly but with greater accuracy and interest, so that phenomena are experienced in new ways; 3. events are not processed in an organized, sequential manner or organized chronologically; 4. the subjective sense of time is altered; and 5. there is a partial inhibition of the ordinary cognitive structures involved in information processing so that vivid memories occur as if they were happening in the present. Each of the alterations of experience described above are also common aspects of the experiences of PS/P participants during structure work.

Hilgard (1968, 1977) has formulated a "Neo-Dissociation model" to account for the effects of hypnosis as well as other dissociative phenomena. In his view, dissociation is an extension of normal cognitive functioning, as evidenced by the fact that the capacity for dissociation is normally distributed in the general population. Information, according to Hilgard's model, is processed by an "Executive Ego" system which monitors and exerts executive control over a complex hierarchical array of cognitive/emotional sub-systems. Ordinarily these sub-systems operate in an integrated fashion with the executive system initiating and monitoring the activity of any given sub-system. Sub-systems associated with particularly painful memories or anxiety-inducing impulses/experiences may, because of their painful associations, function with varying degrees of autonomy from the executive and monitoring functions of the executive system. Hypnosis, according to the Neo-Dissociation model, works through an interpersonal process by which the hypnotist is allowed to assume some of the executive and monitoring functions of the executive system. As a result of this interaction with the hypnotist, the subjective experience of intentionality is diminished, executive monitoring of subsystems is fractionated and/or relinquished to the hypnotist, and dissociated content associated with selected subsystems is allowed expression with diminished executive control and monitoring. Hilgard (1978) refers to his model as a Neo-Dissociation theory because evidence suggests that some cognitive systems, even though not represented in consciousness at the time, continue to register and process information, and when such a system is released from inhibition it uses this information as if it had been conscious all along.

The experiences of structure participants often parallel the alterations of experience described as resulting from relaxation of executive ego functions as described in the Neo-Dissociation model. For example, vivid memories are often recovered of experiences of which the individual was completely unaware, powerful impulses and desires are experienced that would ordinarily seem alien, ridiculous, and/or embarrassing. Participants report powerful effects from structure experiences which they cannot remember or have only the vaguest memories of, and time in the ordinary chronological experience is often dramatically transformed during and immediately following structure work. In Neo-Dissociation terms an important aspect of PS/P is to facilitate the integration of unconscious emotions and memories into the executive ego system, and much of the content of structures includes the recovery and working through of dissociated material.

The structure leader in PS/P does not take over the executive ego functions — known in Psychomotor as the *pilot* — but rather helps to bring dissociated process under the aegis of the pilot. This reinforces the client's ownership of personal history and experience. Done correctly, there should be a clear memory of all experiences within a structure. Like the hypnotherapist, the PS/P structure leader seeks to foster integration.

Unlike Kohn's (1984) description of relaxation as a frequent end-goal of hypnotic induction, the experiences of Psychomotor participants are often intense and consonant with the thematic content they are experiencing. Participants having sensations of bodily tension or elemental feelings are encouraged to intensify their experiences by tightening muscles, making sounds, or moving so that these basic experiences are encouraged to follow the basic formula of energy->action->interaction (the *cycle of becoming*). PS/P participants are often highly energized during cathartic and limit structures, and blissfully relaxed during symbolic healing interactions. The following excerpt illustrates the experience of intense focus, reduced attention to distractions, enhanced imagery, and relaxation that may be experienced during a structure:

> Next I was on my back on the floor and remembering my early, early boyhood. Lying on the floor listening to music and watching the trees swaying in the wind and the grassy earth on which I was lying was heaving under me. I was rocking on the crest of a firm but gentle wave.

The structure experience is also characterized by periods of relaxation of the critical/monitoring attitude; this is perhaps one of the mechanisms by which symbolic healing experiences can be integrated into the adult ego as symbolically real and growth inducing.

One participant, for example, described his structure as follows: "I saw myself curled up inside my mother's womb with my genitals clearly visible. The *ideal mother* confirmed them by touch, saying that she wanted a boy and liked my being a boy." A second excerpt illustrates both suspension of the critical attitude and time distortion that may occur during structures:

> The sequence was that I stated to my parents what I would like, then I got on my hands and knees and crawled around on all fours. They exclaimed what a wonderful baby I was, how wonderfully I was crawling, how skillful I was and in general were very approving, accepting, admiring. The structure did not seem to last long , 5-10 minutes. I remember feeling very proud of myself, successful, and that what I had done gave me joy to do and it won approval from my parents. I remember feeling the warmth of their attention and feeling that I had made them happy just by being.

Brown and Fromm (1986) have attributed the recall of vivid memories experienced as if they were happening in the present to the hypnotic process. Psychomotor participants describe their experiences in similar fashion:

> 1. I was three years of age. I recalled the taking away of my father by the Germans. I experienced the farewells; also the feelings of hatred toward the soldiers.

> 2. I'm not sure what my goal was, seemed like I wanted to work on not always being afraid of other people and this seemed to lead into an operation when I was 3 years old and not being able to get away.

> 3. The first structure dealt with my older brother's death. For years I had never processed the grief and a part of my soul had left with him. The neighborhood we shared in childhood was role-played as I experienced a revisit. A male was chosen to role play my brother as I talked about many of the experiences we shared in childhood. During this structure I had the opportunity to say goodbye.

> 4. Pesso asked me to stand up with some kind of penis symbol between my legs... I don't remember how much time went by before I had the courage to rise. I was so ashamed! Don't be such a silly bitch I said to myself. You really don't have one you only play it. But that did not work, when I arose it was bloody serious.

> 5. I was getting in touch with dangerous feelings in relationship to my dad (from a five year old perspective) and blacked out.

Several of the examples provided above illustrate participants enhanced ability to express dissociated material and to retrieve lost or forgotten memories during structure work. This enhanced ability is also illustrated in the following example:

> I started focusing back on the pregnancy and my husband's claiming it was my fault. Al asked me how I felt about that and I said "shattered". He then asked me who else had shattered me and suddenly I replied "my stepfather." Al asked me how I felt about the early shattering by my stepfather (who was brutal and sexually abusive) and I said despair.

Dissociated material is often expressed in physical signs that, when translated into actions and interactions, lead to the expression of the unconscious issues expressed in the somatic symptom; this process is quite different from the enhanced control of physiological processes attributed to hypnotic subjects. The following examples illustrate the Psychomotor process:

> 1. I told about the pain in my hands and arms. Every night for the past few months I awoke from the pain, more than six times each night, and again in the early morning (usually I am a very sound sleeper). Pesso asked me to do what I felt with them, and I over-stretched them, just as if to hold some very great danger away. I got some *ideal parents* to help me. They were not weak like my real parents were, but protected me and helped me to protect myself against doctors. Then I remembered that I very often dreamed of knives and operations they (the doctors) did to me. The day after the structure the pain was gone.

> 2. I can't remember what happened then, until Al asked me what I was experiencing. My clearly remembered answer was, "I feel like I have an empty box from here to here" and I drew the box which extended from my waist to the top of my chest, including some of my throat, but was mostly in the heart area. Al said he thought that box was the emptiness and loneliness I felt as a child. That made great sense to me and I started to cry...When I stopped Al explained that my compulsive masturbating was a desperate attempt to fill that emptiness and nurture myself and all that made even more sense....At some point I felt a warm tingling in my anus and pelvic area. I reported this and the ideal parents affirmed my right to feel warm in all those areas, thus affirming my sexuality.

PS/P differs from Ericksonian hypnotherapy in a number of important ways. One of the most important is that PS/P includes a dynamic component that provides interpretation and healing experiences, usually in a symbolic family context, during the structure experience. Structures provide a facilitative context for the expression of dissociated material, the provision of the symbolic healing experiences that were not provided earlier in life, and the integration of these symbolic experiences into the ego system. This process and the manner in which PS/P differs from the Ericksonian approach is illustrated in the following example:

> From somewhere deep inside myself I wanted to flail about. Al told me to go with the feeling, try to throw myself around and the ideal parents, helped by their extensions, would keep me "centered". I began an incredible, wild, crazy struggle that shocked me, at first. After that I don't remember all the struggle clearly, except for a panic that grew to terror until I screamed a very loud, shattering scream. Then I collapsed in tears. When I took my hands from my face I wanted someone to hold them and Al had the two extensions do that. I cried until calm started to settle in and gradually, in my mind, I saw an image of an overlapping layer of shingles that seemed to be made of mud. After reporting the image, Al suggested that it might be the clay being remolded. That felt right to me. I was beginning to really feel the presence of those supporting figures. I began to talk about how afraid and alone I always had been as a child. After checking with me, Al had the ideal parents say "If we had been your parents we wouldn't have left you alone and afraid." Somewhere in here I said "You wouldn't beat me?" The ideal parents answered affirmatively and there was more interchange with the ideal parents saying what I needed to hear. Finally, I began to feel their presence more deeply and had a sense of being like a young plant, a slowly blooming flower. Al suggested the ideal parents affirm this growth by saying "If you had been our child, we would let you grow and bloom into a beautiful flower." I asked, "You wouldn't humiliate and trample me?" They answered assuringly, but I

said "really?" in a disbelieving way. Al stopped the process at this point and explained that he suspected there was a part of me that wanted to be trampled, that this happens often in victimized children. There is an erotic drive to go to that which was the source of the punishment. Well, it felt right, fit my history and what I knew about child abuse and incest, but I was also frightened and repulsed by the idea. We talked for a while and Al explained what he wanted to do to help me resolve this. Al's idea was to choose some people to role play "tramplers" and I would try to go to them, but the ideal parents and extensions would act as limiting figures and prevent me. I told Al to choose some tramplers as I just couldn't. He chose two men and one woman. They stood in front of me, about four or five feet beyond the extensions. When they began to stamp their feet I almost freaked out; they sounded like Nazis in boots. All my childhood fear, obsession, and identification with the Jewish victims of the Holocaust came back. But, sure enough I went for them. I pulled one hand free of the extensions and tried to pull myself hand over hand up the arm of the other extension; he held firm. All my other holding figures also held firm and I eventually stopped struggling. The structure ended with a series of dialogues between myself and my ideal parents. Al asked me to visualize a family who would affirm this me in ways that were meaningful to me. Most important was that my family/parents believe in something. My step-father was an avowed atheist and religion, or spirituality, was ridiculed in my family of origin. Permission to be a spiritual person is very important to me in my life. So we had the ideal parents say they believed in something. Another important issue was anger and having the ideal parent say they would handle their anger in non-violent ways, this was very satisfying. We did this until I felt finished and the structure was done.

Conclusion

This paper has described some similarities and differences between Psychomotor and hypnotic process. Psychomotor is not hypnosis, although there are similarities between aspects of the experience of PS/P during structure work and descriptions of hypnotic process. The most important similarities discussed are: 1. alteration of the subjective sense of time; 2. the recovery of vivid memories experienced as if they were happening in the present; 3. reduced attention to surroundings and distractions, and enhanced absorption in one's own imagery; 4. temporary relinquishing of critical/monitoring functions; and 5. enhanced ability to re-experience and express dissociated material, as well as to retrieve memories and to process experiences at different levels of consciousness.

The differences between the two processes are many, among the most important are: 1. Psychomotor structures do not involve direct or indirect suggestions intended to change problems; they do result in experiences designed to foster healing and growth; 2. Psychomotor structures do not include paradox, or strategic assignments; the roles of symbolism and metaphor in the expression and resolution of participants' issues is recognized and an important part of the therapeutic process, however; 3. participants select and provide the content; the therapist helps to choreograph the experiences that facilitate healing and growth, according to an interpersonal formula of energy->action->interaction; and 4. Psychomotor places great emphasis on developmental psychodynamic processes, as well as current relationships, in the origin of problems and their solutions.

References

Brown, D.P., & Fromm, E. (1986). *Hypnotherapy & hypnoanalysis.* Hillsdale, NJ: Erlbaum.

Gindhart, L.R. (1985). Hypnotic psychotherapy. In J.K. Zeig (Ed.), *Ericksonian psycho-therapy, Vol. I: Structures* (pp. 233-268). New York: Bruner/Mazel.

Haley, J. (1976). Development of a theory: a history of a research project. In C. Sluzki & D. Ransom (Eds.), *Double bind: The foundation of the communicational approach to the family.* New York: Grune & Stratton.

Hilgard, E.R. (1968). *The experience of hypnosis.* New York: Harcourt Brace.

Hilgard, E.R. (1977). *Divided consciousness: Multiple controls in human thought and action.* New York: Wiley-Interscience.

Hilgard, E.R. (1978). States of consciousness in hypnosis: Divisions or levels? In F.H. Frankel & H.S. Zamansky (Eds.), *Hypnosis at its bicentennial* (pp. 143-184). New York: Plenum.

Kohn, H.B. (1984). *Clinical applications of hypnosis.* Springfield, IL: C. Thomas.

Lankton, C. (1985). Generative change: Beyond symptomatic relief. In J.K. Zeig (Ed.), *Ericksonian psychotherapy, Vol. I: Structures.* (pp. 81-112). New York: Bruner/Mazel.

Rosen, S. (1982). *My voice will go with you: The teaching tales of M.H. Erickson.* New York: W.W. Norton.

Applications of PS/P

Chapter 14
Abuse

by Albert Pesso

Abuse is a topic of high current interest. We read about it and hear of it everywhere. Children are abused by their parents, their teachers, and others who would ordinarily be expected to be earnestly concerned with their care. Wives are abused by their husbands, and husbands by their wives. And now, in this insane period, ordinary citizens, tourists, and other innocent bystanders are beaten, held as hostages, and even murdered by terrorists.

Abuse threatens and offends all of us. No one, anywhere, feels sufficiently safe to ignore the outbreak of this plague. It disturbs our sense of well-being. It robs us of our birthright expectation of security and comfort in our personal lives. Abuse is more than just another topic for psychological exploration. It is a social phenomenon that can affect everyone and demands that therapists, who are especially involved in the treatment of victims of abuse, most fully understand it so that they may be more effective in their efforts to heal victims' pain and distress.

There are three general categories of abuse:

First, there is physical abuse which comes from damaging blows to the body of the victim from weapons, such as guns, knives, etc., hard objects, such as rocks, sticks, etc., or body parts, such as fists, feet, teeth, etc., used to injure, tear, or disrupt the normal use of the victim's body, muscles, bones, tissues, and organs. In simple words, the victim is physically beaten.

Second, there is sexual abuse which comes from unwanted sexual relationship and stimulation — via sexual intercourse, contact, or penetration of body parts with the abuser's genitals, or other body parts.

Third, there is psychological abuse which comes from unwanted reduction of the victim's self-esteem and value through imposed degradation, humiliation, ridicule, derision, and/or other psychological blows, demeaning to the self image, and damaging to the identity and functioning of the victim. Another form of psychological abuse results from forced submission to the commands and will of the abuser with no possibility of resistance or escape, where the victim must only show obedience.

In brief, *abuse* (ab-use) is an ab-(*normal*)-use of a person, whereby a person is treated as a thing, an object, or a commodity and not as a living soul and ego.

By *soul*, I mean the essential self — the core of a human being. It is the source of all the energies of a person — those energies that arise out of the genes, out of the unconscious. In this definition of soul I include attributes that are similar to what are usually referred to as instincts. Thus, the soul is the source of our emotions, our impulses, our primeval behaviors and reactions to external events. From there, we find pleasure and laugh when things are satisfying, and become angry or sad when things are frustrating. From there, arise the urges to be close to others, to love, and to create. From there, we gain the capacity and willingness to attack or run when we are in danger.

Our soul also gives us our capacity to feel, to sense, to take in the world as food or experience. When we take in the world literally, as food, we convert it to energy, and the stuff our bodies are made of. When we take in the world symbolically, as events and experiences, we neurologically and psychologically digest it and convert it to meaning and the stuff our minds are made of.

In content, the soul consists of the *polarities* of *power* and vulnerability. By *power*, I mean the capacity to move, to act, to transform, or make an effect upon the world. One of the metaphors of power is mass or matter in action. By vulnerability, I mean the capacity to feel, to respond, to take in and be transformed by the world. One of the metaphors of vulnerability is space and receptive emptiness.

The individual soul inherits the treasure of the collected information and knowledge about life and existence that has been accumulated through evolutionary time and recorded and deposited in our genes. Our individual soul, though born in our lifetime, traces its history to the beginning of time.

The *ego* is the agency by which we connect with the energies springing from the soul. It is the encircling band of consciousness, control, and mastery surrounding the soul that enables people to function as individuals in charge of their own lives and destinies. The ego is not ancient, it contains no information rising from the evolutionary past. We are born with the possibility of an ego, with blank slates where our egos shall be written. Our egos are created in our own lifetime.

Metaphorically speaking, if the soul is the protoplasm in the biological cell of existence, then the ego is the cell membrane which holds it together, defines it and separates it from other cells and the rest of the outside world.

The shapes and characters of our egos are formed and influenced by our relationships and contacts with the significant individuals involved with our upbringing, especially our parents and parent surrogates.

From its position as the interface between the outer and inner world — the membrane which separates the soul from the outside world — the ego mediates, modifies, and controls what shall go out of us or come into us. It determines what form the action shall take when the impulses from the soul are allowed to become behavior and what form the meaning shall take when the significance of external events is internalized.

The ego gives us the capacity to become conscious of existence as it gives names, words, images, and measurements to the outer world of events as well as to the inner world of our impressions. The ego has the capacity to make discriminations between things, categories, and emotional states. In that function it assists in differentiating between this and that, inside and outside, self and other, dreaming and awake, thinking and feeling, etc. This discriminating ability is a function of its encircling, boundary-making, and separating capacities.

As the ego is created in the crucible of the family home, it is a reflection of how our parents and significant others have reacted to us. It is a record of what names they have given to what they license or allow to come in or out of us. Simply put, the child, through interactions with its parents, learns to know and to control his/her own emotional range of feelings and actions. Then, having internalized the knowledge gained from those interactions in his/her ego, the child is more or less equipped to handle those ranges of feelings and actions in relationship with the rest of the world. Ultimately, it is the parents who determine the relationship and balance between the soul and the ego.

We are in good balance if our parents and our early history licenses and allows as much as possible of what our souls actually and potentially consist of to be expressed consciously, and to be given names and sanction for expression or experience. For only what is named and sanctioned is made conscious by the ego and given the right to be expressed, have a place in the world, and be experienced as real. All else becomes inadmissable, hidden, or sinks to the unconscious and will not be fully experienced or recognized as coming from the *self*. What the ego has no place or name for becomes psychologically invisible, whether it be inside or outside the self. It is for this reason we spend such a large part of our lives learning to maintain the balance between our souls and our egos.

The ego, from its first development on, is always at work managing the nuclear forces of power and vulnerability within us: containing power, so that we do not explode the world or ourselves with what can come out of us; withstanding vulnerability, so that we can maintain our physical integrity without losing our own shape by merging or making union with the rest of the world.

What Effect Does Abuse Have on the Soul and the Ego?

Abuse dramatically damages the carefully constructed relationship and balance between the soul and the ego. All abuse figuratively pierces the ego (which penetration can be experienced as a rape). As experience is thrust into the victim by the abuser without consent, the ego defenses are broken or burst, and the soul-stuff is left without boundaries, giving rise to omnipotent levels of feeling.

The ego, throughout its lifetime attempting to gain mastery of the self and the outside world, is given a great shock, for the abuser gives the victim's ego no part in the decision-making process determining what shall come into his/her body or consciousness. The abuser may beat the victim, rape the victim, ridicule the victim — or all three — and the victim is absolutely unable to control what is happening.

The ego is thereby damaged. All the ego functions are affected and reduced, resulting in varied degrees of feelings of loss of control, language, consciousness, identity, meaning, capacity for discrimination between inner and outer, fantasy and reality, dream and awake, etc.

As abuse is extremely life threatening, it produces highly charged survival reactions in the soul and figuratively raises the internal temperature to a dangerously high degree. Abuse produces levels of feeling and reactivity (vulnerability and power) that are far beyond what the victim's ego has heretofore learned to cope with. Their normal life histories have simply not prepared them for this amount of response. Since these feelings have had no interaction or contact with any ego constructing figures, they are unknown, not named as their own feelings, thus responded to as foreign. Consequently, victims become uncertain as to who they are and what their true identity is — more evidence that their weakened ego is in great distress and jeopardy.

Most victims tend to become quiet and fearful. They carry a wound that makes them extremely vulnerable. Though some may learn to cover this vulnerability with a facade of toughness and prickliness, underneath they share a terror of their own softness. Their extra sensitivity provides them with a deep capacity for feeling. The outer world has presented them with great danger — they learn to be very alert to what other people are feeling, especially about them.

Their own souls have reacted in ways that are beyond their consciousness and comprehension. The first response is to shut down. The ego shrinks and grows rigid — letting little in or out. Everything is regarded as suspect, foreign, and dangerous.

They become more closed, less willing to let anything of any kind near or into them. Their vulnerability becomes not only unprotected and exposed by the abuse, but dangerously exaggerated and reinforced because of it. To some victims, their vulnerability appears unbounded and without dimension. That may explain why those abuse victims become promiscuous and act out.

In others, the unbounded vulnerability is not acted upon at all. In fact, their vulnerability and openness may be so frightening to them that they don't dare to feel even the smallest quantity of it. Others find the openness of their beings so great that they experience psychosis.

Some abuse victims who don't act on the increased vulnerability in a direct way may express it by being "spacey." (You remember space is a metaphor for the openness of vulnerability.)

I am thinking now of a client who had a long history of incestuous relations with her father. She had learned to be out of her body as a way of coping with the impossible sensations that the sexual contact with her father produced in her. That way, she could say to herself that no matter what he did to her body, it was not being done to her, because she wasn't really there any more. This dissociation added to her appearance of being far away, mysterious, not of this earth. She was also intensely interested and deeply absorbed in things metaphysical. But when she spoke of those matters it was never quite clear what exactly she was talking about.

Her voice was very quiet, almost inaudible. Ordinarily, I think of the voice as an expression of power. In her case it was practically the reverse. Her voice was so soft, it was as if she were drawing words *in* with her breath rather than speaking them *out*. The same quality was true of her gaze. When people look into someone's eye, you can get the impression that they are looking into that other's person's mind or thoughts. That supports the notion that some part of looking has a penetrating quality. Of course, seeing is also taking in images and is therefore an expression of openness. Ordinarily these qualities are balanced in people, but this client's gaze rarely gave that penetrating impression. Only the reverse was true — her eyes were quite open, even enlarged, and had that quality that would make people think they could fall into them.

Her personality and behavior communicated that kind of too-vulnerable message that often produces its opposite in contact with others. It is common that when someone is very powerful, some part of the local environment tends to become less powerful and more vulnerable. Also, when someone is very vulnerable, others become less vulnerable and more powerful. I think of the polar forces of power and vulnerability as tending to pull out or elicit the opposite effect on people. That might explain why some vulnerable people almost seem to literally attract attack.

As a therapist, I have noted my own subtle, not quite unconscious reactions of subliminal aggressiveness toward, and sexual awareness of, this kind of client. I have come to expect those feelings and have learned to apply that information toward the therapeutic work. We therapists have to be on guard not to fall into the trap of reflexive opposite reactions. It is quite a testimony of some abuse victim's paradoxical power that they are capable of arousing responses in some people to do and say terrible things to them. That is not their conscious intention — they hate being hurt. They want that pattern stopped, but other unconscious historical conditionings are also operating which we should be careful not to reinforce in the therapy.

Because of their increased feelings of defenselessness and helplessness, some clients work hard at finding the strength and force that would hold off future abuse. They strive to be strong and able to protect themselves. This counterphobic hardness helps balance their psyche and is important to achieve. However, in order for them to finally feel comfortable with their emotional selves, they must also learn to master the feelings of vulnerability, not only by developing the opposite forces but by corralling them — that is, by experiencing the receptivity within benign, accepting *limits* — which leads to having good ego boundaries around the openness. But to achieve that comfortable state they must first feel fully the force of their super vulnerability in the therapy, and some may not consider that to be a very attractive prospect.

However, interpersonal contact *must* be made with those nuclear forces or there will never be peace between the soul and the ego. The truth of what one has lived through must be felt and experienced consciously, in interaction with ego-making figures, and thereby made real.

It is the aim of Pesso System/Psychomotor Therapy (PS/P), in the treatment of abuse victims, to attend to these problems by:

a) creating conditions that allow the ego to once again be in charge;

b) creating a setting where the victim may bring all those repressed, powerful feelings and impulses to the surface of consciousness and behavior;

c) providing that behavior and those feelings with the necessary validating or limiting interactions with ego-creating, *ideal parent* figures, via the use of role-playing group members.

These steps have the function of allowing everything in reaction to the abuse to be understood, made conscious, given names, given shape, given a place, given acceptance, and therefore made available for internalization in the ego.

Two more PS/P concepts follow, which will help in the understanding of the interventions I will describe in the next section.

The first is *shape/countershape*. A *countershape* is not a mirror reflection of a *shape*. Rather, a countershape complements a shape by having matched surfaces which complete, satisfy, and validate that shape where their mutual surfaces make contact and correspond.

If we think of the soul as having a shape, then a perfectly fitting ego would provide a perfect countershape. Such an ego would perfectly correspond with the soul as it surrounds and contains it. (This would be an instance where there is perfect balance between the soul and the ego.)

As the ego is created in contact and relationship with parents, it is the parents who must first provide appropriate countershapes to every dimension of the soul before there can be an ego countershape. These parental countershapes then get reflected to, and internalized by, the ego.

In ordinary life, parental relationships include touch and action. Therefore, there is an element of touch and action in the process of experiencing countershapes. If the shape of the soul is represented by the action of the body, then the countershape of the ego is founded in the touch and action of the parents' bodies, as well as in their acceptance, naming, and defining of the child's action.

We can conclude then, that the victim's damaged ego requires touch and action to repair it.

If one would attend only to the victim's fear and uncertainty following the abuse, then touch and action might not be entirely necessary, but if one acknowledges and understands that some of the major damage to the ego results from the condition of over-arousal of the instinctual or soul energies which severely buffet the ego, then it becomes clear that touch and action will be absolutely necessary, as those energies and actions must be limited before they can be internalized by the ego.

The second concept is that of *ego-wrapping*. I mean wrapping in the sense of wrapping a package or a gift, or wrapping a blanket around a baby. Wrapping is the countershape around the shape. In this sense, it is the skin of the self, the ego, which wraps around the soul.

Using this metaphor, the totality of soul should be wrapped in ego. That means that every expression of the self — the shape — should be met with the touch and action — the countershape — of those parental figures who assist in constructing ego. Thus, to insure a balanced life, every part of the soul should be met, touched, responded to, named, given dimension, and accepted by ego making figures.

Much of the ego-wrapping of victims' souls may be ripped apart by the harsh impact of abuse. In PS/P, *structures* create the conditions for the re-wrapping and ego repairing of the damaged areas. A structure provides the theory, techniques, and supportive arena which allows clients to symbolically re-experience historical events. During a structure, clients can discover those powerful soul emotions and reactions that arose in response to the abuse that may never have been brought to action and consciousness before.

During the structure, group members, in a function called *accommodation*, role-play *negative aspects*— hated and feared portions of the real figures in the abuse event — and *ideal figures* — symbolic figures (often parents) who would have provided what was missing in the past. The negative accommodators do not fight back when the client symbolically assaults them in the expression of their suppressed fury for the abuse, but respond to the counterattack by moving or falling as if struck and making sounds of pain and defeat. This gives the client the satisfaction of the expression of that suppressed rage.

The ideal figures represent the ones the client would have needed in the past who would have provided benign, respectful, and loving contact, in contrast to the original abusers; or, to represent those who would have been there to stop the abuse; or, following the abuse, to have given the support, protection, and comfort needed for the harsh effects of the abuse to be processed and dealt with by the confused and distressed ego. Thus, the ideal figures furnish the missing ego supports which ultimately assist the soul and the ego to come in better balance. Accommodation insures that sufficient ego-wrapping will be available.

In the next sections I describe the various topics in abuse, attending to the body symptoms and the PS/P treatment.

The Experience of Loss of Control

Inasmuch as abuse denies the client choice and control, those rights must be freely given in the therapy. If the therapist is too rigid and follows a too formal procedure, the therapist and the procedure itself will be further evidence that the world is abusive.

During the therapy, one has to deal not only with the concepts and ideas of power and vulnerability, but ultimately with the physical and active bodily expression of those forces. Power and vulnerability are not just thoughts and feelings, they are the stuff that moves and activates our lives.

But there is a caveat that should be included with the above statements. Since it was imposed touch and action that contributed to the sexual abuse in the first place, those clients are naturally aversive to touch and action. Much time must be spent to help victims feel safe with the therapist and the group itself.

I emphasize group because my experience indicates that it takes many people to do the limiting and contacting necessary to contain all the power that eventually becomes available to the client. Therefore, touch and action must be used with caution and great discretion. Too rapid application of those potentially therapeutic elements could frighten clients and reinforce their belief that their bodies are still not very safe places.

There are two simple PS/P exercises that help clients regain control. These are not set forth as major procedures in the overall healing process, but as simple examples of the kind of techniques and exercises that can be applied to the control issues.

The first exercise is called the *controlled approach*. Clients first choose where to stand in the room and then ask a group member to volunteer to be the figure that is controlled. The rules are that the controlled figure must respond to the commands of clients, given by hand signs. Clients then direct the controlled figure to move closer, away, to one side or another, to stand higher or lower, to move faster or slower, etc. Although it might produce anxiety as they move the figure closer, they soon discover that they can command the figure to move farther away, thus reducing their anxiety. This gives clients practice in controlling another person in their field of sight and develops safety as well as mastery.

This exercise can be repeated many times over the period of therapy and the variety of feelings, reactions, and associations that the distance and direction produce can provide much material for the therapy, as well as be indicators of the clients' increasing safety with physical closeness.

The second exercise gives clients practice in regaining control of their own body. It is called *conscious voluntary movement*. There are four steps in this exercise: 1) Decision, 2) Plan, 3) Implementation, 4) Verification. Briefly, the exercise provides an opportunity to practice mastery and control over one's own body during the completion of a non-threatening, non-emotional, movement task.

Clients must first make a decision regarding simply raising an arm only from the shoulder joint, in a motion devoid of expression or meaning. In the Decision step, the choices are limited to which arm, which direction, and what height. In the Plan step, clients make a mental image of the arm at the decided position and height. In the Implementation step, clients fulfill the plan, using no more than the minimum energy necessary to carry it out, and make sure not to add emotional content to the movement — as well as determining that each bit of motion is a product of conscious choice and execution. In the Verification step, clients, by visually checking the steps as they occur and the final outcome, determine that the action has been carried out according to the decision and plan.

In this way, clients learn to gain control over their own actions, not allowing any other motion than that pre-decided by their own conscious choice. Thus clients practice and learn that at any time, the turbulent emotions, pushing for action beneath the surface, can be held in check while they make their bodies follow their conscious will.

Those who wish to know more about these exercises Diane and I devised can refer to *Movement in Psychotherapy*, (1969).

Having learned more about control of conscious voluntary actions, clients are better prepared to consider allowing unconscious emotions bodily expression.

The Experience of Fear and Terror

Fear and terror are experienced intensely during abuse and, without ego-wrapping, it is felt as boundless, endless, and omnipotent. We see the residue and signs of this unbounded fear in clients when they report trembling in their legs or that their shoulders are tense, both indications that the fear is at the threshold of expression. Trembling in the legs indicates the possibility of an impulse to run; tension in the shoulders suggests an impulse to hide.

Structures provide clients with opportunities for the bodily expression and discharge of that energy. In working on this topic, it is important to understand that the expression of fear will not be finished and satisfied until the client feels safely away from the threat, in a secure place. Therefore, ideal figures must first be established as a completely safe haven, and, if necessary, so designated with power that they can be perceived as being equally or more powerful than the abuser. This arrangement reassures clients that the attacker would not be able to overcome this new possibility of security.

Without such safety, the expression of fear might lead to a feeling of panic and a pit of terror from which the client dreads that the only escape would be madness, death, or a psychological splitting from the body. Safety is the appropriate countershape or ego-wrapping for fear. Without safety, fear can be felt as endless. The expectation of safety releases the suppressed action and provides great relief when it is reached.

In one structure a client began to remember incestuous contacts with her father. She started to feel sick and felt that she would throw up. That reaction occurs when there is too much feeling in her body, more than can be handled. Such moments of nausea may be a reflexive, unconscious attempt to get the unpleasant overcharged feelings out of the body. She was also one who learned how to leave her body because she believed that if she felt what was in there, it would be overwhelming. I know that the route out of this dilemma is to ask persons with this tendency to strongly contract their muscles around the tension, and then to have the action that appears be given *contact* by supporting or containing figures. They provide the necessary countershaping pressure and resistance to the action which gives the feeling to clients that they can be helped in handling it. The physical contact and pressure is both literally and metaphorically a healing seal or cover over the hole in the wounded ego.

I suggested she select some people to role-play just such contact, containing figures so she could process that energy. She chose female contact figures who gently put their arms around her as she sat on the floor with her arms around her knees, and then I suggested that she tighten the muscles around the areas of tension in her body. She began to tremble. The contact figures held her more securely and she began to cry, saying she was very frightened. I understood that she was frightened not only because she was remembering how helpless she felt when her father abused her, but she might also be frightened of the feelings that it brought up in her that she did not understand. It was fear of the inside as well as of the outside. The contact figures are usually asked by clients to say things they need to hear, such as, "We can help you handle how scared you are." "We are not frightened, your fear is normal and we will help you deal with it," etc. Such words of acceptance and reassurance give a cognitive dimension to the experience as well as a license to feelings, making them more handle-able. Further in the structure she needed the experience of an ideal father with whom she could feel safe, protected, and respected.

Another body symptom associated with fear is achiness in the shoulders. When I ask clients reporting that symptom to move in the way the achiness seems to make them want to move, they usually raise their shoulders. The appearance of that movement gives the impression of someone trying to pull their head into their body in an attempt to shrink and hide inside themselves. It is suggested to clients that gentle but firm counter-pressure on the shoulders by the contact figures could assist them in fully accessing the fear that may be locked up there. The expression of this level of fear frequently includes a peculiarly high pitched sound — one you might hear from a terrified person or animal. The therapist and the group must be prepared to hear, and handle calmly, the screams of fear, terror, and helpless-calling-for-help that may erupt. The ideal figures must hold clients tightly during this expression so that clients don't experience even momentary loss of contact in the midst of this terrifying expression. Loss of firm contact would feel like a collapse of the ego.

When that fear is fully processed, the shoulder tension disappears and clients become more relaxed. What was overwhelming fear becomes experience-able, expressible, name-able, finite, acceptable, conscious, and has a place in the ego.

The Need for Protection

The absence of *protection* is a regular factor in abuse situations. Frequently, the abuser is a parent — one who should have been a protection giver rather than a threat. In such cases the child feels totally undefended, unprotected, and abandoned — not only by the abuser but also by the remaining parent, who they feel should have known what was happening and therefore stopped it.

A healing, antidotal, protective experience can be supplied by ideal parent figures, who are most effectively placed as a wall or shield between the victim and the abuser. This positioning provides the victim with a visible defense against the heretofore overpowering force of the feared figures of the past who had such a toxic effect on them. The protective figures are often asked to say things like, "If I had been back there then I would have seen what was going on and I would have not let him/her do that to you," or, "If he comes any closer I will stop him and call the police," etc.

A client in another structure, safe in the arms of the protective figures, was allowing herself to experience deep levels of vulnerability, when she suddenly clasped the back of her neck which had cramped painfully. Such neck cramps are a common reaction when people feel more vulnerable than they commonly are accustomed to. As a kind of unconscious, reflexive alternative to the softness that leaves them feeling so defenseless, some part of the body — frequently the neck or calf muscles — becomes very hard.

I asked her to exaggerate the tension in her neck and in doing so, her head pressed backward. I assumed that this motion needed to be responded to by a countershaping figure. I suggested that a contact or containing figure be chosen to place their hands around the base of her head, so that when her head would press backward again with the tension, it would be met with accepting and responding hands.

This kind of intervention is provided to accommodate the counter-force which the clients call up, in the attempt to balance the too-vulnerable feelings. It is important that when this hard reaction to their soft feelings surfaces, it is not met with limits. *Limits* are that special intervention which stop an action from being completed. In this case a more subtle amount of resistance is offered — with just the right amount of energy applied that allows clients to continue to move in whatever direction they wish. Clients usually welcome the resistance and then, by applying more effort, are able to overcome it. This intervention demonstrates to clients that their strength and force is effective. They are allowed to push the hands in the direction their head wishes to move. The words that the accommodators might be asked to say in connection with it are, "You're strong, you can have an effect on me," or other words that would give a similar message of validating the clients' capacity to increase the amount of power they have at their disposal. The validation of that hard, counterforce strength has the paradoxical effect of giving clients the license and safety to go deeper into their more frightening, vulnerable feelings.

The Experience of Pain, Hurt, and Sadness

The experience of physical pain and the emotional anguish of what had been lived through must also be attended to. The physical symptoms connected with those feelings are often reported as tension or hardness in the stomach, tension in the throat, and pressure in the chest. That is not to say that emotional or physical pain always shows up that way, but deep sadness, grief, and other painful feelings frequently give first evidence of themselves in those areas of the body.

Once again, the technique is to ask clients to tighten the muscles around the distressed areas and then to note what emotions, feelings, sounds, or actions arise. In many such cases clients will begin to cry, for it is those muscles and body parts that are most involved and affected by sadness and grief. The intensification of effort facilitates the expression of the pain that is locked in. Often, what comes is a purging kind of crying, one which might include grieving for lost innocence, lost safety, or whatever other losses the abuse produced.

One client remembered how much she loved her father, that he had been the adored daddy of her childhood — and now could not bear to think that she also hated him. She felt great sadness and loss as she recalled how hurt and confused she was the day he first approached her sexually. It was like the end of her world. When she reported these thoughts — and the sadness and grief connected to them — she began to cry and shook convulsively. She reported that she felt an increase of tension in her belly and lower back. (I must include here that those areas are also the ones affected when there is unconscious sexual energy just below the threshold of expression. For incest victims, the combination of sadness and repressed sexual feelings is not unusual. However, I did not choose to remark on the possibility of sexual energy in that instance).

To facilitate the expression of those deep feelings, the customary approach is to have the hands of ideal figures firmly placed against all turbulent and shaking surfaces of clients' bodies. For if the crying was expressed without solid contact, they might feel the force of their emotions as too great for their bodies to handle. The body shows the strain on its physical integrity at those troubled spots, and needs external support to help sustain it through the storm of feelings that are surging through it. The physical agitation and distress is felt as a strain on the ego, and the external support results in strengthening the ego. If there were not such contact figures available, clients, in an attempt to keep their bodies from bursting or imploding under the force of the tumultuous feelings, might choose to turn the feelings off.

The phrases that the ideal figures may say at this time include, "we can handle how sad you are," "we are not overcome by your feelings," "we can help you handle how sad you are," "we won't let you explode or implode from this feeling," etc.

The Impulse and Expression of Revenge and Sadistic Feelings

Although there is no pre-determined sequence in the expression of feelings during structures, it is usual that clients are more ready to encounter, and attend to, their reflexive impulse to vengefully and sadistically return the insult to the attacker after they feel sufficiently safe.

Nonetheless, these are not easy emotions for clients to find or identify. As the abuser has often been judged as less than human for what they have done, it is repugnant for victims to consider that there is even the remotest possibility of finding in themselves the impulses or fantasies to pay them back in kind. It is a matter of individual judgment as to when it is the right moment to bring up this topic, for I have found that clients do not usually present those fantasies on their own. When appropriate, I offer the information that it is common that sadistic impulses arise to "pay back" the abuser — by penetrating and violating *them.*

Fortunately, the body gives some clue as to the appropriate moment for this intervention. The body sensations that are most closely associated with sadistic aggression are tensions in the calf muscles (similar and related to the hardness mentioned above, when clients attempt to overcome their too vulnerable feelings). Often such clients complain of waking in the middle of the night with severe pains and cramps in the calf muscles. When asked to exaggerate this felt tension, they flex the foot in a way that is similar to the appearance of someone about to stamp on the ground or on some object.

If this interpretation is now acceptable to clients, the therapist can suggest that they could stamp symbolically on the abuser. Clients may then proceed to grind and stamp on a pillow while another group member, role-playing the abuser, provides the appropriate groans and cries of pain.

The therapist should see to it that the pillow clients dig into and stamp upon is not too soft, or too easily compressed —which could result in the clients' heels striking the hard surface of the floor and possibly producing pain or injury. Unconscious guilt feelings about sadistic emotions might incline clients to accidentally punish their own foot for the unacceptable act, even if the act is only directed symbolically and in fantasy toward their abusers.

For the client who might be guilty about this form of expression, it may be useful, or necessary, for the foot and leg to be restrained by ideal limiting figures, who keep the client from carrying out the full motion of stamping. This limiting function is often accompanied by statements such as, "It is all right that you have such revengeful and sadistic feelings, but we won't let you 'literally' do it." This intervention clearly defines the expression as symbolic and conveys the message that its full realistic expression in the outside world, to the real attacker, would not be permitted, but that this expression of the feelings is all right. However, not all clients need to be limited in this fashion as they already have the notion that the action is purely symbolic, not only in the motoric expression, but also in their minds.

Clients might have been beaten with fists, or shot, or cut with a knife; they might have been slapped, or humiliated or tortured; they might have been sexually assaulted or had bones broken. Whatever the form of attack, the therapist can expect and anticipate that these clients have unconscious impulses to avenge themselves using the same method of attack. It seems the unconscious contains a kind of "eye for an eye" attitude — a less loving variation of the golden rule, that would be expressed in words as, "*Do unto others as others have done unto you.*"

Repulsive as it may be for clients to hear of the possibility of such attitudes within themselves, they are relieved to learn that those impulses do exist in others — that they are normal responses, given the experiences they have endured. And when those impulses finally do surface to consciousness and are expressed in this symbolic setting, they find it brings great satisfaction and relief, for, even if only in fantasy, "revenge is sweet."

In order to be accurate in facilitating the appropriate accommodation, the therapist should attend to reports of sensations in clients' hands, arms, or whatever part of the body is receiving the impulses to carry out the revenge. Clients who have been shot might hold their hand as if a gun were in it. Usually, the emotional reaction to imagining shooting back makes it evident to both the client and the therapist that such reversal impulses do indeed reside in the musculature and in the soul. The same procedure would be followed for clients who had been stabbed, punched, etc. They would then play out the reversal procedure with a role-player identified as the original attacker. When clients symbolically carry out those deeds in the structure, the role-player who is representing the attacker must act as if punched, shot, tortured, etc.

Once again, the therapist must be prepared to offer limiting figures, if clients are too frightened or uneasy about expressing those impulses. As in the earlier example, the limiting figures would restrain clients from fully completing whatever action the vengeful impulse had taken. They might make statements like, "It is all right that you want to stab the attacker, but we will not let you literally do it," thus giving validation and permission for the impulse, but not for it being literally carried out. They would then illustrate that by keeping the stabbing action from being completed, keeping the symbolic knife from its target, etc. (The same procedure would be followed whatever act of revenge was imagined, such as keeping the client from pulling the trigger on the gun, or keeping the client from sexually assaulting the attacker — for instance, by placing hands on their hips and restraining them while they attempted to "rape back" the attacker.)

The Expression of Eroticism and *Receptivity*

One of the most unexpected findings in our work with victims is that any kind of abuse produces a reflexive increase in vulnerability that includes an erotic element. The person under attack not only responds with defensive reactions, but will also experience some degree of reflexive bodily impulses, not immediately available to consciousness, that imply a readiness to receive penetration. It is as if some archaic portion of the soul is highly responsive to and receptive of aggression. This level of vulnerability feels like a kind of infinite and omnipotent openness. It includes a chaotic excitement and readiness to take in and absorb everything and anything. Of course in sexual abuse this element is even further heightened. Not that victims want or consciously feel any sexual excitement, but the sexual organs are involved and some unconscious part of their bodies reacts to this stimulation. This factor only adds to the distress, for they have not asked or wanted to be stimulated. By the abuse, they have been denied their rights to mastery over their own feelings and body.

The guilt felt when this stimulated state becomes conscious is enormous — victims then blame themselves for their own predicament. The fact that they found themselves feeling sexual seems proof to them that it was their fault that the abuse occurred. They would kill the offending parts of themselves ("If thine eye offend thee pluck it out"). They would pluck out their own sexual feelings in their guilty thighs and smash the sexual feelings out of their head.

On the bodily level, this state shows up as trembling in the upper thighs and often is associated with pain and tension in the lower back. A client's psychological readiness to deal with this topic must be assessed by the therapist and includes attending to the time when those physical elements are noticed by that client. Clients, while recalling the attack, might report that their thighs are trembling, which they react to by clasping their arms around their knees and holding their legs tightly together. Imagine a client sitting on the floor, knees bent up, chin or face near the knees, arms around legs — in a kind of small ball. It looks protective, and indeed is an expression on the bodily level of: "Keep away from me, I won't let you get to me. I am keeping myself tightly closed."

When these positions and bodily actions are found in female victims who have been sexually assaulted, it is clear that they are closing themselves to keep their genitals from being penetrated. However, one need not be physically and sexually penetrated to get the reaction of omnipotent vulnerability or openness. Psychological abuse and attacks on the ego produce the same out-of-control, unconscious responses in men who have been assaulted or regularly beaten by siblings or parents. These men fight the same battle with their own out-of-control *receptivity* as assaulted women do. With no literal vagina to close, they present the same picture following a physical attack. They report and show the same trembling in the thighs, combined with the same desperate holding together of the legs.

On the topic of eroticism and receptivity, the treatment of abuse should be the same for men and women, whether or not the attack included sexual elements. It is as if the force of the violence created a "magical sexual receptivity" in the victim via the psychological "hole" that was torn in their personal boundaries or in the psychic structure of their ego.

My speculative hypothesis is that the endocrine system, influenced by the unconscious, responds to the feeling of the omnipotent vulnerability, or magical sexual receptivity, by secreting significant amounts of those hormones associated with sexual receptivity into the bloodstream. It would make an interesting research study to measure the shifts in hormone levels in men and women after they had suffered various kinds of abuse.

This unconscious pattern of reflexive receptivity creates great conflict and difficulty for victims. They know that they are very uncomfortable in their bodies following the attack, and they know on a conscious level that they are trying to protect their bodies, by holding themselves tightly. But they don't know that part of the discomfort arises from the paradoxical and unthinkable impulse to open themselves to receive the attack. To repeat, the discomfort in the body is not only from the fear and shame and pain of the attack, but also from the effort of holding down those unconscious and extremely powerful, yet conflicted drives. It is only when the legs are tightly held together by ideal limiting figures that the full force of those receptive bodily impulses can become felt, conscious, visible, and controllable.

The more regularly one has been made a victim, especially by a powerful family member, the more reinforcement there is for the unconscious notion that one has not only a magical sexual receptivity but an *omnipotent* one as well. It is as if the repeated attacks demonstrate to the victim that they "draw" the attacker to them and that the attacker cannot resist attacking them. They may feel that they have become irresistible in their attractiveness as victims. For the attack is attention, even if negative, and is a highly charged form of recognition with much emotional heat attached to it on the side of both the aggressor and the victim.

When working with this aspect of the treatment, I recognize the importance of letting clients know what is behind this interpretation and intervention. Clear, comprehensible teaching is necessary to assist clients to create a cognitive frame of reference that makes sense. I talk about the notion of openness, that I have just described, in such a way that clients do not feel judged or reproached for their paradoxical erotic responses. Rape victims have so often been blamed for what has happened to them that it is important that it does not appear to clients that they are once again being blamed for causing the attack, rather than being sympathized with for its damaging effect.

It must be made evident to clients that victims' reflexive, sexually receptive reactions are not a conscious choice representing their wishes, but rather an unconscious reaction created by the attack. They have to understand completely that they have not chosen to become stimulated by the attack. That they are not perverse and desirous of pain, but that a process has been triggered within them by the attack which overcame their — until then — balanced ego controls of vulnerability and receptivity.

If clients are not told in advance why this intervention of holding the legs together is being done, this act itself could be perceived and experienced as another abusive attack. The abused client's ego, having lost control of both the outer and inner worlds, must be actively included in the treatment. *Everything done in the therapy must include clients' conscious control and choice.*

The intervention that is used to deal with this openness is to provide limits to the impulse to separate the legs via ideal limiting figures. (They may also be likened to or even be enroled as ideal parents). They tightly hold clients' legs together at the knees, so that they "take over" the task of holding the knees together, allowing clients to then be able to feel and attend to the opposite impulse of separating them. It may take more than one person to do this successfully, for it is important that the accommodators keep clients from separating their knees — even the slightest bit — when they attempt to do so.

When all is prepared, clients can attempt to separate their legs with all the energy and wish for doing so that they can find in their body. The scene that usually follows is startling and dramatic. A tremendous energetic struggle begins. With impressive effort clients attempt to separate their knees and with equal and greater effort the limiting figures keep them together.

It is as if the magical sexual receptivity is asked to make its appearance or the omnipotent receptivity is invited to express itself. Although the limiting figures are external, they represent allies for the ego which in this intervention succeed in keeping the legs closed, no matter how hard the effort is made to open them.

It is not exactly accurate to say "no matter how hard the client is trying to open them" for in a way it is not the clients in their ego state that are trying to separate their knees. It is as if the clients have permitted the out-of-control or seemingly "possessed" element within themselves to take over their body. It is that element that fights and ultimately finds that it cannot overcome the limiting efforts of the external ideal figures.

The screams that come out of the client at this time are not screams of terror or pain but screams, high and piercing, like some mythological banshee. "Let me go, you———!!" clients shout. I may stop the process at this point to check if clients truly want to be let go. Almost always, they reassure me in their normal speaking voice, "Oh no, not at all, I just have to say that while I struggle, but please don't let go of me." The struggle resumes.

Finally, after repeated and frenzied efforts, the battle is over. One would not have expected such titanic efforts coming from the timid or quiet victim we began with. There has been no timidity here. Certainly no quiet, as one hears the client's screamed demands for release and the heavy breathing of all involved in the struggle. Even small, seemingly weak and helpless women demonstrate tremendous energy at this point of the structure. Therapists who use this technique should be prepared to confront this great force regardless of the physical appearance or sex of clients. It is as if one were able to literally witness a Freudian, primitive id struggling to escape the grip of a determined ego force. From this kind of experience one learns to seriously attend to the force of the id in its wish to be "free."

At the finish, clients feel relieved and cleansed. They report that the tensions which they have chronically felt in the lower back and in other parts of their bodies have relaxed. It is clearly a relief for them to find that they were not able to break the bounds of their openness. The verbal message of the limiting figures is internalized along with the experience. The limiting figures can say, "It is all right to feel open and to want to be receptive, but we can put limits on it and help you handle your openness and vulnerability."

One can add, when clients have been sexually abused by a family member, "We will not let you be literally penetrated, even if you want it." For in family incest situations there may be some part of clients that might unconsciously wish to submit to the demand for sex and this verbal injunction gives the right for that wish to exist, while emphasizing that the limits shall still be applied.

Those limits and statements empower clients to say to themselves, "It is all right for me to have powerful receptive and vulnerable feelings, or even incestuous sexual wishes. It does not mean that I will submit to those impulses and have them carried out against my conscious wishes of choice and control. I have help in handling those feelings, I can learn to handle those feelings."

The Impulse and Expression of Murder

Victims ultimately have to deal with their own murderous anger at the attacker. Some of that theme was examined in the section about revenge, but now I shall go into that topic further. One portion of the murderous impulse arises out of the outrage for what has been done. Another portion originates from the strongly felt impulse to kill that person who was capable of awakening such powerful and unacceptable feelings in one's self as those just described. I would like to address this second element now. Because their self-esteem as well as ego membrane has been so damaged by the assault, and because so many unacceptable and disturbing feelings are released by that wound, clients — in an attempt to stop that threat from ever happening again — come to the innate conclusion that murder is the only solution.

A third way to understand those impulses is to see the rise of those murderous feelings as an attempt of the soul, in the absence of ego ability to contain its unfettered vulnerability, to balance itself by releasing equivalent antithetical power in the form of unlimited aggression. A primordial penetrating force is set loose — directed, not so much sexually, but aggressively toward the attacker — and if one adds the second element, with this unconscious or possibly conscious thought, "I am not well or safe until the attacker is dead."

In the structure which develops out of this stage in the treatment clients, as before, are permitted fuller expression of the inhibited body impulses which would result in the visible, motoric emergence of those unconscious drives. The body symptoms which are reported at this time are rather global and include rapid heart beat, increased breathing, and tensions which result in extension of the body in many places — tension in the arms, hands and jaws, which produce fists or fingers extended like claws, and bared teeth, resulting in biting actions. It might also include tension in the legs, which when released, results in kicking actions. When clients are viewed in this state, the impression is one of destructive hatred.

The assistance of ideal limiting figures is essential for the release and safe expression of those feelings. Without them, a client might choose to remain frozen and emotionally paralyzed rather than risk releasing the devastating explosion that might issue from the direct, open expression of all that aggressive power stirring inside.

It takes at least six people to limit one person in this state. They must be expertly placed so that no injury to clients is possible. For when clients release those furious emotions into action, the force and speed of the movement are prodigious. Care must taken that there is no chance of accidental wrenching or dislocation of joints, and no possibility of painful contact with people, furniture or other objects. In the holding, they permit some action, but completely check the possibility of harmful outcome. PS/P therapists are trained in this intervention and know how to teach group members to properly hold one another for safe limits. This intervention should never be attempted without taking all appropriate measures beforehand.

The limiting figures might give the following verbal message, "It is all right to want to kill your attacker but we won't let you literally do it." This kind of statement and intervention licenses the emotional impulse while simultaneously making it safe to express it without danger or damage. It communicates to the client that they are justified in their outrage and feelings but doesn't demand the curtailment of the flow of feelings to the muscles. It simply prevents the motoric expression from resulting in the literal death that is emotionally intended.

When clients complete this expression, they feel great relief, and the changed levels of tension in their bodies are not only visible but also announced by them. Now they have learned that even this level of inner fury and penetrating-ness can be tapped safely. The ego is once again in charge. Clients realize that such primitive feelings do not have to cause literal disruption, and that the flow of their vivid, living, emotional rhythms can be attended to safely, without danger.

The Increase of Guilt, Shame, and the Desire for Punishment

Guilt, shame, and self-punishment are processes used by the psyche to bring it more into balance when ego processes have failed. If there had been sufficient ego, that is, ability to handle one's own strong inner forces, then there would be less (or no) need to bring such drastic measures — as massive guilt — to the task. Whenever there is an abundance of guilt, shame, and self punishment, one can assume that there are strong inner forces that are not yet under ego control. Guilt is used to control powerful inner forces in the absence of sufficient ego strength.

Victims, thrown out of balance and out of control by abuse, are ashamed and guilty about how open they are, and, by the law of opposites become rigidly closed. Ashamed and guilty about how angry they are, they become rigidly "nice."

Guilt, operating on the law of turning inward unacceptable forces, inclines victims to punish themselves for their out-of-control, forbidden impulses. The murderous energies directed outward are turned toward the self as a way to reduce the discomfort. Thus, victims have a predisposition to be accident prone or self-destructive.

Paradoxically, that very self-punishment — which is sought to alleviate the distress — allows an indirect but precise expression of the two forces that victims seek to place under control. In that act of self-punishment, both the enactor and the object of those drives are the self, rather than an external figure.

Guilt takes clients' own wish to penetrate their abusers, deflects it from that external target, and directs it back towards the self, resulting in the self-destructive wish to punch one's self or tear one's self apart with their nails, knives or any other penetrating object. When the deflected blow lands on the self, it is the self that is penetrated and thus the possible, unconscious wish to be penetrated is partially satisfied, but by the self and not by the outside figure.

The non-interactive solution of self-punishment leads to isolation, and in an odd way, omnipotence. Since one's penetrating forces are not reality tested and limited by an outside force, one can assume that one is omnipotently penetrating. And, when one's receptivity is not reality tested by an outside force, one can come to the conclusion that one is the most open person in the world, and the very model or paradigm for openness in the universe.

So, while victims feel awful, shamed, guilty, and wishing to destroy themselves, there is a significant secondary gain of specialness and uniqueness. This is unconscious, it is not given up easily. This fact must be recognized in the treatment. Simple verbal reassurance to a victim that they really aren't so bad is not satisfying to the unconscious omnipotent fantasy — and even threatens to take away the pleasure of one's uniqueness. The treatment must include the expression of the force and power of both the penetrating and receiving impulses and meet them head on in their most active forms and levels of expression.

As before, the limiting figures are required. This intervention can be applied when clients exhibit gestures and impulses that indicate that they are about to direct their anger inwardly. For example, clients may have their fists balled up and be preparing to strike in the direction of the attacker. It becomes apparent that the gesture has a tendency to move toward the self rather than toward the object. The therapist can check with clients if indeed there was such an intention. If a client says there was, and also admits feeling a strong inclination for self-punishment for all that happened, the therapist must be prepared to limit that action. With the agreement of the client, the limiting figures place their hands over the balled fist and keep it from landing on the client's body, saying, "We won't let you hurt yourself," or, "You don't deserve to be hurt."

This statement has to be delivered seriously, and acted upon with determination so that there is absolutely no possibility of clients touching their own faces with either their own fists or the controlling hands of the limiting figures. For any touch at that moment is taken as indication by clients that they have succeeded in breaking the limits. Another mighty struggle may begin at this point. The guilt-driven wish to hurt one's self is now allowed free expression as clients, in a self-hating rage, attempt to break loose and attack themselves.

What is also set loose is the penetrating force that has been out of control, and which is now directed toward the self in an omnipotent, non-interactive form. That, too, is blocked by the limiting figures. This very act places them between that part of a client that is punching and the super-receptive part. This limiting obliges clients to recognize that they are not presently in a *self/self* interaction with their energies, but in a *self/other* interaction. They cannot avoid noting that they are daring to tap those energies that they have heretofore kept from external (self/other) interaction, suppressed out of fear of the danger they might cause. They may have also avoided interaction in the past in the service of their omnipotence, in which state they may have found pleasure being the greatest and only force in the universe.

The struggle of the client is impressive and makes me think of some primitive God figure who might be saying, "Get out of my way. I will punch myself, I will kill myself, I will rape myself, for I am the mightiest power in the universe and no one can control me." By being limited, such clients are reduced to the level of being only human and not so elevated.

But they do not give up the struggle easily — there is another element involved. In the midst of it all, clients may imply or directly say, "Let go of me, I am the worst person in the entire world for what happened, it is my responsibility for making it happen — I should be punished." Now impotent feelings seem to follow the omnipotent ones in a kind of balancing maneuver, yet that powerlessness secretly maintains the omnipotence, as clients would be both punisher and punished.

When the struggle finally subsides, clients are both relieved and saddened. The human, interactive part of themselves is relieved. They are not God, they are not the worst person in the universe, they are just another person. In the limiting act they have found people outside of themselves caring enough to keep them from hurting themselves, and that feels good. Nonetheless, the omnipotent aspect may be somewhat frustrated and unhappy, for now it has to give up its solitary, unique posture as the total self joins the world of human beings.

The Desire to Express Love for the Abuser

Having put many of their unlimited feelings under ego control, it is possible for clients to consider feelings of love for the aggressor, especially if the aggressor was a family member. They may now be more able to consider their feelings of tenderness and affection toward that part of the abuser they may have cared about — not the hated part, not the awful part, but the human part they have experienced and remembered.

Imagine a client who has been regularly abused by her father — an alcoholic. In the father's alcoholic periods, he would be savage and violently beat all in the family who came near him. However, when he was not drunk, he would be considerate and even pleasant to be around. Furthermore, when he and the victim were both younger, they shared some very happy times fishing, going for walks, riding bicycles together, etc. The warmth and love felt in those periods may have been buried and never fully savored or expressed, probably because the client hesitated out of concern or fear of when the next outburst would occur.

The figure used in structures to facilitate this expression is called the loved aspect of the real figure. It represents neither the totality of the real figure nor the hated aspect of the real figure, but only the loved aspect, separated from the other parts that the child knew and remembered so clearly. When such a figure is placed before a client in a structure, many feelings — including some negative ones — may rise up in association with the entire, "real" figure. Then it is necessary to have the negative aspect also enroled and present to distinguish it from the loved aspect figure. Thus, the negative and positive emotions both have objects in roles.

When the loving feelings well up, clients can voice and finally openly express the warmth and affection that has been so long suppressed. At the point in the structure when clients might want to touch the loved aspect, tender feelings rise higher than they may be prepared to handle, and they might get anxious. At that juncture it is useful to introduce the limiting figures who would hold clients — bursting with their feelings — to provide reassurance and limits on their tendency to become too receptive and vulnerable in the presence of that figure. The limiting figures might also encircle the clients' legs to keep in check the receptive impulses that might arise with the tenderness.

More typically, they provide flexible restraint as clients reach a hand to caress the loved aspect. This curtailment assists clients in modifying and controlling the level of action that might arise out of the loving impulse that is out of ego control. The words that the limiting figures might say at this time are, "we can help you handle how much you love him," "we won't let you burst with your feelings," etc.

It is very touching to watch clients express this long suppressed love. It is also a great relief and satisfaction for clients. Those feelings are no longer frightening. They may have feared that had they expressed them in the past, the real figure could have made them their "slaves." That is why they preferred to hide those feelings, even from themselves.

In one such structure, the male group member role-playing the loved aspect is asked to sit closer. The client is still being held by the contact figures around her. As she looks at him, her body begins to tremble and she asks them to encircle her legs to help her contain her vulnerability as she feels the love for him. This constraint reassures her. As she reaches her hand to touch him, she becomes frightened by the force of her feelings and other containing figures are enroled to hold onto her wrists as she reaches her hand toward her "father's" face and hair. They exert a little counterpressure, giving just enough resistance so that the effort is not stopped completely. They supply sufficient external resistance so that she does not get paralyzed by her ambivalence about touching so tenderly. This intervention makes it possible for tender feelings to be expressed without getting out of control.

It also helps create a more balanced figure of the aggressor, who no longer looms so large and forbidding. Following such a structure, aggressors are perceived as less gigantic and more human-sized in clients' minds. They appear less charged, because clients are more able to handle all the different range of feelings the abuser provokes in them. Clients no longer feel out of control in their presence and can handle each different emotional response without it getting out of hand — neither too much love nor too much hate. The loving reactions to the abuser are now handle-able and ego integrate-able.

The Need for an Antidote Relationship

After the historical events have been processed through expression of the negative affect and unconscious emotions showing up in clients' bodies, the antidote must be attended to. By *antidoting*, I mean symbolically providing, via *ideal figures*, the needed, wished for interactions that would have been more appropriate in the original event. It is called antidoting because the interactions counter the toxic interactions with the original figure(s). For instance, if the real father had been abusive, the ideal father would be respectful and gentle; if the real mother had been weak and non-protective, the ideal mother would be strong and act as a shield; if the real brother had been incestuous, the ideal brother would only be sexually active with his own peers, etc.

In abuse situations in families, the child often experiences a double loss. If the child is abused by one parent, resulting in the diminution and loss of parenting from that side, the other parent frequently does not come to the defense of the child for fear of retribution from the spouse. The result is the loss of both parents.

A further loss is that of not seeing both parents together in a loving relationship — which sight is necessary for a child to feel related to and identified with both sides of their family.

One client experienced the possibility of the ideal parents as antidotes in the following way. She chose two group members, male and female, to represent the ideal father and ideal mother. They were instructed to sit side by side, entirely opposite to the original situation where the parents were not close at all. She said something about being amazed to see parents together that looked as if they liked each other. She wanted them to say that they respected each other. The ideal figures then repeated, "We respect each other." Then she wanted them to look into each other's eyes as they said that they loved each other. This made her face light up, but she said that it also made her jealous.

I suggested that the ideal parents could say that it was all right for her to be jealous but that her jealousy would not jeopardize the parents' connection to one another or to her. This reassured her and she asked the ideal parents to repeat that phrase.

She looked again at her ideal parents embracing one another and said she had never seen her real parents so close and that it was wonderful to imagine her ideal parents being so intimate. She wanted the ideal father to say, "I would never be sexual with you; I would only be sexual with your mother." It was a great relief for her. It made her feel free — like a child — and now she felt she could have a mother again.

She began to cry and climbed into her ideal mother's lap like a little child, experiencing what she hadn't felt in a long time: being loved and protected by a mother who was only a mother and not a competitor for the father.

Whatever form the abuse took, the ideal figures are there to antidote it. For it is not sufficient to create a *new map* to be used in framing the future by only processing the negative events of the actual history. The symbolic history provided in structures with the ideal figures gives a much needed visualization and modeling for how to approach a future that is not simply a relentless repetition of the travails of the past.

This concludes the list of elements attended to in structures. I have tried to show how we tap the energies showing in the body so that nothing is left unexperienced, unexpressed, unconscious, unlimited, unnamed, and without place. Everything rising from the soul is ego-wrapped by contact with the ideal figures.

The body, no longer the storehouse of frightening omnipotent impulses, can be in balance, and living in it can be a more comfortable, pleasurable experience.

References

Pesso, A. (1969). *Movement in psychotherapy.* New York: New York University Press.

Chapter 15

The Use of Psychomotor Therapy in the Treatment of Chronic Pain

by Gus B. Kaufman, Jr.

The treatment of chronic pain is one of the most difficult and complex problems faced by the clinician. In recent years, multidisciplinary treatment programs have been developed to address the multiple factors which contribute to chronic pain. Psychomotor therapy, as a component of one such program, has been used to attack the physiological, psychological, and social roots of the pain problem. The theory and practice of Psychomotor therapy and the special problems of the pain patient which it addresses are presented here.

Frans Lohman (1978) found psychological factors contributing to the chronic pain syndrome. He was able to demonstrate that patients in chronic pain tend to be more susceptible to adverse effects of stress, have inadequate support systems, and have less effective coping mechanisms than normal controls.

Chronic pain patients (*persons with pain continuing over months or years with 1) physical symptoms and 2) psychosocial disruptions of the patient's and associates' lives*) often suffer the effects of severe, long-standing conflicts (cf. Blumer, 1972; Engel, 1959; Lohman, 1978). These conflicts are perpetuated by being repressed, denied, or somatized, rather than resolved. Denial and repression provide relief from anxiety for a while, but often eventuate in exacerbation of existing pain, increased anxiety, or even injury. Freud discovered that a patient's intellectual understanding of conflicts may not produce a cure. For this, catharsis — an emotional re-experiencing of the conflict-inducing situation — may be required. Psychomotor therapy is especially suited to provide the pain patient with an avenue for catharsis and "working through." (Many psychosomatic patients are unable to express feelings in words; Sifneos calls them alexithymic [Nemiah, 1978]. In Psychomotor therapy these persons may focus on their somatic distress first, and then be helped to find its context and meaning.) Pain patients, neurotic or not, can relive and relieve conflicts in a carefully tailored therapeutic situation.

Psychomotor therapy was developed by Albert and Diane Pesso from knowledge of body movement and emotion, and especially from their experience as choreographers, in helping people overcome inability to physically express emotion. They found (Pesso, 1969, 1973), as had Alexander (1950), that this inability was often symbolized in a symptom (e.g., "a pain in the neck," etc.), and that some degree of symptomatic relief could be obtained if underlying conflicts could be resolved. They hypothesized, as had others, that chronic muscle tension often indicated conflicting intentionalities within a person.

Psychomotor therapy was an essential part of the treatment approach of the Boston Pain Center from its inception. Foulds & Hannigan (1974) and Sokolove (1975) have reported positively on the effectiveness of Psychomotor therapy with college students. However, its use for treatment of chronic pain patients and its effectiveness in this setting have not been previously documented.

Method

At the time of this study, the Boston Pain Center occupied one floor of the 284-bed Massachusetts Rehabilitation Hospital. Over two thousand patients were treated by this center in its ten years of existence. These patients tend to represent the treatment failures of the medical system: those individuals for whom conventional therapies (bed rest, physical therapy, medical/surgical treatment, drug therapy) have offered inadequate relief, people whose lives have been disrupted by pain, disability, discouragement, and depression. Specifically, these patients have endured, on the average, more than five years of pain and two or more surgical interventions. 80% were referred by orthopedic surgeons, neurosurgeons, or neurologists; 72% have back pain. Thus, while a complete medical evaluation is conducted, for most patients the diagnosis is not in question, but rather the patient's failure to respond to therapy. The treatment program is designed to expose patients to resources for dealing with their pain problem beyond those available through medical treatment alone.

Several publications have described the overall treatment program at the Boston Pain Center (Aronoff, 1981; Aronoff & Wilson, 1978) and some of its aspects and principles (Aronoff, Wilson, & Sample, 1978; Aronoff, Kamen, & Evans, 1981; Lohman, 1978; Wilson & Aronoff, 1979). The therapeutic community is particularly important as the context for encountering these resources. Most of our patients have become depressed, inactive, and preoccupied with their pain medication and/or physical dysfunction. In the struggle to become active again, and to deal with suffering as a part, but not the center of their lives, they provide each other with invaluable support, understanding, and encouragement.

Gradual reduction in medication occurs as patients become more active, less depressed, and able to deal with pain without the support of medication. Through biofeedback, relaxation, and meditation training, patients learn to reduce muscle tension and anxiety which often have exacerbated pain and suffering. A thorough physical therapy program uses traditional techniques plus various forms of heat and cold therapy, deep massage, and individual and group exercise programs. Some patients use Transcutaneous Nerve Stimulation (TNS) for pain control. Psychosocial treatment recognizes the complex interrelationships between pain, disability, and life stresses. Accordingly, psychological testing, various types of group therapy, and individual psychotherapy as needed are an integral part of the program. Since what the patients go home to affects subsequent success, family meetings are used to explore feelings, problems, and life-style issues; vocational and rehabilitation plans are developed; post-discharge plans are discussed with each patient. An outpatient aftercare program is available for those in the Boston area, and referrals are often made for those living farther away.

Results

A study in progress of the records of patients treated by the Boston Pain Center indicates that more than two-thirds describe themselves as markedly improved at discharge. Their descriptions typically mention reduced pain, which is no longer viewed as disabling. In addition to feeling more able to cope, these patients are clinically less depressed, experience less insomnia, have increased activity levels, and no longer use narcotics for pain.

These results have been described in detail by Wilson (1980). His intensive study conducted at the Boston Pain Center of 38 successive admissions with chronic low back pain found 35 of them evidenced at least mild depression on entry. On completion of the program, 70% of those with mild-moderate depression, and over half of those with moderate-severe depression were clinically not depressed, a highly significant change. Average daily pain levels were also significantly lower for all subjects, and this was directly related to decrease in depression. Subjects' activity levels in the various therapeutic programs were positively correlated with decreased pain.

A further issue for this, and other multidisciplinary treatment programs in which patients are subject to a variety of therapeutic interventions, is that it is virtually impossible to apportion the effects of each approach. In fact, it is likely that the various techniques have synergistic effects, and that it is neither necessary nor desirable to use only one. Studies mentioned earlier indicate a therapeutic potential for Psychomotor therapy used alone. It is our impression that the addition of Psychomotor to the traditional therapies has provided an outlet for individuals who are less psychologically oriented, to deal with somatized conflict and to express emotions motorically. Those patients who resist active involvement often benefit from observing others work through issues.

All patients at the Pain Center participate in Psychomotor therapy groups. (Entrance may be delayed for persons who evidence thought disorders.) Groups meet weekly for two and a half hours and have a maximum of ten members. Average patient stay is four weeks. Patients view an introductory videotape on Psychomotor theory and group participation. Guidelines regarding comfort, safety, and confidentiality in the group are discussed.

Theory of Psychomotor Therapy

Psychomotor theory assumes that when a person is in pain and does not have acute physical trauma, the pain may be a sign of unresolved conflicts. This theory suggests that the pain can be decreased or eliminated if the patient externalizes the conflict, expresses the suppressed feelings around it, and receives a sympathetic and accepting response from significant others.

The stages of this therapeutic process are:

1. Location of the conflict. A conflict may be located through the verbalization of a memory or a conflictual event. More frequently, however, the conflict is experienced as a body sensation, e.g., pain, heightened muscular tension, numbness, tingling, spasm, etc. Members of a Psychomotor group are helped to become aware of these indicators through focusing exercises (Pesso, 1969).

2. Expression of the conflict. In this stage the conflict is expressed verbally and physically, and tension thus begins to be released.

3. *Satisfactory response*. As a person's suppressed feelings — anger, sadness, fear, need for warmth and closeness, nurturance, etc. — emerge, they are responded to in a validating manner by group members designated to represent the appropriate target figures. These will usually be either negative aspects of remembered punitive figures or positive (ideal) figures, who can provide satisfaction for unmet needs. Often, these figures will be designated negative or positive parents. This process is called *accommodation.*

The emphasis on parental figures stems from the fact that negative treatment or neglect by parents often leads to symptom formation much later. This can happen in two ways: through "acting-in" (somatization), often a factor in ulcerative colitis, peptic ulcer disease, labile hypertension, brittle diabetes, arthritis, asthma, tension headaches, etc. (Frazier, 1965) and through "acting-out," as in injury caused by self-abusive action such as lifting something too heavy, certain traffic accidents, etc. To break up the patterns of "acting-in" or "acting-out," the parental figure's negative response or neglect which was internalized must be countered with a more positive response. This new response can then be internalized, clearing the way for future healthy expression and satisfaction, as opposed to continued suppression, tension, illness, or acting-out.

This paradigm of conflict resolution can be diagrammed as follows:

ENERGY—> ACTION—>
INTERACTION—> INTERNALIZATION

For powerful emotions to be expressed in action, a safe environment must be created. Pillows and mats serve as objects on which anger can be vented safely. Group members agree to help each other feel safe and comfortable, and to keep confidential what others express. With these safeguards, group members let themselves experience and report most tensions, and with encouragement, try active expression.

At this stage, a difficulty often arises of a sort Freud termed the "repetition compulsion." This refers to a person's tendency to re-enact past behavioral patterns, even when these are self-defeating and self-destructive. In Psychomotor therapy these patterns are recreated symbolically in the controlled setting of the group, using other members to represent negative aspects or "parts" of the original figures. The full affect of the original scene may now be experienced and expressed, so that it need not linger as unresolved conflict. There is, of course, no repetition of actual injury (such as beating or falls), but affects from these — anger, grief, and fear — do emerge. Longings for closeness commonly emerge also and can now be satisfied by the alternative, *ideal parents.*

Psychomotor therapy thus allows the creation of a new, more positive alternative solution to a situation of conflict or deprivation, so that unresolved needs can be met symbolically.

Case Example I

A man with back and shoulder pain experienced an impulse to strike with his fists. When questioned about past anger he remembered his rage at his father who beat him and his siblings. He then expressed this symbolically by hitting pillows, while a male group member in the role of negative aspects of his father reacted as though being struck and hurt. This reaction, called *negative accommodation*, was performed at a safe distance. The action and accommodation provided considerable tension reduction. This man then felt weak and tremulous; he was asked to recognize a need for support from his father which had never been satisfied. It was suggested to him that he use another male in the group in the role of an ideal or positive father who, if he had been there, would have been supportive and affectionate with his son. Upon receiving this positive interaction, accompanied by the statement by the ideal father: "I'll be there to support you when you need me, son," this man was able to internalize supportive qualities, so that he did not need to hold himself up rigidly against feelings of weakness.

In this vignette, the specialized nature of the interaction — the use of "negative" and "positive" or "ideal" figures — is demonstrated. A pain patient needs to come to terms with historical traumas before new learning can easily occur. A person angry from past mistreatment often suppresses this feeling due to guilt. This person does not feel right expressing anger at someone on whom s/he has depended. The guilt can be minimized through a deliberate splitting of the target figure. We tell the patient to define the negative figure as a "part object" — those parts of the parent which were perceived negatively.

On the other hand, the patient's use of ideal, positive, or good figures — usually parents — depends upon innate patterns and cultural learning, perhaps more than specific, historical knowledge. Positive figures can sanction expression of anger, without being threatening or disapproving. This is often counter to the person's historical experience, yet it may induce feelings of relief. The therapist helps the patient recognize *basic human needs* (nurturance, support, protection, limits, etc.) and how they might be satisfied. This learning of healthful patterns coexists with the knowedge of particular historical experiences, which for the pain patient may have been deprivation and/or abuse (Blumer, 1972).

When the power of negative experiences has been dissipated, the patient is free to contact and activate healing patterns, reinforcing them through interaction with ideal parent figures. This experience addresses the deepest part of the self, and leaves feelings of health, wholeness, and satisfaction in its wake.

In such a procedure, called a Psychomotor *structure*, the patient can find an alternative to pain for satisfying one's deepest needs. Blumer (1972), in his study of 383 patients with chronic atypical pain, summarized their core issues as "the denial of infantile needs to be dependent, to be spoiled and physically catered to on the one hand, and of hostile, sado-masochistic strivings on the other." Pain behavior and the interpersonal transactions accompanying it satisfy these needs so thoroughly, as Blumer and others point out, that psychotherapy is typically rejected by such persons. Psychomotor therapy, however, offers the pain patient a more direct and non-destructive avenue to the satisfaction of these emotional needs.

Case Example 2

Stan was a thirty-year-old separated male admitted with a medical diagnosis of intractable low back pain and abdominal pain. He was unusual on our unit in that his back was "virgin," as he put it; he had not had surgery. Stan injured his back lifting a heavy object.

For several sessions Stan volunteered little, but in the third week he asked to speak about a personal problem. Years before, he had served in Vietnam as a medical corpsman. He reported that others in boot camp had told him, "Don't make any friends." He disregarded their advice. When his company went into combat, Stan's one friend was shot. Stan wanted to rescue him, but the lieutenant in charge forbade it as too risky, and had three men restrain him and take his rifle. Stan struggled while watching his friend die. Speaking of the lieutenant,

Stan told the group, "I'll kill that guy if I ever see him." When asked what he was feeling, Stan reported anger, but also sadness, and guilt that he hadn't rescued his friend. He was trembling and clenching his fists. The group therapist suggested that Stan have someone play the negative aspects of the lieutenant. Stan first chose the group leader, who replied that it would be difficult to give assistance from that role. Stan selected a group member, and began pounding, with tremendous force, the pillows and mats provided for this purpose. The "negative lieutenant" responded to each blow with gasps, groans, and moans. The group leader encouraged Stan to express himself more openly (he had been clenching his teeth). He began to curse, yell, and growl as he hit.

After his rage subsided, Stan no longer had a "knot" in his stomach, but felt "shaky" and had back pain. Another group member, in the role of a positive figure, "backed him up" with an arm around him and verbal support. Stan was thus able to relax and reflect on his experience. He spoke of his friend's having been shot in the stomach. He felt great relief. He had never told anyone about this incident before. Stan felt less hate toward the lieutenant, and no longer felt bound to kill him.

Stan subsequently experienced no further chronic abdominal pain. His discharge diagnostic summary mentioned: (1) intractable lower back pain, presumably based on discogenic disease with local psychophysiological musculoskeletal effects, but with little abnormality noted on examination; condition much improved; and (2) probable psychophysiologic gastrointestinal reaction, condition improved.

What can be learned from Stan's problem and his dramatic improvement? We hypothesize that Stan's pain symptoms were multidetermined. In terms of the healing paradigm we have presented, we can think of Stan's stomach and back pain as encapsulating meaningful tension. Through avoiding others, Stan denied himself opportunity for expression, thus protecting himself against the possible release of his homicidal impulses. When we encouraged him to focus on his feelings, he began to experience them emotionally as anger, sadness, and guilt, and physically as shaking and fist clenching. His expression of anger and its accommodation led to a release. His underlying need for support was also allowed symbolic satisfaction. We can hypothesize that the pattern of these needs had antecedents in Stan's family of origin, but in this case it was not necessary to refer to that context. We speculate that his particular background mediated his symbolic internalization of his friend's wound through abdominal pain. We also hypothesize a conflict related to authority in which rebellion-submission and activity-passivity themes with Oedipal overtones were prominent. Evidence for this can be adduced from: the proximate cause of his injury — lifting a heavy object (see section entitled "Macho and Martyr"); Stan's rage at the lieutenant who had him held down; his selecting the group leader for the lieutenant's role; and in Stan's reference to his back as "virgin." Stan's murderous rage at having been held down while murder occurred was perhaps restrained by the "k(not)" in his stomach. His outrage and fear concerning violation warred with dependency needs which may have helped keep him a patient. Stan's conflicting impulses could be expressed and resolved in the structure, rather than remaining encapsulated in the compromise solution of the symptoms.

Special Problems of Work with Pain Patients

All chronic pain patients are not difficult to work with. Some, however, have made "a career of suffering" (Szasz, 1975, p. xviii). They are "among the most reluctant to accept psychiatric referral and to participate in psychotherapy if they do so" (Engel, 1959).

Our experience has often corroborated Szasz's and Engel's impressions. We believe that related issues of role and defensive style militate against expeditious cure of many chronic pain patients. In our experience, certain pain patients have rigidly circumscribed role expectations they are attempting to fulfill — the most typical male and female forms of which we have labeled "macho" and "martyr." Role maintenance for them is based on a defensive constellation of suppression, repression, and denial. Repressed feelings are expressed through the pain symptom and behavior.

Supression, Repression and Denial. Persons with circumscribed role expectations and rigid defenses may be thought of as maintaining a façade. In Psychomotor therapy, where physical activity, stance, posture, etc. are regarded as meaningful, this is likely to become evident. These patients are likely to "explain away" manifest signs of body tension, saying for example, "It's just a nervous habit." In discussing themselves, these patients frequently maintain that they always tell other people what they feel when they feel it, so they have no past "hangups" and furthermore, they had "perfect" parents and "happy" childhoods, so their pain has nothing to do with that. Blumer's (1972) and Engel's (1959) research, our own clinical experience, and even common sense tend to cast doubt on such statements, and to highlight their defensive qualities. These defenses may gradually be relinquished in the context of a group in which others with painful histories are seen to be benefiting from therapeutic work.

Rigid Roles: "Macho" and "Martyr." Patients who are angrily defensive toward questions about their personal and family life and upbringing are often males steeped in a "macho" culture — one which emphasizes male strength and nonemotionality. The immediate etiology of their pain is often a work-related accident. Injuries from falling or lifting excessive weights are common. Persons with this character style have often carried enormous burdens (physically and/or metaphorically) from an early age, without the relief of emotional discharge. Many women with chronic pain have parallel backgrounds being, for instance, a "parental child" (Minuchin, 1974) who had to help raise younger children (and received little care themselves), or perhaps having been raised in foster homes or sent to parochial schools. Often, having experienced rejection or neglect, they have adapted by becoming "givers" who do not expect or ask for anything in return. Often, too, they were taught not to complain and to suppress many emotions; not only neediness but also anger, ambition, sexuality, etc. This pattern may persist until a "real," i.e. physical injury in adulthood reawakens early feelings of deprivation and despair, and legitimizes being taken care of by others. In such circumstances, the pain of an injury will often persist beyond the anticipated healing period, and the person may "require" further medical attention. Blumer (1972) and others have indicated that in such cases the injury itself, surgical procedures sought to correct it, and the strain the patient places on the family, can fit sadomasochistic character patterns.

The rigid self-concepts of many chronic pain patients seem to lead to inflexibility, which in turn makes them more susceptible to self-abuse and injury. Injunctions which contribute to an inflexible self-image can be noted in homilies we have heard from pain patients: "Crying is a weakness." "I don't want to depend on anybody." "The past is past: it should be buried and forgotten. Nothing can be done about it anyway." "It's wrong to get angry." "It's wrong to have sexual feelings outside of marriage."

The last two statements are often heard from persons raised in strict religious settings. Two-thirds of our patients were raised in the Catholic faith, which may be explained in part by New England demographics. Yet it is clear that many pain patients have scripts (Berne, 1961), derived from familial, church, and parochial school experience, which seem to emphasize "martyr" qualities — self-denial, suppression of feelings, and so forth. Male patients sometimes have had these scripts reinforced in military training (Eisenhart, 1977).

Script behavior, rigid self-concept, global defenses, and the secondary gains attached to the pain sufferer's role all make the therapeutic endeavor more difficult, but by no means impossible. There are incentives for therapeutic work. These include the genuine desire for relief of pain; seeing treatment at the Pain Clinic as "the last resort" (traditional medical treatment having failed); and the support, encouragement, and example of other sufferers' improvement through participation in the group (Wilson & Aronoff, 1979).

Conclusion

Psychomotor therapy capitalizes on these motivations, especially group support and the example of others facing past traumas and experiencing subsequent pain relief. Moreover, since in Psychomotor therapy basic needs can be symbolically gratified, the patient is likely to feel better following participation. This is important for both the active group participant and those observing, since their frequent disappointments in treatment have led to negative, fearful expectations. They need this reassurance.

The chronic pain patient is "feeling the pain of his life which he has not experienced" (N. Hollister, personal communication, 1976). Psychomotor therapy provides him a manageable way to confront and begin mastering that pain. Its effectiveness requires not only skill and sensitivity, but also a therapeutic community in which staff, patients and patients' families can be part of the therapeutic effort. With this support, a career of pain can be sacrificed for a healthier life.

References

Alexander, F. (1950). *Psychosomatic medicine: Its principles and applications.* New York: W. W. Norton & Co.

Aronoff, G. (1981). A holistic approach to pain rehabilitation: The Boston Pain Unit. *National Institute for Drug Abuse Research Monograph,* 36.

Aronoff, G., Kamen, R., & Evans, W. (1981). The relaxation response: A behavioral answer for chronic pain patients. *Behavioral Medicine, 8,* 20-25.

Aronoff, G., & Wilson, R. (1978). How to teach your patients to control chronic pain. *Behavioral Medicine, 5,* 29-35.

Aronoff, G., Wilson, R., & Sample, S. (1978). Treating chronic pain: The team approach. *Nursing Care, 27,* 12-13.

Berne, E. (1961). *Transactional Analysis in psychotherapy.* New York: Grove Press.

Blumer, D. (1972). Psychiatric considerations in pain. In P. Rothman and F. Simeone (Eds.), *The spine,* Vol. 2. Philadelphia: W. B. Saunders.

Eisenhart, R.W. (1977). Flower of the dragon: An example of applied humanistic psychology. *Journal of Humanistic Psychology, 17*, 3-23.

Engel, G.L. (1959). Psychogenic pain and the pain-prone patient. *American Journal of Medicine, 26*, 899-918.

Foulds, M.L., & Hannigan, P.S. (1974). Effects of Psychomotor group therapy on ratings of self and others. *Psychotherapy: Theory, Research and Practice, 2*, 351-353.

Frazier, S.H. (1965). Psychosomatic illness: A body language form of acting out. In L.E. Abt & S.L. Weissman (Eds.), *Acting out: Theoretical and clinical aspects.* New York: Grune & Stratton.

Lohman F. (1978). *Stress factors and support systems in pain patients.* Unpublished doctoral dissertation, Caribbean Center for Advanced Studies.

Minuchin, S. (1974). *Families and family therapy.* Cambridge, Mass.: Harvard University Press.

Nemiah, J.C. (1978, October). Alexithymia and psychosomatic illness. *J. C. W. Psychiatry*, 25-37.

Pesso, A. (1969). *Movement in psychotherapy.* New York: New York University Press.

Pesso, A. (1973). *Experience in action.* New York: New York University Press.

Sokolove, R.L. (1975). *Verbal and motoric styles of therapy: An outcome study.* Unpublished doctoral dissertation, Boston University.

Szasz, T.S. (1975). *Pain and pleasure* (2nd ed.). New York: Basic Books.

Wilson, R.R. (1980). *The relationship of depression, pain and therapeutic activity in chronic low back pain patients.* Unpublished dissertation. The Fielding Institute.

Wilson, R.R., & Aronoff, G. (1979). The therapeutic community in the treatment of chronic pain. *Journal of Chronic Diseases, 32*, 477-481.

Chapter 16

Working with Suicidal Clients[1]

by Albert Pesso

The metaphors and imagery that I use in this article are kept in mind as background when I work with clients who may be suicidal, have had poor early rearing experiences, or endured toxic intra-uterine history. Experience with people of diverse cultures and from many countries has led me to believe that the metaphors used below are generally useful, and perhaps even archetypical. For many clients these images are meaningful and believable on the emotional level. With those clients who are not traditionally religious, I replace the term god with other similar concepts such as the cosmos, nature, the void, Buddha, etc. Those readers who are put off by religious terms may feel free to replace them with their own terms and images which carry similar meanings.

Basic Images

Before we are born, when we are pre-existent and not yet alive, we are in the arms of God. There, we are immersed and embedded in bliss and oneness that provide total pleasure and security. There, we cannot die, for we are not yet alive; we cannot be hurt, for we are surrounded by safety and power; we cannot be lost, for we are not separate beings.

To be drawn away from God, to be willing to live on another level — on earth — to be born into flesh and reality, we must be led with sweetness and good tasting things, like those found in God's presence: unending love, warmth, security, and blissful feelings. Why else should a child-soul be willing to come to earth and be alive, if life would not be as attractive as being in heaven with God?

The uterus is perfect as the heaven-earth bridging vessel. It provides the closest approximation to the experience of being sheltered in the warmth and lovingness of God. Embedded in the warmth and closeness of a fleshly, child-longing mother (whose uterus, might in fact, be the earthly equivalent of God, and provide, perhaps, the original experience out of which images of God are created), the soul hardly notices that it is now on earth and no longer with God in heaven.

After the child is born, the arms, hearts, and fond gazes of the parents have to sustain the effect of the sweet, loving embrace of the uterus. The parents must let the child know that God also lives in their hearts, their arms and their gazes — for the child has known nothing but love, and will miss it and long to return to it in heaven with God if it is not found and experienced on the living plane.

These metaphors and images have clinical application, for if clients' experiences of the uterus in their original history have been foul, and the arms and hearts of their parents rejecting, the clients long to go home again — to where things were right and good tasting. In their emotional center, they know they are not in the right place. *Souls* know what it is they have experienced and what is their birthright. They long for the comfort and pleasure that was — before life — and they struggle to find ways to return.

Clinical History

Children who have had illness at an early age, one month to six months, and who have had to be separated from their home and placed in hospitals, have a rather stereotypic response to this circumstance. Especially if the illness was life-threatening, the experience seems to separate them (their souls?) from their bodies and keeps them from trusting and relating to their parents. It is as if they have come close to death and, by implication, God, and have become, consequently, that much less connected to and invested in earthly living. They seem to be far away and longing for some other place that seems more ultimately and legitimately real than what they find for themselves on earth. Such children, when they have become adults and have not yet overcome the effects of this early trauma, tend to be dreamers, fantasizers of other worlds, prayers to God. They are fascinated with otherworldly topics, alienated from ordinary experience, and show other such signs of cathexis to something and someone other than ordinary living people and places. They speak of never feeling at home either in their bodies or in the houses and cities of their upbringing.

It is as if their transition from being in the arms of God to being in the arms of their parents has been disturbed and they land somewhere in between. They are not fully in the arms of God, yet they seem always to be yearning for and closer to God than to people. And in the past, they were not fully in the arms of their parents, for their parents typically describe them as aloof and unwilling or unable to let them become close and intimate with them. They long to feel intimacy, trust, and lovingness with people, but seem never to fully be able to accomplish these steps.

During the time of illness, when life is almost gone from them, when they are struggling to remain alive, they find no familiar face to turn to — only strange nurses and, frequently, no one at all. The infant child, at those times, turns to something within itself, or to something transcending itself, that can sustain it. Such children become, without even noting it consciously as adults, extremely religious. This is especially hard to discern if the person is not raised in an orthodox religious setting. However, such people, when asked further, will usually recall extended, important periods in their lives when they were active in something like meditation, communion with nature, or some other such activity of intense "connectedness" to something not human that is never matched by their human contacts.

Here, I am describing children and people who survive these traumatic events. Those who do not, having found insufficient symbols of God in their survival-seeking process to enable them to stay alive on earth, simply succumb to the temptation and necessity, to them, of a return to God. Such unfortunate children may simply die.

The child's developmental needs must be met by figures outside the self. When a child survives a life threatening situation totally alone and separate from his parents, he learns too soon to depend upon himself and his own resources. Instead of it being the *ideal parents* inside himself who have taught him how to *nurture*, *support*, *protect*, and *limit* himself, he has had to inflate the interior outlines of what the ideal parents should behave like, into the very figures themselves. He has had no external models for the internalization of positive forces. He becomes self reliant too early. Thus, no one outside is of trustworthy value. He becomes his own object, his own caretaker, his own "other." He tends not only to move toward God but to become identified with and indistinct from God itself.

Clinical Approach

The difficult task, then, arises of how to bring that person back to the possibility of trusting others as God-containers. For if this does not happen, the child will never be able to trust outside himself and will remain a separate, isolated world apart — waiting till literal death for feelings of connectedness and communion.

The way back is to find the symbols and images of what it is that the child turned to, whether it be light, sky, moon, clouds, water, or whatever. Then the child (living now in the adult client) must dialogue in a believable, cathected way with those symbols. Without those symbols brought to life in a structure, the client will always remain removed from intimate contact. That is why the symbol of death is so important. For there, in death, they project that symbol and hope of final homecoming, peace, and connectedness.

Clients who are suicidal, depressed, and living miserable lives long for more than the end of life; they want to feel once again the pleasure that they sense was theirs. They anticipate the end of pain in the end of life. They long for the peace to be found when they are dead. They no longer anticipate that life and living will give them what they yearn for. They are moving away from life and looking towards death.

With such clients, I suggest that the act of symbolically dying in a structure can be a way of applying the energy behind the conscious suicidal wish toward a good therapeutic outcome. I clearly tell them that I do not want them to literally kill themselves, and that I do not see this act of symbolically dying as a rehearsal before the real thing. I let them know that when I lead such structures I do not encourage clients to pretend to shoot or hang themselves as a way of dying but rather ask them to submit to the inner wish to let go and be "dead". (Usually, clients, following such impulses will simply just let their bodies go limp and slump to the floor. This is most safely done if the client begins from a sitting position.) I remind them that in this way the symbolic act is not a rehearsal of the act of a literal suicide but more the symbolic act of surrendering and giving in to the wish for peace. I often tell them about my own belief in life and that I would prefer to help them to find their own hope in life rather than reinforce their wish to be actually dead.

The acceptance of the client's wish to be dead is of itself healing. Then the client does not have to hide those impulses and can feel still part of the group for having them. By only negating and blocking the suicidal wish, or only encouraging such patients to "hold on," therapists may not be so successful in either keeping patients alive or improving their lot in life, especially if the suicidal wish is strong and their daily feelings miserable to the extreme. It comes down to having fundamental trust of the energy in the body as the source of healing, even if the energy of the body seems, on the conscious level, to be moving toward the embrace of literal death.

There is a class of clients for whom the above intervention is simply not applicable. There are other clients, who, in the midst of a structure, will suddenly turn upon themselves with intense rage and hatred and attempt to claw at their faces or begin to pound on their bodies. The major impulse here is not a longing for peace and communion but rage and hatred. I don't offer these clients the option of symbolic death. They are full of fury towards another for which they have insufficient limits and it is therefore turned back upon themselves. They also hate themselves for being so hateful and feel that they deserve death as punishment for their awfulness. Offering such clients the option of symbolic suicide is evidence that the therapist agrees with them that they are unworthy of living. The PS intervention for those clients is to provide limit figures who block blows from landing and who say that they can help the client handle how angry they are by providing limits so that the blows do not land on the body. (This kind of intervention is covered more completely in the article on abuse — Chapter 14.) Offering the possibility of symbolic death to those self-hating clients is not recommended.

The intervention that I am presenting now is for those clients who are not so angry and guilty, but depressed and impoverished in their history of satisfying contact with parental and parent surrogate figures.

When given the freedom, choice, or possibility of symbolically dying, these clients will generally do something like "giving up" or "giving in", or whatever it is they imagine dying to be like. When they have "done" it, to "die" or whatever they need to do to give up life, they may end up lying down, curled up on the floor, or wrapped up in a blanket. I have come to notice that whatever mode they choose, they typically present a body posture that is reminiscent of intra-uterine existence, early mothering, or some expression or symbol of embedded-ness.

The effect of the submission to the idea of finally loosening the hold on life as they approach death, with the anticipation that the end of pain is to be found there, is dramatically visible on their bodies. Pleasure and relief suffuses through them, just as their unconscious conditioning has taught them to expect. Usually tense and uneasy, they go limp; their breathing becomes quiet and relaxed; their faces light up with the first outlines of satisfaction, relief, and pleasure.

In this expression of symbolically dying, the high energy in their bodies is released as action. PS/P procedural techniques demand that action must always be followed by an interaction (*ENERGY-ACTION-INTERACTION* are the first three steps in the Psychomotor *cycle of becoming*). The client is then asked to choose someone to role-play whatever, wherever, or whoever it is that it is they are with, now that they are dead — the cosmos, Buddha, nothingness, death, void, God, or whatever. This PS/P structuring process makes their symbolic death interactive and not isolated and solitary, and thereby provides the therapeutic possibility that they can have a dialogue with that figure that represents the place where death brings them.

When they are overcome with feelings of relief, the client may say things like, "Finally, peace — it feels such a relief, so good," etc. That allows the role-playing figure to say, "You can feel peace and relief with me." Thus the client is in a position to experience that this relief is a function of a relationship and not simply the consequence of dying as a solitary experience.

The client is permitted to stay in this condition for as long as they like, for they are finding the kind of peace that has eluded them in their image of what life has had to offer. Only the symbol of death, for them, permits the possibility of relief and pleasure. Only there, in the midst of death, do they expect to taste the sweetness of safety and love. Yet, what is death but that aspect of God that is overseer to that which is not alive, whether it be dead things or non-living things. God oversees life and death, for God is on both sides and is neither dead nor alive — in the common sense.

As the client stays within this image of having died, which includes the expectation of eternal safety, the relief and pleasure that they feel in their bodies (perhaps for the first time in a very long while) may come as a surprise to them. For they may have thought, until now, that such feelings had been literally dead for them.

And, once there is pleasure from literal life felt coursing through their bodies, they become interested and curious about actually living. For a function of life is to want to go on living and to feel, to know, and to understand life. This new sensation of pleasure puts them in conflict: if now they choose life, why should it be different than it was before? Won't it soon become, once again, as horrible, black, and bad tasting as their lives, till now, have been?

At this juncture, I help them construct a loving God, who may say something like, "I shall keep you here with me and shall not let you go back to earth unless and until I find the exactly right mother and father whose life I shall place you in." Then God, perhaps with the help of angels, would carry the client to the ideal mother and place him in her uterus.

If the client's actual mother has not been loving, or had not wanted to be pregnant, the client might resist the notion of being in any woman's uterus, all women being generalized as unloving and uncaring. Such clients (only if they have had experience with a loving father) may be offered a kind of way station to the ideal mother by being placed in the scrotum of the ideal father, who promises not to ejaculate them until he finds exactly the right woman to put them into. Then such clients can curl contentedly in the embedded-ness of their image of that condition, in the same manner they might have in the arms of death or God.

Similarly, when placed in the uterus of an ideal mother by God, she may promise to find him an ideal father to counter memories of a non-accepting, invalidating father.

Slowly, such clients do choose to be carefully placed into the loving lives of the ideal parents (either in this or subsequent structures, following the processing, reviewing and handling of the negative experiences the clients found in their original family early history). But first the search must be made in earnest, for the exact qualities the couple should have. God goes about searching seriously, avowing that the client would never be allowed to fall into the hands of the wrong people. Only those who have the God-like quality of loving and caring would be chosen.

 The pleasure that such clients have found in the image of God embracing, caring, and loving, while searching, provides a new platform for earthly existence on the literal, sensate level. The juices of good feeling, flowing once again inside such clients in association with their image of God, provide the hope that such feelings also can be experienced in their images of living people (the ideal parents) — for in fact they are feeling good with living people. It is not God that is holding them, but a living, supportive group member role-playing such clients' images of God.

Slowly these clients can be brought into contact with the ideal parents, with images of being embedded in the uterus of the ideal mother. If necessary, this includes their picture of God overseeing and validating the ideal mother's containment and incorporation of the God-like qualities in herself. Thus, there is no cessation of the continuity of God's loving embrace, only a transition in images from one form of loving to another: from the God-like unearthly form to the living and earthly form.

Knowing that the client's real life history has been painful, the return to life from death and God must be re-approached with great care, minding that no diminishment of God's love will be a consequence. For if there is disruption in any of the transition moments, it might appear to the client that life still remains unsafe and only death and literal contact with God will be the dependable route to peace.

These kinds of *structures* can never be rushed and must be treated with great care and sensitivity. It is not an "off the shelf" structure and the therapist must constantly be on the alert for disruptions that might inadvertently occur due to falling into unexpected pitfalls where the structure process itself might seem suspect, or where the accommodation might be inaccurate or troubling to the client.

Properly handled, these structures can lead to a process of re-connection with the world of people. However, it may possibly take several structures to complete the process. Some clients have needed to stay in the embedded feeling with the ideal mother for more than one time. Other clients have needed to stay with the figures of the cosmos for more than one time, and it is important that the therapist accurately track this process so as not to leave the client in a limbo condition — neither in the world or out of it — reinforcing their already tenuous connection to humans.

These ideas are quite useful in allowing me to understand and to assist clients who have important connections to the "other world." Although it is delicate and difficult work, I have found it to be rewarding for all concerned — the client, the group, and myself as therapist. Clients feel recognized and known in their condition which allows the trust that develops from that relationship to be translated into the trust of the accommodators and the structure procedures offered.

Chapter 17

PS/P and Recovery for Adult Children of Alcoholic Families

by John Crandell and Gail Hagler

PS/P, when used in conjunction with 12-step programs such as Alcoholics Anonymous and Al-Anon, is the treatment of choice for people who have grown up in alcoholic family systems. PS/P provides *ideal parent* messages to counter the prior experience with inadequate parenting; it encourages the expressive self-exploration which fosters self-acceptance and integration for clients whose core self has never been adequately affirmed. But PS/P should not, in our view, be the exclusive vehicle for recovery. Many, probably most, adult children of alcoholics (ACOAs) have problems with addiction. The compulsive behavior must be stopped — and any primary addictive disease process addressed — before PS/P or any other psychotherapy is attempted. The recovery process requires spiritual growth in the context of ongoing relationships, which 12-step programs provide. PS/P is adjunctive, especially in the early stages of recovery. But PS/P and 12-step programs work synergistically to assure full integration of inner resources for the ACOA in recovery.

After describing the ACOA experience, and its link to addiction, this article will detail the relationship of PS/P and 12-step programs. The contribution of each approach to the recovery process will be noted. The article will present a model for using PS/P with ACOAs in an outpatient group. It will outline the sequence of structure work that is likely to ensue. It will also highlight the importance of the non-structure work, and the accepting attitude that pervades the Psychomotor group process, to the healing that occurs in recovery.

The ACOA Experience

Adult children or grandchildren of alcoholics typically show a fundamental failure in self-care based on their alienation from feelings and their shame over the inadequacy of early primary relationships (Crandell, 1989). Blocked from discovering and expressing their true selves, ACOAs relate to the world through false selves, crafted in childhood to secure attention and insulate from pain. But these false selves prevent the hidden core of their souls from being affirmed in interaction so that true self-esteem can develop. ACOAs live in doubt about their worth, unaware of or afraid to express their inner feelings, and meeting their needs indirectly through manipulating relationships. They may give heroically: vicariously participating in providing to others as the closest approximation of giving to themselves without feeling selfish. They may be people-managers: doctors, ministers, therapists, all codependently focusing their energy on controlling the behavior and emotions of another, often addicted, individual. Or they may become "Lost Children" (Wegscheider, 1981), retreating from relationships to protect themselves from a repetition of the disappointment and abandonment that characterized their early family experience. Each choice represents a failure to develop an identity separate from their family of origin. Brown (1988) notes that:

> people who spend their days reacting to another rather than following their own inner voice, will lose, or never develop, a sense of independent self. Instead, a false self develops — one tied to the needs or dictates of the dependent person, and thus not easily recognized nor relinquished (p. 60).

Effective self-care cannot be learned if the true self is not expressed. The experience of the childhood family must be reworked if the client is to have a separate identity (Hibbard, 1987).

The family of origin is characterized by failure of the parental models. The addicted person is obsessed with the compulsive behavior, and the codependent spouse is preoccupied with the addict. Neither is consistently available to attend to the children. There is emotional abandonment (Black, 1981; Bradshaw, 1988). What parenting is available is inconsistent and driven by the parent's needs rather than the child's. This lays the groundwork for subsequent addiction as well as codependency.

ACOAs and Addiction

Children need time, attention, direction, and love from their parents. If these needs are not met, the ego becomes disabled and the development and expression of the *true self* cannot occur. Addiction develops readily in this family climate:

> Abandonment sets up compulsivity; (children who do not get their needs met) grow up with a cup that has a hole in it...This hole in the soul is the fuel that drives the compulsivity. The person looks for more and more love, attention, praise, booze, money, etc. The drivenness comes from the emptiness. (Bradshaw, 1988, p. 94)

When people come into therapy, whatever the presenting problem, we ask questions about addiction in the client and in the client's family. It is very common for alcoholism to skip a generation, so we ask about grandparents and even great-grandparents. Whenever there is a history of sexual or physical abuse, familial substance abuse is suspected. We know that denial is a central characteristic of alcoholism, and shame and guilt reinforce denial, so we expect clients to minimize the impact of addiction or abuse in their lives.

Whenever substance abuse is present, we educate clients about addiction as a primary disease and the effects this disease has on all family members. Much of our initial focus is on providing information (Crandell, 1987). We also work with clients to help them become established in the appropriate 12-step program. Today there are a growing number of such programs fashioned after Alcoholics Anonymous (AA). Others include Al-Anon, for families of alcoholics; ACOA groups, which are Al-Anon offshoots specializing in the experience of having grown up in the addicted family; Overeaters Anonymous (OA), for persons with eating disorders; Narcotics Anonymous (NA), for persons with a primary addiction to prescription or street drugs; and O-Anon or Nar-Anon, for their families. There are 12-step programs for addictions such as gambling (Gam-Anon) and sex (Sex and Love Addicts Anonymous). All are based on the same Twelve Steps of AA: "a group of principles, spiritual in the their nature, which, if practiced as a way of life, can expel the obsession to drink and enable the sufferer to become happily and usefully whole" (*The Twelve Steps and the Twelve Traditions,* 1953, p. 15).

There will be resistance: to identifying the addiction, to the suggestion of abstinence, and to the necessity of altering lifestyle through involvement in self-help groups. We expect it and work with it. Psychotherapy may be unnecessary once the recovery process has begun; it is contraindicated for anyone who is chemically addicted and still attempting to use.

Not all ACOAs become addicted, although there is evidence that they run at least four times the normal risk of alcoholism (Goodwin, 1979). Addiction is not necessarily based on childhood deprivation. But the association of the ACOA background and subsequent compulsive behavior is strong enough that it must be carefully examined in initial assessment of new clients. Even those ACOAs who escape chemical or food addiction are prone to adult symptoms etiologically grounded in their exposure to dysfunctional family norms.

ACOAs and Codependence

The stress of trauma and abandonment, the faulty models offered by addicted parents, and the child's suppression of natural reactions when the family environment is unsafe all contribute to an enduring pattern of dysfunctional behavior known as codependence (Cermak, 1988). Children learn to suppress their feelings when the parents are unavailable, to reverse roles and parent their parents (Brown, 1988), or to adopt the survival roles that will most reliably attract attention (Black, 1981; Wegscheider-Cruse, 1981, 1985). The real self atrophies as the false self develops. Children often experience overt trauma from abuse or neglect (Gravitz & Bowden, 1985). This destroys trust and sets up a fear of emotions (Krystal, 1977). Since children egocentrically assume responsibility for all events surrounding them, they internalize the abuse and neglect as proof that they are unworthy and shameful (Bradshaw, 1988; Brown, 1988; Subby, 1987). The children imitate the immature defenses of denial and projection modeled by their parents. As a result they grow up with a distorted view of the world and a blurring of boundaries between people. They believe themselves to be responsible for others' feelings, as if their own emotions were magically omnipotent (Bepko, 1985; Cermak, 1986; Cermak & Brown, 1982). They respond with hypervigilant self-denial and codependent overinvolvement in the experience of others (Beattie, 1987; Norwood, 1985; Schaef, 1986). Lastly, family loyalty and shame enforces an unspoken oath of secrecy and isolation that keeps the child of the alcoholic or otherwise dysfunctional family from seeking more effective models. When they leave home, even if they cut contact, adult children remain unable to individuate and are prone to repeat the dysfunctional pattern learned in their family of origin (Bowen, 1978; Bradshaw, 1988; Miller, 1981).

This pathological upbringing leaves ACOAs alienated from their true selves and inner resources (Crandell, 1989). The childhood rules remain: "Don't talk, don't trust, don't feel" (Black, 1981). Perception and emotion are ignored or mistrusted. There is an underlying feeling of shame that no outer success can ever fully disprove — and ACOAs often achieve outward success in their attempts to defend against this chronically low self-esteem. Fear of abandonment obstructs relationships with dependency and clouds the affect with unresolved grief. So the inner life is repressed in favor of preoccupation with the outer life. Internal resources remain unavailable, and self-care suffers. Failing to individuate adequately or to find a secure base of identity, symptoms develop and failures accrue until the ACOA becomes desperate enough to overcome the prohibition against asking for help and therapeutic assistance is sought.

Twelve-step Programs and PS/P in Recovery from Addiction

Common Elements in PS/P and 12-Step Programs

Recovery from addiction is a process which includes self-discovery, increased consciousness, and spiritual awakening. PS/P and 12-step programs foster the ongoing recovery process because they share the essential goals of wholeness, self-acceptance, and living in the body in the present moment.

Both PS/P and 12-step programs are based on the belief that the primary drive of the human *soul* is to become whole — to become ourselves — and that this is, essentially, a spiritual process. Spirituality is about wholeness and presentness (See Chapter 9). Recovering people are encouraged to live in the here-and-now and to take life as it comes: "one day at a time." The Serenity Prayer is said at every 12-step meeting: "God, grant me the serenity to accept the things I cannot change, courage to change the things I can, and wisdom to know the difference."

Central to both Psychomotor and Alcoholics Anonymous is the idea of consciousness: awareness of the immediate present. Carl Jung expresses this in a manner familiar to PS/P therapists:

> if we reconcile ourselves with the mysterious truth that spirit is the living body seen from within, and the body the outer manifestation of the living spirit — the two being really one — then we can understand why it is that the attempt to transcend the present level of consciousness must give its due to the body (1933, p. 220).

As PS/P demonstrates, the soul is discovered within the moment and within embodied experience. In recovery, people learn that addiction is spirituality gone awry, that the addict's quest is for transcendence or, as Jung wrote in a letter to Bill Wilson, one of the founders of AA:

> Craving for alcohol is the equivalent, on a low level, of the spiritual search of our being for wholeness; expressed in medieval language: The union with God... "Alcohol" in Latin is 'spiritus,' and you use the same word for the highest religious experiences as well as for the most depraved poison. The helpful formula therefore is: spiritus contra spiritum (1987, p. 71).

Contributions of 12-Step Programs

The Twelve Steps of Recovery, as practiced in any of the 12-step meetings, are a powerful adjunct to our work as Psychomotor and family therapists. The family rules — "don't talk, don't trust, don't feel" — need to be broken. This happens as people attend meetings and work the Steps. It is at meetings that people begin to talk to each other, to trust, to feel, and to break the patterns which were necessary in childhood but which prevent them from living their lives fully as adults. People who have grown up with addiction need the support of others who have had similar experiences. Twelve-step meetings provide this support so that psychotherapy can occur.

In Psychomotor we refer to the *basic needs*: *nurturance*, *support*, *protection*, and *limits*. Twelve-step programs supply these needs — through abstinence (from the addiction), attendance at meetings, the sponsorship link with a veteran of the program, working the Steps, and the principle of anonymity — in a concrete way over a long period of time. Through this process of recovery the person's basic needs are met, much as would happen for a child growing up in a healthy family. In both Psychomotor and the 12-step programs we believe the soul (or true self) is always in a process of becoming. For this to occur, the person needs a *place*, loving attention, and acceptance by others.

AA is, essentially, a spiritual program which provides a *place* for recovery to occur. AA and the other 12-step programs have groups all over the world, meeting at all times of the day and night. Alcoholics, codependents, and other addicts learn that they will be accepted automatically at any of these meetings. Acceptance — the sense of belonging, being seen, being understood — provides the platform for healing.

Addicts and codependents (relationship addicts) have difficulty with relationships and use their "substance" to deny this. Withdrawal from the substance leaves the newly abstinent person extremely vulnerable. This is the experience of powerlessness which is referred to in *Step 1*: "Admitted we were powerless over alcohol, that our lives had become unmanageable." Alcoholics and ACOAs suffer from low self-esteem; most admit, after attending some meetings, that they never felt they "belonged" any place before. For most people, the experience of acceptance and love at the meetings is new and healing.

From the beginning, the newcomer in AA or other 12-step programs is encouraged to find a sponsor. It is in this special relationship that the addict experiences real acceptance, often for the first time. The sponsor (who is any person who has had some time in the program) shares her or his "experience, strength, and hope" and helps the newly abstinent person with the problems of early recovery. In many ways the sponsor becomes a kind of *ideal figure* — the parent, sibling, or friend who helps the newcomer learn to live a sober life. In Al-Anon, the newcomer learns to keep the focus on the self rather than on the addict. The sponsor teaches about the Program, encourages as many meetings as possible, and may literally sit with the newcomer through periods of extreme anxiety, depression, or relapse. Always the newcomer is challenged to live *one day at a time*. People learn that it is impossible to guarantee abstinence on a permanent basis, but it is possible to abstain from that pill, fix, food binge, or controlling comment for this moment. This is how the addict learns to live in the present, with the sponsor as a kind of spiritual guide.

The recovering individual slowly learns to trust others as s/he lets go of the self-will that lies at the root of all compulsive (addictive) behavior. For recovery to occur, the addict and codependent must accept, in depth, his or her powerlessness over alcohol as well as all other aspects of life. Total surrender is necessary for recovery; paradoxically, it forms the basis of liberation. It is through a continuing process of acceptance and surrender that the individual begins to form a belief in a Higher Power. *Step 3* — "Made a decision to turn our will and our lives over to the care of God as we understood Him" — asks the recovering person to let go and put trust in something or someone other than self-will. This very critical step cuts away at *omnipotence* and forms the basis for trust. At first, the Higher Power might be the group, the sponsor, or someone seated nearby at a meeting.

In the Program people develop their own concept of Higher Power, which some call God. Most find their idea of a Higher Power changes as their awareness deepens with recovery. People are encouraged to use prayer and meditation to develop an awareness of Higher Power or spirituality (*Step 11*). People often report imagery of parental figures who are loving, kind, all-powerful, and accepting. The similarity to the Psychomotor concept of the ideal parent is striking. As Han Sarolea has said: "Apparently each of us knows what would have been ideal for him" (1986, p. 1). But this knowledge must be developed:

> Only when the client is receptive to his needy side... is the accommodation of the
> ideal parents a meaningful possibility...Prior to their capability for working with ideal
> parents, (people) must be able to reclaim their own souls (p. 6).

The 12-step programs lay the groundwork for trusting relatedness that makes recovery possible.

Acceptance from outside eventually provides a basis for self-acceptance. Re-education through the twelve steps leads one inward; the locus of control is no longer external (the codependent position), and the person becomes more inner directed. Psychomotor fosters this process.

Contributions of PS/P to 12-Step Work

Once relapse is no longer a threat on a daily basis and the person has become established in a 12-step program (usually a year for chemically addicted people), Psychomotor, with its emphasis on feelings and bodily energies, deepens self-exploration. Addictive behavior is an effort to control feelings, and when the compulsive rituals are withdrawn the body must learn to experience feelings which have been denied for a lifetime.

Structure work in Psychomotor is a valuable aid in "working the steps." The "searching and fearless moral inventory" of *Step 4* and admitting "to God, to ourselves, and to another human being the exact nature of our wrongs" through *Step 5* require that we stand right in the *center of our truth*. *Step 6* - being "entirely ready to have God remove all these defects of character" — and *Step 7* — "Humbly asked Him to remove our shortcomings" — are acts of faith and humility, requiring of us openness and honesty and the willingness to let go of defenses so that we become ourselves. The dramatization of our *true scene*, with all our impulses and resistances enacted about us, makes the PS/P structure a powerful vehicle for discovering our selves. Pesso recognizes that the soul gets stuck if the ego is unwilling to acknowledge its truth (see Chapter 4), "and Psychomotor is set up on the principles of how to get the soul moving" (Pesso, 1985). *Steps 8 and 9* — "Made a list of all persons we had harmed and became willing to make amends to them all," and "Made direct amends to such people whenever possible..." — are about our relationships with others. These steps require honesty, courage, and emotional balance. The PS/P structure provides practice in the encounter with the enacted other. Through this spiritual process we call recovery, people become alive to their feelings, the soul moves again, and they become "response-able" in their relationships with others.

The PS/P Group for Treating ACOA's

The essential task of psychotherapy is to restore authentic identity by reestablishing contact with the inner child (Bradshaw, 1988; Subby, 1987; Wegscheider-Cruse, 1985). This entails a shift from an external to an internal focus (Beattie, 1987). The result is access to new resources:

> Adult children rediscover and reclaim the wisdom of their inner experience. Instead of perceiving feelings as treacherous undercurrents in life, they see them as valuable messages... Most important, an underlying unity develops among their thoughts, feelings, and behaviors. What were once conflicting associations and separate processes now merge into integrated experiences (Gravitz & Bowden, 1985, p. 85).

But the access to feelings must be validated in interaction with parent figures. There must be a corrective reworking of the old experiences with inadequate caretakers, one which now allows the naming and expression of emotions that were originally suppressed and denied (Bradshaw, 1988; Wegscheider-Cruse, 1985). Therapy is a process of recovering the real self through genuine emotional encounter in supportive relationships in which the true self is cherished.

Psychomotor is uniquely suited for aiding ACOAs. It provides the safety and permission to return to authentic childhood experience. It provides the corrective focus on feelings and impulses to act, accessing the inner constituents of identity. It provides an experiential framework for an encounter with the parents of childhood. Through the *ideal parents* it provides validating messages that encourage the use of resources and loving limits that make it safe to tap the uncovered wellsprings of energy.

Therapeutic Factors in the Process of the Psychomotor Group

There are various models for outpatient PS/P groups. In common, these models recognize the impossibility of each client doing a structure weekly and hence that continued attendance must be motivated by other advantages of group involvement. One model (used by J. Crandell) has weekly sessions of two-hour duration. Once working norms are set, there may be two structures weekly. More commonly there is a period of sharing, then a single structure, then sharing of issues triggered by the structure topic, then an exercise or group discussion to explore themes from that session, and then a concluding group hug. There are typically seven to ten participants, with the opportunity to work being extended first to the one who has attended the most sessions since last doing a structure. Clients can expect to do a structure every six weeks. Another model (used by G. Hagler) has six participants per group. Each member does a 30 minute structure every other week. Groups begin and end on time, with weekly check-in and check-out. Group process sessions are interposed as needed, continuing until structure energy is present.

Clients gain a great deal from the group process in addition to the personal structure work. First, there is a tremendous sense of loyalty to the group and the climate that it creates. Clients emphasize the importance of the sense of safety and the permission to live their feelings openly in the group. The PS/P group provides a family of choice to which members can remain firmly attached while disentangling their ties to the families of birth. ACOAs develop cohesive groups quickly, as an antidote to the old fears of abandonment (Brown & Beletsis, 1986). The climate of acceptance is a treasured experience.

Second, there is a cautious fascination with sharing emotion. Old rules often made any expression dangerous; at the very least, clients learned to pay more attention to the reactions of significant others than to their own feelings. Having emotions witnessed and named is an important corrective experience (Brown, 1988). To discover that they will not be judged or abandoned for being expressive is a tremendous relief. Perhaps for the first time, there is an opportunity to experience the function pleasure — the joy of satisfying expression — that results when inner tension is brought forth into action. To entrust the group with one's rage or vulnerability is a gradual process, but the risk-taking becomes an important part of the shared quest that heightens group cohesiveness. In the safety of the group there is the repeated opportunity to witness intense affect without clients feeling overwhelmed with responsibility or seeing some feared catastrophic reaction. Authority does not punish, and emotional expression does not lead to omnipotent destruction or loss of self. Emotions that are brought into interaction and accommodated can be assessed more realistically. This is a critical corrective experience for ACOAs.

Third, *accommodation* provides an important opportunity to learn. Positive accommodation provides a model of effective parenting. The nurturing, supporting, protecting, and limit-setting functions of the ideal parents are exciting to clients who may never have experienced them. Members cherish not only the opportunity to experience ideal parenting in the role of children, but also in the role of parents. They use the group to practice a new model of fostering the growth of others, and then they apply it outside of group in relationships with their children and friends.

ACOAs come to group with an impaired sense of boundaries, and accommodation teaches interpersonal boundaries. At first it may be difficult for group members not to take in the angry and rejecting messages expressed to them when they are in the role of negative figures. The group helps participants distinguish the role from the self. In time they learn not to personalize: The client is responsible for his or her own feelings in the structure, and the accommodator is a symbolic stand-in who is not being personally addressed with the feelings directed at the role. Positive accommodation is also an opportunity to give without codependent mind-reading; the accommodator experiences the efficacy of responding directly to stated needs, of providing what is requested and no more. Accommodation fosters a more realistic sense of the limits of responsibility in relationships.

These learnings, needed correctives to early experiences, take time to become securely internalized. For this reason, the outpatient group should probably not start doing structures during the first months of its existence. Initial group process and movement exercises develop trust and attune clients to bodily experience. As group members process reactions to Psychomotor *exercises*, they learn to accept feelings without judgment — an antidote to the shame that is so characteristic of ACOAs. Focused exercises should replace structures as needed throughout the life of the group. *Movement in Psychotherapy* (Pesso, 1969) is a good source of ideas. But the therapist is invited to be creative. During the first group session, I (J. Crandell) asked members to draw a picture about a troublesome childhood event. To suggest the norm encouraging controlled regression, I sought to create a childlike experience by asking them to draw with their nondominant hand and then to conclude the exercise by folding the drawing into a paper airplane and trying to glide it into the wastebasket. When group members later expressed the difficulty in being dependent, they were offered the opportunity to do a 10-minute exercise in which they could imagine being very young and receiving exactly the type of attention desired. This proved a fascinating diagnostic exercise. Some revelled in vigorous touch and frontal contact with the accommodating group; others wanted to be lovingly watched with minimal touch; the most impaired could tolerate lying in the center of the group circle only when the members faced away, enclosing without contact. In response to the special needs of ACOAs, the selection of exercises should be guided by the most relevant of the goals of heightening group cohesion, building trust, sensitizing to inner tension or feeling, encouraging direct expression of emotion, and teaching controlled regression to early modes of experiencing (what one client calls "the return to baby-mind").

The Typical Cycle of Structures for ACOAs

Each structure is as unique as the individual and the specific issues at the forefront at the time of the work. Nonetheless, there is a typical sequence that seems to characterize the progression of structure work done by ACOAs.

Overcoming Prohibitions to Expressing Needs and Emotions. Initial work is often characterized by an uncertainty about what to work on or by a denial of affect despite the presence of evident physical tension. Interpersonal energy is being channeled through the body. Suppression often shows in hunching the shoulders, biting the lips, rocking the upper body, or pressing hands forcefully against the mouth or eyes. This energy is brought into action and interaction. Most often this can be accomplished by exaggerating the gesture or applying gentle counterpressure. The tension usually proves to be a reaction to disparaging inner voices which represent prohibitions against being "selfish" by attracting attention or "bad" for having feelings.

Once the disparaging voices are externalized there is the prospect of therapeutic work. While they may be enroled simply as "negative voices," the accommodators are usually recognized as specific individuals. When the message is repeated from the outside, one of two reactions tends to result. At times there is an immediate sense of anger and rejection which can be directed at the negative target and accommodated. More often, the message triggers shame and fearful acquiescence. As the client becomes aware of successive levels of self-accusation, these messages are externalized and located in the negative voice. Therapy must avoid traumatizing with repeated accusations or overriding the *pilot* by relying on provoking messages to elicit feelings the client may be choosing to suppress. The goal is to externalize messages that are present but which have been interpreted as internal truths.

When fear becomes prominent, either in reactive ducking and stiffening or as a conscious feeling, the client will accept protective accommodators. These figures are more often called "allies" at the outset, although they often re-enrole as ideal parents before the end of the structure. For this reason, I encourage a male and a female ally. The allies may encircle the client with their arms, protectively interpose themselves in front of the negative accommodator, or verbally dispute the disparaging messages. This crossfire of negative and positive messages dramatizes the conflict and heightens the client's experience of the resulting bodily tension. Anger is likely, evident in clenched fists or constricted breathing if not consciously apparent to the client. The rising emotion can be noted and validated by the *witness figure*.

When this anger is acknowledged and expressed, the client has broken the "don't talk, don't trust, don't feel" rules. The anger work is typically partial. If it is directed at the negative accommodator, it is likely to trigger fear of retaliation or uncertainty about the appropriateness of anger. Or it may be directed inward as rage at the self, which must be limited (by allies now re-enroled as limiting figures or ideal parents).

Important progress has been made. Inner feelings are given credence. Supportive parent surrogates have been sought out for limits, protection, reassurance, and approval. Any degree of self-assertion can be condoned, and the right to have and express emotions can be affirmed. The structure reaches its resolution when these affirmations are accepted in a congruent fashion by the client.

Accepting Nurturance. The supportive figures from the first structure are seldom fully accepted as ideal parents. This is because shame makes the client feel unacceptable (Bradshaw, 1988). The next phase of structure work involves regressing to the point at which *nurturance* is acceptable. This may be at an actual age and with an actual person with whom effective nurturance was available. It may be an imagined age which the client considers to have been innocent. Those who have had the advantage of self-help work often will have a photograph or self-portrait of the lovable inner child. In our experience, this child has always been younger than five. In many cases, the structure work involves a symbolic rebirth: the encircling womb is played by the group as an extension of the ideal mother.

This phase of structure work is initiated when the client, often out of fear or loneliness, begins to seek a nurturing figure. Ironically, the requested contact with the positive accommodator may be rejected or unsatisfying. This is subtle work; the client may act *as if* satisfied with the nurturance while remaining tense or physically contorted so as to minimize contact with the ideal mother. In this eventuality, the truth of the body must be made conscious for the client's pilot: The client is profoundly ambivalent about nurturance. The structure unfolds based on the careful exploration of the individual's particular blocks regarding nurturance. At times the presence of the ideal father has raised unresolved issues of parental conflict or incestuous pressures that must be worked through (with negative parent figures enroled to accommodate the polarized feelings). At times the ideal mother is imagined to be disapproving or incompletely available. Often the child/client feels guilt about neediness because of early maps indicating she or he should be caring for the mother. There are often breaks in contact at this point, with the client stiffening or supporting his or her own weight in symbolic expression of premature self-sufficiency. As the obstacles to nurturance are explored and resolved — often over the course of several structures — the parents are repeatedly polarized into loved and hated aspects, with ideal parents available when acceptable. Through this work, the ideal parents are "purified" as successive issues are resolved, and the child feels more worthy with repeated validation of his or her experience of truth.

This phase of structure work comes to fruition when the client can unreservedly accept nurturant messages, often in a configuration in which the ideal parents are cradling or nursing the placid child. When this experience can be symbolized and internalized, then there is an enduring antidote to the historical identity based on shame.

Expressing Anger and Grief Over Abandonment. Anger work must be completed, often interspersed with the shame work described above. Yet it is difficult for most ACOAs to acknowledge the depth of their anger. Instead, clients report somatic pain such as a headache, back ache, or a tight jaw. Often, aggression gets turned against the self in a flurry of self-condemnation — perhaps accompanied by suicidal fantasies. Motoric free association, in the first case, and interacting with negative *fragment figures*, in the latter, surface the anger. Free expression is usually blocked by one of three issues. First, there is the fear of hostile counterattack. This is handled, as described above, by securing protective allies (see Chapter 14 for an extended discussion of countering a history of abuse). Second, there is shame for feeling a forbidden emotion. This seems to be a pivotal issue for the many ACOAs whose identity is based on meeting the needs of a parent (Brown, 1988). They fear that any confrontation would devastate the parent, leaving the client with no protection against the experience of abandonment. Here it is critical to have ideal parents who can model self-care and reassure the client that the expression of anger will not jeopardize their love. It is then safer to acknowledge the anger toward the negative parent for the emotional neglect that accompanied the role reversal. Third, there may be fear that any expression of long-suppressed anger may lead to destructive loss of control. Pesso has noted that "all unexpressed emotions seem to amplify the longer they remain unexpressed" (1973, p. 72). In this case, the ideal parents need to convey the message that "we can handle your anger; it will hurt neither us nor you." The limit structure that follows provides the reassuring messages that the client is not destructively omnipotent and that the anger need not remain suppressed.

As anger can be expressed toward the negative accommodators, other feelings surface: sadness about emotional neglect and unmet needs, or hunger for nurturance. Through this phase of the work the client finally faces and grieves the many losses from childhood (Black, 1981; Bradshaw, 1988).

PS/P is an excellent vehicle for teaching boundaries, and ACOAs have had distorted experiences with boundaries. The existence of boundaries is graphically illustrated in the limiting/containing hands which reassure that anger can be expressed without destructiveness and in the contact/resistance figures who permit strength to "push up" in erect posture and full intake of breath. The witness confirms which feelings belong to the client, while various fragment figures embody the messages which were originally external and no longer need to remain internalized if they violate the soul's experience. Through touch and sight and words, boundaries are concretely experienced so that the individual can be validated as a separate being in the interactive field of her or his significant relationships. Having clear boundaries heals the codependent tendency toward loss of self when involved with others.

Authentic Emotional Expression as Survival Roles Are Dropped. In this concluding phase the structures become more diverse in terms of the emotions and the period of life history covered. The organizing focus is on acting from a grounding in authentic emotionality rather than playing the survival roles adopted in childhood. Those who are used to denying or autistically soothing their needs are urged to explore how the energy could be expressed and resolved in interaction. "Lost children" (Wegscheider, 1981), who learned to stay invisible, are encouraged to accept attention. The over-responsible "hero" explores overt dependency and playfulness. During this phase there is more spontaneity and emotional range: joyful dancing and horseplay mix with requests for praise and reassurance. The guiding principle in the structure work is that all experience is to be brought into interaction, often with validation from the ideal parents. With this work, the permission to track and act on inner experience is internalized. Mature self-care is established.

Special Issues with ACOAs in Psychomotor Groups

The group in which a majority of clients is from alcoholic families will present the therapist with several characteristic challenges. These can be resolved if the therapist is alert for their occurrence. First, it will be difficult for new clients to join an established group. The permissive attitude and the overt emotionality of the group will be very threatening to newcomers living by survival defenses which overcontrol emotions. They are especially likely to dislike in other group members their own split-off, unacknowledged feelings (especially anger or dependency). All clients are in concurrent individual therapy or active in a 12-step recovery program such as Al-Anon or AA. This affords support. Entry into the group is timed to coincide with willingness to explore emotions in individual therapy, and after there is a well-developed understanding of the rationale for expressive work.

Second, the permissive atmosphere can become an excuse for shutting down during another's structure work. Observers are as likely to drift off to sleep or to watch impassively as to cry quietly. This may seem bizarre to the newcomer, who may mistake passivity for callousness. In reality, it is the ACOA pattern of handling emotions internally. Hence, it is important that there be ample time to process reactions to each structure, including the opportunity for accommodated emotional expression if strong feelings are unresolved after the discussion. Members are encouraged to reach out for reassurance from others observing the structure. At one point there was the "baby animals" corner, in which three participants huddled together when the work stirred up vulnerable feelings.

Third, when in the structure, ACOAs are unusually likely to rely on self-nurturance rather than acknowledging their need for others. Conditioned to expect frustration or abuse when emotions are shared, ACOAs historically have found it safer to shut down their feelings rather than to interact based on them. ACOAs typically isolate or act out when "unacceptable" feelings occur. This is especially true for emotions such as anger, sexual attraction, or vulnerability, each of which alter the boundaries between people. So there may be abrupt shifts from emotionally and physically expressive work to uneasy quietness. We query closely any apparent turning inward, especially if there are gestures (e.g., pushing the fingers against closed eyes) that direct energy back to the body. The therapeutic corrective is clear: *All energy is an invitation to interaction.*

Fourth, the blurred interpersonal boundaries can cause trouble. Accommodators must be checked to assure they are not personalizing negative messages when role-playing negative figures. Likewise, accommodators often have to be cautioned against elaborating on the messages or contact they have been asked to provide. For example, a positive figure may start nurturing before more than a supportive presence has been requested. We see this as well intended, often responsive to real needs for nurturance, but mistimed out of codependent compulsion to be helpful. Lastly, boundary blurring may lead to transference acting out. The ideal mother in a structure may become an ideal mother after group. While we encourage out-of-group contact (many have outside relationships through self-help groups that predate the PS/P work), we urge people to be alert to transference and provide time in group to talk about it. The difference between the role and the individual playing it are highlighted by making a clear ritual of enroling and de-roling, including a change of physical placement to mark transitions.

Psychomotor meets the need for an experiential reengagement with childhood relationship patterns that allows ACOAs to face and resolve the developmental arrests that inhibit effective self-care. The experience in the structure work and in the group process encourages clients to break the limiting "don't talk, don't trust, don't feel" rules; to value inner experience; to get past shame and blocked grief work; to express feelings actively and to ask that others respond to felt needs; and to internalize the permission to act in self-affirming ways. In this, Psychomotor makes a major contribution to the remediation of the problems that confront the many adults who grew up in alcoholic families.

References

Beattie, M. (1987). *Codependent no more*. Center City, MN: Hazelden.

Bepko, C. (1985). *Responsibility trap: A blueprint for treating the alcoholic family*. New York: Free Press.

Black, C. (1981). *It will never happen to me*. Denver, CO: MAC.

Bowen, M. (1978). *Family therapy in clinical practice*. New York: Aronson.

Bradshaw, J. (1988). *Bradshaw on: The family: A revolutionary way of self-discovery*. Deerfield Beach, FL: Health Communications.

Brown, S. (1985). *Treating the alcoholic: A developmental model of recovery*. New York: Wiley.

Brown, S. (1988). *Treating adult children of alcoholics: A developmental perspective*. New York: Wiley.

Brown, S., & Beletsis, S. (1986). Development of family transference in groups for adult children of alcoholics. *International Journal of Group Psychotherapy, 36*, 97-114.

Cermak, T.L. (1986). *Diagnosing and treating co-dependence*. Minneapolis, MN: Johnson Institute Books.

Cermak, T.L. (1988). *A time to heal*. New York: Avon Books.

Cermak, T.L., & Brown, S. (1982). Interactional group therapy with the adult children of alcoholics. *International Journal of Group Psychotherapy, 32*, 375-389.

Crandell, J.S. (1987). *Effective outpatient treatment for alcohol abusers and drinking drivers*. Lexington, MA: Lexington Books.

Crandell, J.S. (1989). Brief treatment of adult children of alcoholics: Accessing resources for self-care. *Psychotherapy, 26*, 510-513.

Goodwin, D.W. (1979). Alcoholism and heredity. *Archives of General Psychiatry, 36*, 57-61.

Gravitz, H.L., & Bowden, J.D. (1985). *Guide to recovery: A book for adult children of alcoholics*. Holmes Beach, FL: Learning Publications, Inc.

Hibbard, S. (1987). The diagnosis and treatment of adult children of alcoholics as a specialized therapeutic population. *Psychotherapy, 24*, 779-785.

Jung, C.G. (1933). *Modern man in search of a soul*. New York: Harcourt, Brace and World.

Jung, C.G. (1987, summer), Spiritus contra spiritum: The Bill Wilson/C.G. Jung letters. *Parabola*, 71.

Krystal, H. (1977). Self representation and the capacity for self-care. *Annual of Psychoanalysis, 6*, 209-246.

Miller, A. (1981). *The drama of the gifted child: The search for the true self.* R. Ward (Trans.). New York: Basic Books.

Norwood, R. (1985). *Women who love too much.* Los Angeles: Jeremy Tarcher.

Pesso, A. (1969). *Movement in psychotherapy.* New York: New York University Press.

Pesso, A. (1973). *Experience in action.* New York: New York University Press.

Pesso, A. (1985). *Introduction to Psychomotor training.* Lecture given at the Dimele Center. (Available through the Telles Institute, P.O. Box 52246, Atlanta, GA 30355-0294).

Sarolea, H. (1986). Ideal Parents. *Pesso Bulletin, 2,* 1-9.

Schaef, A. W. (1986). *Co-dependence: Misunderstood-mistreated.* San Francisco: Harper and Row.

Subby, R. (1987). *Lost in the shuffle.* Pompano Beach, FL: Health Communications.

Twelve steps and twelve traditions. (1953). New York: Alcoholics Anonymous World Services.

Wegscheider, S. (1981). *Another chance: Hope and help for the alcoholic family.* Palo Alto, CA: Science and Behavior Books.

Wegscheider-Cruse, S. (1985). *Choicemaking.* Pompano Beach, FL: Health Communications.

Chapter 18

Using Psychomotor in Private Practice with Individual Clients.

by Carl Telles Clarke with Doris Chaves

Purpose

This chapter is written from the perspective of a private practitioner who uses Psychomotor with clients. My purpose is to highlight some of the issues, the benefits, and the scope of application of PS/P principles which I have experienced in my private practice. I will describe the use of Psychomotor strategies primarily with individual clients. I bring to my therapy with individual clients a grounding in Psychomotor theory and methodology, which I acquired by the experience and training necessary for my certification in Psychomotor therapy with Al and Diane Pesso. This experience included guiding approximately 500 *structures* in the context of weekend Psychomotor therapy workshops of 8 to 10 participants each (conducted nationally) and in the context of ongoing weekly Psychomotor Therapy groups.

The psychotherapy clients in these weekly groups I had also seen or was currently seeing in individual therapy. I developed, as part of the therapy process, specific strategies to prepare persons for structure work in individual sessions. Before actual structures are done many adaptations from Psychomotor theory and procedure are employed. My current preferred methodology of working with clients is a unique combination of bi-weekly individual and group sessions. The eight clients in the group I work with this week, I will see in individual sessions next week, then in the group again the following week. In both settings I am now utilizing a broad range of applications of Psychomotor theory and technique, some of which I will attempt to describe.

Goals of Therapy

I have come to the realization that I have specific goals relative to the personal growth of my clients and that the specific applications of Psychomotor therapy I use in my private practice are in the service of reaching those goals.

At present, four psychotherapy goals guide my selection of Psychomotor technique in ongoing individual therapy sessions. My first goal is to teach clients to use their symbolic processes in the service of integrating the use of the *ideal parent* symbol into the adult self for personal parenting. The goal is reached when the symbols of ideal mother and ideal father, which are central to Psychomotor therapy, and the adult that the person knows him/herself to be, become one and the same: The adult self learns how to parent the part of the self which is still immature, still child. Without the role model of ideal father/ideal mother, the adult self is much more vulnerable to being influenced by the negative role model of the original inadequate parenting in place of learning the appropriate parenting response.

This first goal is in part dependent upon attaining the remaining three goals which have to do with expanding the use of consciousness in the service of personal growth.

The second therapy goal is to teach the client to be more aware of his/her own inner guidance. This is a process of learning that involves the person identifying the range of mental experiences s/he trusts and calls guidance, or inner guidance. The person learns how to differentiate what part of that range of experiences is trustworthy, and what is untrustworthy; i.e., what leads to personal growth and contributes to individuation, and what does not. Through the therapeutic process, the person also learns to identify those inner experiences that s/he does not trust, but which need to be trusted for wholeness of personhood to be accomplished: forms of innate inner guidance that in childhood were rejected, disowned, and misidentified as untrustworthy. These rejected innate forms of inner guidance include the instinctual, the intuitive, the creative, and the emotional impulses of body energy.

My third therapy goal is to teach the client to be aware of being "in a child state of consciousness" while being in it. Being in a child's state of consciousness is living by an unconscious adaptive pattern created by the child in response to a *basic need* deprivation. For example, being in such a state is feeling rejected by another when actually that person is being loving. A child state of consciousness is a marker, indicating a point at which the emergence of some part of the *true self* was interrupted. Every such pattern — however detestable and abhorrent, or however acceptable and respected — is a marker for unrealized potential: potential that is yet to grow, and that will need parenting as it grows.

Parenting is nurturing, supporting, encouraging, respecting, protecting, limiting, and guiding: all different behavioral expressions of the interactive energy called love. The client's learning includes recognizing the pattern and responding to the pattern as a marker that points to an unfulfilled basic need. The essential resource the person has for learning how to be the parent of the child s/he still is comes by way of inner guidance.

The fourth goal is to teach clients to access all the love they have within — healing/ guiding energy — for the benefit of growing-up the parts of the true self that still need the parenting that was absent. It is my belief that as organisms, we maintain our biological integrity by the constant production of an organizing energy at the cellular level. When experienced consciously, this energy is called love. The child states of consciousness are unable to access conscious awareness of this love. When experienced consciously, this energy is beneficial and healing. I further believe the cellular energy of love carries the information by which the person can change everything that is blocking the articulation of the full range of the person's genetic endowment.

I find that Psychomotor enables me to work toward these personal growth goals with great effectiveness and economy. To me, Psychomotor is a therapy grounded in a theory of being and becoming that directs the therapist to look for the innate growth process in the clients. Upon finding that process and forming an alliance with it, the therapist teaches clients to follow their guidance. I believe Psychomotor is a more evolved way of addressing the dynamics and the issues of the natural process of growing up: to unlock it, to release it, to liberate it, to nurture it, to cultivate it, as needed. When I use metaphors that are based on parenting and child functioning, I am able to convey information about the truth of the client's experiences with greater economy and more power. I see the "growing up" that I am referring to as the important unfinished process of adulthood; it is life being itself at this stage of its individualized becoming. The ultimate effect of achieving these four psychotherapy goals is the possibility of persons functioning in the full range of all their maturing capabilities.

Description of the Therapy Room and its Contents

In support of the application of Psychomotor techniques in individual and group sessions, the therapy room by design has the appearance of a room in a home. It has wall to wall carpeting adequately padded for comfortable sitting and floor level therapy work; with table lamps suitable for living/bedroom use located on small tables in several corners; with a variety of potted plants here and there including a Ficus tree that almost touches the ceiling; with a two person sofa and therapist's chair; and a miscellany of objects visible to the client for use in a variety of roles. The therapy room lends itself 1) to being enroled in many ways, parts of it or the whole of it; 2) to therapy done in the customary sitting position in chairs and sofa; as well as 3) to structure work that often is more appropriately and safely done while seated on the floor.

Both individual and group sessions are conducted in this same room. In group sessions, other group members are enroled to symbolically represent the content-aspects of the client's consciousness (*accommodation*). Sometimes objects in the room are also enroled along with the accommodators. In the individual sessions, in place of other group members, anything and everything in the room can be enroled. The soft, large-armed, two person sofa becomes the lap of ideal mother. Add a large cushion in upright position on the sofa with the client's arm encircling it and the *supporting* or *protective* ideal father is also present. Currently, there are twenty cushion/pillows to choose from, in all sizes and shapes and with covers of many different colors and designs. All aspects of the therapy room are chosen to support a broad range of symbolic possibilities.

While the vulnerability of the plants silently calls attention to the need for protective limits in the interactive resolutions of structure work, their obvious symbolism of life and nurturance offer many clients very powerful external representation of what they have yet to find and connect to within: the support, hope, and trust to be; the sense of place and intrinsic worth; and the link to a long lineage of those who passed on the keys of life from one generation to the next.

The objects are a few large and many small items of obvious functional value or seemingly irrelevant meaning. There is the tape recorder with flashing lights and cords to mikes here and there; the fan, the clocks, and the window unit air-conditioner; a traveled foot locker, now base for several plants; the five foot long piece of drift wood sculptured by nature's hand leaning in the furthest corner behind the ceiling-high Ficus tree; the whitish-grey skull of a small animal hiding under the thorn-tipped leaves of a potted plant; and the hideous-hilarious face on the blue pogo ball. All of these objects are here and there in their usual places in the room. But in a small area, the size of a large dinner plate (at the corner of the foot locker), is an assortment of some 70 items laid out in an ever-changing pattern: polished stones; sea tumbled fragments of ancient shells; small plastic figures of ninjas, mermaids, and humans; several colorful little wooden cars with big wooden wheels; a small segment of sheep skin; polished wood and crystal curios; some tiny fossils; a Kakua nut; etc.

A client is seldom unable to select some object to symbolically represent a place, a person, a principle from her/his personal experience. The cushions, mattress, and pillows form an "on the floor" sitting area along three sides of the room with the walls holding up the back-supporting cushions. In a moment's notice any or all of these support objects can be incorporated into the client's symbolic work.

As therapist/Psychomotor *structure leader,* I am sitting in my customary chair, on the floor on my white sheep skin, or leaning against the wall, all depending upon where the client chooses to sit at the beginning of the session and by the client's movement into and out of structure work. I am flexible as to where I sit, how I sit, and how long before I change slightly or altogether.

Working with a New Client

Part of the assessment I make while getting acquainted in the first few sessions is to identify where I may begin using Psychomotor theory and techniques with the client. In my mind, I am asking: "What are you ready for in Psychomotor therapy?" I may, in a given moment, ask the person to do something that is Psychomotor just to assess what s/he may do with that.

I check for the entry level ability at using symbolic processes, and I test for the level of readiness of the client to project on to objects in the therapy room the symbolic meaning of thoughts/feelings/memory processes/fantasies/dreams. While assessing the person's ability to accept support from me as his/her painful/scary feelings surface, I may also explore with the client the readiness to use a symbolic source of support as well.

To establish the body awareness level at which the client is functioning, I will offer some of the focusing suggestions and questions of Psychomotor structure work: "Be aware of the tension in the front of your body. What might be the meaning of it? How might you use that energy?"

Assessing Ability to Use Symbolic Processes

In specific moments, I target assessment questions from those aspects of Psychomotor that have to do with using symbolic process in the service of the therapy process. For example, is this person able to imagine a different experience from the one he lived? As a client is telling me about his mother, how it was in childhood with her, I might ask: "How did you need her to be in that situation?" The response will tell me if he knows, from within, the parenting that was needed and can imagine that happening (can symbolize it). Some people are so disconnected from that knowing that they cannot imagine what they needed. If so, I will slightly modify the assessment question and say: "Well, what would it have been like if your mother could have done such-and-such?" What I am doing is presenting the knowledge which I recognize the person has but is unaware of at this time. I am at this point checking to see if he can recognize it; giving him a model on the outside to facilitate the inner connection.

A basic assumption in Psychomotor is that the needed parenting is inherently known by the organism and responded to by growth. When this basic knowing cannot be articulated upon request, then the next step is to offer a picture of the needed parenting to call forth the recognition of it out of the inherent knowing. When clients recognize what they needed, their bodies will acknowledge that recognition emotionally. A person may sigh, or tear-up, or begin verbalizing an emotional response. When these responses occur, I know that this client can imagine the good parenting that was needed and will be receptive to using the symbol of ideal parents for corrective re-parenting experiences.

I may then assess the form in which the *antidote* might need to be for the client to accept it. For example, I might check out if s/he can, having assessed the symbol of good parenting, put the symbol outside. Is the client able to use the mental process of projection to effect a corrective parenting experience. To do so, I ask the client to pick an object in the therapy room to symbolically represent a mother who would have done "such-and-such." I suggest s/he follow inner guidance to know which object to pick for enroling. If the client is able to respond positively to these suggestions, I know that the person's ability to use the symbolic process to experience ideal parenting is potentially accessible. I anticipate the opportunities in subsequent sessions to activate and develop that ability as part of the on-going therapy process and as preparation to do structures in the context of individual psychotherapy sessions. From the above assessment procedures and others like them, I anticipate where and how I can help a client use specific aspects of Psychomotor. Multiple applications have an enriching effect to the therapy/growth processes of the client as well as prepare him/her to do structure work.

Assessing Use of Support

Another important ability to assess early in the developing therapy relationship is how ready the person is to accept support. For instance, if the person starts to cry and I see her/him blocking it, I may say something that is supportive of the feelings and permission-giving to the expression of them. The resistance to consciously experience supportive emotional energy indicates that the client's process of becoming is being blocked by a child's state of consciousness, of a specific age, and of specific beliefs and decisions. I know I am observing this person being controlled by a pattern created by the child mindset. I am already wondering what the family of origin *countershape* was to the *shape* of the adaptation I am now observing. I begin anticipating what ideal parenting will be its antidote. If the client can take support from me through my verbal expression of it, that response will tell me about what this person may be able to do with the symbol of ideal support figures. I might, even then, introduce the thought of "what would be the effect if you had someone who gives you permission to have your feelings." I am exploring not only whether the person is ready to use the figures, but whether or not the person is receptive to have support through his/her own symbolic process in addition to the support coming from me.

Assessing Level of Body Awareness

Through my experience with structure work, I am growing more sensitive to the flow of guidance energy which is clearly manifest in the body. For example, energy may be showing up in the body through the tension that effects the way the client holds the hands or a foot, but the person seems not to be aware of these emerging motoric expressions. When attention is directed to where in the body the energy is manifest, there is the potential for increased awareness and possible movement toward a satisfying resolution. Insight and integration of new meaning about self usually follow a satisfying interactive motoric expression.

Selectively, there is a series of questions that I might ask to establish an awareness of this body energy. I may ask: "Can you become aware of tension in your hands as they clasp together?" If the person reports being aware, I become curious how s/he might be able to utilize that awareness. I may ask what the person considers the meaning of the tension to be, what movement might express that meaning, or with whom might the energy want to interact if it was free to move. Whatever their answer, I am assessing the person's readiness to use specific, entry level procedures in doing Psychomotor structure work. An outcome effect of asking such questions is often that the person begins to learn to become more aware of his/her body when there are such emergent energies.

Sometimes the flow of emotion takes the client into memories that I know to be important, but that this session is not the time to work with them. If sufficient trust is not established, I know that the person is going to be too defended and not prepared to take in support and bring the emotional arousal into therapeutic healing. So, the "entrance place" to the work can be acknowledged without having to go into it immediately. In words appropriate to the specific person, I would say, "I can see how close you are to that, how present that is to you. We will first do the preparation work we need to do for you to move through this feeling state into the resolution you need."

Assessing the Ability to Use the Symbol of Ideal Parents

One of the fundamental tasks I set for myself in the therapy process is to teach the person how to use the symbol of ideal parents beyond the therapy session. I know I am going to teach the client to do self-parenting following the role model of the ideal mother/ideal father symbols which s/he will create and evolve in the course of therapy with me.

To accomplish a functional personal use of the symbol of ideal mother/ideal father, I will offer the possible use of the symbol at every point in the therapy process where I see the client could experience ideal parenting. Sometimes this will be in the context of a formal structure, but more frequently it will involve the immediate and brief use of visualization: "If you had an ideal mother right now, what would you want to hear her say to you?...How would you want her to hold you?," etc. As the client's ability to employ the symbol grows, I begin to encourage the use of this ability in connection with his/her awareness of being in specific child states of consciousness. From session to session as they give feedback regarding the outcome of such personal use of the symbol, I continue to teach and coach for improved effectiveness.

I observe clients learning to use these symbols 1) to access positive emotional potentials which formerly were seldom felt, 2) to reprocess original negative experiences, being able to antidote the deprivations of them, 3) to activate the adult state of consciousness in the service of dealing therapeutically with the reality of being in a child state of consciousness.

As part of learning the self-parenting process, I will check with clients whether or not they are ready to use the reality of the way they are functioning at a mature level, as adult, as the parent to take back into their childhood. I would say: "If the part of you that understands what you are saying to me right now about what you needed in childhood, if that part of you could go back and be with the child that you are telling me about, what would you do, what would you say to him/her?" The main objective I have is to check out the person's capacity for compassion and love. Or, I will ask: "If the adult that you are when you are doing such-and-such with so-and-so could go back and be with the child that you are describing right now, what would be your response as that adult? How would you respond to that child?" If the person is able to feel love and compassion for that child, it will pop right out. But, if s/he is not able to feel love, then I know that this is another one of the areas of personal growth we will be focusing on in the therapy process.

What I am trying to establish is this capacity to transfer adult functioning back in time to the child who needed assistance. I know that what I am going to teach clients to do, in parenting themselves, is to learn how to utilize the adult functioning they have already developed to parent the inner child that has not developed. Knowing their capacity for self-love guides in the introduction and development of a functional symbol of ideal parents for the adult to model after in place of the inadequate model of the real parents.

Starting With Fragment Figures

Early in the development of the therapy relationship, the function of affirming and validating emotional expressivity can be moved from the person/role of the therapist to the symbol of the *witness figure*: one of the many *fragment figures*. The witness figure sees and understands all emotions without judgment. Since this figure and its use in setting the true scene at the beginning of a structure is described in detail elsewhere, I will only describe my applications of it in individual therapy sessions.

Introducing the symbol of the witness figure and teaching the use of it in individual therapy sessions is often the place of beginning the creation of the symbol of ideal mother/father. Learning to feel accepted and affirmed by ideal parents while experiencing and expressing emotions that were rejected in childhood can begin from hearing that acceptance and affirmation in the therapist's voice while his/her voice is enrolled as the voice of the witness figure: "I can see and understand how sad you feel while remembering what happened to you when..."

The selective use of the witness figure when the client is expressing herself with observable affect is a dependable first step toward developing the ability to activate bodily responses by projected symbols. The response that occurs as the witness figure becomes believable and functional is the beginning of learning to respond to the symbol of ideal parents. The witness function of validating the feelings is a fundamental ideal parenting function. Likewise, from the experiential connection with the witness figure can evolve the use of the other fragment figures of the ideal parent symbol that give permission, protection, comfort, support, containment, limits, etc. Clients for whom the ideal parent is, at first, too good to be true, can accept a protection figure, support figure, etc. Out of the seed of such a fragment figure grows the symbols of an ideal mother and ideal father.

As the witness figure can be used independently of structure work per se, so can all of the other voices of the various fragment figures: the voice of caution, judgement, personal truth, etc. Traditionally, the employment of the positive and negative voices of fragment figures results in an internal crossfire leading to the establishment of the client's true scenes early in the structure. But in individual sessions, long before structure work is introduced, many applications can be made of fragment figures to increase body awareness and to intensify the experience of structure energies for recognition and exploration of meaning. Most clients need the assistance of taking tiny new steps of awareness before entering the expanded self-awareness and self-expression that can result from full structure work.

Minimizing Transference in Individual Therapy Sessions

The caveat of Psychomotor therapy is to redirect the transference off of the therapist onto an accommodator or object. The Psychomotor method intends to involve the client in the conscious choice of temporarily projecting an aspect of her/his symbolic process onto an *accommodator*, who has agreed to be the external representation, or onto an object of choice.

In a Psychomotor group the functions of an accommodator are taken on by other clients. With the accommodator symbolically representing the object of the client's child feelings, thoughts, desires, or expectations, the client can psychomotorically express repressed experiences. Because the identities of significant others are projected onto the accommodators, the client keeps at a minimum the transference of those identities unconsciously onto the Psychomotor therapist. The intent of the structure is to consciously utilize the projection process (transference) for an agreed upon limited time frame. At the end of the structure, the symbols are intentionally withdrawn from the accommodator and the meaning taken back inside by the client.

In individual therapy sessions, in the place of clients functioning as accommodators, various objects are in the therapy room for enroling. And with caution, the therapist can also enrole as an accommodator or enrole her/his voice, representing the voice of a specific figure.

However, as therapist, I limit the extent to which I enrole myself as an accommodator. I do not enrole myself to symbolically represent the total figure. While there have been exceptions to this standard limitation, experience has taught me to enrole an object first to symbolically represent the total person. My enrolement then is limited to extensions of the enroled figure with parts of my body as: "the voice of," "the hands of," "the leg of," "the foot of." In this manner I remain the therapist as a total person, having only a part of me being used as a symbol.

When speaking as the enroled figure, it is important for the therapist to make that representation very clear. For example, I would say: "I'm using my voice now as the voice of the ideal father;" or, when using my voice as any of the fragment figures, I will say: "I'm using my voice now to speak as the voice of your truth, etc." Even clients new to Psychomotor structure work have little difficulty keeping the voices sorted out as long as I am identifying how I am using my voice symbolically. As stated above, experience has taught me to enrole an object as the total person. After doing so, I determine with the client that the symbol has been projected onto the enroled object by asking for feedback as to the effect of the enrolement. When projection is effected, then I enrole my hands, voice, arm, etc. Only while my hands are enroled as the hands of an ideal figure will I be touching the client.

If I enroled as an accommodator, using my entire body on every occasion that a support/ protective/containment figure were needed in an individual session, taking the symbol off of me at the end of the work would be less likely to occur fully and a more active transference would likely develop. Enroling some other object and only a part of me reduces that likelihood. Also, by meeting in a Psychomotor group every other week and using different group members as accommodators, clients learn the intentional use of projection. Then, in the individual sessions where I have to sometimes be involved in touching, holding, providing containment, or resistance, the symbol is more easily taken off of me when the symbolic work is completed. With clients who have not yet done structure work in a group context, I am even less likely to enrole my total body as an accommodator.

Before any physical touching in individual sessions is employed in the accommodation process, the possibility of this happening and the need for it will be discussed and the variety of reactions and meanings considered. The client needs to be comfortable and confident that the real and symbolic meanings can be differentiated by client and therapist. Again working alternately in individual and group sessions from week to week provides an experiential learning laboratory in which to develop the mental capability of utilizing the realness of the body contact. The contact is in the service of creating the needed symbolic meaning and transferring that meaning back to the historical context in which it is the adequate and sufficient antidote.

Another essential safeguard to reduce transference is the process of enroling and de-roling. Anything and everything that is used as symbolic representation of the client's experience must be consciously enroled and then consciously de-roled from that symbolism. There needs to be conscious involvement in taking the symbols off of the objects and off of me and taking them back inside.

The de-roling process includes not only taking the symbol off of, but also returning the object, person, or part of the person to its original place and function. In this way if, as a therapist, I have enroled my voice as a symbol, at the end of the structure I will de-role my voice as that symbol. If I have moved in the direction of the client, I will return to my original place and posture. If I sense that the client may not have made the shift from symbolic to literal thinking, then I will ask the client to say the de-roling statement again and discuss the need to take the symbol back inside.

One may keep in mind that the statement of enroling has some effect on mental functioning. The desired effect is a shift in the state of consciousness to symbolic functioning in which a symbolic representation of reality has the same stimulus power to activate all levels of organismic responsivity as does a perception of reality. De-roling is the process of taking the symbol off of what or whom it has been projected onto and shifting back to a state of consciousness where the symbol is no longer related to as if it were a perception of reality. The de-roling statement is an announcement to the symbolic process that its work is finished for now. In individual sessions, not only does the client say the de-roling statement, but I will also say the de-roling statement about the object. Hearing the de-roling statement from an external source assists the client in the removal of the projected symbol and the shift in consciousness back to a literal orientation.

Limits to Structure Work in Individual Sessions

The greatest challenge to me in guiding structures during individual sessions has been to become effective in limiting the scope and depth of the structure work to fit within the varying time limits which are encountered from session to session. Structure energies emerge throughout each individual therapy session. Plus, there are frequent opportunities for me to ask questions or to give suggestions that lead into structure energies. Deciding which of the many structure issues to focus on requires a certain sensitivity to one's own intuitive guidance.

Working to a positive resolution in the remaining session time, which may be anywhere from 5 to 40 minutes, requires a continuing commitment to precision in guiding. Having to rush through the end phase of the structure, in the interest of stopping the session on time, often leaves the client still in the past, not yet ready to function in the present. Seeing this happen to a few clients was enough for me to know I wanted to learn to guide with precision so that whatever the time limits, a satisfactory closure would be effected. Learning how to move quickly to the resolution (end) phase of the structure when there is less than 10 minutes in which to get closure has been essential.

Of course there have been sessions in which the client began by asking to do a structure on a specified issue. But comparatively speaking, planned or spontaneous structures that begin early in a session are a luxury. Most structure work in individual sessions has to be done within a much tighter time limit.

Actually, a subsequent structure can begin right where the work had to stop in a previous session. The same objects can be enroled, the same positions taken, and the client can usually return to the unfinished aspects of the previous structure work. Knowing this has made it easier to identify stopping places in the work where closure can be achieved, in the brief time remaining, with the assurance of returning to this point and resuming the work. And the work done to this point is acknowledged as precursor to a longer structure in some future session in which a more adequate expression of the structure energies can be accommodated.

Some clients need more post-structure time in the session before "hitting the street" than do other clients. The therapist learns to identify this need and limits the structure time accordingly. I am also sensitive to the occasional need for asking the client not to drive for a given time after leaving the therapy room.

There are those critical moments in the use of Psychomotor in an individual session in which judgements are made whether the effects of some specific touching techniques will be more beneficially experienced by delaying their utilization until the next group session rather than attempting them in this individual session. For instance, when a client needs the hand of the ideal father to be placed over the chest or when the hand of the ideal mother is to be placed over the navel. Also, when the structure energies call for more limits or resistance than the room and I can provide, we limit our work in the individual session to doing only that which is precursor to addressing this issue in the group context where adequate accommodation is assured.

A different kind of issue that also requires the accommodation of group members is that, for some clients, the use of inanimate objects as ideal parents is too close a reconstruction of the original parent-child relationship in which the parent was physically there but emotionally was totally unavailable....absent! Initially, these clients need to connect with the emotional energy of the accommodators who are enroled as ideal parents. After they experience the range of their possible emotional reactions to the accommodators' emotional presence, the newly emerging response capabilities can be evoked with enroled objects in the individual sessions.

Allying with the Child Within as the First Step Toward Ideal Parents

My Psychomotor orientation enables me to be more effective in making alliances with the child parts of the client as they emerge. Very early in the therapy I begin discovering and developing the language (words, metaphors, stories) by which the client and I can talk about and with the child within.

When there is sufficient trust, I will use statements and questions that help clients become aware that the thinking or feelings being experienced represent a younger emotional part of themselves. With some clients I will ask the question, "How emotionally young are you, thinking or feeling that way?" This is often the client's first step in expanding awareness toward being able to make this discrimination personally, both in and out of the therapy session. As soon as I can, I point the new client to the fundamental truth encoded in the metaphor of the "child within/the children within" by communicating in one way or another: "Once we have reached adulthood, our greatest challenge is to discover all the ways we're still children and to take the responsibility for learning how to grow-up those parts of ourselves." For most clients, this communication immediately evokes a personal truth that is felt at once to be self-evident.

With each new client, I also assess his/her understanding of the concept of a child state of consciousness as a fixed "pattern of being" learned in childhood in order to protect some yet-to-be expressed part of the *soul*. My ultimate goal is to help the client develop the ability to recognize the child's thoughts, feelings, and beliefs; to establish connections with the child/children within; and to develop the symbol system for communicating with this inner truth in order to develop an effective adult/parent-child relationship.

Once I have made a personal connection with the child within and the child part talks to me, I will, on occasion, explore the child's ability to relate to ideal parents. When I know I am talking with the child directly, I will talk to the child about her/his understanding of what parenting was wanted; if needed, I may suggest the parenting by asking the question, "If you could have had a father who would have..." When the client can create such a symbol of an alternative positive parent-figure, there are observable body reactions which cue me that the child is connecting with the symbol and is feeling parented, or is resisting connecting with the parenting. If the ideal parenting is resisted, I know a defensive child state of conscious is in control in this moment. If the good parenting can be symbolized, the next step toward Psychomotor structure work would be to suggest that some object/plant in the room be enroled as ideal mother and/or ideal father. The suggestion is addressed in a style so as to involve the adult part of the ego (called the *pilot* or observing ego) in making the selection and in the process of enrolement and placement, and at the same time maintain the alliance with structure energies, that is, the child's feelings.

Learning How to Parent Oneself

In therapy I know that learning how to use the symbol of the ideal parent is often an essential precursor to the ability to parent oneself. Once the client can use the symbol of an ideal parent, s/he then has a newly emergent role model from which the adult s/he is can learn to parent the child s/he is. With the role model of ideal parents, the innate principle of parenting can be evoked in the service of the unfinished work of maturation. Without the inclusion of the ideal parents, the client is much more likely to maintain much of the unquestioned negative parenting style of the original parents.

In structure work, when the ideal parents validate the child that the client still is, they model the groundedness, the support, the encouragement, the protection, and the wisdom the client can learn to find within. Since one of my goals is to help the client learn to use the symbols of ideal mother/father outside of the therapy session, frequently I will attempt to find a way that is believable and acceptable to the client to use the symbol of the ideal parents. I will illustrate this process with a short description of the work one of my clients experienced.

One of this man's growth/parenting issues was that, in his family of origin, he got little or no recognition for any of his own creativity, intuitive insights, or inner being. In one session, he was saying something to me that I knew was coming out of his intuitive process. From the content, the way he was talking, and the way he introduced the subject, I knew he was thinking right at his creative edge. He began to recognize it also, and said: "You know, this is really good. What I just said is really right on. It's the truth."

Keeping the orientation in the present, I said: "What if right now you were to have ideal parents who would say, "Great, Charles! How intuitive you are! What a bright idea that is..." This exclamation was chosen to include within it recognition, acknowledgement, and celebration. Immediately, his energy responded and I knew he had already connected with the symbol in response to my enactment of the ideal parents. So I said, "Well, you could just enrole something, right now, as ideal mother and ideal father, and I could use my voice." He was sitting on the floor, leaning against the couch for support; so when I observed: "Well, you are leaning against the couch...", he made the further connection: "Yeah, I can enrole the couch as my ideal father and ideal mother."

There was a cushion already on the couch, he picked up another cushion, enroling them as extensions of the ideal parents; and he wedged them back behind him with the corner of each cushion protruding under an armpit. He positioned himself, snuggling right into them and had me use my voice; at that moment a lot of energy showed up in his feet, and we looked at that and wondered what that might mean. He had a sense of wanting to be grounded. I pointed out that, usually, that is the function of the ideal father. So, we enroled a cushion as the feet of the ideal father and placed that cushion against his feet. I enroled my feet as an extension of the ideal father and placed them against the cushion, providing the literal resistance to effect the experience of groundedness in the ideal father as he used the energy in his feet to push into the cushion. While pushing, he started telling me what he wanted to hear, and I used my voice as the voice of the ideal father. Immediately, he became aware of being "Little Charles," and he was able to get it clearly framed that now he was in his child and receiving what he needed to hear back then.

He wanted and received beautifully affirming statements about being intuitive and instinctual, about how trustworthy that is, and about the wisdom that comes in that way being just as important as any knowledge he will ever get from the outside. After about ten minutes of working with the symbol of ideal parents, he reached closure and de-roled everything.

Without the Psychomotor framework, I might or might not have made some acknowledgement about the fact that he was being intuitive at that moment. Without Psychomotor, I certainly would not have been able to shift from the present time frame and the behavior that was going on in the present frame to an historical frame. When that same instinctual behavior occurred in childhood, it had not been recognized and affirmed, or if it was recognized at all, the child was related to in a punitive, negative manner.

In using the ideal parenting procedure, this client moved from being oriented to the present to a historical set of conditions where a basic need had not been met, and we were able to work there in a reparenting, healing way. Because the original parenting was not adequate, his adult trust in his intuition was very limited and many creative potentials had never developed and had not become part of this self system yet. With the effective repeated use of the symbols of ideal mother/father, that potential can be activated and those parts of the self can mature, developing the sense of growth toward wholeness.

I believe that much remains to be done in learning how to use the ideal parent symbol to enhance the healing to the mind, to open new vistas of potentiality for people. Through the use of the ideal parent symbol some of what is now accomplished in group structures can also be done in individual therapy in a variety of applications that do not require the presence and participation of accommodators.

Summary

This chapter discussed some of the core issues, the benefits, and the evolution of my experience in the application of Psychomotor therapy principles and strategies in the private practice setting. Most of the discussion centered around the private therapist and a single client. The great potential for the private therapist to use multiple applications from the Psychomotor system was demonstrated. The theoretical underpinnings of specific strategies were elucidated. The power of imagery, interaction, symbolism, and the use of contents of the private office as interactive figures were described. The self-parenting capabilities that mature from a personal use of the symbol of ideal parents was emphasized.

Chapter 19

A Pastor's Use
of Psychomotor

by Armen Hanjian

Pastors are often the first to be approached by persons needing help with life. This is so in that the pastor is usually a trusted person; his or her services, at least initially, are free of charge; and persons often sense a connection between their problem and their spiritual life.

In this chapter I share my developmental use of Psychomotor as a pastor in the United Methodist Church. In a twelve year period, I have administered 60 weekend workshops (eight clients per weekend) involving over 200 different individuals. Some persons have come to only one workshop; others have participated with regularity. Some have entered into Psychomotor training.

I am not suggesting this pattern for all pastors. I do believe all pastors can benefit personally and in their counseling to the extent they are comfortable with this powerful modality.

My introduction to Psychomotor came in setting up a weekend workshop in my community. I invited a clinical psychologist who had begun training in the Pesso System to be the guide. My mind set was this: "This would be good for those I recruited for the workshop." In fact, it was also good for my wife and me. We were able to assess the Pesso System both by observation and experience. Thus, we began a journey which has not ceased in terms of enabling our own personal growth, dealing with our own hurts and deprivation issues, and even recapturing warm positive experiences from the forgotten past and celebrating them.

Soon the Psychomotor guide was coming to our community a couple of times a year. It was not long before I shifted in my mind from "What can I receive personally" to "How can this be beneficial in my interactions with other people and my understandings of other people?" In observing the guide I began asking, "What interventions would I make?" I got captured by the way the system was readily usable in my counseling work, how it was so congruent with real life. It rang true!

Training in Psychomotor produced a major shift in my counseling methodology. This was the shift to being with a person at the *center of his or her truth* as opposed to advising a person to move from where they were to where I thought they should be. I discovered experientially that when I am with people in the center of their truth and when that truth is set up outside them where they can see it clearly, their internal energies are mobilized and the movement begins of their opening, of their trusting, of their expressing — a movement toward finding the *antidote* for their dilemma.

All this is very much an expression of my Christian attitude toward life; namely, that God accepts us just as we are and where we are, and, in response to that, life unfolds with gratitude and with self-development. The two work together very harmoniously. Psychomotor, in many respects, became for me an expression of Christian caring.

Persons of most faith communities would appreciate that Pesso System/Psychomotor honors the biblical attitude that creation, all of life, is good, that each person/soul is of value. This therapy system regularly confirms the values of full parenting with both male and female parents, of family, and of caring community.

As a Christian pastor, I find this system congruent with the beneficial truth that Jesus accepts us just as we are. Although Jesus was critical of the "religious" leaders of his day, he did relate in a non-judgmental way to tax collectors and prostitutes, to intruding children, and to the criminal on the cross next to his. He always seemed to be with a person in his or her center. A universal truth seems to be that in accepting persons where they are, energy emerges to move them toward wholeness and healthier relationships.

Similarly, this therapy system is accepting of the client in two ways that are very clear to me. First, the therapist stays in the center of his or her truth. There is a place for transference; however, that is peeled off and placed on a *fragment figure* in the structure who states an old tape of an injunction, or on one who is witnessing the person's affect. In addition, the therapist's countertransference screen informs the therapist with truth regarding the immediate reality.

Secondly, the client is guided/allowed to stay in his or her own center. This is done by letting the person stay in charge of the work with the help of the therapist who works at not letting the person readopt an old pattern (a negative reconstruction) or hurt him/herself or another. The work provides unconscious information to be surfaced and owned by the client. Clients are enabled to be congruent with their own feelings — to be in their *true scene* from moment to moment so that they may fully own their shifts in understanding and own their healing.

I understand this process to be what was operative when Jesus used parables to help people see truth, own it and "repent" — that is, make a change of direction in their lives. The parables of Jesus in the New Testament usually have interpretations added. However, when read without the interpretations the parables have a timeless value in that they offer not answers to some life situation, but a provocative stimulating paradox or statement or picture that requires the hearer to reconsider his or her own life situation.

For example, consider Luke 18:2-5 (verses 1 and 6-8 are interpretation):

> [2]He said, "In a certain city there was a judge who neither feared God nor regarded man; [3] and there was a widow in that city who kept coming to him and saying, 'Vindicate me against my adversary.' [4] For a while he refused; but afterward he said to himself, 'Though I neither fear God nor regard man, [5] yet because the widow bothers me, I will vindicate her, or she will wear me out by her continual coming.'"
> (*Holy Bible, Revised Standard Edition*)

Or consider Luke 8:5-8 (verses 9-15 are interpretation):

> [5]"A sower went out to sow his seed; and as he sowed, some fell along the path, and was trodden under foot, and the birds of the air devoured it. [6] And some fell on the rock; and as it grew it withered away, because it had no moisture. [7] And some fell

among thorns; and the thorns grew with it and choked it. [8] And some fell into good soil and grew, and yielded a hundred fold." As he said this, he called out, "He who has ears to hear, let him hear."

Parables have the potential for activating a shift in consciousness. With parables as with this therapy system, unless the work is processed by the person and owned by the person, it has limited life changing potential.

Now I want to shift to practical applications of Psychomotor in my world as a pastor.

The spectrum begins with understanding where people are coming from: seeing them as children at times — as hurt or deprived children. When a parishioner has an explosion of feelings — whether positive or negative — I've grown to see that a large measure of it is projection. They were not "in love" with me or "angry" at me, rather the emotions are related to someone I remind them of from their past. Seeing that, I am freer to respond appropriately.

In terms of counseling situations, I begin by being primarily the listener rather than the communicator of truths. I move along the spectrum, I will help people see the sources of their problem which they had not been able to see previously. They come to see how much of their past directs their present interactions. In a short span of time, this can be accomplished by using parts of Psychomotor exercises such as experiencing persons at varied elevations or in a *controlled approach* setting (Pesso, 1969). Face affirmation (face telling: the fond naming of parts of the face) would be a further step in letting people shift to a structure place — letting them be in a child place and then giving them affirmation as an *ideal parent*. Following a few exercises, I suggest the person consider attending a weekend workshop. For most, that seems the most effective route.

At the workshop they benefit from being part of a community. Sharing at a feeling level, the community is quickly bonded. They see how others are affected by historical pains and deprivations and are thus more readily accepting of that dynamic in themselves. They discover a safe community and a caring one, that there is no forcing of people to do what they fear to do and there is gentle encouragement allowing people to do what they need to do in terms of expressing and moving through to their new *map* for life.

My Psychomotor involvement also includes finding someone in my office in structure energy and inviting them to do a single client structure.

Thus the spectrum moves from understandings, to exercises, to a taste of structure work in terms of some of the exercises, to participating in workshops, to doing a full structure. All these are possible interactions of a pastor with whoever comes by — parishoner, client, friend, or stranger.

References

Holy bible, revised standard edition (1952). New York: Thomas Nelson and Sons.

Pesso, A. (1969). *Movement in psychotherapy.* New York: New York University Press.

Chapter 20

Psychomotor Therapy in the University/College Setting

by Ruthann Fox-Hines

I want to point out from the outset of this chapter that the applications described are adaptations of Al and Diane Pesso's work and do not strictly follow the method as taught in their certification program. Although I have participated twice a year for about ten years in a Psychomotor therapy group for therapists run by Al Pesso, I have not gone through the Certification Training Program. My applications are an amalgamation of Psychomotor therapy and the many different therapies I've incorporated into my practice as a doctoral level, licensed counseling psychologist.

As a psychologist in a University setting, I have found Pesso System/Psychomotor Therapy to be an effective approach with many of the intelligent, highly verbal students who use the Counseling and Human Development Center's services. The majority of the Center's clients are in their mid- to late twenties; the range extends from 17 to 65, but, typically, it is the somewhat older student who acknowledges a need for psychological services. Depression, anxiety, relationship problems, self concept difficulties, and issues of sexuality are the most frequently presented problems. Seriously disturbed individuals are usually referred to psychiatric services, which allows much of the Center's work to relate to developmental issues and lends itself well to the Psychomotor approach.

There are, however, some clients for whom the approach does not appear to be appropriate. Research using Holland's types found that Realistic, Investigative, and Conventional types may find disclosing with people uncomfortable and favor more cognitive-behavioral approaches; whereas, Artistic, Social, and Enterprising types prefer interactive approaches (Mahalik & Kivligham, 1988).

The hypothesis I would like to investigate empirically is that individuals with certain profiles on the Myers-Briggs Type Indicator would be more responsive to Psychomotor therapy than individuals with other profiles, e.g., Extraverted, Intuiting, Feeling, Perceptive types versus Introverted, Sensing, Thinking, Judging types. In my clinical experience, I have found Sensing types to be highly resistant to the applications of metaphor required by the Pessos' approach; they tend to respond better to much more externally directive, concrete, here-and-now, behavioral approaches. Clients who are more intuiting and interested in possibilities, however, tend to appreciate metaphor and are open to exploring the childhood origins of the difficulties that bring them to my office.

In working with students, I explain concepts in terms I have found they can easily assimilate instead of employing the Pessos' precise terminology, e.g., I will use phrases such as "traditions that are dysfunctional" and the "need for replacing old tapes, reprogramming," or the "need to let go of old traditions and establish new ones."

I also talk about "treating the child within," explaining that the adult keeps trying to get others to meet needs the "child within" did not have met; that it is the "child" who needs treatment; and that a major function of *ideal parent* figures is to provide the "child" with experiences of having those needs met. I explain the need for positive and negative aspects of "significant others" in terms of one set of feelings — love, honor, respect — getting in the way of or clouding the other set of feelings — anger, hurt, frustration — when we try to deal with the significant others in our lives as whole individuals. When we try to express the negative and sometimes forbidden feelings such as anger, messages like "I should honor my father," or "I am supposed to love my mother," block the negative feelings. When we try to feel love, gratitude, or respect, the hurts, frustrations, and anger intrude. By separating the negative and positive aspects, we can "protect" the loved aspect, reserving it for a time when we feel clearer about our positive feelings, keep it "safe" while we deal with hated, hurtful, frustrating aspects: "Let's put your mother's good intentions over there in that bean bag and the fact that she criticized you all the time and helped you feel inadequate in this bean bag. That bean bag over there represents the part of your Mom that you do care about, your positive Mom; this bag represents the part of your Mom you're angry with, your negative Mom."

As a supplement to my oral explanations, I provide clients with a handout that describes in simple terms the process of the Psychomotor approach.

In my work with University clientele, I have applied the Pesso's approach or aspects of it in three settings: 1) individual counseling or therapy, 2) group counseling or therapy, and 3) in an experimental therapy group for graduate students and faculty from the helping professions. Also, for use in the group setting, I have developed what I refer to as "Mini Structures." Descriptions of application in these three settings and of "Mini Structures" follow.

Individual Therapy

During the initial sessions of individual work, when issues are explored and defined, I typically use a genogram — a form of family-tree chart with comments — to assist in the identification of dysfunctional family patterns, "traditions," negative messages, unmet needs, etc. and/or time-line charts to focus on specific issues. For example, in dealing with sexuality with a female client unhappy because her husband has had a series of affairs I use the genogram to show a family pattern of passive wives accepting philandering husbands. With a sexually confused male, I identify through the use of a sexual time line early negative messages and proscriptions from his mother regarding men in general and sexuality in particular. As these patterns are uncovered, I suggest the Psychomotor approach as a possibility, explain it, provide the handout describing the approach and invite the client to join the therapy group where the Pessos' approach is the dominant approach. With some ongoing clients, a humorous awareness occurs; we both spontaneously conclude that something we're dealing with would be best faced in a structure, and the client says something on the order of "Oh, darn, this would be a good *structure*, wouldn't it? I don't know if I'm ready to deal with this. Oh, damn, it is important, isn't it? Well, OK, I guess I'll do it. Yes, I know, there's a lot of *energy* around this issue. All right." And I, the therapist, haven't said a word. As they have learned to listen within and to their bodies, they know and I know, and with shared humor we move on with the work.

In a majority of cases, deciding on structure work means taking the issues to the group therapy sessions. A luxury in a university setting is a clientele with relatively flexible schedules which allow both individual sessions and participation in an ongoing group, and the back and forth flow appears to be most beneficial; issues, such as transference, that arise in group can be dealt with individually.

For Psychomotor therapy, the group setting is ideal; however, some clients' schedules do not fit and some clients resist participation in a group. So, with chairs, bean bags, pillows, and other props (a brilliantly colored Guatemalan cloth has represented God) we do structure work one-on-one. The props are used as negative and positive aspects of significant others. I operate as director and take on *ideal* female roles — usually an ideal mother. Although the Pessos, in their training program, discourage therapists from taking roles, I have, at times, found it necessary in cases such as that of a client who needs the experience of an ideal mother holding her as she cries or deals with old fears. In order to help the client maintain a distinction between myself as psychologist, therapist, director, and me when I enrole, I make sure to change my position, allowing the client to place me when I enrole — usually beside him or her — and return to my chair when there is a need for interpretation, clarification of messages, etc. Typically, I leave something to represent the ideal figure — a tissue, small pillow, or even the client's own hand placed where mine had been and asking them "Let me go back and be Ruthann for a minute."

When we are dealing with ideal male figures, I have a large, brown overstuffed backrest with arms that I enrole as that ideal figure. The client decides where to place it, sometimes leaning against it, sometimes hugging it; and I phrase things in this manner: "Your ideal father would tell you ..."

At times, the backrest is enroled as ideal father and I am enroled as ideal mother. In those structures, I use phrases such as "We ...," unless, of course, the issue is a silent or absent father and a domineering mother, in which case I usually stay with separate work on the ideal figures, or if it is possible, call upon a male colleague to join the session and enroll as the ideal male.

One interesting application of Psychomotor therapy in the individual setting is the addition of hypnosis with clients who are familiar with and comfortable with it, and who have had relatively extensive individual and group experience with the Pessos' approach. We first identify the negative messages and then together write a script for the ideal figure, deciding the appropriate age the client needs to regress to under hypnosis in order to take the message. The hypnotic state is then induced.

I then enrole as the ideal figure (if male, a male colleague enroles) and move and make physical contact with the client in a predetermined manner — frequently a hand on the shoulder or upper chest. Although this physical contact diverges from the Pessos' teachings — they encourage the minimization of therapist-client touch — the physical grounding of messages, as recommended in psycholinguistic therapy, has been useful with clients from a university population.

Next, I communicate the script. When the script has been gone through once, I ask what more is wanted; most often, a repetition is indicated. Conclusion involves suggestions regarding holding onto to the new messages, letting go of the old ones, and a count indicating when I will de-role and return to being the therapist and the client will "return" to the session. We then process the experience and during the next session follow up with reports on the effects; typically introjection of the messages is reported as stronger than in regular structure work.

Although groups are the preferred setting for structure work, structures can be effective in the one-on-one settings with some creativity on the part of the therapist, high levels of rapport between therapist and client, and a relatively high level of imagination on the part of the client.

Group Therapy

For almost fifteen years, I have run a therapy group through the Center. At first it was a women's group; then a male colleague joined me and we opened it to men. Gradually, as I participated in Psychomotor groups, I introduced the Psychomotor approach into this group, and currently the Pessos' approach is a frequent — although not exclusive — approach employed.

Since four of the seven psychologists on the Center's staff have had or are still involved in Psychomotor training with Al Pesso, appreciation of the approach is strong, and a large majority of the participants in the therapy group are referred to the group by myself or one of the other three. Thus, most participants are experiencing both individual and group counseling/therapy, and the flow between the two settings, mentioned earlier, is a given in the majority of cases.

The therapy group is an on-going group with participants joining throughout the year. Inclusion of new members is a stated norm of the group so the fact that it is not a closed, exclusive group has not created any noticeable problems with regard to a group spirit.

The previously mentioned explanatory sheets are provided to new participants — usually during individual therapy — as an introduction to the approach. Upon joining the group, members are also given a sheet which explains the purpose of the group and the "rules." New members learn about enroling, *accommodation*, etc. as they watch or actually participate in another member's structure work and through the processing that follows.

The group proceeds in a manner similar to Al Pesso's groups. Each session begins with a "check in" period. Old members are responsible for making new members feel comfortable, report on how their week went, describe effects of previous structure work, and, if desired, ask for time to deal with personal issues during the session. New members are asked what they are hoping to get from the group.

Asking for time is an important part of the check in process. Frequently, when members ask for time they are requesting time to do structure work. However, there are times when participants simply want some time to talk about a situation, get feedback, or merely ventilate. Since encouraging individuals to assume responsibility themselves is an important goal of therapy, the asking-for-time aspect and the acceptance of the choice for structure work or not is a major feature. Participants are directly informed that the leader will not play at being a mind reader, pull feelings or needs or wants from them, or push them into action — although, at times, with humor, seeds are planted: "It sounds as if that might be something you'd like to do some work on; down the road, you might want to ask for some time to do something with that — when you're ready, of course."

Because the group is limited to two hours, when structure work is done, usually only one person gets to work. If more than one member asks for time, the usual procedure is the democratic take-a-number approach. However, some members will express the feeling that they'd rather allow another to go ahead of them. Participants quickly learn that if they want time, it is best to jump in right away rather than sitting and looking to the leader to indicate with whom the check should begin.

An issue several participants have worked on over the years is uncovered by the process of asking for time. After several sessions of not asking or of letting others go before them, the issue of how the reticent individuals view their own needs in relation to the needs of others arises and some fine structures have evolved.

My experience with Al Pesso's work has been to see the emphasis move from dealing with the negative figures to a stronger focus on provision of *antidotal* experiences with the ideal figures. With this change, Psychomotor structure work has become more appropriate for use in our relatively public group facility with its poor sound insulation — cathartic experiences with negative figures have, in the past, caused much talk in the office: "What's going on in there?" To avoid such embarrassing reactions, I have tended to emphasize the use of negative figures in their role of clarifying what antidotal experiences and messages are needed, and with few exceptions, focused on permission giving, validating, nurturing experiences with ideal figures rather than a great deal of work calling for accommodation by negative figures or limiting structures.

The rare use of limiting structures is also related to the practical fact that I am a small female and the group is predominantly female — usually four to six women and one to three men. Others may have found a way around this. I have not.

Other differences from the work I have seen in Al Pesso's groups with active therapists is on the level of emotional expression and with regard to sexual issues. With the student population, there appears to be a general reticence to go very deep or to deal too directly with sex in the group setting. I accept where the clients are, work with them individually, and help them in group to build "safe" structures related to their issues. A supporting notation on this is the fact that a fair number of new participants have been scared away even with the level of structure work present in this group.

After check in, the group moves into structure work or whatever other work participants have requested. Structure work is followed by sharing time — a connecting, process time. Most participants do validate the work of the individual through sharing feelings about how the work touched them, their benefits from the work, etc. However, participants occasionally slip into commenting on the structure itself, evaluation of the individual's feelings, etc. Intervention and redirection is a must on these occasions. Reminders of the individual's vulnerability and a need to stay with one's own issues touched by the work are sometimes needed. These situations are usually avoided by an opening statement along the lines of: "What within you did so-and-so's work touch?" "Is there anything about your own issues that connects with so-and-so's work?"

Although there is never a formal termination to the group because it is an ongoing one, each session ends with a pulling together into a tight circle where the question is asked: "Is there anything else someone wants to ask for or to give?" Responses vary from inclusion statements made by old members to new ones, through expressions of gratitude for the work a member has done to requests for "energy" by members who will be facing difficult situations.

After the circle, individual hugs are exchanged. Students seem to need formal permission and leader role modeling of touch and closeness. As hugs become the norm, the contact needed in structures becomes easier for them.

The aforementioned flow between individual therapy and work in the group is a major asset of having an ongoing group in which Psychomotor therapy is the predominant form of therapy.

Experiential Therapy Group Specifically for Helping Professionals

Graduate students in psychology, social work, rehabilitation, counseling, and nursing typically have therapy and group theory courses, but they have minimal experience in therapy themselves or participation in group therapy. In past years, each semester some would participate in the on-going group in order to gain that experience, but didactic and process components were still missing. Two years ago, a colleague and I decided to offer a group specifically for graduate students in the helping professions — a group in which they could get experience plus instruction and processing. I have continued the group with a formalized organization. Prior to the beginning of each semester, I send out a letter to faculty in the helping professions inviting them to recommend the group as a supplementary experience. Faculty are also invited to participate on a space-available basis and several have responded.

The formal organization is as follows: During the first two sessions, participants are given the explanatory handouts and a list of terminology for reference during lectures. Videotapes of my own structures with Al Pesso are shown; lectures on my adaptations of theory and goals as well as terminology and processes relating to the videotapes are given; demonstrations and practice of aspects such as accommodation are provided; discussion, questions, comments are encouraged; and, of course, sharing time by members is included as part of the basic group building process.

Interestingly, reactions to the videos include much more than simple process questions. Participants spontaneously begin to connect my work with issues in their own lives, and without formal instruction they have begun to engage in the follow-up sharing, validation process. As members connect with my structure, they share more and more of who they are, and the group builds trust. Also, my willingness to self-disclose through the videotapes inevitably brings comments regarding comfort, rapport, trust, and decreased anxiety regarding involvement in what for many participants is seen as an alien experience.

In the group, each participant, rather than asking for time, is required to work at least one time during the semester, and the remaining sessions are devoted to this work. A take-a-number approach is employed. Usually there are members who have either been in the therapy group or in the training group before and they take the lower numbers, leaving later numbers for the newer, less comfortable participants.

Unlike the on-going therapy group, the training group is a closed group, usually with seven to ten participants, and does have a limited number of sessions: one or two introductory sessions, one session per number of members, plus one or two closing sessions. The work sessions last two hours, the first half hour of which is check in time; during the next hour, one participant does a structure with an additional fifteen minutes to half-hour devoted to connecting, sharing time; the concluding time is used for process questions and comments. As with the therapy group, each session concludes with a pulling together and hugs to desensitize participants to closeness and touch and to contribute to the building of a group feeling.

The closing sessions include time for "Mini Structures" (described below); time for further discussion of theory and applications; information on the Pessos' program in New

Hampshire; and time for participants to react to their experience and to express whatever they need to express to fellow members — usually some form of gratitude and appreciation for the closeness and support. Many of these students and faculty members elect to return to this group for one or more semesters.

Mini Structures

In both the on-going therapy group and the group for helping professionals, there are sessions in which no one is scheduled to work or in which no one has asked for time. During these open sessions, I lead the group through what I refer to as "Mini Structures." These are approaches I developed consisting of approximately twenty-minute structures which can be used to add pieces to previous structures, to deal with specific incidents from the past, and/or to set the stage for future full structures.

A relaxation exercise is used as a group starting point — eyes closed, focused breathing, and verbal inductions to relaxation. The participants are then asked to allow themselves to go backwards in time and identify progressively further back events when they were emotionally hurt, negated, invalidated, "Xed," provided with dysfunctional role models, etc. As they travel back in time and note these incidents, they are asked to note their reactions: Around which incident do they feel the most energy? Those participants that wish to are invited to do a "Mini Structure" focused on that incident. Frequently individuals return to previous structures and express a need to do something more with the issues involved.

When an individual does a "Mini Structure," he or she moves to a bean bag in the center of the room — often the choice of the color of the bean bag is important. For example, a young woman who had had a series of relationships with exciting but unstable individuals and whose mother is an exciting but unstable woman chose a bright orange bean bag in which to sit. Part of the conclusion of her work included both the experiencing of an ideal mother who could be exciting *and* stable plus having the experience of owning her own excitement as symbolized by the orange bean bag she had chosen.

The individual then asks another participant to role-play the negative aspects of the hurtful person, the invalidator, the "Xer," the poor role model, etc. and places that negative figure. The remaining members of the group enrole as ideal support figures and move to form a close semi-circle in back of the individual working. They give permission and support as needed for the person working to confront the negative figure, with the negative figure, of course, accommodating. Often the person working asks the support figures to join in the confrontations and they do. This enrolement of the remaining members of the group as support figures appears to provide the energy for the individual to move to a resolution in a relatively brief period of time. As the individual working feels success in the confrontation, she or he requests from amongst the ideal support figures a participant to add the role of a specific ideal figure who will provide the antidotal experiences and messages.

Following the de-roling process and a brief connecting period, another individual is given time for a "Mini Structure." In a two-hour session, with check-in and closing exercises, up to three "Mini Structures" are possible. The suggestion is given to those who would have liked to work but time did not permit, that they may want to claim time during the next session for either a "Mini Structure" or a full structure related to the incident identified. If this occurs at the conclusion of the time-limited group these individuals are invited to join the on-going therapy group to complete their work.

Conclusion

One of the strongest assets of working within a university setting is the opportunity to establish a flow between individual counseling or therapy and group therapy. Related to this is the fact that university clients are able to experience this flow over an extended period of years which allows the possibility of individuals doing as many as a dozen or so structures.

Since the majority of participants are in the developmental stage where they are still dealing very directly with significant others in their lives, usually parents, they have the opportunities to test out the effects of their structure work and report changes in themselves and their interactions with these significant others to a supportive and validating group and/ or therapist. A major effect reported is the development of a healthy emotional distance between the individual and the significant others. They report being able to "observe" their parents' behaviors more clearly and feel less controlled by them. They observe rather than introject their parents' — or other significant persons' — role models or messages. They report being freer to enjoy the positive aspects of those significant others and even begin to find humor in the persistence of the manipulative behavior: "Boy, when I was home this past weekend, she tried a beautiful guilt trip. I just said, 'Yes Mom, I know,' but I was laughing inside the whole time. Otherwise, we had some good close moments. She really does know how to have fun at times."

My experience within the university setting supports the applicability of the Psychomotor approach with a relatively young population and supports the possibilities of its application both in one-on-one sessions and in group with a flow between the two being the most successful application. Also, I would recommend further investigation of the use of hypnosis coupled with the Pessos' approach.

Reference

Mahalik, J.R., & Kivligham, D.M. (1988). Self-help treatment for depression: Who succeeds? *Journal of Counseling Psychology, 35*, 237-242.

Chapter 21

Preparation for Pesso System Group

by Robert Beloof

I

No doubt each therapist prepares people for group work in a somewhat individual way, a fact which lends the writing of this chapter a problematic quality. What I shall attempt to do is touch on the most common issues which one will encounter, regardless of how the individual therapist approaches the matter.

Before proceeding with a look at preparing the client, it is necessary to look at the preparation of the therapist. Learning to lead a Pesso System group is a lengthy process. A certified PS/P therapist has spent a minimum of three or four years receiving a thorough training, and that is beyond whatever academic and supervision requirements he or she has fulfilled to become a competent clinician. This training includes: an extensive training in noting emergent body energies and identifying their probable etiologies as well as their probable "structural" antidotes; training in special exercises designed to bring the worker[1] to an awareness of his body, its feelings and energies; thorough knowledge of Pesso System theory; experience in facilitating the efforts of the worker and the efforts of the group in supporting the person who is at that moment the worker.

So let us assume that the therapist is thoroughly trained. What does he do to prepare persons for group? Before he comes to that point he must decide whether or not the person would benefit by group work (the usual and most effective form of PS/P). And that decision will in part hinge on information which emerges in the history taking.

II

Before proceeding to any actual therapy, it is important for the therapist to take a case history. The usual professionally important reasons hold here, with emphasis on certain aspects beyond the usual. Since PS/P arises in large part from emergent body energies, a thorough medical history takes on special import. Disturbances in autonomic as well as voluntary systems will take on compensatory features which may well affect the movements the

---

[1] In this article I shall use the term "worker" when referring to that member of the group who is working as client, and is engaged in direct work with the therapist in his own designated hour. See also *enactor*.

therapist later observes in structures. Surgeries are invasions leaving their symbolic messages in the psyche. In like manner a history of accidents as well as non-accidental body trauma is very important, for there is a significant body of Pesso theory centering around the psychological effect of such insults. A detailed sense of family — genealogical and emotional — is vital, since Pesso work centers around issues of inadequacies of protection, support, nurture, limits, place, respect and validation within the family matrix. Deaths, divorce, abuse (both violent and sexual), and abandonment are among the more dramatic of such events. But quite important are such elements as being preferred by a parent to his or her mate, being typecast, being more or less loved than a sibling. The above data will aid the therapist in his efforts to assist the client's understanding of emergent body energies.

III

Many PS/P therapists require an introductory period of exercises before proceeding to structure work. A PS/P exercise is a procedure whose specific rules of behavior, described by the therapist, are followed by the worker in voluntary agreement. It is by these specific rules, requiring a narrow focus on a limited ground, that an exercise is distinguished within the therapeutic arena from an unstructured talk or movement on the one hand and structure-time on the other. Its goals may be one of several: to awaken a connection between the worker's body feeling and his or her conscious awareness, to reveal to the worker that that connection carries an historic meaning, to lead to a desire on the worker's part to explore further the implications of that illumination. The nature of these exercises is described elsewhere in this book (see Chapter 22 and also *Movement in Psychotherapy* by Albert Pesso, 1969). Suffice it to say here that they are designed to give the worker information concerning his specific bodily responses to certain carefully delimited movements in order to develop sensitivity and awareness of the inner feeling that accompanies movement or the impulse to movement. (They are also valuable to the therapist in the process of assessing whether or not a potential client is sufficiently in touch with body sensations to do structures without preparatory therapy.) The utility of these exercises in preparing for a structure is that they familiarize the person with, and validate the utility of, the subtle feelings and impulses that signal movement or the desire to move. Other exercises focus on the outer environment. In those exercises one comes to a keener awareness of feelings and impulses for movement that arise in the presence of persons and objects in the space around one.

Exercises are grouped around three foci: *reflex movement* (those movements which occur more or less automatically, can occur with awareness, and are importantly centered around gravity); *voluntary movements* (those movements which occur as a result of conscious command and are largely centered around responses to the external world); *emotional movement* (movement in response to feelings, largely centered around the internal world of the individual's affective reality). There are several comments that need to be made concerning both goals and procedures in relation to these exercises.

1. Nowhere in Pesso System structures or exercises is a person led to or trained in any attitudes or skills that might be seen as relinquishing the responsibility for his or her own actions.

2. It is essential for the therapist to create an environment in the group that is safe for each group member, so that these exercises and their results may be freely executed and experienced.

3. The group leader must have experienced and expressed the sort of powerful emotions that may emerge from members of the group and be comfortable with them as they appear.

The exercises, if used by the therapist, lead easily into the teaching of *accommodation*. The ability to accommodate is an essential skill in PS/P group participation. Its teaching in one manner or another is a necessary pre-condition to group work. Accommodation is at the heart of the *structure* work in Pesso therapy, and the structure is the chief instrument for change.

IV

It must be remembered that unlike practice in the standard group, in which members speak in a conversational give-and-take, each member of a PS/P group has his own distinct period of time (usually 45 or 50 minutes) during which (with the exception that the therapist reserves the right to prevent negative events) he is in complete control of his therapy. During his time he uses others in the group as role-players. That is, members of the group will be asked to role-play a figure in his distant or recent past, or various *ideal figures* (which would include ideal mother, ideal father, ideal lover, ideal friend, etc.).

Accommodating is in itself therapeutic, and not the least therapeutic aspect is the opportunity to learn what it is truly to assist another person. It is an interesting speculation, in fact, whether outright viciousness does more damage than well-meaning but inappropriate help. For many people learning to accommodate, it is the severest of disciplines to learn to do nothing that the worker does not want done, to add or subtract nothing to or from what has been requested, to wait in patience when not needed. Yet that is the essence of good accommodation. As Milton wrote, "They also serve who only stand and wait" (Sonnet #19).

The first thing the potential accommodator must learn is to take care of himself. It is extremely important for the person who is the worker that he have no need to worry about the physical or emotional well-being of the accommodator. Part of what brings many people to therapy is a confusion about the appropriate focus on their own welfare, and an accommodator whose self-care seems inadequate will often pull the worker directly out of the structure time-space. While the therapist will pay as much attention to the welfare of the accommodator as possible, that attention must of necessity be focussed on the worker. So if the therapist misses something related to the accommodator's welfare, it is always that person's responsibility to see to his or her own well-being by bringing whatever is necessary to the therapist's attention. For it is the prime directive in PS/P work that no one in the group feels in any way, at any time, unsafe.

It may happen that the worker begins with a request that certain roles be at once assumed by members of the group. Indeed, it does happen that sometimes the worker will know from the beginning what direction the structure will take, and after briefly checking with the therapist, will proceed to request certain members of the group to play certain roles. More commonly, however, an appreciable amount of time is taken in talking to the therapist before such a request is made. In general, structure work begins the moment the first member of the group enroles, although structure energies may surface in the talk with the therapist. Enroling and de-roling is a ritual which the accommodator must not vary. The worker says, "Will you role-play the negative aspects of my mother?" The accommodator responds, "Yes. I will role-play the negative aspects of your mother." Sometimes the role required is more narrowly defined. But the same principle applies; the accommodator should repeat, with only the necessary pronoun variance, the words of the worker. "Will you role-play the negative aspect of my mother that paid little attention to me?" "Yes. I will role-play the negative aspect of your mother that paid little attention to you." The worker then places the accommodator in some present space symbolically equivalent to the place which that figure occupies in his psychic life at the moment. At the end of the structure, the accommodator must de-role in the same terms as were used in enroling, with the addition that her real identity must be re-established. Worker: "You are no longer role-playing the negative aspect of my mother. You are Jane." Accommodator: "I am no longer role-playing the negative aspect of your mother. I am Jane." De-roling marks the departure from symbolic space-time, and hence from the structure.

So it is that enroling and de-roling is a necessary ritual to emphasize, on the one hand, the special symbolic play of the structure in which all one's positive needs are honored and responded to, and, on the other hand, the giving up in de-roling of the symbolic controlling position vis-a-vis the other group members. To understand the power and originality of Pesso System structures, one may reflect on how far our culture has gone toward excluding the life of symbolic play, as opposed to fantasy (including movies and television), rational or pseudo-rational intellectualization, empty ritual, competitive play and leisure play (where we play with ever more sophisticated and expensive toys). Symbolic play is what children do often in their daily activities and also in child-play therapy, when they arrive at new decisions about life by reaching the symbol-making level of their psyche through symbolic interaction with named, external figures. The structure is, similarly, a "play for mortal stakes" where "love and need are one" (Frost, 1949, pp. 357-358), where body and mind as unified being work together in mutual respect. Working so, and using external reality as a symbolic role-playing world under its safe control, the sentient self can be moved to profound hope and on to profound restructuring.

There are other elements of accommodation that need to be explained, having to do with the use of the voice in structure work, and I shall address these as simply as possible.

1. The accommodator never adds any words or vocal sounds of his own origin which are not directly given him by the worker, or which are not directly appropriate as a response, in a negative role, to hostile words or actions coming from the worker.

2. Further, the accommodator never leaves out any words or sounds requested by the worker.

3. In short, the accommodator is to say neither more nor less than he is requested to say by the worker. (The only exception will be discussed when we examine the accommodator's task when "in" a negative figure.) This is an instruction which appears easy to follow, but is, in practice, not easy at all. One may learn a good deal about oneself by looking inwardly at what it is one wishes to add or subtract to that which is requested by the worker.

With certain exceptions the accommodator will be required to play two kinds of roles, *ideal figures* and *negative figures*. Negative figures are nearly always aspects of historic persons in the life of the worker. Indeed, one of the central distinctions made in PS/P work is that between the destructive effects of emotions and actions of historic persons in the worker's life, and the loved or positive aspects of such persons. Thus a person might enrole two people to role-play simultaneously a negative and a loved aspect of the mother. The goal here is to get an almost surgical exactitude in clarifying the negative, so that when the worker is empowered to attack that figure, and we see the accommodator respond appropriately to the beating of an extension (a pillow), the energy mobilized is expended with as great an accuracy as is possible at the appropriate target.

Accommodating in such negative roles, then, is primarily a process of responding accurately to the angry words or actions of the worker. Accuracy includes both amount and quality of response in both corporeal and oral aspects. Let us take three examples.

1. The worker has so much guilt toward or fear of the negative figure that only a small, almost gentle "I hate you" can be uttered. Under these circumstances the accommodator will, in matching that energy, make only a slight physical movement, like a wince, and the verbal response, if one is deemed appropriate, would be a quiet, pained "Oh," again designed to match exactly the amount of energy coming from the worker.

2. The worker, in a rage, is beating a pillow representing, in extension, the head of the negative figure. The accommodator will make successive major physical movements representing some one being beaten around the head. These movements of the body will be coordinated with the blows so that as the blow lands on the pillow the accommodator responds at that precise moment. Each movement will be accompanied by a loud sound appropriate to a person being beaten on the head.

3. The worker has a pillow in his hand and is wringing a portion of the pillow symbolizing the neck of the negative figure. Here, the accommodator will make writhing movements with the body and will utter sounds imitative of a person being strangled. In each of these examples the accurate response of amount and quality in both body and voice is the key to effective accommodation. There are other aspects of negative figure accommodation, such as taking care never to appear to attack back, which the therapist can assist the accommodator in avoiding or accomplishing.

Negative figures are the principal means in Pesso System for the worker to clarify how and by whom he has been damaged in the past, and then to validate his own anger and his power to express that anger effectively.

Ideal figures are, in PS/P work, the principal means of healing. Ideal parents, for instance, provide a visible and physically felt filling in of deficits suffered by the worker in his development. Such deficits may appear at any developmental stage and ideal figures will be involved in structures which help the worker to feel a new sense of adequate response from parental or other sources. Such responses will generally fall in, or be combinations of deficits in *support*, *protection*, *nurturing*, *limits*. As an example, support might include such diverse structural activity as: approving of the worker's anger at a negative figure, physically support- ing the worker in a manner appropriate to the particular developmental stage experienced by the worker at that moment, displaying understanding of behavior for which the person in the past has been made to feel guilty. Again, the key to effective accommodation in ideal figures is to respond verbally with the exact words requested by the worker and, in physical terms, to be there for all of the worker's energies without being hurt by them, (generally to be physically positioned so as to suggest that one can contain the worker's energies), and to be careful never to allow the worker physically to support or defend the ideal parent or otherwise take on a more powerful (i.e. parental) contact or position. In short, not only do ideal parents fill deficits, they also limit any learned tendency of the worker toward parenting his parents. As a result of thus relinquishing that inappropriate role, the worker is free to concentrate on the symbolic and healing re-creation of his developmental needs and on their satisfaction.

There are other kinds of roles that will occasionally appear. Enactment of these roles will follow the basic rule of saying and doing only what the worker wishes and the therapist approves. But beyond the responsibilities of the individual as accommodator, there are also responsibilities as a member of the group. For the most part these fall under three headings;

behavior during a structure, behavior after a structure, and dress and hygiene.

As a member of the group not at that moment engaged in a structure, it is necessary to conduct oneself so as not to detract from the energy focussed on the worker. Minimum movement and no talking are the simple rules here. After the structure the worker is usually in "gape time," a kind of transition space-time between the symbolic and the now. He is absorbing the new body feelings, the new interactive possibilities he has just encountered. While there is sharing immediately following the structure, the worker is not addressed directly. He is left alone till he volunteers re-entry into the group. During sharing time, or at any time, avoid comparative comments ("This was more powerful than his last"). Avoid not only comments during the sharing time which might detract from the worker's former work but also, at any time subsequent to the structure, those comments which call in question his new structure experience. (Suppose you were an ideal figure giving support during the structure, and several hours afterward you were overheard by the worker to say, "I got really cramped in that position." Such a comment will undercut the worker's trust in his sense of having been supported, and will hence undercut his new but delicate gains.) In sum, it is safest at any time to leave the initial contact concerning his structure to the worker and, in sharing, to restrict one's comments to feelings as they, perhaps, were opened to one concerning one's own life or structure work, or such statements as are confirmatory of the experience of the worker in the structure. And finally, it is important that the members of the group not only avoid comparisons ("his structure seemed to do what Joe was trying to do in his") but must avoid being so emphatic and charged as to overpower the worker's experience and hence "claim" his work as somehow one's own. Remember that the worker has just made a hard-earned gain. A safe rule is this: if you are in doubt about the propriety of a comment, then don't make it.

The third responsibility as a group member arises from the circumstance of PS/P work. The group will work in an enclosed space where, for reasons of noise control and privacy, the windows often must be kept closed. Further, accommodators will be holding people, and there may be structures of high energy and perspiration. In consequence, a bathed body and fresh clothes are appropriate. Clean, short fingernails; absence of lumpy rings and bracelets, dangling earrings, delicate clothing, all contribute to comfort and safety. Women will need to remember that structure work is done on the floor, and that skirts may prove awkward in several ways. Common sense, in short, is a valuable commodity in thinking of one's person and dress in relation to Pesso structures.

V

There are concerns that are frequently expressed by people who are about to enter their first structures. Some of these questions arise before any structures have been seen, some after structures have been described or observed. The therapist must address these anxieties, and it is best to start that educative process as part of the preparation. Here are a few of the more common issues which arise, with possible responses:

Should I decide ahead of time what I want to do in the structure, or should I just let happen whatever will happen? There is no "proper" approach — there is no approach to which one could even faintly attach a "should." Some people seem more often than not to have a theme or problem chosen. Sometimes they go so far as to envision the shape of the structure's beginning. But even these people will often change to something completely different as their energy begins to emerge in the early moments. Some people seem seldom to have anything planned when they move out on the floor to start a structure. One suspects that even these people have, at least in the unconscious, a broad area with which they are, at the time, concerned. In any case it is important to understand that one's approach to this issue will reflect one's general personality, and that that is all right.

What about confidentiality? Persons preparing to start any therapy should realize that even in private one-on-one work the option for confidentiality is in many places limited by law, and they would do well to acquaint themselves with these limitations. In many states, for instance, comments relating to danger to others, child abuse, and danger to self are among the issues concerning which the therapist is by law required to ignore confidentiality. Apart from such legal and ethical issues, the therapist holds in confidence what is told him in the therapy hour. However, where the person engages in a group therapy such as PS/P, then the therapist clearly cannot absolutely, despite group agreements, guarantee confidentiality. There is always the option to begin working in private with the PS/P therapist on those issues deemed to require guaranteed confidentiality. Usually such work leads ultimately to a comfortable way of opening up the problems in group, or, alternatively, working in private sessions till one can move beyond them and return to the group.

How long will it take? How long is a piece of string? Or to pose the answer in a form less like a koan, what piece of string is long enough? Certain sorts of issues with a rather narrow target, quitting smoking or drinking, for instance, might best be handled in other contexts and with other techniques. For another instance, those problems which are primarily focussed on how to use social agencies and resources to resolve areas of stress, might better be dealt with outside a PS/P group.

A part of the function of preparing someone for structures is, in fact, to determine if their goal is suited to PS/P work. Often the problem is for therapist and worker to achieve some kind of agreement that the problem may require more time than was initially hoped. A person asks to work with the therapist on an inability to write the introductory letters which are necessary for the success of his particular business. A little conversation reveals that this is a kind of problem that has been repeated, in various guises, throughout the worker's life, thus indicating a deeper, symbolic decision governing the temporarily troubling behavior. Such deeper issues underlying the presenting problem are frequently met with. The possibility of permanently altering surface manifestations will then depend on whether or not the therapist and the worker can come to a mutually agreeable goal regarding the more profound level of symbolic decision.

I have seen a specific memory and its concomitant pain remedied in a structure or two. But I have seldom if ever seen a major characterological or neurotic pattern altered in a brief therapy.

Is my problem susceptible to change? Any well-trained PS/P therapist should be able to make broadly-based distinctions between the sorts of mental states suitable to treatment by PS/P and those which are not. Certain conditions, for instance, such as manic-depression (bipolar disorder), require management which includes medication. A PS/P therapist who is also a psychiatrist could join the medical management with the therapy, if he deems it suitable. But a Pesso System therapist who is not a psychiatrist would pass such a person on to a physician, or would work closely with one.

Apart from such distinctions, it should be noted that PS/P has a rather complete developmental theory. It allows us to look at people in terms of critical deficits in the environment, centrally the home environment, which have resulted in defensive modes of life. These defensive modes have left the person with too little adaptive capacity to allow for fulfillment. *Antidotes* to these lacks or distortions lie in using members of the group to role-play such appropriate symbolic figures as can fill the deficit or clarify the distortion through physical interaction on the symbolic level. It is from a knowledge of these tools that the Pesso therapist will discuss the suitability of the person for this form of therapy.

Can I get used to the emotions, actions, and language which I have heard of as happening, or have seen taking place, in a structure? PS/P is often concerned with the taking in, from ideal figures, of the softer emotions and gentler interchanges which the client did not receive as a child. It is easy to be accepting of such structures. It is also true that history has left many people with crippling rages, damaged sexual energies, enthusiasms which were not only invalidated but which were often labelled as evil. The symbolic expression of these natural energies which have either been labelled as bad or which have been inadequately limited can indeed lead to expressions of emotions on the part of the worker which are very powerful. The best assurance that one can be comfortable with such scenes is that, through extensive training, the PS/P therapist is himself or herself comfortable with such intense emotions, knows what they mean, knows how to assist the worker to deal with them, and knows how to create a safe environment.

But this general question raises issues which need to be addressed. The Pesso therapist is aware that there are culturally learned standards of behavior which may be affronted, and which certainly must be the object of his or her concern in the environment of structure work.

Take, as an instance, the issue of touching. In general, Asian cultures train people to be uncomfortable with touching except under very specific circumstances. On the other hand there are cultures, Mexican culture for example, where physical closeness and touching are deemed necessary aspects of relationships. There are more specific cultural issues that can arise in a therapy such as Pesso work where physical interaction is the norm. For instance, it is an insult to pat a Thai on the head. Each culture has its own sense, not only concerning touching in the narrow sense, but on the larger issue of the use of space in relation to the proximity of bodies.

Apart from the physical issues, different cultures will teach different attitudes about family and friends. For instance, people from those Asian cultures where reverence for parents is a prime issue will often have a difficult time remembering negative family patterns, or recalling specific damaging moments.

It is clear that in a country such as the U.S.A., whose peoples come from such diverse backgrounds, an exceptional sensitivity both to the family and to inter-active bodily issues must be practiced by the Pesso therapist. Beyond the necessity to avoid offending people, the whole area of the meaning of space and inter-activity on the symbolic level undergoes subtle and not-so-subtle alterations in light of such cultural realities. On the other hand it is important for all persons who engage in PS/P to understand that it is based on a theory of general or universal developmental needs and that it may be their part to observe or participate with equanimity in structures working through interactions to which they are to some degree unaccustomed. Their assurance is that PS/P is designed to be safe physically for all, and that all members of the group have the right at any time to decline to take on, or to continue in, a role.

VI

It is for many participants an amazing fact that despite all their questions, they find themselves falling quite easily into structure work. I believe that is because humans are not merely *Homo Sapiens*. We are more broadly, more profoundly and hopefully what the Dutch scholar Huizinga (1955) labelled us: *Homo Ludens — Man Playing*.

References

Frost, R. (1949). Two tramps in time, in *Complete Poems of Robert Frost* (pp. 357-358). New York: Holt.

Huizinga, J. (1955). *Homo Ludens, a study of the play-elements in culture*. Boston: Beacon Press.

Milton, J. (1647/1940). Sonnet #19. In A. Quiller-Couch (Ed.), *Oxford book of English verse*. (p. 352). New York: Oxford University Press.

Pesso, A. (1949). *Movement in psychotherapy*. New York: New York University Press.

Chapter 22

Structured Exercises as Therapeutic Tools in PS/P

by Lowijs Perquin[1]

In the field of psychotherapy, it is rather unusual to inform clients in any detail about the method the therapist uses. It is even more unusual to find clients being extensively trained in the technical aspects of the psychotherapeutic approach concerned. At the very least, the *exercises* in Psychomotor Therapy are intended as this sort of training. The exercises prepare clients for the individual sessions in the group, which in Psychomotor Therapy are known as *structures*.

In the initial years of my training as a psychotherapist, I found learning to use the exercises a dead weight. To me, the exercises were a relic of Al and Diane Pesso's dancer past rather than valuable therapeutic instruments. On the other hand, I found the structures impressive therapeutic work. That was what I so badly wanted to learn. To my mind, the exercises, which seemed so simple, did not have much to do with psychotherapy. It took several years before I began to see the therapeutic sense of the exercises. Looking back, I allowed therapeutic moments to slip by because of this. I only later realized that some of the structures I had led had taken place at a purely cognitive level. Other structures were like a leap into the emotional depths and the unconscious of clients, who were later unable to comprehend what had happened during the session. What really set me thinking was conducting workshops for both clients and professionals: Over and over again, it turned out that the participants had found a number of selected exercises more important than I had expected. I gradually became convinced myself. Greater insight into the therapeutic possibilities of the exercises, and more practical experience applying them, have helped me to balance cognition and emotion in therapy. This has strengthened the foundation of my therapeutic work.

This chapter discusses a number of arguments in favor of the therapeutic use of the exercises:

1. The exercises offer the client cognitive support.
2. The exercises are valuable instruments for self-diagnosis.
3. Group cohesion is enhanced by the exercises.
4. The exercises have a direct therapeutic effect.

---

[1] Translated by Harold Alexander, Alexander Translations, Amsterdam.

Examples of exercises are presented to highlight these points. For further exercises and a more detailed discussion see: A. Pesso, *Movement in Psychotherapy*, 1969.

1. The Exercises Offer the Client Cognitive Support:

The way the exercises are divided into categories is understandable for clients; it offers a logical frame of reference. There is nothing mysterious about it and it feels self-evident. As an example I will discuss the subdivision into three modalities of movement. This subdivision gives the client a handhold while exploring the relationship between mental and bodily states. The subdivision is as follows: *reflex movement, voluntary movement* and *emotional movement*.

Reflex movement is what we do when we use our bodies in a more or less automatic way. We trust our motor reflexes. We walk, stumble over a doorstep, lose our balance and, without realizing how, we land on our hands without hurting ourselves. Examples of exercises that have been designed as tools for experimenting with this modality are the reflex-relaxation exercise and the fall-catch exercise. Both exercises provide clients with the opportunity of experimenting with trusting their own bodies. In the reflex-relaxation exercise the participants are instructed, while in a standing position, to let go of the restraint of their muscles as far as they can without falling on the floor. Their head will bend forward to their chest, their belly bulges out and their legs will be straight but relaxed, with the knees unlocked. The clients experience that their reflexes prevent them from falling down in this position of optimal relaxation. Meanwhile, they can let their thoughts drift away. With a sort of free-floating attention the clients can follow what their bodies are telling them: a tension at a specific spot in the neck, a trembling in the legs, a warm feeling in their hands. They can also attend to thought-associations and visual pictures as they come and go. Purposely giving up conscious control and trusting reflex physical control will create room for memories, impulses and emotions as they are located in the body.

In the fall-catch exercise, the participants, still in the standing position of the reflex-relaxation exercise, let themselves lean slightly forward till they lose their balance. The clients purposely wait till one of their legs catches the fall of their body in a reflex reaction. They experience that they can postpone the reflex reaction of their leg by willpower. At the same time the clients notice that the reflex that protects them from falling down is stronger than their conscious decision to postpone reaction. Exercises in reflex movement can be used as a metaphor for trust in the body. Confidence in the body can be generalized to trust in the possibilities of the *self*.

Voluntary movement exercises are a training in conscious control of the body in a non-expressive way. These exercises highlight the human capacity for fine motor control and assist in the effort of conscious mastery of the body. In these exercises, decision making, programming, implementation and verification of plans are trained as basic functions of the *ego*.

One example is the *conscious voluntary movement* exercise. The group members are instructed to stand in a relaxed, neutral manner and to make a conscious decision to move one of their arms to an angle — of their own choosing — from their bodies. The next step is to concentrate on raising the arm to that pre-selected position with minimum effort. Not quickly and habitually, but slowly, concentrating on how it feels, with little or no awareness of anything else. The aim is to bridge the distance between the intention and the execution of an act or movement. We tend to use so much energy for movement in everyday life that it is surprising to experience how little effort may suffice. Doing this the exercise shows the client the logical order of the following steps:

1. To make a plan: "Which arm do I want to choose and what angle do I want to raise it to?"
2. Programming: "How do I get my arm to that position and how fast shall I move it?"
3. Implementation: "I am busy carrying out the exercise, using the minimum of energy that is needed. I am concentrating on that."
4. Verification: "Did I complete my plan, did I achieve my goal, did it satisfy me?"

This framework is simple and gives clients something definite to hold on to. It is a fact of life that, on whatever scale, we are continually engaged in making plans, either carrying them out or not, and either evaluating the results or not. Here, too, it soon becomes clear to the clients that the exercise can be a metaphor, that it can provide them with essential information about their own attitude toward life. This becomes particularly apparent when the exercise is discussed in the group. "I forgot to check how high I'd raised my arm at the end. That often happens to me, I put a lot of effort into doing things, but I don't pay any attention to whether it was all right in the end." Or: "I had the feeling that my arm just went up of its own accord, but I couldn't concentrate on what was happening." The latter example makes it clear that voluntary control had been given up.

In this exercise in conscious voluntary movement, the clients experience that they are in control. They can choose to behave in a particular, controlled way. This underlines the notion that they can be in control of their impulses and emotions and can decide for themselves whether or not to express them and in what form they wish to give them. When awareness and control are possible, impulses and emotions can be experienced and expressed in the service of the ego. This is why the exercises in voluntary movement come before the exercises in emotional movement.

Emotional movement exercises are the first step toward expressing emotions. Clients are trained to express emotions in physical action. The group acts as a "holding environment." It is receptive and provides acceptance. The clients experience that they are safe, even when control over their reflexes and voluntary muscle reactions are reduced.

The cognitive support that is given by the subdivision into three modalities of movement and the exercises related to them can be summarized as follows: Clients experience that psychotherapy in which the body plays an important part is not something obscure and mysterious. What happens during physical experience and bodily movement can still be comprehended. Only three modalities are distinguished: reflex, voluntary, and emotional. This simple subdivision directs the exercises and indicates limits. It is reassuring that there is not an infinite number of motor possibilities. Moreover, the subdivision offers a reasonably adequate, if somewhat simplified, model of what actually takes place in the nervous system.

In everyday life, modalities of movement are continually interchanging and supplementing one another. By the very fact of continually emphasizing different modalities in the exercises, clients learn to differentiate between them and deal with them more flexibly. They learn that in a totally unexpected situation, they can trust their reflexes. If they feel overwhelmed by emotions, they can move in a controlled way and act voluntarily. In familiar surroundings, they can let go of voluntary control and reveal an emotion by means of bodily expression. Because in everyday life the different movement modalities are constantly intermingled, the subdivision helps clients to distinguish and to be more aware of choices.

This can be compared with a piece of music for three different instruments. In varying combinations, each of the instruments plays part of the melody. The several voices are heard in unison but can also be heard separately. There is flexibility and structure, space, and limitation. The composition is a whole.

2. The Exercises Are Valuable for Self-Diagnosis:

Exercises that are aimed at the body are a means of reducing dissociation: experiencing and knowing are brought closer together. The tension in the participants' necks or the empty feeling in the pits of their stomachs is taken seriously and examined to find out what it means. The clients are invited actively to attend to this bodily experience — these signs and symptoms — as a source of information about what is going on inside. They can gain knowledge about the strong, healthy sides of themselves and about the vulnerable, conflicting parts from the exercises.

The *controlled approach exercise* can serve as an example. This exercise evokes and illustrates internal programs of potential behavior patterns. Attention is focussed on the internal reactions of the clients to external stimuli in a structured setting. From long experience of their body, they have made unconscious estimates of their strength in each part of the body. The clients know how hard they can hit and how softly they can touch with their hands. Through long experience, the clients have built up a series of programs that reflect their history and anticipations in the use of their body.

According to the instructions of the exercise, the *enactor*, who is in a standing position, should indicate with a hand that another member of the group, in the role of neutral *accommodator*, is to walk slowly towards the enactor in a neutral fashion. The enactor stands still while the accommodator is directed to move only as indicated and to stop when told to. In one case, we see the role figure follow the enactor's instructions exactly. When he has been allowed to approach to within a meter, the enactor sends him back to his place with an abrupt gesture. In the discussion that follows, the enactor says: "At first it didn't bother me at all that he came closer. But when he was really close, I suddenly felt a tension in the calves of my legs." When the therapist asks what his body felt like doing, he says, "I might have kicked his shins, if he'd come any closer."

This might suggest a conflict between his desire for and his fear of intimacy, which is actualized in the exercise. The client recognizes his tendency to let the other person cross the boundary of what is, to him, acceptable physical closeness. While the other person is coming towards him, he does not become aware of the effect this has on him: "At first it didn't bother me at all." When he has allowed the distance between them to grow too small, he is suddenly unable to tolerate the closeness. He experiences a violent motor impulse and abruptly sends the stimulus figure away. After some further exercises, this client made the connection between his urge to kick out and his anger at his father, who abused him as a child. In other words, as a result of the exercise, the client experiences a form of self-diagnosis. The client's observations of himself extend further than what he could have discovered by verbal, cognitive reflection.

Important features of the exercises are their clarity of structure and simplicity of instructions. Only one variable is introduced during instruction. In the controlled approach exercise, this is the distance a neutral role figure assumes in relation to the clients. After the experiment other variables may be introduced, such as having the accommodator approach from the left or right, the effect of different speeds of approach, or the gender of the role figure. The last part of the instruction for this exercise provides limits and offers the prospect of a satisfactory conclusion: "When you have experimented with various distances, bring the exercise to a close by placing the accommodator at the distance that suits you best." As soon as the clients deviate from this simple instruction, meaningful information is presented: the abrupt manner in which they send the accommodator away becomes diagnostic information. The clients can observe this for themselves. It is just the well-structured setting of the exercise with its clear limits that makes it into a laboratory in which important experiments can be carried out. These experiments may lead to new discoveries about oneself.

Self-diagnosis and self-evaluation do not imply that the therapists do not make any observations for themselves. On the contrary, they gain a wealth of information from the exercises. For instance, during a positive accommodation exercise, the therapist might notice that the client hardly dares to ask the accommodator for physical support. It may also be diagnostically significant whether the client has a strong unconscious preference for one or other of the modalities of movement. The therapist may gain an impression of how the client moves in real life. Does the client have a marked preference for voluntary movements? This may be connected with over-accentuation of rationality and fear of loss of control, or little faith in the naturalness of reflex movement, spontaneity and emotions. A strong preference for reflex movement may be connected with the wish to relinquish ego functions, to hand over control, to give up thinking, and to avoid attributing meaning to experience. One-sided interest in the emotional movement exercises may indicate an attempt to satisfy the emotions and needs of early childhood in the reality of the present. Another possibility is that the client, as a child, had too little experience of secure *protection*, containment, and *limits*.

It is important that such diagnostic considerations are only wielded as provisional hypotheses. The therapists must be prepared to drop their hypotheses quickly and to incorporate new information into new hypotheses. In this way an interactive process emerges between: 1. what the clients observe about their own bodily processes; 2. what the clients report about them; 3. what the therapists observe; 4. what the therapists experience as discrepancies between what they observe and what the clients report; and 5. how the clients handle the therapist's observations. This may lead to hypotheses that can be checked with the clients by way of suppositions. All of which is set against the background of the information a therapist has from the client's biography and previous therapeutic work.

Another example in which self-evaluation and diagnostic considerations on the part of the therapist come together is the ideal parent exercise. In this exercise, the clients have the opportunity of experimenting with how it feels to have two group members in the roles of the kind of parents they would have wished for as a child: a new father and mother who accommodate perfectly to what the participants ask them for and who respond totally beneficially. This can help the clients to build up and integrate pictures of parents that fit into the needs of the young child. *Ideal parents* have never existed and will never exist. They are archetypal figures, symbols brought into action to let the clients construct very accurate models of what would have been ideal for them in early childhood. It is striking how most clients, when confronted with this possibility, know how to create ideal parents. They manage to picture them in great detail: the way the ideal parents should sit and look, what they should say and the kind of physical contact they should offer. Everybody seems to have some notion of what would have been ideal for him or her and what his or her genuine needs and wishes are. To experience this with group members can support the belief in the possibility of the principle of ideal parents. This human principle of caring contact is very real and is directed to the child part of the client still living in the body and the mind of the client. Later on, in the *structures*, the ideal parents will offer the client the right verbal reactions and the appropriate physical contact in response to unrecognized and unfulfilled childhood needs. That does not mean that the traumatic events and experiences of neglect and disrespect will be erased. What will happen is that the clients will enrich their inner world with new experiences consisting of satisfying interactions that are the opposite of the old, real history. This helps the clients create a new symbolic history and offers them an alternative to old patterns and expectations. It opens the perspective of more optimistic prospects and new opportunities in real life. How the clients handle the *ideal parent* exercise tells them and the therapists a lot about their life history, present condition and expectations. During the ideal parent exercise, one client places the father figure close and the ideal mother some distance away. This choice lifts the veil and reveals some aspects of the original object relations and unfulfilled needs of the client. With the help of the therapists the clients can make progress in this exercise by experimenting with having the mother come closer.

During the ideal parent exercise, discrepancies may emerge between what the therapists observe and what the clients report. It may be of therapeutic value to mention some of these discrepancies to the clients. Of course, the timing, dosage and subtlety of the interventions are important. "Am I right in seeing that you are reluctant to lean fully back into the hands of the ideal parents?" to a client who reports feeling perfectly supported. "Could it be that the way the ideal father is supporting your neck might be holding you down in some way?" Discrepancies are of prognostic value: are the clients capable of integrating new experiences? Or are they undergoing all sorts of experiences which the therapists seem to understand better than the clients themselves? In that case, the therapists will have to appeal to the clients' ability to consciously take small steps and watch themselves doing so.

Observation and self-diagnosis, as described here, form a process in which clients and therapists build up a cooperative therapeutic relationship, with the group available as a medium. The term "body reading," which has sometimes been used, does not adequately express the subtlety of this process.

3. Group Cohesion is Enhanced by the Exercises:

Defined simply, group cohesion is the attraction the group has for its members. The exercises contribute to an attractive and safe therapeutic climate by their simple form and the way individuality is guaranteed within the group. The simple form of the exercises contributes to the individual differences between the participants and their ability to emerge lucidly and with respect for these differences. The therapist's manner, which clearly indicates that the self-observations of the group members always contain important information, contributes to an atmosphere of acceptance. In one of the circle exercises, one group member reported a feeling of shock when she asked all the group members to make the gesture of extending their arms with the palms of their hands toward her. Even though she knew beforehand that this gesture was coming and had previously decided that it did not refer to her, she felt rejected and believed that rejection was really communicated by the group. Another group member had a completely different reaction to the same gesture: she felt safe, and surrounded by people who clearly demanded nothing of her, and this was a great relief. Both reactions were genuine, authentic programs of the particular group members concerned. When they are revealed, the projections can be clarified. The therapists can communicate acceptance and understanding of the many different reactions. By doing so they communicate this attitude to the group members.

One important characteristic of Psychomotor psychotherapy — individual therapy within a group — is also expressed in the design of the exercises. The exercises are individual experiments; the group members follow the instructions of the enactor closely. The implication is that, in principle, there are people who can offer you what you ask for. This can be done without the distortion or interference that is always present when the other person's needs have to be met at the same time.

One of the circle exercises aims to sensitize clients to the emotional influence and meaning of the spatial arrangement of other people. Each client in turn has the opportunity to vary the size of the circle of group members, and can investigate the effect of the different positions. The group members follow exactly the instructions of the client whose turn it is. As enactor you have the freedom to get in touch with the needy, demanding child in you. In accommodating, an appeal is made to the giving, available, adult parts of the group member. Everyone has a turn. The exercises are not experiments in group dynamics. The group as such, and the play of forces within the group, are not the primary focus of attention. Doing things together, and acting instead of talking, ensure an atmosphere of cooperation and solidarity. "I can both offer and receive" becomes an implicit group norm. The members of the group undergo the essential experience of being able to ask for a great deal while at the same time having a great deal to offer.

When they carry out an exercise, every member of the group is engaged in the same simple task, each in their own way. No one can fail, there is not just one right way of doing the exercise. "It is all right to be different, and I am not as odd as I was afraid I was" is the way one client put it. The emergence of an unfamiliar, hidden or feared part of one's self does not lead to rejection. An exercise provides clear aims and boundaries, within which failure is impossible. Members of the group make no comments, do not offer confrontations, nor do they evaluate what others say or do during an exercise. They are invited to give their own points of recognition and their own associations during the process of sharing. The sharing is aimed inside, at oneself, not out towards the other. An atmosphere of possibilities is created in which the implicit message is that whatever emerges is important and meaningful, that it will not be rejected. Seeing the many differences between them underlines individuality. Discovering that many parts of themselves are recognized by others highlights universality.

Some of the above-mentioned factors contribute to the therapeutic climate in every form of group therapy. Specific to Psychomotor is that respect for individuality and the experience of universality are greatly enhanced. This is a result of the direct form by which the participants, stimulated by the safe structure of the exercises, reveal themselves. The use of bodily expression, bodily contact with symbolic meaning, and fulfilling a significant role for another person as accommodator, ensure that the above-mentioned factors occur extensively in Psychomotor Therapy.

4. The Exercises Have Direct Therapeutic Effect:

Let us return to the client who suddenly sent the role figure away during the controlled approach exercise and who felt like kicking the accommodator's shins. On further verbal exploration, he faces his current conflict. He recognizes the pattern he has of continually breaking off relationships after allowing the other person to get too close. He learns to see the connection with his desire for his father whom he found threatening as a child, but also dauntingly attractive. During a year's participation in a weekly therapy group, the client regularly repeated the exercise described. By paying more attention to his physical reaction, he discovers how he can determine the distance to the role figure that best suits him and communicate this. He discovers different ways of reacting to varying role figures. He will not allow one big, strongly-built man to come too close, even though he is able to take note of his own fascination and express it in words. He allows one somewhat older, strong female member of the group to get close. He expresses his desire to be hugged and protected by her. He is able to relate this desire to his need for a strong mother who could have protected him from his threatening father when he was a child.

In a number of structures, the client explores, expresses, and clarifies his confusing emotions and attitudes toward his father. The client's awareness of his own ability to set the pace at which he wants to make contact increases by working with the ideal father figure, who respects the pace at which he explores his need for safe closeness and distance. Gradually, his present relationships stabilize. All the while, the exercise in controlled approach — often carried out by him as the start to a structure — is an instrument of self-research and a guideline in his therapeutic process. In this example we can see the following therapeutic aspects of the exercises:

- The client learns to attend to his own physical experiences, which provide him with direct knowledge of inner, mental processes. He is better able to observe himself.

- Physical sensations and reactions grow from being alien symptoms to providing valuable information about needs and desires that are part of the client, ego syntonic and legitimate.

- The client learns better to differentiate between fear, aggression, and the need for intimacy.

- By using an exercise, he can face both current and old conflicts and the connection between them.

- He is offered a *possibility sphere*, in which it becomes possible to express repressed emotions in an adequate context.

- The exercise can serve as a tool for monitoring the progress of the therapeutic process.

Conclusion

I started this contribution with a look back at the first years of my training. I was only interested in the exercises to the extent that they were a direct preparation for the structures.

If the participants learned to accommodate quickly, we could get down to work. In this way, I unwittingly devalued the starting phase of a new group. Training the members of a group so that they would, as soon as possible, be able to act as ideal parents and negative role figures for each other contained a denial of their cautious attempts to get to know themselves, one another, and their therapist: to gain trust and become a group.

The exercises gradually became instruments that I introduced for the benefit of the group members and not merely for the sake of the method. I now see the exercises, more than I used to, as a means in the hands of the clients. They are therapeutic tools which develop their attention to bodily information. This may help set a process of change in motion.

Chapter 23

Participants' Descriptions of the Effects of Psychomotor Therapy

by Glenn Shean

The focus of this paper is on participants' reports of their *structure* experiences during Psychomotor therapy and the changes that resulted. Historically, self-reports have been included in studies of psychotherapy as both global estimates of therapy-induced improvement and of specific target-based improvements. Readers can make their own judgments about the credibility of the evidence reported in this paper. Much remains to be done to adequately describe and document the changes that occur during and after Psychomotor therapy. Nevertheless, the range of content of the evaluations, as well as the anonymity, suggests respondents tended to provide candid evaluations of their experiences.

There are two major aspects of the therapist's expertise that influence the effects of interventions (Schaffer, 1982): (a) the extent to which the therapist is adhering to a particular set of technical operations, and (b) the level of competence manifested by the therapist. PS/P represents a complex theoretical system and set of intervention strategies that requires extensive training, experience, personal maturity, and expertise to practice effectively. Individual participants also vary in their ability and readiness to benefit from psychotherapy. Pesso System/Psychomotor therapy requires sufficient ego strength by participants to move toward a positive outcome in their structure work, to maintain boundaries between the work of other group members and their own issues, and the ability to assimilate powerful emotional experiences without loss of ego function.

There has been little research conducted on the process or outcome of Pesso System/ Psychomotor therapy. A summary of research is provided in Chapter 1.

Method

A mailing list of individuals who had participated in one or more Psychomotor workshops with Al and/or Diane Pesso was obtained. Of 92 packets sent out, 34 were returned completed in varying degrees of detail. These questionnaires provide the basis for this report. Each questionnaire included the following directions:

> "You may respond to the following questions any way you wish. If you have completed only one or a few structures you might choose to respond to the questions

differently for each structure experience, or group them into one response. However you choose to respond, please provide as much information as you can."

The questionnaire included the following items:

1) approximate number of structures completed;
2) approximate time or number of years since you first participated in Psychomotor group;
3) general issues/concerns you wanted to work on;
4) description of structure experience(s);
5) the effects of structure experience(s) on your life (think in terms of body functions, specific behavioral patterns, subjective experience, interpersonal relationships, spiritual issues; any, one, or all).

Results

Participants varied widely in the amount of information provided. Many respondents chose to provide information about the effects of their experience with no structure description or background information. Survey results are therefore organized according to the amount and type of information provided. Responses were grouped and are presented as follows:

A. responses that included a relatively detailed description of structure experiences and effects are presented verbatim,

B. participants reports that were critical of some aspects of psychomotor or its effects are presented verbatim,

C. brief reports of structure effects are presented.

A. Detailed Positive Reports

REPORT 1. (Two structures, ten months apart)

Issues/Concerns. Developmental issues, such as sense of self, family trauma, concerns about sexuality, and relationships with men.

Description of Structure. I started by sitting on a pillow in front of Al Pesso, the way most structures seem to begin. In giving him an inventory of my bodily sensations I reported a lot of anxiety, felt primarily in my chest and throat. Also, my hands were cold, which is unusual. I had a desire either to wring my hands or hide them in the pockets of my favorite "protective" jersey jacket. Then I brought in a lot of information. I wanted to work on my sexuality and told a story of how after my son was born, when I was seventeen, I slowly lost my ability to orgasm. My ex-husband blamed me for the pregnancy, our second child. I was deeply hurt, and angry and had made a vow never to have another child. I had recently worked on this issue, releasing the energy block with my regular therapist and thought it all had been resolved. But in some way I must not have forgiven myself for getting pregnant. I began remembering other events, all traumatic, which happened during those years between 17 and 21. When Al stopped me, saying I seemed to be getting scattered, overwhelmed, and overstimulated, I started focusing back on the pregnancy and my husband's claiming it was my fault. Al asked me how I felt about that and I said, "shattered." He then asked who else had shattered me and

I replied, "my step-father." This information seemed to give Al a focus for the structure. Al asked me how I felt about the early "shattering" of my stepfather (who was brutal and sexually abusive) and by my ex-husband. I said I felt "despair." When questioned about the despair I began to cry. It seemed like my life was, at some deep level, shattered beyond repair. First the abuse of my stepfather, then my mother when she became an alcoholic when I was 12, and finally by my own actions. Getting pregnant at 15, having to marry, and then getting pregnant again at 17, had been devastating.

Al said that I was like a vase that had been shattered and lacked a sound center or base. He explained, "A child is like clay that is shaped at the core by the parents. The parents act as a potter's wheel, centering the pot and letting it grow in their hands." Al felt that giving me a base/center would be the best use of the structure. He suggested I select *ideal parents* and two extensions. The ideal parents and two extensions would sit on all sides, holding me as I threw myself around, and they would keep me on center, in firm but caring hands.

Coming out of my tears, I listened, understood and finally trusted. Al has worked with me once before and knew that in my chaotic family my needs were not important or recognized. But, at first I protested. I wanted to do "something" on my sexuality. Earlier when telling my story, I talked of how I had discovered masturbation at an early age. The masturbation has been very compulsive, and I felt great shame about it, especially when an adolescent. And, then there was the orgasm problem and some fantasies! Al assured me it would all come and tie together. So, I chose a young woman I knew slightly, but had warm feelings toward, as my ideal mother. My friend who is gentle and kind and completely unlike my step-father was my ideal father. I placed the ideal mother on my left side and my ideal father on the right, the extensions were placed in front and back of me as caring but limiting figures. I sat cross-legged on the floor. When all the figures were in place, each holding and/or supporting a side, I felt like I couldn't move but wanted to. From somewhere deep inside myself, I wanted to flail about. Al told me to go with the feeling, try to throw myself around and the ideal parents helped by their extensions would keep me "centered." I began an incredible, wild, crazy struggle that shocked me, at first. After that, I don't remember the struggle clearly, except for a panic that grew to terror until I screamed, a very loud, "shattering" scream. Then I collapsed in tears. When I took my hands from my face I wanted someone to hold them and Al had the two extensions do that. I cried until a calm started to settle in and gradually, in my mind, I saw an image of over-lapping layers of shingles that seemed to be made of mud. After reporting the image, Al suggested it might be the clay being remolded and that felt right to me. I was beginning to really feel the presence of all those supporting figures. I began to talk about how afraid and alone I had always been as a child. After checking with me, Al had the ideal parents say, "If we had been your parents we wouldn't have left you alone and afraid." Somewhere in here I said, "You wouldn't beat me?" The ideal parents answered affirmatively and there was more interchange with the ideal parents always saying what I needed to hear. Finally, I began to feel their presence more deeply and had a sense of being like a young plant or slowly blooming flower. Al suggested the ideal parents affirm this growth by saying "If you had been our child, we would let you grow and bloom like a beautiful flower." I asked, "You wouldn't humiliate and trample me?" They answered reassuringly, but I said "really" in a disbelieving way.

Al stopped the process at this point and explained that he suspected there was a part of me that wanted to be trampled. That this happens often in victimized children. There is an erotic drive to go to the source of the punishment. Well, it felt right, fit my history and what

I knew about child abuse and incest, but I was also frightened and repulsed by the idea. We talked for awhile and Al explained what he wanted to do to help me resolve this. Al's idea was to choose some people to role-play "tramplers" and I would try to go to them, but the ideal parents and extensions would act as limiting figures and prevent me. My trust in Al and something inside me that wanted to finally heal over-rode my misgivings and I told Al to choose some "tramplers" as I just couldn't. He chose two men and one woman. They stood in front of me, about four or five feet beyond the extensions. When they began to stamp their feet I almost freaked out, they sounded like Nazis in boots. All my childhood fear, obsession, and identification with the Jewish victims of the Holocaust came back. But, sure enough I went for them. I pulled one hand free of the extensions and tried to pull myself hand over hand up the arm of the other extension, but he held firm. All my other holding figures also held firm and eventually I stopped struggling.

I can't remember what happened then, until Al asked me what I was experiencing. My clearly remembered answer was, "I feel like I have an empty box from here to here." And I drew the "box" which extended from my waist to the top of my chest including some of my throat, but was mostly the heart area. Al said that he thought that "box" was the emptiness and loneliness I felt as a child. That made great sense to me and I started to cry. My ideal parents comforted me. When I stopped Al explained that the compulsive masturbating was a desperate attempt to fill that emptiness and nurture myself and all that made even more sense. We talked a little about this and my shame about the masturbating began to fade away. But, what to do about the emptiness? Al asked me what I felt would fill the emptiness and the tentative answer "Love" sort of fell out of my mouth. Al told me to take a hand of each ideal parent and place them where I wanted to fill the emptiness. I placed one hand of each parent over the center of my chest (the heart area) and put my hands over theirs. The area under their hands began to feel warmer and warmer and when I closed my eyes, I had an image of a small, perfect sun which seemed to be radiating light and warmth into my heart center. Then I saw a cross of light through the box with parts around the cross still empty. Al suggested I press still harder with my hands, feeling the hands of my ideal parents and imagine all the area filling up with light and warmth. I did and it did.

At some point, I felt warm tingling in my anus and pelvic area. I reported this and ideal parents affirmed my right to feel warm in all those areas, thus affirming my sexuality.

My back began to hurt, a spot in the middle, right side. Slumping did not help, neither did leaning against the support offered by one of the extension figures. In Psychomotor you always go with the body pain and Al suggested that I do that. I did and slowly began to sit very erect and proud and the pain disappeared. I said " What I feel is pride." And what a beautiful feeling. I felt proud, confident, beautiful, a little shy and very new.

The structure ended with a series of dialogues between myself and my ideal parents. Al asked me to visualize a family who would affirm this new me in ways that were meaningful to me. Most important was that my family/parents believe in something. My stepfather was an avowed atheist; religion and/or spirituality was ridiculed in my family of origin. Permission to be a spiritual person is very important to me in my life now. So we had the ideal parents say they believed in something. Another important issue was anger and having the ideal parents say they would handle their anger in non-violent ways was very satisfying. We did this until I felt finished and the structure was done.

Effects. How about finally being able to have a firm base and center? That is how I feel and all growth, particularly spiritual, has come from that base.

REPORT 2. (One structure, 3-4 years previous to completing questionnaire)

Description of Structure. When asked what I would like to do (I don't really remember how it was set up) I almost immediately thought of crawling. It was simple, uncomplicated, and developmental (I did not analyze it as such at the time). It seems that I had a hunger for recognition and approval from my parents and even today love having my husband make a fuss over me. The sequence was that I stated to my parents what I would like, then I got on my hands and knees and crawled around on all fours. They exclaimed what a wonderful baby I was, how wonderfully I was crawling, how skillful I was and in general were very approving, accepting, admiring. The structure did not seem to last long, 5-10 minutes. I remember feeling very proud of myself, successful and that what I had done gave me joy to do and won a feeling of approval from my parents. I remember feeling the warmth of their attention and feeling that I had made them happy... just by being me. In general these statements as I write them seem to reflect me as a person. I recall times in my life feeling that I had to "perform" or do something extra special in order to be "OK" as a person. I resented the feeling of society (my parents) that I was not OK just because I existed... you don't count unless you do something extra special. Thus I have been a doer most of my life... making the extra effort.

I am considered to be very active, productive and energetic by my friends and work associates... also very joyful most of the time. I guess that structure allowed me to see how important that theme has been in my life and to know that perhaps I didn't have enough or all that I wanted of my parents' attention and approval when I was little. When I was born I had a sister who was 3 years old and a brother who was 1 year old. My mother was in her early 30s and I don't think really wanted to have so many children, and probably was not at all pleased to have me when my brother was so young. I imagine that I got strokes for helping out by playing "little mother." I had value because I could make mother's life a little easier... perhaps to make up for my feeling that I was an extra burden to her. I have a brother who was born 6 years later... much to my mother's dismay (my parents never said these things...I just think it was so from watching and feeling) and I took on the primary role of "mothering" him. My mother had a nervous breakdown when my brother was 6 yrs. old and was not with our family much for the next 5 years and died when I was 18 yrs. old.

Effects. Well maybe in the above I have elaborated on how that structure fed a missing link in my life. I guess in doing the structure it made me realize that I had an issue to deal with which was my "OK-ness" with myself. I had worked my butt off to be successful in society's eyes — college, graduate school, Peace Corps, employment, marriage,... then divorce. The divorce represented a change in that I now wanted to start doing things for me, because I liked it. Through the structure experience I was able to let go by thinking, "There, I have it! My parents think I'm wonderful and I don't have to do anything except be me." I remember when I was crawling, I had great fun twitching my head and back-end and just crawling away with gusto... a bit of a showoff. The more my ideal parents exclaimed the more wonderful it was. It was like we were all working together as a team to produce some wonderful feelings and experiences. I like remembering it... it was so simple and so innocent.

Whether it was from that structure or not, during the past few years I saw myself needing to come to the rescue of others less and less. Some friends commented that they had always been able to count on me for a back rub. It was because I tuned into the needs of others so well — legitimizing myself that way. Some expressed disappointment that I no longer had this need so they got fewer back rubs. More and more I've come to enjoy myself with others on whatever level I happen to be. Watching, listening, feeling but not always taking charge to fix things or make something happen. I choose how I act more now rather than acting where I see need. I no longer have the illusion that I must or can do it for others. Finally, I've learned how important it is to express my own feelings of approval when I like or enjoy what someone is doing. In my present relationship with my husband I try to be very positive, providing approval and support rather than criticism.

REPORT 3. (Three structures during several months some years ago)

Description of Structures. I recall my very first structure. Although I had seen many structures, accommodated in many of them, and understood the format, when my first personal turn came I was terrified. I firmly resisted any role-playing of parental figures although I was keenly aware of my anger toward my father. As the therapist made suggestions, guilt and betrayal feelings overwhelmed me. I obviously had difficulty separating reality from role-playing. Slowly, patiently, the therapist was able to set up a delightful scene in which I was seated playing with an imaginary playmate. My father in real life gave me mixed messages about playing. Often he chided me for spending so many long hours reading. Conversely, he ridiculed sports, resented money spent on toys (actually resented spending money on anything). He often shouted at us (my sisters and I) when we were playing for making too much noise. So that first structure gave me permission to just play.

It was a few years after that, that I had another structure turn and began slowly and painfully to seriously work on the father/anger issue. In the beginning it was still difficult for me to have negative aspects of father role-played and I resisted, after trying to sabotage the therapist. Even more difficult was the introduction of ideal father. I only let that figure happen close to the end of my allotted time. Gingerly would I allow ideal father to have minimal contact and even today I have not in any structure been able to fully "take-in" that figure.

The second structure centered around the theme of money for schooling. I was refused tuition for school. I wanted desperately to go as it was a way to get out of the house and learn a way to make a living. Consequently, I worked for a year and saved every penny except what I paid for room and board and entered on my own. I lived a meager existence, having only a few changes of underwear (I stopped wearing underwear altogether by the end as well as sleepwear). I had no winter coat and never went to a movie or out for an ice cream. My resentment was very high as the money was there, but my father did not want to finance me. After 18 months, he saw my determination and the state of my wardrobe and offered me a stipend. I refused.

I was able to express much anger around this issue in a very ungracious way and it was extremely exciting and satisfying. I still feel badly that the ideal figure was so hard for me to let in. The money issue evolved into my being very conservative on dates — ordering the least expensive item on the menu, and that type of thing. It was hard for me to believe a fellow would want to date me and spend money on me.

Pre-Psychomotor — and this includes pre- and post-marriage experiences with men — I was abrasive, always ready for a fight. I was challenging verbally, nasty, argumentative and petty. When a man was nice to me, I could not bear it. I would try hard to antagonize him so that we'd have an argument. Of course, there would be angry words. I got very energized by these arguments (they were almost constant at home) and in a crazy way, felt good when I was arguing. I guess it was exciting and it felt like "home." I would concurrently feel bad and upset — cry and be miserable — but that was like home too!

Effects. Post-psychomotor I am much less argumentative with my husband. I do not see all his actions as threats. Arguments are no longer so thrilling and exciting when they do happen. I am much more able to accept his love and believe in it. I am able to spend money on myself with less guilt. I recently (after a 28 year hiatus) returned to school and earned two degrees. I was able, with minimal guilt, to use some of our savings and pay tuition. For me this was a big step.

In general, with men other than my husband I am friendly and sociable and far more at ease than before. I certainly am not always (as before) on guard and looking for a fight. And I can accept with pleasure an expensive dinner!

Another theme of my structure work was the physical abuse my father handed out. I was able to address this issue with all the righteous fury it deserves. The energy I spent on this issue (it was several structures) was enormously cathartic. However, my ability to accept a non-violent ideal father was marginal.

In the early marriage years I was often afraid my husband might strike me. He never did. Nor did he ever make a motion to do so. Yet, I expected (hoped?) he might. It is no longer something I fear.

In one structure I found myself standing at the foot of my father's grave wanting to lie down beside him. I did so. What evolved was a wonderful peaceful feeling. That experience was powerful and was quite important. Through that structure I was able to realize his death and several important points: 1) physically he can no longer harm me; 2) emotionally he cannot harm me; 3) I have come to terms with my past. Since that structure I have found myself to be more accepting of my husband's behavior when it is negative. I no longer view negative behavior from him as the totality of our relationship but simply a part of it — as it is in all relationships. That has been a freeing and vital learning experience for me.

REPORT 4. (Ten structures during the past two years)

Issues/Concerns. Issues from my personal history. A not understandable pain I suffered in my hands and arms for months. A very peculiar experience I had that frightened me.

Description of Structure. Number 2 stands out most clearly. I told about the pain in my hands/arms. Every night for the past few months I awoke from that pain, more than once each night and again in the very early morning (usually I am a very sound sleeper). Pesso asked me to do what I felt with them, and I over-stretched them, just as if to hold some very great danger away. I got some ideal parents to help me. They were not weak like my real parents were, but protected me and helped me to protect myself against doctors. Then I remembered I very often dreamed of knives and operations they (the doctors) did to me. In fact everything was all right (but not in my dreams!).

Effects. The day after the structure the pain was gone. I never had it any more.

REPORT 5. (Eight structures during the past few years)

Issues/Concerns. Experiences from my youth, especially during World War 2; also later periods of childhood and adolescence. Later on some feelings and relationship issues with my children and boyfriend.

Description of Structures. Three years of age: the taking away of my father by the Germans. I re-experienced the farewells, also the feelings of hatred toward the soldiers. This was the most important structure done with Pesso which was good because it was a very "heavy" structure and he could handle it. Age 5-6 years: This was about the bad treatment I received in the foster family. Age 15-16 years: I often was ill and in the hospital, feeling deserted and lonely and that my parents had no interest in me. Friends were kept away and could not visit me. I was hated for being ill. I re-experienced this with understanding parents. Boyfriend: When my boyfriend decided to go abroad for a year I had a hard time with that, being deserted by men during all my life, first my father, then my ex-husband. I experienced this as a disaster or a leaving forever. My structure helped me accept this. Children: Having had much responsibility as a child, for my parents and later, for my own children, I was able to give the children more independence, especially my 18 year old son who had the hardest time after my divorce a few years before.

Effects. I accept now that I have no father anymore and don't think about that all the time anymore. I accept my mother's behavior better and can understand it better as a result of her experiences during the war. I have come to the realization that youth is the most important experience in the formation of one's personality. This helps me in my work as a social worker in a therapeutic community. Relationships: I think the structures contributed to the fact that I have become a more trusting person, more accepting and responsible toward people who are dependent or attached to me in some way.

REPORT 6. (Three structures during the past year)

Description of Structures. I approached each training session, except the first, prepared to go with my body and feelings at the time of my work. Prior to the first session, I thought I wanted to work on my love relationship, but when I settled into going with what I was experiencing in my body, I immediately began dealing with issues related to my father and later my mother. For my third and most recent structure, I knew my father's death a few months before would be the focus.

The first structure dealt with general issues with men and power via my father, and with issues with my mother's early death (age 49) and the scripting that caused me.

The second structure focused on my mother's modeling of women as sickly. I experienced an ideal mother who would have been healthy and who would have taught me how to be soft and strong, and an ideal grandmother and great-grandmother who would have passed on to me healthy genes.

The third structure allowed me to let go of some of the deep grief I had from my father's death. I also discovered the set up I had — to have him as the ONLY man worthy of me. Lastly, I discovered I was still battling with choosing life or death — I had my mother waiting for me in heaven. Again I chose life with the help of an ideal family who would enjoy life here.

Effects. Personal health: During the last structure I was at the end of pneumonia and pleurisy. During the three day training session, the pleurisy disappeared. When I had a chest X-ray a few weeks later, my chest was clear. I realized then that a pain in the upper left chest that I'd experienced periodically over time was a signal that I was dealing with the life/death choice. I now know that if I experience the pain again, I need to stop and look at that theme.

REPORT 7. (Two structures, both during one workshop last year)

Description of Structure. Started with a shaking in the legs, I went into a structure about my sexual identity. I saw myself curled up inside my mother's womb with my genitals clearly visible. The ideal mother confirmed by touch, said that she wanted a boy and liked my being a boy.

Effects. Clear expression and experience of the wish/fantasy/action that women can like my genitals. Realization of a connection between sexual feelings, anger, withdrawal, and loss of sexual contacts/experiences. I feel that the structures initiated a new stage or phase of my life. I had been stuck in a cycle of withdrawal and anger about being rejected (which I am still partly stuck in). However, after having worked on issues, I felt motivated by the strength and depth of the structures to explore new vistas.

REPORT 8. (Two structures during the past month)

Issues/Concerns. At the time of initial structure, I had no sense of really having a self or of being an adult. Closely related has been the feeling of not having the right to be, of being afraid. Poor self-esteem. Afraid to be real. Not taking my space or feeling I have any rights.

Description of Structures. The first structure started out with the goal of allowing myself to be. To my surprise, what quickly surfaced during the structure was the fact that the foster children my parents had given a home to (about 17 in the course of my childhood from birth to around age 13) had been a problem for me. So I got ideal parents who would have felt I was enough for them, they would never have all those kids, etc. About the time we "got rid of all those kids" — which was done by tearing up a cardboard box, I was overwhelmed with a feeling of sadness, but since one has to bring a structure to a positive end in the time allotted and this seemed like something for future exploration we didn't look at it. The structure ended with ideal parents playing with their one child who would have been enough for them. They would not have gotten all those other kids.

The second structure got into the fear — I'm not sure exactly what my goal was, seemed like I wanted to work on not always being afraid of other people and this seemed to lead into an operation when I was 3 yrs. and not being able to get away and the structure worked on limits and the ideal parents would not have had me have an operation.

Effects. Both structures seemed to leave some things undone. After the first one I acquired, or perhaps I should say a pain in my neck/shoulder area surfaced, and I have not since been able to get rid of it. It lessens or worsens, even seems to change location but no thought, image or whatever will make it totally go away. I have a hunch it is connected to the torn up box and whatever loss that represented when all the kids did finally leave and there was just my brother and myself. My mother had a nervous breakdown, which was a pretty frightening experience for me, and she went uncared for by any professional. The second structure had about a two week after-effect of my wanting to test and believing I could break through any limits — that I couldn't be limited. This eventually simmered down but I have a hunch there is more work to be done on limits, too. However, I have a self now. I'm not always sure of what my space or my right to space is in the world but this seems to be growing stronger. I think too there is less fear in my encounters with other people. I find myself in very small ways behaving in new ways — it's exciting when it happens. I expect to be returning to do another Psychomotor workshop shortly. I hope to get rid of the "pain in my neck" — but I don't know what will surface.

I have the sense that one structure is easily equal to 6 months to a year of weekly sessions with the traditional psychiatrist. And what surfaces is often surprising and a real "aha."

I like PS/P. I like the feeling of respect for each other that one feels doing a structure, a sense of how important it is to feel and to express one's feeling and there is this respect you feel participating in another person's structure. I like the responsibility being on the person doing the structure, it is your structure, not someone doing it to you. I like the clear-cut role-playing and being told what to say instead of trying to guess what someone needs to hear or how they need to be touched. I like letting something go, or expressing something negative and then having a positive to replace the emptiness which would be there if you just let it go.

REPORT 9. (Three structures during the past two years)

Issues/Concerns. The first structure dealt with my older brother's death. For years I had never processed the grief and a part of my soul had left with him. The neighborhood we shared in childhood was role-played as I encountered a revisit. In a subsequent structure the part my grandmother played in my life and the impact she has had on me was the focus.

Description of Structures. A male was chosen to role-play my brother as I talked about many of the experiences we shared in childhood. During this structure I had the opportunity to say goodbye. In dealing with my grandmother someone role-played her husband, whom I had never known, and I got in touch with incredible anger/rage as limits were set on me.

Effects. After the first structure I could easily remember my brother and talk about him. It was the first time since his death that I had mentioned his name. The life experiences which we shared were easier to discuss with my parents. The second structure really made me aware of the lack of grandfathers/male relatives in the former generation and how much dying there was. I'm not sure where the anger came from, way down deep, but getting in touch with it and having it limited and focused made me aware of other work I need to do.

As a result of my work with Psychomotor I have been able to talk with my parents more about the past: family history and the period of time when my brother died and I was leaving the "nest." It was a difficult time for all of us. There seems to be a lot of strong emotional stuff involved yet with that issue. During a recent visit home, I brought up my mother's apparent inability to get enough of me during my stay and how each visit caused her a lot of sadness, especially when I readied to leave. I confronted her and processed her perception of the problem. It became clear that she associated my leaving with my brother's death and had been laying a lot of stuff (anger/hurt) on me. The results of the confrontation were amazingly good.

I used to have periodic back pain, but have felt none since the visit home (6 months). I've also learned to meditate and have returned from the "cosmos" since those two experiences. I know without the work I've done in Psychomotor my present state would not be possible. I feel more grounded, more here, less anger-projected and no back pain!

REPORT 10. (Three structures during past the past two years)

Issues/Concerns. Worked on feelings about my Dad.

Description of Structure. I was getting in touch with dangerous feelings in relationship to my Dad (from a 5 year old perspective) and blacked out. While not remembering the details of what happened in that particular structure, nor how Al managed to gently lead me back to awareness, I did have the strong feeling that I was being supported and cared for by a group of loving people. That feeling of "being cared for" was very real when Al called me the next day from out of town to see how I was feeling. Those cared for feelings have been there for me to recall.

Effects. (a) No longer personalizing responses in job-related experiences and allowing myself to feel OK and affirmed; (b) I respond less frequently to my "boss" as the child seeking his approval and never doing enough to feel his approval. I try to remember the new *map* I have to follow and know that I am a loved person. Therefore, I feel less need for his direct words of approval; (c) I do more "reality testing" in looking for ways to affirm my OK-ness; for instance, in noting the way clients provide good feedback about the way they are treated in our office; (d) As I remember the new map of the feelings that come from safe and secure parenting, I am able to relate to my two staff assistants in ways similar to what I would want from my boss. As a result, our office "team spirit" is reflected in the cheerful and cooperative way we respond to clients.

Citing these examples is not to say I can always recall the option of the new map I have, for some days I still walk along on the old map. But I have more days on the new map than the old, and each experience of well-being gives me more security in moving ever closer to a goal of wholeness and well being.

REPORT 11. (Three structures during the past three months)

Issues/Concerns. To understand where my extreme distress over violence that leads to death comes from, my distress is triggered even if the violence is symbolic as in structures when negative parents are killed.

Description of Structure. Got in touch with feelings that my brother is literally killing my dad. This freed me to explore feelings toward my brother that I was afraid to deal with. I found myself being OK with being physically abusive myself in my structure. It felt good not to hold back and being totally out of control. Then had trouble accepting support; finally was able to accept.

Effects. Have been able to let go without letting things build up until I am totally out of control to the point of exploding. Realized that my fear was if I let myself get in touch with my need to be taken care of I feared I would lose my freedom, control and independence. Have been able to get closer to people without my fears getting in the way.

B. Critical Evaluations of the Psychomotor Experience

REPORT 12. (Six structures)

Issues/Concerns. Self worth, personal power, validation of being. Having girlfriend as content. My tendency to prefer separation and distancing.

Description of Structure. Last structure was three years ago. It involved acting out of feminine content and turning to parents for support. I experienced inhibition to the extreme. Two hours after my structure I freaked out, was confused, disconnected. Had sex/slept with a woman in the group the night before she was in my structure and I had not separated clearly. Still had her as my content.

Effects. Very short lived benefits. Very superficial, Pesso works at a very shallow content level. After the last structure it took four months to clear the confusion and feel whole and well again. Mostly the structures catalyzed a process at the surface; deep closure had to come through my own processing. Pesso seems to have definite tendency to structure too soon; doesn't allow deeper content to surface before he begins to guide. Had a sense that he was doing too much guiding and steering.

The people role-playing parents have feeling content beneath the messages they convey that is received by the person doing the structure. Pesso ignores this. My sense of Psychomotor is that it is a fairly good emotional clearing process for surface emotions, but doesn't reach or deal with deep feeling content and therefore could never bring anyone to wholeness and wellness completion.

REPORT 13. (Two structures during the past year)

Issues/Concerns. The general, constant tension between my wife and me.

Description of Structure. The first structure eventually came to issues with my father, working toward an experience that he would hold me. The second structure dealt with my mother and her sexual seductiveness; I was put in a limits structure to be shown I could not get her.

Effects. The only effects I'm aware of are feelings of dissatisfaction with the experiences, that they didn't touch the real issues I wanted to work on, and that Al and I led ourselves and the others away (seduced them away?) from these issues. I didn't like these results and have decided to do no further work for now.

REPORT 14. (One structure during the past year)

Issues/Concerns. Grief work surrounding a tragedy.

Description of Structure. I wasn't in the space to do the above work, and showed that by leaving my body and going off on some "trip." I did try another structure about my brother — sadness at his having been scapegoated as psychologically unfit for most of his life.

Effects. To date — since my structures weren't really complete — I have noticed no change. I guess I wasn't ready for this experience with Psychomotor, though I believe in the process.

C. Summary Reports of Positive Effects

REPORT 15. (First workshop experience, first structure)

Issues/Concerns. Tendency to be ungrounded.

Description of Structure. I was on my back on the floor and remembering my early, early boyhood, lying on the floor listening to music and watching trees swaying in the wind and the grassy earth on which I was lying on my back heaving under me, rocking me on the crest of a firm but gentle wave. The whole thing led to much sadness for me. The sadness was later replaced by a sense of peace. I cried a bit during the structure — and therapy or no therapy, that doesn't happen very often.

Effects. Its effect on me was profound, but I cannot tell you what the effect has been in specific terms because I don't know myself at this point.

REPORT 16. (Approximately five years experience with psychomotor)

Effects. Phase 1. Helped me to be more comfortable, less anxious about being close, physically and emotionally, to others. I can now distinguish between a desire for nurturance, affection and a sexual, sensual desire. This has greatly reduced my anxiety about being close. Two years after this Psychomotor work, I married for the first time, and some of these issues have resurfaced, but were clearly recognizable and less anxiety producing. Behavioral effects: I less often initiate sex as a substitute for other forms of emotional closeness. I no longer retreat from people for whom I have an attraction (which I used to experience as only sexual).

Phase 2. Psychomotor helped me reduce my fear of my own anger, excitement, sexuality, play, power. I trust myself to go further with each, without putting my own lid or brakes on.

Phase 3. Helped with integration of strong, thinking, male aspect and receptive, feeling, female aspects of my personality.

REPORT 17

Description of Structures. I am still shocked at the strength for me of unknown experiences, feelings and that it is terrifying to reveal them, become aware or express them. Every structure was a kind of shock to me. I don't remember much except pieces.

Effects. Some proof of change can be found in the fact that after my first structure — all of a sudden my place in my therapy group changed. I had more pride, was more free and less dependent and the other members seemed glad with that.

I feel more at ease with myself, and with others too. I'm less eager to please, complain less, and can be aggressive. The curious thing is a lot of people tell me I'm a lot more feminine now! There is a lot more self acceptance. Since I grew to understand my own personal history and accept it as being unchangeably mine, the feeling of being sorry for myself disappeared. I now like my own strength and power and am less afraid of it. There are more friends in my life now. As persons, they are more direct and mind their own boundaries. I feel there is a lot less to hide. I can stand up for myself more.

REPORT 18

Issues/Concerns. Depression/rage and self-destructive thoughts were my first order of business. Later I dealt with emptiness and lack of focus and goals, experienced following loss of significant relationship.

Effects. I have had considerable training/therapy of the cognitive variety and have difficulty sorting out what were the elements of Psychomotor which made an impact for change in my life. The group permission to act on impulses connected to death wishes and to experience the consequences, i.e., peace of mind, absence of demands, stability, enabled me to integrate these experiences and feelings and to experience them as consonant with my value system. Sleep time increased and a sense of emotional and physical well being began immediately after my structure and continues. I suspect the social permission to "be" without accomplishing helped me to see options as to how I might satisfy my needs.

Having been trained to disregard physical needs in order to "accomplish the task" my Psychomotor structure has had the most significance in reversing that mind set. Al was the first therapist who talked about my *soul*, finally raising an issue which seemed worth fighting for, and turned me from a victim into an actor.

In the 2 years since my only Psychomotor experience I have sold my house, moved to another city, taken my first trip abroad, resigned my job of 10 years and feel more in tune with my spiritual goals than ever.

REPORT 19

Issues/Concerns. People and relationships, marriage relationship, release of anger, dealing with people in business who I supervise, father relationship with my daughters, feeling more positive about myself.

Description of Structures. At first lots of nurturance and having a sense of ideal parents who are connected to each other. Later structures focused on limiting of anger, and accommodation of anger.

Effects. Able to, for periods of time, accommodate personal attacks; with more structures these periods have become longer. I even started to like people. I take stronger responsibility for my own actions. I have made a commitment to being male instead of alternately switching. I have thrust myself into situations requiring me to grow and have managed several job advances with the acquired people skills.

REPORT 20. (Seven structures during the past year)

Issues/Concerns. (a) Accepting myself as a female; (b) Issues with my mother — about accepting my body (my breasts) and bodily functions (elimination). Dealing with my hostile feelings toward my mother; (c) Being at ease, reaching out to people with touch.

Description of Structures. (a) I chose ideal parents. I was "reborn" and they were glad I was girl. They held me, rocked me, sang me a lullaby. I continued to work on accepting my femininity. I also had the opportunity to hug my mother very tightly and she was accepting of my doing this. I felt a lot of sadness at this time, because I thought about the fact that I had never allowed my daughter to hug me tightly.

Effects. I am now letting myself be on time more often than before. I am feeling more at ease in relating to other people and am experiencing more pleasure in sexual intercourse. I am able to negotiate better in working out problems with my husband.

REPORT 21. (Two structures several years ago)

Effects. Though I was about 33 years old, I felt like a little girl trying to please daddy whenever my path crossed that of male doctors (the "daddies" of the hospital). In my structure Al asked me to rearrange the people in the room so that I could feel more comfortable. I created a circle of the men and me. I could tell each person where to sit without having to be cute or coy or flirtatious or fearful. I felt I became an equal. We all became grownups. That moment of being in control was the important one, and since then I have been more aware of my options to choose between feeling like a "girl" and feeling like a "woman."

REPORT 22

Issues/Concerns. At the beginning, no clear motivation; later I wanted to work on my relationship with my father. Since my structures my relationship with him has improved.

Effects. Change in life style; more concerned with my work; less with unhappiness. I might marry within a year. Clearer choice of what sort of partner I like.

REPORT 23

Effects. Can release my mother and father to be who they are and accept them there. Am able to integrate my female, receptive side with an overdeveloped aggressive side.

REPORT 24

Issues/Concerns. Feelings of anger and depression. Overinvolvement in fixing up my house to the exclusion of relationships; making contact with others.

Effects. Generally, I either ran into the parts of my life in which I was stuck and didn't realize it or I moved through some feelings which were in the way. The first structure I did really cleared me up for a month or so, and the effects seemed to remain for quite a while after that. In later structures I really struggled with parts of myself I barely understood.

REPORT 25

Effects. Able to have adult-to-adult relationships.

REPORT 26

Effects. I'm not sure that I very often reached the child within me in order to absorb the message from the ideal parents in my structure. I certainly feel that at the very least I gained knowledge about my body tension, posture, etc. and feelings. I also felt the support of the group and was able to see that my problems were not terribly unique, which was reassuring. I gained insight into my own feelings, many of which had been long buried.

REPORT 27. (Two structures during past two years)

Issues/Concerns. Body signs, self/self activity, self punishing tendencies.

Effects. It is hard to be specific, but my family — wife and kids (4 kids 25-15 years old) — have told me that I am an easier man to live with, and that is something, isn't it.

REPORT 28. (Six structures over the past two years)

Issues/Concerns. Relationship to my little son and to my wife, self-acceptance, sexual behavior.

Effects. It brought more awareness of deep-rooted motives, Oedipal desires, narcissistic projections on my son, insights about deep longings and also a lot of therapeutic skills and sensitivity for my work as a psychotherapist.

REPORT 29. (Two structures during the past two years)

Issues/Concerns. Depression, family issues.

Description of Structures. Both times I moved from focus on bodily sensations to issues with mother and father figures, and in particular an event in childhood where my father tried to choke my mother to death. The second structure was a progression from the first.

Effects. The structures have given me insights unavailable by other methods, allowing me to move ahead at a faster pace.

REPORT 30. (Ten structures during past year and one-half)

Effects. The series of structures has opened a new way of internal seeing for me — the particular changes involve greater freedom of expression of all kinds of emotions and energies (sexual, aggressive, etc.).

REPORT 31. (One structure)

Issues/Concerns. Allowing myself to get closer to a man who can be significant in my life.

Effects. A sense of relaxation about the issue. Less sense of "I need to do something."

REPORT 32

Effects. Until I experienced Psychomotor structures I did not know what good parenting was. I did not know what good therapy was. I believe the Pessos have made Freudian, Jungian, and Object Relations therapy truly usable. For they have developed a theory of therapy as well as a theory of human growth.

REPORT 33. (One structure during past year)

Issues/Concerns. Depressed off and on.

Description of Structures. I felt about 8 years old, and wanted my parents. Was held by positive figures. Negative parents were inaccessible and this was very upsetting. I felt alone and angry. At first I rejected them back, then expressed anger, hurt. Ideal parents gave me love, acceptance, and relieved me of any responsibility for their problems.

Effects. I have experienced only one day of depression in the past few months, which is much less than before. I also experienced much less teeth gritting and jaw clenching — both awake and asleep — which was a very common area of body tension for me for many years. Keeping my mouth shut was part of holding that anger in. It's fantastically nice to be rid of that tension.

REPORT 34. (One structure during past year)

Issues/Concerns. I have experienced much stress and many frustrations in my family over the last two years related to the birth of a new (wanted) baby, because my husband has not been available.

Description of Structure. My structure was related to the lack of support/protectiveness by my parents. As the oldest child, my mother depended on me in an almost reverse relationship in which I was set up and felt obligated to support and protect her. My father basically disapproved of me — he offered only criticism if he did interact verbally with me, which wasn't very often. I could never do enough to please either of them, it seemed. My dad showed fairly obvious favoritism to 2 younger siblings.

Effects. My overall mood has been happier. I feel I have "taken care" of some of those negative situations, as if by the actions of righting the "wrongs" in a structure I have symbolically dealt with them. I feel more ready to let go of the negative feelings associated with them. I feel better about myself as I feel I can better leave the past behind.

Conclusions

The variety and richness of self reports of the experience and effects of Psychomotor structures provide a valuable source of information and evidence for the effectiveness of this approach. The majority of the participants who responded described important life changes that they attributed to participation in Psychomotor. This evidence is particularly impressive in light of the fact that one structure experience lasts only 50 minutes. A great many changes were attributed to the effects of a single structure.

These results suggest that Psychomotor is a potentially powerful therapeutic approach that requires sensitivity and expertise on the part of the leader, as well as commitment and responsibility on the part of participants, to see to it that their structure work is complete and comes to a positive end. A positive outcome with beneficial results was not reported by all respondents. In some cases the content of the report suggests possible reasons for the disappointing or negative quality of the outcome reported. These reports illustrate the significance of the contract made before each Psychomotor group: that each participant is responsible for bringing their structure experience to a positive outcome during the time allotted. Overall, reports suggest that Pesso System/Psychomotor therapy is a powerful, effective and efficient process for change.

We need many more detailed self reports to learn about the details of the effects of structure work and to obtain long term follow up descriptions of the effects of these experiences. A catalogue of this material could provide a rich source of insight into the process of Psychomotor.

Finally, I wish to thank each of the respondents who unselfishly took the time to respond to the questionnaire material and granted permission for it to be included in this paper. Further reports would be welcomed by the author.

References

Schaffer, N.D. (1982). Multidimensional measures of therapist behavior as predictors of outcome. *Psychological Bulletin, 92*, 670-681.

Chapter 24

Psychomotor Therapy:

A Client's Perspective

by Debra Antari

I experienced my first Psychomotor *structure* in January, 1985. PS/P has effected profound differences in my life since. In this chapter, I will describe these changes and tell a little about some of the structures that brought them about.

At that time I was withdrawn, insecure, depressed, and frozen — arrested in a time warp of early childhood abuse. This inner prison was erected by my own *soul* to combat the atrocities perpetrated against one too young and fragile to bear them. The best defense I could provide for myself was withdrawal. I saw my brother and sister beaten and abused by our brutal father with no forthcoming protection from our scared, insecure mother. I was abused also. The world was too hard and unsafe for a three year old, and so I withdrew within. I was good, I was quiet, and I was emotionally dead.

Four years ago, the same inner gatekeeper that imprisoned me for my own survival came in contact with Psychomotor and realized the time had come to unlock the fortress — that same soul knew that here was a path — a way back to the life I had shut down as a small child. I am grateful to Albert and Diane Pesso for creating this system, to Dr. Carl Clarke for first introducing me to it, and to the powers of my own inner *self* which first protected me by withdrawing a part of my emotions into safekeeping and subsequently, through Psychomotor work, resurrected those lost aspects.

I was newly divorced, the mother of two babies, and filled with frozen fear when I went to my first Personal Growth Workshop led by Carl Clarke. Personal Growth Workshops were developed by Carl and utilize almost exclusively PS/P techniques.

I remember in vivid detail that first workshop and the struggles it held for me. I had never felt comfortable speaking in groups and I found myself in the midst of a group of twelve strangers to whom I was expected to expose my soul. I was a good actress and my acting ability served me well in the initial check-in of the workshop, as I pretended I felt comfortable. As I calmly related the facts of my life at present — that my husband had left me and that I knew I needed to make changes in the way I lived my life — inside I felt frightened, sick, and dissociative.

The first part of the workshop that really "got" me was an ideal parenting exercise, led by Carl, which we participated in on Friday night. I was instructed to place my hand on the back of a complete stranger and enrole as her *ideal mother*. Ideal mother? Those two words seemed so incongruous to me, but I was accustomed to obedience and so I said the words. Then something happened. The person I was partnered with was a veteran of Psychomotor workshops and had had the experience of working with the ideal mother symbol before. As she began to experience within herself the nurturance and tenderness of what the words "ideal mother" meant to her simply by reacting to the placement of my hand on her back and hearing the enrolement statement, I began to feel a strong bonding to her. I felt protective and nurturing. I was not acting, I *felt* it! Somewhere, deep within me something was stirring — some inner longing of my own needs as a child was being projected outward, allowing my adult self to understand and provide for the needs of my partner. Through involving myself in providing for the needs of this other woman, yearnings and sensory memories of being an infant and being nurtured by my own real mother were being recalled. I was strongly affected by these feelings.

Then we switched roles and she placed her hand upon my back. The effects were nowhere near as profound. I found it much more difficult to take in the meaning of the symbol of ideal mother than it was to take it on. It was easier for me to give nurturance than to accept it.

Already, without my conscious knowledge, groundwork was being laid for what I would work on in my structure. The issue I dealt with when I had my turn was how hard it was for me to be touched by others. In retrospect, I see how much information about myself was being offered to myself and to Carl as workshop leader, through participating in this exercise which seemed so simple but whose results seemed so profound to me. I could touch another and feel warmth, but blocked feelings of nurture while being touched.

I remember feeling very connected to Carl Clarke early on that weekend. The persona he exhibited was not at all what I had pictured. I had envisioned a pompous, big, "here I am to fix you" doctor type person, not this small, gentle, loving man whom I first encountered tangled up in the wires of his audio and video recording equipment. Carl was funny, warm, and nurturing. Men in my life heretofore had not been of this ilk and I was able to develop a trust in Carl — this psychologist who referred to garlic bread at dinner as "stink bread" and who seemed to genuinely enjoy hugging.

Then came the second day of the workshop and *structures* — whatever the hell they were. My structure turn came fourth on a snowy January afternoon. I will never forget it. The first words out of my mouth as I sat on the floor facing Carl to begin my structure were, "I've never been able to allow myself to feel people." This provided the basis for all the hard work I was to do within the next 80 minutes.

The first 40 minutes of the structure were spent with me going to very regressed states and with Carl requesting I "come out" and make eye contact with him. Through doing this preliminary work Carl was establishing a trust between us, as well as teaching me to work via the Pesso System. The client needs to develop a part of himself that can report to the guide what his feeling and experiences are, as well as to be feeling them at the same time. Al Pesso now refers to this part of the client as the *pilot* — the supervisory ego that works in alliance with the Psychomotor guide and makes decisions as to how the structure should proceed.

I, as most survivors of abusive families, was so numbed out that there was little of this pilot part developed. I was accustomed to decisions being made for me and following them blindly. In my family, were I not to do this, I could have quite literally been killed. Carl and I had to work hard to "prime the pump" and set this long dormant aspect of myself in motion. To me, it seemed as if I were developing some sort of life-line connection that was prodding me towards the top of an abyss of dark, non-feeling in which I had spent almost all of my life. I knew how to numb out and retreat to an emotional never-never land very well. I had no experience in the reporting of this to another. Carl was teaching me how to develop this pilot part of me by calling upon it when I went to those regressed states during the structure and enlisting its help in bringing me "back out" to talk and make eye contact with him. The "adult" part of me was encouraged to be present and in alliance with Carl while connecting with the part of my self that so needed to regress in order to repair and illuminate instances of early trauma. This was a struggle for me. I was so afraid to be seen, yet so wanted to be whole.

Carl asked me why it was so difficult to keep present and not retreat within myself. I was able to tell him of my knowledge of my sister being raped by our father when she was eleven and I was seven. Carl asked if I had been sexually abused. My verbal answer was no, but something deep within me in that instant knew I was not telling the truth. When I view the video tape of this structure, I see myself saying "no" in answer to Carl's question, while my head, indeed, almost my whole body, is nodding in the affirmative. The body never lies. That the body is a storehouse of information that can be used to bring about healing is a basic tenet of PS/P. The knowledge I gained from my body in that one instance has been invaluable in my journey of personal growth. During the structure I was not able to consciously deal with the possibility that I had been sexually abused, but the gatekeeper part of me must have been both groaning from the fear of being found out and applauding in anticipation of the fortress opening at one and the same time.

I was able to arrive at an *antidote* to my opening statements of never having allowed myself to feel other people by coming to a point of being receptive to suggestions made by Carl that I enrole people from the group to be "persons who could touch me and rub my back" while I remain in a curled up fetal position on the floor. This intervention provided a motoric, tactile undoing to the opening statements of my structure. The final step involved extending the roles of two people into ideal parents. The only male I would allow as ideal father was Carl, and Vicky, a dear woman and friend, was enroled as ideal mother. As these people took on these roles I noticed a striking difference in the lightness of the room. Although my eyes were closed I experienced everything getting about four degrees of light brighter. I reported this to Carl and he laughed gently and said, "That means we've made soul contact," and I knew he was right. As I was allowing my body to be touched by so many of the people in that room, so, on a deeper level, was my soul opening to be touched.

The structure ended by my having the ideal parents make the statements, "Here with us, you can feel supported and safe." As I think of those words, I can still experience those feelings — feelings of other people surrounding me in a cocoon of love, safety, and warmth that was so new for me to feel.

As I write this, I am aware for the first time how profoundly those words and feelings of my first structure have affected me since, and of how magnificently they provided the antidote to my words as I sat down as client in my first Psychomotor structure — "I've never allowed myself to really feel other people." My God, did I feel other people at the closing of that structure.

It now seems as if those good feelings I had immediately after doing my first structure were the calm before the storm. Later that evening a turmoil like I had never known arose within me. Somehow, through struggling to enable myself to take in the symbols of ideal parents who would make my world supported and safe, a part of me recognized the time was now to look at why I had chosen to shut down as a defense against allowing others to touch me emotionally.

I recalled an incident of being sexually abused by my father at around age three. I was not able to relate this to anyone yet, indeed, not even fully to myself; that would happen in subsequent structures. But I knew I had been violated in this manner.

I could not sleep that evening. I saw flashes of images of my father and I had conscious memories of what had happened so long ago that caused me to view my world as unsafe. I knew my father had forced me to have oral sex with him while still a baby. This knowledge just came that evening. I was scared. It took seven months before I could speak of what I was recalling. I clung like a marsupial monkey to the good symbols and feelings I was left with at the end of my structure. These new images of abuse were so terrifying and strange to me that I attempted to push them out of my head. I so wanted Carl to wake up that night and magically know what was going on within my brain, because I knew I was not ready to speak of these troubling pictures yet. I could not go and get Carl — I was so habituated to not bothering anyone with my needs that I didn't even consider reaching out to anyone. Carl did not awaken, and I did not go to sleep. I couldn't eat the next and last day of the workshop.

I left for home that evening in a daze. The stupor lasted for two weeks. Exhaustion and elation at the good work I had done kept incongruous company with the terrifying flashes of sexual abuse I had seen. The world seemed totally new to me. The feelings of support and safety of the ideal parents wafted me through the uncomfortable feelings that foretold of hidden realities lying barely beneath my consciousness. The world actually looked sharper. I saw things quite literally differently. Al Pesso says this new 3-D vision that some people experience after a structure is indication that the person is in integrative contact with a part of the self which had not been lived. I knew I needed to do more of these things called structures.

It's now 1989. I've done about 30 structures. Each pointing me to more worlds of possibility. Not all growth needs to be done through pain — I've done riotous, hilarious, gut wrenchingly funny structures; structures whose meaning (like that first one) started quietly and crept up on me with soul changing impact; and lots of structures where I've nurtured myself with the milk of just what I needed. I have dealt openly with the demon of early sexual abuse that I came upon in that first workshop, as well as many other issues. My soul has known, with intricate exactness, just what I've needed to do in each and every structure.

In one structure, with Al Pesso as guide, I was not in a place emotionally where I could enrole other people. I started playing a childlike game of peek-a-boo with him — averting my eyes and surreptitiously glancing at him to see if I could catch him not looking at me. My soul needed to be seen and somehow I had enroled Al as an ever present figure who would see me even when I was not aware of my own existence. Through hearing this figure say the words, "I am aware of your existence, even when you don't know you exist," a deep need of a watchful, ever guarding parent was being met on the symbolic level of the structure. I experienced that Psychomotor could be just as effective in one-to-one therapy as in groups through this work. Here the usual structure form was varied, so that work on the relationship and transference levels complemented the role-taking.

Between this last structure and the one previously described, there have been a myriad of others. Structures in which I became more aware of myself and my feelings. I've found that even in dealing with the most serious issues my body and soul can help me heal in most unexpected and delicious ways. In one rollicking structure which dealt with the issue of my early sexual abuse I "became" a little doggie who almost by chance bit off the bone-like cock of an unsuspecting negative father. As I write of this, I still smile with the glee of that moment. My soul was aware that I was not yet ready to handle the depth of outrage and anger I felt towards my father on a reality level, so it created a safer fantasy version. Through the safe symbolism of Psychomotor I was able to taste (any pun not intended) a bit of that outrage in a more tolerable, fairy tale manner. I could feel the beginnings of the sweet, vengeful feelings towards my father, but was able to try them out via a safer fantasy structure.

Another structure I have vivid recall of is a nurturance structure in which I suckled at the breast of an ideal mother. The image I brought from that structure was one of a breast that seemed the size of a bowling ball coupled with feeling my head to be infant sized. Although physically, of course, I maintained my normal size during the structure, intrapsychically I felt myself to be the size of a tiny infant. The breast and nipple (in truth, the thumb of the woman enroled as my ideal mother) seemed immense. To this day, I swear I was truly that small, infant-sized being that afternoon. As I recall that structure, warm feelings of nurturance, acceptance, and love flow through me and I re-experience the safe vulnerability I felt allowing myself symbolically to be that small and helpless.

The recall of these sensory feelings captures the long term, life changing effects of Psychomotor. The client is often asked by the guide to make images and symbols of the good feelings experienced at the end of the structure. These images are concrete sensations that can be encoded within a person's innermost being and serve to form new patterns and guidelines for living life to the fullest. These symbols can be recalled to consciousness long after the actual time of the structure, to allow the client a re-experiencing of the positive new feelings in an intrapsychic, re-programming manner.

My life is new. I am alive in every sense of the word, coming to realize my power and glimpsing my potential. Psychomotor has helped me see how much there is for me to be, how good it is to feel. This has happened in my "shit cannon" structure which allowed me to shoot shit at the world in a riotous, passive aggression intervention; through helping me symbolically dislodge my father's cock from deep within the depths of my throat; and through giving me the model of an ideal mother, who in full awareness of her own sensuality could teach me of mine by shaking her shoulders at an attentive ideal father who looks on in love and sanctioned lust. All these images and many more have transformed me back into the person the universe meant for me to be before my growth was stunted at age three by outrageous sexual abuse.

These changes are apparent in almost every part of my life. The way I look, act, and am are different from the way I was four years ago. One of the most amazing testimonies to these changes is an incident that happened one Sunday afternoon upon returning from a workshop. Easter was approaching and I stopped to buy goodies for my boys at a drug store. I went to pay for my items with a check and provided my license as identification. The clerk looked closely at the picture of me on the license, taken about six months previously, and then back into my face. With disbelief she said, "this can't be you." I had changed so much that even the appearance of my face looked different to a total stranger. I still have that license. I take it out every so often to show people how I looked before I "started to grow."

I am confident and learning to express and know my feelings. I love who I am, yet I also accept and love the tiny three year old I was who did the best she could to keep me safe by shutting down a large part of me. I have been alone for these past four years but am feeling eager to enter into a love relationship when the opportunity arises. I am a much better mother and I have so much more love to give to my children now that I am more able to love myself. I have been in graduate school these past three years (my entry into higher education coincided with my starting Psychomotor) and I will enter into the PS/P Training program after I receive a Masters degree this May. Perhaps this is to be the last piece of writing I will be able to do strictly from a "client's perspective."

The withdrawn, shy, intimidated, unassertive girl of four years ago is changing into a confident, assertive woman and psychotherapist. The most amazing part of all this growth is that I feel deserving of it. I have setbacks and times when the hurt little girl comes back, but now I know how to take care of her. I can visualize images and symbols from the endings of my structures, I can put on a relaxing tape or meditate, or I can call out to someone for help if I need to. I am feeling these changes and growth deep within my being. I feel I have neurobiologically changed somehow. None of this would have happened if I had not ventured alone on that snowy Friday in 1985 to participate in a Psychomotor Personal Growth Workshop.

I believe we all start out as whole, functioning entities, but sometimes things happen that shut us down or cause us to function in other defensive ways for a time. I was shut down by a protective, overriding subconscious when the world became too brutal and unsafe for me to negotiate. Through PS/P and my inner strength and determination, at thirty-five years of age, the override is finally no longer necessary. The life I stopped feeling at three is coursing through me, emanating from within my soul in the form of joy, pain, anger, terror, laughter — a score of emotions so long held in. It is wonderful to be alive!

Glossary of PS/P Terms

Accommodation - The act of a role player responding in a way that matches and satisfies the impulses and action requests of the client in a structure. (See also **Negative Accommodation** and **Positive Accommodation**)

Antidote - The healing (antidotal) interaction provided by the ideal figures to counter the toxic effects of the negative history experienced with the original historic figures. The antidote usually provides directly opposite or contrasting elements found in the negative event. For instance, if the original parents were alcoholic, then the ideal parents would be sober; if the originals were abusive, the ideals would be respectful and loving, etc.

Basic needs - People have four basic emotional needs: nurturance (oral/tactile), support, protection, and limits. Secondary needs are the need for respect and a sense of place. Basic needs must be satisfied by parents during childhood in order for a child's ego to develop and for the child to be and become his or her true self. (See also **Nurturance**, **Support**, **Protection**, **Limits**, **Respect**, **Place**)

Center of Truth - The position from which the client is in touch with all the internal information about his or her personal existence that is available for consciousness and experience. The polar elements found there include emotional information regarding moment to moment affective states (inherited personal aspects — the soul) and information regarding values, attitudes, and injunctions resulting from experience during significant, life shaping events (individual learned aspects — the ego).

Contact figure - A symbolic role-played fragment figure who is called upon when the client has more feelings showing on the body level than appear to be comfortably experienced and contained. The contact figure places hands or body parts against those distressed surfaces, assisting in the acceptance and ownership of the experience.

Controlled approach - See **Stimulus figure.**

Countershape - See **Shape/Countershape**.

Cycle of Becoming: Energy-> Action-> Interaction-> Meaning - The four major steps which constitute the way we ideally process the emotional experiences that happen to us. In the first step (Energy) we have an emotional feeling and body response to the experience. Second (Action) we express our feelings. Third (Interaction) we interact with the type of people toward whom the emotion seeks to be expressed. Fourth (Meaning) we create a conscious and/or unconscious prediction model regarding how to anticipate and handle similar situations in the future.

Direct emotion - See **Movement modalities.**

Ego - The psychological boundaries of a person (skin of the self) created through interactions with significant others. It "decides" what to let in and what to put out based on historical learning. It attempts to define and assess reality. It "chooses" what is manifested as the "I." It is conditioned by cultural and historic events. It works with symbols and abstractions. It is the source of consciousness. It is the psychological organ which makes differentiations such as: self and other, reality and fantasy, dream and awake, etc.

Ego-wrapping - The act of applying consciousness, names, acceptance, and place on a portion of the soul or self when it makes an appearance in a structure by means of a witness figure, an ideal figure, or a permission giving figure, etc.

Enactor - The person who is having the structure, also referred to as the "worker," "client," or the "protagonist."

Energy - The source of emotional behavior showing up in structures as shifts in physical sensations such as tension, pain, heat, etc.

Fragment figure - A figure that is just a fragment of what was originally a highly complex figure. For instance, a containing figure would be a fragment of what would be a quality in an ideal figure such as an ideal mother or ideal father. Or a reproaching figure would be a fragment of what might have been included in a negative father. The fragments are easier and more precisely used rather than applying the entire complexity of those rather monolithic total figures. Includes: contact, limiting, and resistance figures, as well as voices of dissociation, negative prediction, and truth.

Ideal father - The wished for, missing father with attributes that were longed for in one's childhood, role-played by a group member. (See **Ideal figure**)

Ideal figure - Figure role-played by a group member that is constructed so as to match the needs of a client in a structure so that those needs can be symbolically experienced and satisfied. (See **Ideal Figures Described**, Page 295)

Ideal mother - The wished for, missing mother with attributes that were longed for in one's childhood, role played by a group member. (See **Ideal figure**)

Limiting figure - A symbolic figure, role-played by a group member, applied to helping the client with non ego-wrapped energies. When a client is feeling out of control with anger or sexuality, the limiting figure holds the client in such a way as to allow the impulses to be felt in the body and then those movements and efforts can be pushed against or towards the limiting figures who keep that potential action from reaching the wished for or tabooed figures. They allow the experience and feeling of the energy but not the negative or destructive consequences to occur.

Limits - The act of physically restraining or constraining the infant or older child from doing damage to itself, others, or valuable objects. In later years this translates into verbal or psychological limits. (See also **Basic needs**)

Map - The combination of memory and emotions that result in specific patterns of perception and response to present events associated with historical events which shaped the personality. (See also **Remapping**)

Movement modalities - The three basic ways of neurologically organizing and motorically carrying out human movement. In actual life people use all three modalities in varying degrees and in complex coordination. For clinical and self-diagnostic purposes, clients are taught to move as clearly as possible in each modality while reducing to a minimum the other two modalities. Structures evolved from the exploration of these modalities. (Refer to *Movement in Psychotherapy*, NYU Press, 1969)

1. **Reflexive modality** (Basic motility) - Moving under the influence of the body-righting reflexes and gravity.
   Reflexive movement exercises:
   a) Reflex relaxed stance (Species stance)
   b) Columnar walk (Reflex relaxed walk)
   c) Torso twist
   d) Fall catch
2. **Voluntary movement modality** - Controlled movement using maximum conscious choice.
   Voluntary movement exercises:
   a) Conscious voluntary movement
   b) Habitual voluntary movement
   c) Voluntary patterns
3. **Emotional movement modality** - Moving under the influence of primary emotional states.
   Emotional movement exercises:
   a) Direct emotion - Most direct, spontaneous, unrepressed expression of emotion short of hurting self or others.
   b) Consciously generated emotions - Imagining or fantasizing situations which would produce emotional states and then moving under the influence of those states.

Negative accommodation - The act of responding accurately, congruently, and appropriately, with sounds of pain and movements indicating the landed impact of a blow, kick, or other angry expression directed by a client in a structure (without literal physical contact) toward a remembered, hated aspect of a negative historical figure.

Negative reconstruction - The inadvertent creation and reliving in a structure of an original negative event which underlines the life-denying learning reinforced by that event, without the inclusion of a positive, symbolic, antidote experience. This is to be avoided.

Nurturance - The act of caring for those infant needs that literally sustain life — such as nursing, feeding, grooming, washing, petting, caressing, etc. In later years this translates or transposes into symbolic feeding and grooming in a way that psychologically sustains life — such as giving "strokes," valuing, appreciating, admiring, etc. (See also **Basic needs**)

Omnipotence - The feeling of unlimited and unstoppable power or openness resulting from a history of absence of parenting or ego-constructing figures during important developmental stages.

Pilot - The designation of the highest order of ego processes, the aspect with which the therapist makes an alliance. In touch with both affective and cognitive content, but often unaware of soul energies expressed in the body, the pilot functions as the coordinating and choice-making center of the personality.

Place - The livable, benign, accepting space for the infant to live within. This is first provided by the uterus, then after birth by the arms of the parents, the hearts and minds of the parents, and one's own space available in the homes of the parents. In later years this translates into having a place in the world. (See also **Basic needs**)

Polar qualities - The two basic modes of human means for interacting with the world: action and receptivity. Everyone, male and female, has the capacity for feeling and expressing both types of polar qualities.

Positive accommodation - The act of responding accurately, congruently, and appropriately with words, movement, and touch to satisfy the expressed needs of a client in a structure.

Possibility sphere - A psychological space within which the client is invited to work. It is an empty space that invites the client to bring out the portions of the self that have been in hiding and never before consciously known, named, validated, and internalized into the ego.

Power - One of the polarities of the soul. Represents the active, massive qualities of the client which can make an impact on the outer world both for beneficial and harmful ends.

Protection - The act of defending the soft vulnerability of an infant against physical injury by parents providing the hard shield of their own bodies between the infant and possible contact or impact with hard or dangerous surfaces. In later years this translates into psychological defense or protection, as in blocking verbal or psychological injury. (See also **Basic needs**)

Receptivity - One of the polarities of the soul. Represents the open, non-moving qualities of the client which can react and be affected by the outside world, both for beneficial and harmful ends.

Remapping - The creation of antidotal symbolic events during structures which may offset the life negating, negative patterns of perception and response created by traumatic events.

Resistance figure - A symbolic figure used to make contact with a clients's motions when the motion is just at the verge of further expression, but withheld from action due to fear or doubt about the extent or consequences of the action which would follow from the interior state experienced. The resistance figure does not stop the action but gives some resistance to the action, at the very least ego-wrapping that action to some extent — giving it a kind of preparatory countershape of consciousness and control.

Respect - The psychological act of recognizing the value of the child in having a right to live in the world as the child actually is. It implies the child being "seen" and valued for what it is and not over-run as if it were not present. In later years this translates into feelings of self-worth and self-esteem. (See also **Basic needs**)

Self - What a person has become. What is perceived as a person's identity and personality. The "I" may or may not be congruent with the true self. (Also referred to as "What I Call Me")

Self/other interaction - The antidote experience for deprivation of needs which is aimed for in structures.

Self/self interaction - The kind of self contact during structures which suggests a history which taught that gratification of basic needs from others would not be available during those developmental stages when it should have been forthcoming from caretaking figures.

Shape/Countershape - If the shape is the emotion/action of a client, then the countershape is the wished-for, satisfying response to that emotion/action.

Sharing time - The period immediately following the structure when the group members are invited to share their own experience and emotions which were initiated by watching the structure. It is not a time for feedback, analysis, or confrontation with or toward the client who just worked.

Soul - The innate, central qualities of the personality arising from the genes, including the polarities of power and vulnerability.

Stimulus figure - A neutral, role-played figure, that is directed to stand or move in manners directed by the client in order for the client to observe his/her own changes in emotional states or body sensations that might be indicators of unconscious emotion, such as tension, pain, etc. A self-diagnostic way for clients to monitor their inappropriate body preparations for interactions.

Structure leader - The therapist or person who is overseeing and facilitating the structure, providing the possibility sphere, the information about the body that will be commented on by the witness figure, the frames within which the work will be done, the review of the accommodation process, etc. Some therapists refer to this role as the "Guide."

Structures - The primary therapeutic vehicle in PS psychotherapy. In an interactional structure an individual client under the supervision of a PS therapist uses group members to play role figures to create interactional settings. Negative figures are used to create the opportunity to re-experience painful events from the past and to discharge feelings of pain and anger. Ideal figures are used to provide (on a symbolic level) the positive experiences that were deficient in a person's history.

Support - The act of supporting and carrying about an infant too young to hold itself upright and move about. The arms and laps of the parents provide this support. In later years this translates into psychological support, as in "backing up," or "standing behind," etc. (See also **Basic needs**)

True scene - A scene sometimes created in the beginning of a structure, utilizing witness and fragment figures that graphically illustrate for the client his/her present state of consciousness, including emotional states, rational attitudes, and defenses.

True self - A person's human potential. What a person would become under ideal physical, emotional, and societal circumstances. The true self constantly reacts to the events in a person's life, although the person may not be consciously aware of this reaction.

Unmet needs - A state of emotional deprivation which occurs when a person does not have one or more of the four basic emotional needs met adequately during childhood.

Validation - The act of sanctioning, approving, and accepting as good an emotional quality that is being manifested. One of the two major functions of parents is to validate the positive, healthy, emotional qualities that their children display.

Violation - An event or person which overcomes the function of ego to control what comes inside a person and what goes out. It may be emotional, such as humiliation, or physical, such as beatings.

Voluntary movement - See **Movement modalities.**

Witness figure - A symbolic, caring, compassionate figure role-played by a group member who sees and responds to the affective states of a client and gives them names, dimensions, license, and blessing.

Ideal Figures Described

Positive ideal figures are new people designed (with certain ground rules) by each client so they can experience the positive experiences they need and want. They do not contain any elements of a real person.

Ideal parents accept and sanction all the client's feelings but may limit the outcome of some of them. Eventually all clients use ideal parents.

The design of positive ideal figures is not bound in any way by the actual circumstances in a person's life. Clients can create for themselves the emotional environment which could have occurred under ideal circumstances. Ideal figures can be used to represent anyone or anything which a client feels would be meaningful. By far the most important ideal figures are the ideal mother and ideal father. Other figures often used are siblings, grandparents, aunts, uncles, friends, lovers, and mates.

Clients are free to individually tailor the actions and world of the ideal figures as long as they stay within certain certain ground rules. First, they must remember that ideal figures bear no resemblance to the real people in their lives; they are entirely new. Second, ideal figures never do anything negative or harmful to the client. If that is required, then negative role figures are utilized.

All ideal figures, whether mother, father, sibling, or so on, have the following characteristics:

- Respect the space, autonomy, and integrity of the client.
- Do not use their power to attack or violate a client.
- Enjoy and appreciate the client.
- Are available for interaction and learning.
- Give approbation to (validate) the way the client is developing.
- Have had all their basic needs satisfied by their own parents.
- Do not expect the client to fulfill their needs.
- Help the client to explore his or her powers.
- Will never relate sexually to the client (unless the figure is a mate or lover).
- Have control over their own sexual feelings; so while they may have sexual feelings for the client, they will not act on them.
- Have their own loving partner.
- Do not reject or humiliate the client.
- Do not violate the client.
- Are warm, supportive, and caring.

The ideal parents each have the following additional characteristics in common:

- Wanted the child to be born.
- Are responsive to the child's indications of need.
- Are available to satisfy needs, but do not decide when it must be done or the type of need that should be satisfied.
- Do not offer assistance in a way that produces dependence or inhibits autonomy.
- Receive pleasure and satisfaction from caring for the child.

- Enjoy being the child's parents.
- Have experienced their own parents giving them everything they are giving to the child.
- Regard the child as a separate individual.
- Non-imposing (i.e., do not force food on the child).
- Provide an environment which allows the child to develop in his or her own unique way.
- Strong.
- Able to limit the child's power when to do so is in the service of the child.
- Restrain the child from doing harm to him or herself and to others.
- Will frustrate the child's omnipotent attempts to go beyond its own space.
- Do not permit the child to overwhelm or penetrate them.
- Allow the child to move and affect them.
- Permit the child to have power in relationship to them (validate the child's power).
- Give to the child out of an innate desire to pass on love, not to provide things they did not receive.
- Have respect for the wholeness and integrity of the child in actual or potential form.
- See the child as separate and valuable in and of his or herself, not as a carrier of their own unfulfilled ambitions.
- Are willing to be platforms for the child to spring off from without feeling defeated by the child's development and accomplishments.
- See the child as having a unique soul which cannot be known beforehand and without the child expressing who it is.
- Do not injure, beat, or use harsh physical attacks on the child.
- Do not give the child pain, humiliation, or ridicule as a substitute for love and attention.
- Have friends who provide appropriate peer functions.
- Do not attempt to assume the parental function of the spouse or to diminish him or her in the eyes of the child.
- Love and adore their spouse.
- Wanted the spouse and view him or her as a peer and equal in value as a human partner.
- Live better for being married to their spouse.
- Are sexually passionate about, satisfied by, and bonded to their spouse.
- Enjoy their sexuality.
- Acknowledge the sexual attractiveness of the child, but do not make sexual advances or have sexualized contact with the child.
- Enjoy life.
- Are intelligent, creative, spontaneous.
- Are complete individuals.

The ideal mother has the following additional characteristics:
- Carries the child in the womb.
- Nurses the child.
- Provides nurturance through food, physical contact, and emotional means.
- Provides maternal-type support and affection.

- Gives the experience of softness.
- Enjoys being a woman.

The ideal father has the following additional characteristics:
- Provides paternal-type nurturance.
- Provides support through carrying the child and through emotional means.
- Creates a safe living environment and protection by giving the child, through his strength and emotional means, a shell of hardness to keep out dangerous elements of the world.
- Gives the experience of strength and firmness to be leaned on, climbed on, and pushed against.
- Enjoys being a man.

About the Authors

DEBRA ANTARI received a Masters degree in counseling from Southern Connecticut State University in 1989 and is now practicing psychotherapy at a clinic for the developmentally disabled in Carmel, New York. Debra is busy "momming" two sons. Any spare time she may find is spent learning, meditating, growing, and writing. She is working on a book entitled *Structures*. Antari is a spiritual name which means "God Within."

JUDITH BARNITT is a Licensed Psychologist in private practice in Minneapolis, Minnesota. Active in Bioenergetic Analysis, she has trained and facilitated groups in the United States and Europe. She served on the faculty of the International Institute for Bioenergetic Analysis from 1980-1987. Judith has her MA in Human Development from St. Mary's College in Winona, Minnesota.

ROBERT BELOOF is a certified therapist and trainer in Pesso System/Psychomotor. Retired as Professor of Rhetoric from the University of California at Berkeley, he has authored many poems, articles, and books on literary criticism. He has been a Fulbright Professor of American Literature in Naples and recipient of a fellowship from the Institute of Creative Arts. As a conscientious objector, he worked during World War II as an attendant at a State Mental Hospital. His clinical interests led to obtaining an MSW. He began work with PS/P in 1975 and in 1980 became the only certified Pesso System trainer in the western part of the United States. He continues with clinical work and writing, currently completing a book on ego defenses as they relate to and are discovered in literature.

DORIS CHAVES is an Associate Professor at the University of Tennessee, Memphis, College of Nursing, and a Nurse Therapist with Simmons, Kelman and Associates, a private psychiatric clinic also in Memphis. Doris has many years' experience as a teacher and therapist, both in the national and international area. She works closely with Carl Clarke, both learning how to parent the child within and how to teach others to use the nurturing of their own adult self for personal growth. Doris is presently doing research on happiness as a strategy for emotional connection and motoric response to ideal parenting.

CARL CLARKE resides in Atlanta with his wife, Nara, loving living in a city built in a forest, and doing his private practice there for 18 years when not hunting for fossils in the mountains of northern Georgia. He developed a weekend communications workshop for couples in 1970; for 20 years he has been Director of Training for his program, first with the United Methodist Church and then with Marriage Enrichment, Inc. He regularly conducts weekend Psychomotor workshops in New Jersey and Michigan. As Executive Director of Telles Institute, he is dedicated to the development of more video, audio, and written materials for training in PS/P. Certified as a Psychomotor therapist in 1987, he is currently in Supervisory Training with Albert Pesso.

JOHN CRANDELL is a clinical psychologist in private practice in Winchester, Virginia, where he lives with his wife and two children. He specializes in family therapy and the treatment of substance abuse. Educated at Loyola University of Chicago, he received his doctorate in 1981. He has directed Concord Counseling Services, served on the faculty of the Psychiatry Department of the Northwestern University Medical School, and designed and delivered employee assistance programs and treatment programs for drunk drivers. He wrote *Effective Outpatient Treatment for Alcohol Abusers and Drinking Drivers* in 1987 and has written and lectured on psychotherapy for alcoholics and codependent families. Since first being exposed to Psychomotor in 1977, Dr. Crandell has used it for personal growth and for providing individual and group psychotherapy.

RUTHANN FOX-HINES, PH.D., is a psychologist on the staff of the University of South Carolina and in private practice in Columbia. Enough years ago (she does not want to mention) she earned her doctorate and taught at the University of North Carolina in Chapel Hill. Ruthann has been participating in a Psychomotor training group with Al Pesso for over 10 years. As they watch each other's children grow, leave home, and marry, Ruthann and other members of the group offer the common prayer that their children will get into similar therapy to heal their inevitable issues with their parents.

GAIL HAGLER, MSW, is a family therapist in private practice in Atlanta. She specializes in working with families with problems of addiction and has a particular interest in the relationship between addiction and violence. Gail is a fifth year trainee in a Psychomotor Certification group. The mother of four grown children, she is an aficionado of skiing and all-terrain biking.

ARMEN HANJIAN is the pastor of the First United Methodist Church of Montclair. Educated at Union College, West Virginia Weslyan, and Drew, he has a Masters of Divinity. Married to Vicky, with whom he has been training group leaders for Marriage Enrichment, he is the father of 3 grown children. Armen offers personal growth workshops in the community as an expression of his interest in counseling, the focus of his continuing education the last 12 years. He has also served as camp counselor and conference director for summer youth events. He is skilled at playing hymns, calling folk dances, and building a log cabin.

VICKY HANJIAN is an ordained deacon in the United Methodist Church, presently completing her studies in the Master of Divinity program at the Theological School of Drew University in Madison, New Jersey. She serves as the student assistant pastor at St. Mark's United Methodist Church in Montclair, where she resides with her husband, Armen. She and her husband are certified trainers for the Marriage Enrichment Program. She is presently pursuing training in PS/P.

LOUISA HOWE received her Ph.D. in sociology from Harvard. She lived in Washington, Topeka, Berkeley, and Kauai, and had three children (now grown) before returning to Boston and settling down to work mainly in the field of community mental health. Over the years she has taught, done research on vocational adjustment, pregnancy, mental health consultation, and addiction, and worked as a practitioner in penology, public administration, community organization, and psychotherapy (mostly psychoanalytic). Her contributions were recognized in 1989 when she received a Distinguished Career in Sociological Practice Award. She has known the Pessos for nearly 30 years. Since her certification in 1976, she has been in private practice as a PS/P therapist and has also done some Psychomotor training and supervision.

Gus Kaufman is a PS/P trainer in independent practice in Atlanta, Georgia. With Al Pesso he co-leads certification programs in Atlanta and Basel, Switzerland. He moved to Boston in 1974 to train in Psychomotor with the Pessos. Along with Louisa Howe, Ph.D., he was certified as a Psychomotor therapist in 1976. Gus is also clinical director and cofounder of Men Stopping Violence, Inc., a private nonprofit organization working to end male violence toward women.

Dr. Tilmann Moser studied sociology, politics, and social psychology at Frankfort and Giessen — completing his Ph.D. dissertation on juvenile delinquency. From 1969 to 1978 he was an assistant professor on the law faculty at the University of Frankfort, simultaneously receiving psychoanalytic training at the Sigmund Freud Institute. Since 1978 he has had a private practice in Freiburg integrating body therapy into his psychoanalytic work. He has been in training with Al Pesso since 1985, has translated *Experience in Action* into German, and is writing a book on PS/P commenting on transcriptions of structures. He has published books on criminology and therapy, including a description of his own training analysis which appeared in the United States as *Years of Apprenticeship on the Couch.* He is now studying the mental damage of living in the totalitarian communist regime in the former German Democratic Republic.

Dr. Jörg Müller is professor of law at Berne University and consultant to the Swiss government on constitutional matters. As Director of the Federal Claims Division, he serves as an ombudsman in litigation between the public and Swiss radio and television stations. He has served as an Associate Judge in the Federal Court. His special interests are legal philosophy, constitutional law, and international law. He has participated with Al Pesso in an experimental training program between 1984 and 1989.

Lowijs Perquin, M.D., is senior psychiatrist of the Faculty of Medicine of the Free University of Amsterdam and the Psychiatric Center of Amsterdam — the Valerius Clinic. He studied medicine at Groningen and psychiatry at Amsterdam. He was trained in Psychomotor in 1980 by Al and Diane Pesso, Han Sarolea, and Tjeerd Jongsma and is now a registered supervisor, prospective trainer, and chairman of the board of the Dutch Association of Pesso Psychotherapy. He conducts a regular weekly therapy group, gives workshops, supervision, and training for professionals on Psychomotor. Married to Harmina Muggen, he is the father of Moniek and Pieter.

Al Pesso is the cofounder, along with his wife, Diane, of Pesso System/Psychomotor Therapy. He has written about it in many articles and two books: *Movement in Psychotherapy* and *Experience in Action.* Most of his time and energy at present is devoted to training professionals in the use of Psychomotor. He travels regularly throughout the United States and Europe to train and supervise several generations of practitioners.

Born in 1929, Al's initial interests were in dance. He studied with Martha Graham, took classes at Bennington College, and obtained a BS Degree from Goddard College. He danced professionally before becoming the Director of Dance at Emerson College in 1961. He and Diane established their own dance school and began to develop Psychomotor in 1961 in an effort to give students tools of body and of feeling which they could use toward communicating. As this set of exercises evolved into a form of expressive psychotherapy, the Pessos began working with psychiatric patients through McLean Hospital, the Boston Veterans Administration Hospital, and the New England Rehabilitation Hospital, and then in demonstration and treatment groups offered in the Boston area. Now based in New Hampshire, Al continues to evolve Psychomotor.

GLENN SHEAN, PH.D., is Professor of Psychology at the College of William and Mary in Williamsburg, Virginia, and Professor of Psychiatry and Behavioral Science at the Medical College of Hampton Roads. He has published extensively about family systems and schizophrenia. He has been involved in learning about Psychomotor since 1974. He lives on the Chesapeake Bay with his wife, 2 children, and a 27 foot sailboat.

HAN WASSENAAR, PH.D. was educated in neuroscience, completing his Ph.D. at the University of Groningen. He began research on the relationship between catecholaminergic synapse systems and psychoactive drugs. This work brought him in contact with biological psychiatry and cognitive psychology. After attending several PS/P workshops, he was impressed with the effectiveness of the approach and interested in the neuro- and psychological principles underlying it. In collaboration with Al Pesso, Han has developed a model integrating neurobiological and PS/P elements. Han has published articles and chapters in the disciplines of neurochemistry, synapse physiology, and existential psychotherapy.

Index

(Italicized terms are listed in the Glossary)